Teaching College English and English Education

CEE Monographs
Conference on English Education

The Conference on English Education is the organization within the National Council of Teachers of English most centrally concerned with the preservice and inservice education of English language arts teachers. Through this series of monographs, CEE encourages discussion of critical issues in the professional development of literacy educations, including theory, policy, research, practice, and innovation.

Series Co-editors: Robert C. Small Jr., Radford University, and Patricia P. Kelly, Virginia Tech

CEE Executive Committee: Carol Pope, Chair, North Carolina State University; Patricia P. Kelly, Vice Chair, Virginia Tech; Richard Harmston, Recording Secretary, Utah State Office of Education, Salt Lake City; Miles Myers, Secretary/Treasurer, NCTE; Susan Hynds, Syracuse University; Rosalie Black Kiah, Norfolk State University; Nancy McCracken, Kent State University; Peter Medway, Carleton University, Ottawa; Susan Ohanian, Schenectady, New York; Maria de la Luz Reyes, University of California; Tom Romano, Utah State University; Hephzibah Roskelly, University of North Carolina; Bonnie Sunstein, University of Iowa; Don Zancanella, University of New Mexico; Karen Smith, NCTE Staff Liaison

Teaching College English and English Education

Reflective Stories

Edited by

H. Thomas McCracken
Youngstown State University

Richard L. Larson
Lehman College, The City University of New York

with Judith Entes
Baruch College, The City University of New York

Conference on English Education

National Council of Teachers of English
1111 W. Kenyon Road, Urbana, Illinois 61801-1096

Prepress services: City Desktop Productions, Inc.

Staff Editor: Zarina M. Hock

Interior Design: Doug Burnett

Cover Design: City Desktop Productions, Inc.

NCT0E Stock Number: 50373-3050

Library of Congress Cataloging-in-Publication Data

Teaching college English and English education : reflective stories / edited by H. Thomas McCracken, Richard L. Larson with Judith Entes ; Conference on English Education.
    p.   cm.—(CEE monographs)
    Includes bibliographical references (p.).
    ISBN 0-8141-5037-3
    1. English philology—Study and teaching (Higher)—United States.
2. English teachers—Training of. I. McCracken, H. Thomas, 1935– . II. Larson, Richard L. (Richard Leslie), 1929– . III. Entes, Judith, 1951– . IV. Conference on English Education (Organization: U.S.) V. Series.
PE68.U5T39 1998
428'.0071'173—dc21
                                       98-4862
                                          CIP

Contents

Foreword

As a profession over the past thirty years we have been trying to decide if the term "English" is a useful name. Going back to the Dartmouth Conference of 1966, we note that one question dominating the discussions was "What is English?" Each subsequent decade has provided its own responses, from professional leaders such as John Dixon (1967, 1975, 1986), Richard Lloyd-Jones and Andrea Lunsford (1989), and Peter Elbow (1990). While their documents have been widely read, we still note that the question prevails in many different contexts. The ERIC (Educational Resources Information Center) Thesaurus, the proverbial bible for cataloging articles on education, notes that although it included the term "English Education" from 1967 to 1980, it now considers this an "invalid descriptor." The reader is advised to "see the more precise terms 'english teacher education,' 'english instruction,' and 'english curriculum.'" While we might sympathize with the vagueness of the original term, the substitute descriptors do not seem any more precise. ERIC still uses the term "English" as if it were a transparent term.

The National Council of Teachers of English has been publicly considering changing its name for more than ten years, but the name of English prevails to this date. Being perhaps more assertive, the National Conference on Research in English has renamed itself the National Council on Research in Language and Literacy, substituting "Language and Literacy" for the term "English." This name change, however, has not clarified the meaning of the word "English."

The members of the NCTE Task Force on College English and English Education decided that defining "English" needed to be our primary task, recognizing that our discussions would continue to be circular until we clarified the meaning of the term "English." Consistent with the current trend of seeking autobiographical narratives of those with extensive experience as a database for exploring the basic tenets of a culture, we decided to compile narratives providing a forum for exploring the diversity of perspectives on English Studies and English Education.

What fun to read these personal narratives and find out about the professional evolution of our colleagues—those who attend the same conferences we do and those who have been influencing our practice. *Teaching College English and English Education: Reflective Stories* is rewarding reading for this objective alone, but this volume serves a greater purpose. The Task Force sought to document what we do: What is it that people who teach "College English" do? What do people who teach "English Education" do? Implicitly, at least some of us believed that there might be commonalities, but we were "data poor" and needed more information to guide us in possibly coming to a consensus as a Task Force. We thought that these chapters might facilitate our identification of common goals and a common philosophy. The personal narratives provide a rich database, which English specialists will find comfortably familiar. The passionate stories that follow honor our professional practices and offer insights into who we are: the paths we have traveled to arrive at where we are today; our professional values and philosophy; and our hopes for the future.

While there is not one explicit definition or label that emerges from these texts, there are important threads that connect many of the separate texts. I have read these stories as an authentic resource to continue our research. In the process, I have developed tentative hypotheses, which I encourage others to do as well. I offer my general gleanings as a starting point.

We seem to use an infinite number of labels in naming our academic discipline: language arts, communications, drama, humanities, writing, composition, creative writing, literature, reading, literary theory, pedagogy, media, speech, and, of course, English.

Many authors in this volume note the important influence of others who have moved us to change our beliefs and practices from when we started. Frequently mentioned are colleagues, parents, family, friends, texts, and professional organizations, including the National Council of Teachers of English and the National Writing Project. We remember having started quite "conventionally." We did not enter teaching to rebel, although many of the changes we have come to advance have been interpreted by our colleagues as evidence of our rebelliousness. Rather, we retrospectively perceive change as inevitable. As explorers, risk-takers, inquirers, we tell stories of constantly interrogating our practice and seeking to change that which seems to be an obstacle to realizing our envisioned practice.

Our stories reflect an upbeat and optimistic perspective while simultaneously trying to be realistic as well. We admit errors, missteps, and compromises as ways of understanding our personal evolution. We seem to be lifelong learners—learning from and with our students, on whom we seek to have an even greater impact.

But we are disheartened by the resistance to change among our colleagues because this resistance challenges us to become more covert in our thinking and our practice, while inevitably denying us the collegial support that is useful, if not essential, in sustaining our energies. And we are disheartened when students drop our courses, when students are upset, and when students' ratings of our teaching are lower than we expected. When our colleagues in other departments and in other educational settings isolate or ignore us, we are displeased. We are passionate about having an important effect on our students' lives and have fairly recently become aware of the influence of the political environment (locally and nationally) on our classroom practice—although we are not sure what to do about this. Our unquenchable thirst for learning is, perhaps, the overriding commonality in these narratives.

An analysis of these texts suggests then, that English Studies and English Education is about caring for our students as learners; our love of personal, lifelong learning; and our predisposition to seek to improve and, inevitably, to change. These hypotheses might be useful in our continuing dialogue on "What is English?" These hypotheses may serve to move the stalled conversation for the Task Force and for the profession at large.

Whereas committee-created texts are almost universally criticized for their lack of a uniform focus, in this instance, diversity is one of this text's strengths. We were not seeking a consensus; in fact, we intentionally sought a wide range of views. *Teaching College English and English Education: Reflective Stories* provides a totally new perspective for responding to the prevailing question: What is English?

Some could have predicted this volume would result in another installment in the pursuit of an essential, but seemingly intractable, issue, but, perhaps fortuitously, these stories provide a new way of entering the conversation. We have new perspectives to consider and new issues to address as we continue to consider the issues: What is "English Studies"? What is "English Education"? What is "English"? Despite numerous rethinking efforts, English in its many forms, like schools in general, seems to endure unchanged. But that is not inevitable. The tentative hypotheses I offer from my reading of these texts, and those which others will offer, potentially validate the wisdom of the Task Force and of the editors in pursuing this enterprise. What an inspired and inspiring volume Tom McCracken, Dick Larson, and Judy Entes have given us. I commend *Teaching College English and English Education: Reflective Stories* for your immediate attention. It speaks to our common concerns—which will endure as long as schools endure. And it will serve to focus our continuing conversations about "English" or "Learning" or "Life" or whatever we decide to name what we do.

Rita S. Brause
Fordham University

References

Dixon, John. 1967. *Growth through English: A Report Based on the Dartmouth Seminar 1966*. Reading, England: National Association for the Teaching of English.

——. 1975. *Growth through English: Set in the Perspective of the Seventies*. 3d ed. New York: Oxford University Press.

——. 1986. *Growth through English Revisited*. Paper presented at the 4th Convening of the International Federation for the Teaching of English. Ottawa, Canada.

Elbow, Peter. 1990. *What is English?* New York: MLA.

Lloyd-Jones, Richard, and Andrea Lunsford, 1989. *The English Coalition Conference: Democracy through Language*. Urbana, IL: NCTE.

Introduction

This is a volume about teaching in college, and it is about the joys, the frustrations and the battles in getting there and doing it. We wanted to show, through the stories of our colleagues, how it is done. We also wanted to show beginning teachers and veterans alike that it is worth the struggle and that it takes a strong sense of mission for teaching in order to make it happen. This is what happened.

The co-editors thought that a statement or series of principles about college teaching might constitute a contemporary version of Volumes IV and V of the Language Arts Series, a series begun in 1952 and sponsored by the Curriculum Commission of NCTE. Volume V, *The Education of Teachers of English,* edited by Alfred H. Grommon (Appleton-Century-Crofts, 1963), was actually published two years before Volume IV, *The College Teaching of English,* edited by John Gerber and John Fisher (Appleton-Century-Crofts, 1965). Those volumes represented a previous generation's thinking and position about English and English Education. Their value for us was in both how thinking and practice has changed and how it has not changed in over thirty years.

The parts of Volume V, *The Education of Teachers of English,* which are pertinent to this volume are chapters 10 ("The Undergraduate Education of the Future Teacher of College English," 513–36) and 12 ("How the [doctoral] Candidate Learns to Teach," 565–83). In Chapter 12 we read: "To be sure, if he has had the time, the energy, and the interest, the candidate may have applied himself to reading about the art and practice of teaching" (573). This is not a very reassuring attitude toward the place of teaching in college and it has not completely disappeared with time. Two of the popular teaching references of the day were given as such examples: Jacques Barzun's *Teacher in America* (1945) and Gilbert Highet's *The Art of Teaching* (1950). Highet's was the most popular, but the kind of class prejudice contained in it is not explicitly fashionable today. Other recommendations are more forward looking: examples given of colleges which employ observation of teaching and a seminar in college teaching.

Volume IV, *The College Teaching of English* (1965), was sponsored by NCTE, MLA, CEA, and The American Studies Association. It is a group of essays by thirteen college teachers giving direct advice to the reader about programs and teaching. Perhaps significantly, it took that volume over ten years to come into print, not many years longer than this one. One possible significance is that all the groups continue to be separated by one common title: English. Statements in that volume ranged from John Fisher's "[There is a deep] cleavage between those concerned primarily with English as a skill and those concerned mainly with the English language and literature in English as a content" (3) and "the terminus, the ultimate objective of English both within the profession and in the eyes of the public, remains what it always has been—extensive and perceptive acquaintance with major literature" (5) to Wayne C. Booth's "coverage of subject matter is not in the least what we have in mind when we think of competence or distinction in our field" (202). Fisher's reference to skill, as McCracken himself heard at a large-hall presentation by Fisher at NCTE in Knoxville in 1978, applied to those who taught language and composition (how to use language and composition, not the study of them as subjects) and to those who claimed to pay attention to the teaching of English. The advice about teaching from the writers in that volume was various and at times contradictory, but it was primarily about organizing content and what should have priority. The volume generally reflected the beliefs of its day, representing the maturing of the Young Turks (New Critics) who had fought against the *ancien regime* (Literary Historians) and who now were turning their attention to what other aspects of the discipline should have priority, as Krieger characterized it (Murray Krieger, "The Discipline of Literary Criticism" 181) and what elementary and secondary schools should do (an essay by Donald J. Gray called "Articulation Between High School and College English" 256–82).

Several years ago, the Executive Committee of NCTE created a Task Force to explore the desirability of developing guidelines for the preparation of college teachers of English and English education. Rita Brause of Fordham University was appointed to chair the Task Force. But after much deliberation the Task Force elected not to try to develop such guidelines. Instead, it decided to produce a volume of essays about how people *became* teachers of English or English education. The Task Force thought that a didactic and definitional approach such as that taken in the earlier volume would seem to be little more than business as usual. It would leave out most of those who have been influential in shaping the views of college teaching since the beginning of the English Language Arts Series, in particular the English education and college composition groups. We thought of a volume showing who college teachers are and how they got that way. Gradually, we determined that one of the key queries would be: "What has influenced and formed your current teaching practice and attitude?" And most of the essays answer that question.

We still held on to a belief with which we started: that a comprehensive set of principles might be useful to college teachers in their classrooms. An obvious place to look for a current example of such principles was the *Guidelines for the Preparation of Teachers of English Language Arts* that the Council had issued in 1976 and revised in 1986. These NCTE Guidelines had proved widely influential. They had been used as the source for the combined NCTE/NCATE (National Council on the Accreditation of Teacher Education) guidelines that are used as standards for colleges preparing teachers of English for the schools. Approximately 45 percent of the 1,200 colleges and universities which prepare teachers were affected by the NCTE/NCATE Guidelines. As this volume goes to press, the 1996 NCTE Guidelines and NCTE/NCATE Guidelines are being completed.

While such a set of guidelines for college teachers seemed wholly appropriate, indeed desirable in the minds of some leaders in the profession, the very mention of guidelines for college teachers suggested to others that a particular approach or philosophy of teaching would be privileged, so much so that it would affect academic freedom. Those objecting thought that the freedom to approach teaching and learning in their own classrooms and in their own way would be challenged. One of the divisions in the Task Force was between those college teachers who had elementary or secondary teaching experience and those who had not. Another division was over many basic assumptions about how teaching and English are defined. In that respect, the Task Force was a microcosm of the profession. And in that respect your co-editors reflect the profession as well. McCracken and Larson read most of the essays quite differently, one of the many causes, as it surely was for its predecessor in 1965, for the time it took to prepare this volume for publication.

Some members of the Task Force believed that college teaching ought to reflect a variety of teaching styles, instead of what they believed some others wanted: a prescription for one style (e.g., the teacher as facilitator). It was felt by some that college teachers generally do not want to study teaching and even if they do, they don't want to be told to apply what they learned to their own teaching. College teachers work in an environment that many believe is, or should be, a meritocracy. If one is to be meritorious, that line of belief goes, it should be in the realm of what Learned Societies value. It is toward Learned Societies that legislators often look to determine public value. And that means financial support. While pedagogy has recently entered the fringe of this realm of value, it does so only as theoretical inquiry, not as practice in classrooms. That is, in many departments and professional journals, pedagogy is discussed and studied, but often not with the intention of applying conclusions to individual classrooms. So, divisions in the Task Force about what to value and how to define English and teaching quickly slowed the fast start with which the Task Force began and denied the fast finish that every Task Force is expected to have.

One of the profession's impulses is to divide beliefs about teaching along departmental lines (English, teacher education) or specific roles with departments (e.g., composition teacher, literature teacher). In this division, English education folk study teaching and try to practice what they have learned; English folk study something called "the subject" and have relatively little interest in learning theory. Or, it is the view of teacher teaching subject to student, as compared to the teacher teaching students a subject (priority is the point of this canard). Another view is that the students teach each other and the official teacher contributes goals and helps to achieve the goals, as opposed to the lecture format. Such divisions don't hold, at least in the minds of those who completed the national survey by Collett Dilworth and Nancy McCracken. The reader is directed to that survey on this point. Teaching styles and attitudes can be grouped, but not by departments and colleges, and not with any reliability by teaching roles.

Nationally, broader divisions occur, divisions which are usually papered over, as it is not in anyone's financial best interests to insist upon what divides us. The National Council of Teachers of English was created in 1911 in major part because the study of teaching and learning in English was being ignored by the Modern Language Association. The division which each organization represented was characterized in one instance by the belief that English can be studied without reference to how and why it is studied, as against the belief that teaching and English are indivisible in schools and colleges. That broad division persists today. The Task Force mirrored the national divisions as well.

The Task Force did agree, after two years of meetings, that it would not continue to try to produce the consensus statement about the preparation of college teachers of English and English education that it had aspired to write. Recognizing the diversity of the routes taken by members of the profession in reaching their current positions and in their teaching philosophies, the Task Force decided to undertake preparation of a volume in which individual faculty in college English and English education would tell the story of how they became the kinds of teachers of English and/or English education that they considered themselves to be—in other words, a volume of intellectual professional accounts or stories by some leaders in the profession of college teaching. Instead of recommending a monolithic view of college teaching and a common path for all to follow, the volume would recognize and, indeed, highlight the diversity of paths taken by professionals to their current convictions about college teaching. We leave it partly to the reader to determine how diverse those paths are; however, a note follows on the organization of the essays in the volume. For further explanations and interpretations of the essays, the reader is invited to turn to the conclusion—separate essays by McCracken and Larson.

Tensions embody and reflect the profession in four categories in this volume: **Personal** essays which show, through their lives and thinking, some insights about how to live and breathe in the profession (the first essay in each section); **Departmental** essays which show how some aspect of our subject reveals awareness or impedes it (the second essay in each section); **Historical** essays which give us long-range perspective on how it was and how the past informs what we do now (the third essay in each section); **Teaching** essays in which interpretations of background and spirit combine to illustrate parts of current classrooms (the fourth essay in each section). By reading one chapter, the reader should get a cross-section of the volume, or the reader could read the third essay of each chapter, for example, and get a sense of the history contained in the volume (chapters 4, 6, and 8 drop departmental).

This volume will, we hope, encourage current and future college teachers to recognize and analyze their interests, study the several influences that are coming to bear on them, and consider for themselves their stances toward teaching. We also hope that experienced college teachers will find a renewed sense of commitment and enthusiasm from these stories and reflections. The members of the Task Force agreed that such a volume would constitute the most informed and cogent report on the preparation of college teachers of English and English education that it could compile. Later, under the chairship of Rita Brause, Fordham University, the Task Force appointed McCracken, former Chair of the Conference on English

Education, and Larson, former editor of *College Composition and Communication,* as co-editors. The volume consists primarily of first-hand stories, rather than autobiographical narratives—the main difference perhaps being that the stories include perspectives on teaching and represent a particular kind of research that we are proud to sponsor. The stories, as a whole, represent a study of theory and applied theory grounded in personal experience and academic study over many years. We, the co-editors, hope you find the volume thought-provoking and a reflection of the spirit of all of us who persist and take enjoyment in teaching and learning for the sake of our students, our profession, and our own well-being.

H. Thomas McCracken
Youngstown State University

Richard L. Larson
Lehman College, The City University of New York

In memoriam

Robert E. Shafer
1925–1997

and

Donald C. Stewart
1930–1992

I Ways We Have Been Affected

I learned to hide my feelings about what I read, especially from myself, and to transmute the energy into work that was acceptable.

Jane Tompkins

1 Facing Yourself

Jane Tompkins
Duke University

Most of my training in college and graduate school and most of my experience during the first ten years or so of teaching pointed me away from talking or writing about what was most important to me. Away from seriousness, away from risk, away from leading with your chin, or wearing your heart on your chin, or wearing your heart on your sleeve.

Although the process had no doubt begun a long time before, my memory in this regard logs on in detail at age sixteen, when I was introduced in twelfth grade English class to the poetry of T. S. Eliot—"The Hollow Men," to be precise—

> We are the hollow men, we are the stuffed men,
> Leaning together
> Headpiece filled with straw. Alas!

When I read this poem now, I feel the outrage and despair that must have motivated it, and every bone in my body protests the paralysis and ineffectuality it describes. But in high school what sunk in was something different. This poem taught me, more effectively than anything else I can remember, that enthusiasm; perfervid sincerity; desperate, joyous earnestness; and prehensile longing for the truth were jejune, nerdy, and tasteless.

By the limp fall of its lines, by its dry croaking voice, the poem taught me, and in the end just came out and told me:

> This is the way the world ends,
> Not with a bang but a whimper.

I had thought we were supposed to be engaged in a struggle for the truth; I had thought we were going to be grappling with big things. But no. It had all been lost and won long ago, apparently. Now, the only correct posture was a refined, well-educated despair.

This was the first institutionally-delivered body blow to my love of seriousness. The second came the following year. In freshman English studying *The Love Song of J. Alfred Prufrock* and the *Preludes*, I learned that if an image made me feel stupid, numb, depressed, it must be sophisticated and poetic. I learned that if writing were difficult, dry, emotionally perverse, and rasping, that made it good—the best. Eagerly, I glommed on to the ragged claws, the yellow feet, the patient etherized upon his table. They made me feel factitiously world-weary. I had enthusiasm to burn, so I burned it. I was rewarded for this. But still I remember that every time I came to the line "No I am not Prince Hamlet, nor was meant to be," I inwardly screamed, "You *are* Prince Hamlet, I *am* Prince Hamlet, and was meant to be. I *am* somebody. Things *do* matter. Life *does* mean something." (Or screams to that effect.) In the same class we read Katherine Ann Porter's *Noon Wine*, a story about the drastic consequences of going all out too soon (that was what my teacher said it was about; I didn't get it on my own). If going all out would kill you, I would hold back.

The next year in an upper-level course in modern literature, I tried to love the moment in the rose garden from the first of the *Four Quartets* where Eliot says that humankind cannot bear very much reality. But I *hungered* for reality, or thought I did. By then I'd read *The Waste Land* and *Gerontion* and *Ash-Wednesday* and all the rest. I could quote "Because I do not hope to turn again" and the Italian source in *Guido Cavalcanti*. I memorized lines which I have never to this day understood and I could think, with a sigh, "Weave, weave the sunlight in your hair," though these lines from *La Figlia che Piange* were suspiciously melodic and full of feeling. I had learned from my professor, Miss Woodworth, about the malaise of modern life and I tried to convince myself that I knew what that meant, and that I knew what someone named "Mistah Kurtz" had meant by his deathbed pronouncement about "the horror." I didn't know, of course, but had to pretend, to myself most of all, that I did.

Still, it took massive doses of repressive cynicism and academic cool administered continuously throughout graduate school to dampen my ardor for big subjects, moral commitment, and quasi-religious enthusiasm about literature. But I learned to hide my feelings about what I read, especially from myself, and to transmute the energy into work that was acceptable.

Three years ago, I began to get a series of migraines, first one a week, then two a week, that were so bad there were times I didn't want to live. The headaches came in conjunction with an experimental course I was teaching on emotion, a feminist theory course offered at the graduate level to students in the humanities. The course itself was traumatic—that was the headaches' immediate cause—the underlying cause was my life.

I started doing the things people do in that situation. I went into therapy, again, started getting massages, began to do meditation, took more frequent walks in the woods. I read self-help books: Louise Hay, Hugh Prather, Stephen Levine. I thought I was trying to get rid of some headaches, but the change thus set in motion was more general than that. It took place in my heart, somewhere between me and the trees in the area where I walked; in the air of the room where I meditated in the mornings; in the way my dog would lick me when I gave her breakfast and said "Thank you, Ribbon," meaning, thank you for existing—I was so glad to have this dog in my life. It also happened inside my head, where I began to watch my thoughts.

Today what matters to me most in teaching is the way things are done, the presence of the teacher and the students to one another, how they inhabit a common space. I want to know what happens inside students when they sit in class, how their breathing is, whether their heartbeats accelerate or slow down, how their stomachs feel. I want to know what they learn from their interactions with each other, according to the codes of academe, within the ethos of a particular school, within the system of American higher education. I want to know what their hearts' desires are, what they would give their lives for.

I want to know how the instructor is doing, all alone up there; watch her grade papers, track her cycles of exhilaration and discouragement, her satisfactions, her doubts, her dreams, her unmet needs. I want to know why people become college professors and how they think their life-plans are working out.

These are not research interests but practical concerns, an outgrowth of my own development. I ask these questions not because of doing a lot of reading, but to answer a desire for more intimacy and connectedness to the world.

These needs make me feel vulnerable to criticism. "Isn't what you're talking about something like . . . *group therapy*?" I hear people ask. And they do ask. The word "therapy," with "touchy-feely" not far behind, lurks in everybody's mind. They can't wait to say it. "Practicing psychiatry without a license," someone recently threw at me. "What is this," I say to myself, joining them, "kindergarten?"

These are questions I can't answer except to say that, slowly, I've come to think school should be a different kind of place from what it's been, at least from the way it was for me; more like the way home was supposed to be—a safe place, somewhere where you belong, where you can grow and express yourself freely, and where people matter more than information and ideas.

It is Christmas, 1958. I have come home from college and am having Christmas dinner with my family. Sitting across the table from me is Delly DeLaguna, formerly a professor of philosophy at Bryn Mawr College, now retired. She, along with her daughter Freddy, a professor of anthropology at Bryn Mawr, are dinner guests at my parents' house, friends of my parents. Delly has just asked me a penetrating question about my studies (I am a sophomore at Bryn Mawr) and I am about to answer. I have been talking about T. S. Eliot and she has asked what I like about him or what I find important. I no longer remember the exact question, but I get up from the table to remove a dish, and on the way into the kitchen pause by her chair and recite the following lines from *The Family Reunion*:

> You are the consciousness of your unhappy family, its bird sent
>   flying through the purgatorial flame.

As the lines came out, I felt a sudden twinge; I had an uneasy sense that they might have been inappropriate, or might have been misinterpreted by others at the table. I had honestly believed I was making a literary judgment, innocent and high-minded, which exhibited both my taste and Eliot's profundity. In truth, I do not think I had any notion at all that I liked those lines and thought they were important because they were about me and my parents and my general life situation. I do remember, though, that there was a moment of silence from which I escaped by passing through the swinging doors into the kitchen.

That moment can stand as well as any other for what I'm trying to teach myself. It is the moment I want most to avoid: unconsciously reenacting on the scene of my present life an inward drama of which I have no knowledge.

I sit down and reread *Ash-Wednesday* after all these years. I get more out of it now than I did in college. I hear the poet's voice speaking and it speaks to me in a new way. He is praying for himself. The poem is an act of surrender, a plea for mercy, and a whispered hope of forgiveness, though he isn't able yet to let himself hope for that.

> Because I do not hope to turn again
> Because I do not hope
> Because I do not hope to turn
> Desiring this man's gift and that
>   man's scope
> I no longer strive to strive towards such things. . . .
>
>   Wavering between the profit and the loss
> In this brief transit where the dreams cross

The dreamcrossed twilight between birth and dying
(Bless me father) though I do not wish to wish these things. . . .

And even among these rocks
Sister, mother
And spirit of the river, spirit of the sea,
Suffer me not to be separated

    And let my cry come unto thee.

It's the suffering that attracts me to this poem as it attracted me in my sophomore year when I suffered and didn't know it. The poem allowed me to have my feelings vicariously, gave solace because it acknowledged suffering's reality. If only Miss Woodworth had said something about that, had encouraged us to speak of what we felt as we read it, instead of trying to sound knowledgeable about literature. If only she could have taught us the poetry without denuding it of its emotional and spiritual freight. I look back through my cerulean blue hardback copy of *T. S. Eliot. Collected Poems and Plays 1909–1962* and see the notes I'd made in the margins of *The Waste Land*. Next to the phrase "a broken Coriolanus," I'd written "Symbol of proud idealism." Next to "Burning burning burning burning" I'd written "Lust—an image used by both Buddha and St. Augustine." They were desperate times, trying to understand T. S. Eliot, which you had to be able to do if you were in college in 1958, especially if you were an English major. I wrote down the dry bits of information the teacher gave us, trying to make sense. It was like eating dog kibble. "These fragments I have shored against my ruin," Eliot writes at the end of the poem. That was me.

Turning back now to *The Hollow Men*, looking at those dead lines, I see what they say and I can hardly take it. What irony. It was Eliot, after all, who was able to bare his heart in verse, in death's dream kingdom. But the reality was too much to bear for myself, for my teachers, so we lost ourselves in explication. We said: these lines are from Kyd's *Spanish Tragedy*; these are from Gerard de Nerval. "Those are pearls that were his eyes," a reference to Shakespeare.

There must be ways of teaching literature that don't turn students into hollow men.

Returning to Eliot, heart on sleeve, he seems more human and approachable. I don't always understand what he says—

At the first turning of the second stair
I turned and saw below
The same shape twisted on the bannister

but I feel what it means.

> *Weave, weave the sunlight in your hair.*

Of course, it's a mistake to look back with a sense of superiority, as if now I could judge from a secure position my own old self and T. S. The poetry had a haunting duality; it cried out for love while hiding its need for same. But I saw only the judgment and not the need. All along, I was afraid of being judged by Eliot; judged naive. Like Prufrock I was afraid.

Like Eliot, I was afraid.

And in short, I was afraid.

I read the conclusion to *The Love Song of J. Alfred Prufrock* and its sadness is too much for me. I love Prufrock and see in him my father, my self, anyone who has ever not had the courage. Eliot says in *The Waste Land*, commanding us:

> *Come in under the shadow of this red rock*
> *And I will show you fear in a handful of dust.*

I obeyed. For years, in an attempt to brighten grim surroundings, I had a cheap red rug in my university office, and upon entering, like an automatic reflex, I would say—

Come in under the shadow of this red rug—

but never the second line, "And I will show you fear in a handful of dust," which I had forgotten, since I lived it every day. Afraid that my classes wouldn't go well, afraid that my students wouldn't like me, afraid that I wouldn't be thought well of by my senior colleagues. Living under the shadow of this red rug was hard to do! The fear of my students and of my colleagues was, after all, a fear of myself. The same shape twisted on the bannister.

My relation to Eliot's fear and sickness is different now—mainly in that I know how I feel when I read the poetry, whereas before I couldn't let myself know. Perhaps, if I could have read Eliot in full consciousness of what I was feeling as a freshman, as a sophomore, I could have begun to face myself. But instead I was like the character at the beginning of *The Waste Land* who, only vaguely aware of her disease, says, "I read, much of the night, and go south in winter." I knew I was like that woman and that her reading and her vacations were a defeat: half-hearted, polite, well-behaved.

Who would have thought death had undone so many?

Old T. S., old recondite and remorseful, practical cat man and backstage artiste, at long last I have come back to you and, with your help, recaptured a piece of my old lost self.

But this recapture leaves me stymied where teaching literature is concerned. Having rediscovered the powerful emotions associated with the reading of poetry, I no longer know how to teach it. My stock has gone down to zero and nothing that I know seems to do me any good. I have to start all over again. In relation to literature, my ostensible subject of expertise, I feel a little bit like Prufrock at the end:

> We have lingered in the chambers of the sea
> By sea girls wreathed in seaweed red and brown,
> Till human voices wake us, and we drown.

Works Cited

Eliot, T. S. 1963. *Collected Poems 1909–1962*. New York: Harcourt Brace and Company.

Eliot, T. S. 1939. *The Family Reunion: A Play*. New York: Harcourt Brace and Company.

Porter, Katherine Anne. 1937. *Noon Wine*. Detroit: Schuman's.

2 Surprising Myself as a Teacher in Houghton, America

Art Young
Clemson University

I have just finished my twentieth year as a full-time college teacher of English, and what surprises me most, I think, is how much my actual teaching activities and responsibilities have differed from conventional models of teaching undergraduate and graduate students. As I worked as a graduate teaching assistant in the 1960s, earning first my M.A. and then my Ph.D., I imagined a particular kind of life as a college professor of English. I would teach my three or four courses a semester, serve on a departmental committee or two, and work on scholarly publishing—doing the latter mostly in the long chain of placid summers that lay before me. But things happened to me, and, in some instances, I caused things to happen, that took me quite far from this genial image of the classroom teacher and yet, paradoxically, positioned teaching as the center of my professional life in ways I had not predicted.

In June 1971, I finished my Ph.D. in British Romantic Literature at Miami University in Oxford, Ohio, and in August of that same year I was a tenure-track assistant professor at Michigan Technological University in Houghton. I felt fortunate in a number of ways. I had a wonderful experience in graduate school; I was actively involved in, and committed to, the writing of my dissertation on the nonviolent philosophy of the poet Shelley; I was thoughtfully and compassionately mentored by my advisor, Roland Duerksen, and many of the other faculty in Miami's English Department; and I had landed a "permanent" faculty position in a very difficult job market. Although most of my faculty and graduate student colleagues at Miami had never heard of Michigan Tech, it turned out to be a fine engineering college located in the beautiful, remote Lake Superior region of Michigan's Upper Peninsula. Ann Greene Young and I had become enamored of small-town college life in Oxford, so we both looked forward to an adventure in a romantic new place with black bears, otters, and two hundred inches or more of snow each year: a place to be grown-ups rather than students for the first time, a place to begin and to raise a family.

Things began predictably enough. My first quarter, I was assigned to teach three sections of English 101 and a section entitled "The Romantic Period." I was so pleased to be teaching my specialty my first year out, I barely noticed that under Tech's quarter system I would be teaching twelve courses every nine months and that nine of the courses would be in composition and only one of the twelve, if I continued to be fortunate, would be in my specialty. For example, during the winter quarter I was scheduled to teach three sections of English 102 and Introduction to Ethics. Most every day began in my office with a leisurely cup of coffee and reading the daily newspaper, *The Milwaukee Journal*, a newspaper from our nearest metropolitan area—only 450 miles away. I read the hell out of *The Milwaukee Journal*, and my first published "article," an opinion piece on POWs in Vietnam and "Hogan's Heroes" on television, appeared in its illustrious pages later that year.

In the spring quarter of that year, Bill Powers, my department head and another of my most important mentors, poked his head in my office during my morning ritual and asked me how I would like to be Michigan Tech's first Director of Freshman English. I said sure—why not? This opportunity, and the decision to pursue it, changed the course of my life's work. From that point onward, I gradually moved from being primarily a literature specialist to being primarily a composition specialist; from being primarily a classroom teacher to being primarily a program administrator; from writing newspaper editorials to writing grant proposals; from reading the *Journal* and drinking coffee to reading *College Composition and Communication* and eating Rolaids; from thinking of summers as leisurely times to read novels and scholarly essays to working each summer to fulfill assigned administrative, as well as scholarly and pedagogical, responsibilities. The following year, Bill Powers served as Acting Dean of the College of Sciences and Arts as well as our department head, and he asked me to serve as Assistant Head. Three years later, Bill was appointed Dean and I was named Department Head of Humanities, an interdisciplinary department with forty tenure-track faculty. I served as department head for eleven years, until I moved from Michigan Tech and accepted an appointment at Clemson University.

Yet throughout my career odyssey, teaching has been the center of my professional life, although my conception of a teacher's responsibilities has expanded dramatically. While much of my energy has been focused on administrative and programmatic matters, my knowledge and experiences as a teacher have guided my participation in decision-making processes on educational policy beyond my classroom's door. It has been a symbiotic process: what I learn from my students and my teaching informs my other professional activities—research, administration, mentoring, faculty workshops, curriculum development—and what I learn from these activities informs and renews my teaching. This process developed over many years, of course, but this retrospective may be of interest to new and prospective college teachers of English. Not all college professors become department chairs, of course, but many soon realize that participation in creating an academic department, its plans and its programs, its values and its culture, is central to their lives as teachers. I see those activities that often appear to take me away from my primary goal, teaching English to college students, as opportunities to strengthen my personal teaching of English as well as the teaching of English within the communities I inhabit: my department, my university, my profession, and my nation.

What Is an English Department, Anyway?

My teaching at Michigan Tech influenced my perception of what our department collectively should be doing, my perception of what our department, with some sensible planning and a little luck, might look like ten years down the road. It was a matter of listening to our students, collaborating daily with faculty colleagues, and being sensitive to the needs of our campus. At Tech, I and the other twenty-five English faculty taught similar loads: twelve hours per quarter and 75 percent writing courses. We taught mostly engineering students; 67 percent of Tech's six thousand students were engineering majors. A liberal arts major within the department had been instituted, but was not attracting more than a handful or two of majors; there were no education majors in language arts and social sciences, only a small number pursuing secondary certificates in mathematics and the sciences. Faculty talked about designing an English program for our students and our university. What would it look like? How would it be different from those in more traditional English departments, such as the University of Illinois and the University of Wisconsin, where most of us had done graduate work? Why would the state of Michigan, with more than twenty other public and private colleges offering degrees in English, need yet another? I was appointed department head in June 1976, and I was expected to hire six tenure-track faculty before school began that September. Three were to be in English and three in other areas of the arts and humanities. The job market in those days was abysmal, so there were plenty of talented candidates available even at that late date. Because Tech had a different educational mission than institutions with large numbers of undergraduate and graduate students in English and other liberal arts, the faculty in English, with the support of the administration, came to the unexpected realization that we did not need to hire as such institutions did. In English, instead of reviewing the traditional curriculum and seeing where we had "gaps"—say in eighteenth-century British and modern American fiction—we decided on a practice we called "redundant hiring." We looked beyond the candidates' various academic specialities and hired people who were willing to make their main areas of specialization, in teaching and research, those general areas in which the department did most of its work: the teaching of writing, the teaching of literature and reading, the teaching of interdisciplinary humanities. We recruited faculty who had similar interests, so that they could collaborate easily in teaching, research, and program development. We further reasoned that we would not have the resources to support a publishing scholar's library in Shakespeare, Milton, early American, contemporary fiction, etc., nor should the state of Michigan, with three Ph.D. granting institutions in English, provide it. We also didn't want to hire faculty members and require them to publish in specialized areas of literary study when the nearest academic libraries were several hundred miles away and when they would seldom have the opportunity to teach their specialities; and when they did teach them, it would be to engineering and science students whose interests in reading literature are often different from those of liberal arts students. We wanted to make our unique situation at Michigan Tech a strength rather than a liability. If we hired faculty who saw their specialty as "composition studies" or as having a direct connection to it, including connections between reading, writing, and literature, then we could build an adequate library to support both their teaching and research interests, and we could give them teaching assignments in composition and literature in which they could become teacher-researchers, reflective practitioners, and be supported and rewarded for integrating their teacherly and scholarly lives.

And that is what we did. We quickly recognized that our faculty hiring plan was unique and offered exciting opportunities for teaching, research, and program development. In 1976, most other colleges and universities had one or, at the most, two composition specialists, if they had any at all. Little or no collaborative research and publication was being done by English faculty nationally. By 1978, Michigan Tech had more than a dozen such faculty; in 1979, more than twenty MTU faculty participated in the College Composition and Communication Conference in Minneapolis; in 1982, fourteen faculty in the department published a book introducing the profession to writing across the curriculum (*Language Connections: Writing and Reading Across the Curriculum*, NCTE); and in 1986, nine faculty (including five who recently joined the department) published a second book describing our multi-faceted approach to WAC assessment (*Writing Across the Disciplines: Research into Practice*, Boynton/Cook), with several chapters coauthored with colleagues in biology, civil engineering, electrical engineering, mathematics, and psychology. These books were written by teachers for teachers, and they synthesized our experiences as teacher-researchers and writing-across-the-curriculum program administrators. Classroom observations and writings by students were quoted and discussed to demonstrate the essential contribution our students made to our understanding of language and learning.

Creating a Sense of Place

To write of such activities in hindsight is to make the process seem much more orderly than it was. My colleagues and I did several things that enabled us to develop a sense of place and a sense of ourselves as contributing residents to Michigan Tech and to the community we affectionately dubbed Houghton, America. Ironically, at the same time (but not at all foreseen by me), focusing on our local campus enabled us to make a larger contribution nationally to the discipline of English.

First, we listened to the students we taught everyday in composition and literature classes—students who often had ambivalent attitudes toward English. On the one hand, they saw little value in English courses in terms of their career goals, and on the other hand, they found themselves unexpectedly attracted to reading, writing, and the study of literary and other texts. Indeed, some of these students decided to change majors to one of the liberal arts areas, which inevitably meant they would transfer to one of the state's other colleges to pursue that degree, even though such changes meant significantly delaying graduation—since their numerous credits earned in engineering, math, and science courses would not all count toward degrees in English, communications, or political science. Rather than develop an English program for students that we wished would come to Michigan Tech to study English, like those who attended Kalamazoo College and the University of Michigan, we focused on developing a program for those students who had already chosen to attend Michigan Tech.

Second, we listened to faculty in other disciplines and to university administrators. Michigan Tech was looking for ways to decrease the dropout rate, and campus administrators were supportive of programs designed to retain bright and capable engineering students looking to change majors. Faculty generally, however, wanted to maintain Tech's historic focus on engineering, science, and related areas; there was little interest in emulating a multiversity.

And third, we listened to our professional selves. We heard that engineering students found little value in English courses, but we also heard that English faculty often saw little value in teaching "service" courses to engineers. Traditionally, English faculty prefer, and are rewarded for, teaching their specialties, say Chaucer or Milton, to English majors and graduate students who have declared their interest in literature by their choice of curriculum, rather than to nonmajors who often doubt the value of literary study. If we were serious about making connections between science and the humanities in a technological university, we knew we needed to change faculty perceptions, our perceptions, so we could envision new possibilities for teaching English and new possibilities for implementing reward systems that encouraged innovation, both on our campus and within our profession.

The role of serendipity in the planning and implementation of programs that followed cannot be denied. Circumstances that enabled the hiring of a dozen or more tenure-track faculty in English, the miserable job market that made an isolated engineering school seem attractive to outstanding applicants, the rise of composition studies as a major scholarly and pedagogical endeavor within English studies, and the quality and enthusiasm of an adventuresome faculty, all combined to transform the teaching and study of English at Michigan Tech. The first person I hired the summer I became department head was Toby Fulwiler (who also authored a chapter in this book), a recent Ph.D. in American literature from the University of Wisconsin. Other faculty, who have developed national reputations in composition studies followed: Carol Berkenkotter, Marilyn Cooper, Elizabeth Flynn, Randall Freisinger, Diana George, Nancy Grimm, Jack Jobst, Robert Jones, James Kalmbach, George Meese, Bruce Peterson, Philip

Rubens, Peter Schiff, Cynthia Selfe (also a contributor to this volume), and Billie Wahlstrom. In addition to revitalizing composition and humanities instruction for all students on campus, these faculty and their colleagues developed two programs appropriate to the place that is Michigan Technological University: technical communication and writing across the curriculum. Both programs had a locally-acclaimed and documented impact on improving education on campus, and both programs, in ways that surprised all of us who nurtured them on a day to day basis, attained substantial national recognition.

MTU faculty developed what shortly thereafter became the largest undergraduate degree program in technical communication in the nation with over 150 students, many of whom transferred from majors in engineering, science, or computer science. The department now offers Master's and Ph.D. degrees in Rhetoric and Technical Communication as well. And simultaneously, beginning in 1977, in response to needs expressed by the entire campus, the department developed an ambitious and far reaching writing-across-the-curriculum program based on the work of James Britton, Peter Elbow, Janet Emig, Nancy Martin, Donald Murray, Lee Odell, Jay Robinson, Mina Shaughnessy, and a host of other composition scholars, who provided us with mentoring as well as a theoretical foundation. Central to our program was a series of multi-day, interdisciplinary faculty workshops constructed by Toby Fulwiler and several others, workshops that quickly became popular with faculty and became a laboratory for making connections across disciplines, developing interdisciplinary teaching and research projects, improving undergraduate education (including our own teaching of English courses), and, most importantly for a dozen or more of us involved in administering the program, providing us with a sense of common purpose and a sense of community. The program centered on teaching, but it did so in a way that enabled us to develop as scholars and administrators as well. We grew as teachers within our individual classrooms, and adopted new leadership roles as teachers outside of our classrooms. In addition to our work in technical communication and in WAC, we pursued numerous other professional activities—all of which are important forms of teaching—such as conducting faculty workshops on other campuses, publishing regularly, developing new courses, and housing three professional journals: *Computers and Composition; Reader: Essays in Reader-Oriented Theory, Criticism, and Pedagogy;* and *Writing Center Journal.* Indeed, the diversity of these journals—one in technical communication, one in literary study, and one in composition—recognizes the common foundation and the sense of place on which the department was built: the teaching of reading, writing, and literature within a technological university. I've lingered over the activities of a small group of faculty at a single university because I want to suggest that institutional culture is a crucial factor in an individual's development as a teacher and a professional. My intent has not been to recommend Michigan Tech's program as a model for every institution, but rather to suggest that established models, such as those at Harvard or the University of North Carolina, will not be appropriate for all institutions. All of us need to join with others in creating a sense of place, one in which we recognize the needs of our students, colleagues, and institutions even as we aggressively work to construct a supportive environment in which teachers and students alike can lead productive lives in that place.

Creating Ourselves as Teachers

By developing a technical communication program for majors and a writing-across-the-curriculum program for all Tech students, we reversed a familiar faculty perception. We took areas that most English faculty in the 1970s viewed as "service" areas of little professional value and even less professional reward and made them the central focus of our efforts to improve general and professional education on our campus. In doing so, we moved them to the center of our professional lives as teachers, scholars, and program administrators, and in the process we discovered new ways to teach and contribute knowledge to the profession of English. Rather than dreaming of teaching "real" English courses to real English majors at some other campus, we discovered ways to work with each other and with our Tech students (and their interests in technology) to build a rewarding life teaching English in Houghton, America. And by focusing broadly on composition studies, we assured ourselves that teaching would remain central to our work, for a scholarly interest in composition studies almost always means a direct connection to students and to teaching. It goes with the territory. Making teaching the center of our professional work reverses another familiar stereotype still prevalent in many English departments, that if the purpose of a course has anything to do with pedagogy (e.g., with teaching literature rather than analyzing literature), then in some fundamental sense it is not truly an English course, not worthy of English credit, or if a scholarly work deals with pedagogy, then it is somehow less scholarly for doing so and thus less worthy of scholarly recognition. With the support of the Tech administration, we were able to build an institutional reward system that included merit pay, tenure, promotion, and status; one that rewarded achievement in the role we envisioned for ourselves on our campus and within our profession. We were no longer hostage to a reward system constructed elsewhere for other purposes. In the process of establishing our role on the Tech campus, we were able to substantially reduce class size and teaching loads and to substantially increase the size of the faculty and to create an environment in which faculty could fulfill their expanding responsibilities in teaching, research, and service.

If a professor's responsibilities can be briefly summarized in the phrase "teaching, research, and service," then "service" is usually acknowledged as the least important and least respected part of our professional lives, similar in this regard to the service courses that we teach. Yet, for most faculty in composition studies, service, in the form of program administration, is integral to who we are and what we do. It, too, goes with the territory. Senior faculty often advise junior faculty not to get involved with service and administration because it is not valued within the profession or the department and will not count at tenure time. And certainly, depending on the local context, this might be good advice. However, in such cases, it usually means that the senior professors also do their best to avoid administrative assignments, thus perpetuating the belief that program administration is neither significant nor rewarding; or if they take an administrative assignment, they do so realizing that their effort is perceived to be of little value by their colleagues. In such an environment, to spend a minimum amount of effort and to do a mediocre job of training and supervising Graduate Teaching Assistants (GTAs) in the teaching of composition (isn't this one of the most important forms of teaching that we do?), for example, is considered a very satisfactory performance in a department made up of colleagues grateful they didn't have to take on this thankless chore.

The status of such work is tied up not only with the poor status of service, but also the poor status of composition within most English departments. To do an excellent job of directing the writing center does not seem to "count" as much as authoring two minor articles on the poetry of Andrew Marvell. This was another faculty perception we were compelled to change at Michigan Tech. Most of our faculty in composition studies were untenured, and yet the role we were developing for our department needed faculty to administer, and to take pride in and to be rewarded for administering well, such programs and responsibilities as WAC, Technical Communication (undergraduate), Technical Communication (graduate), required first-year English courses, the Writing and Reading Center, the Center for Computer-Assisted Instruction, the Center for Research on Language and Learning, the local National Writing Project site, training and supervising GTAs, arranging and supervising student internships with industry, organizing conferences, and managing grant projects. In a supportive environment, most composition faculty are eager to play such roles because they realize that such roles are an important form of teaching. They wish to lead rewarding professional lives in which teaching, scholarship, and service are seen as integrated, valuable, and central to their department and their profession. If we had not created such an environment in our department, our communal and individual lives would have been less vital and less fun.

My enthusiasm for teaching deepened as my service responsibilities and scholarly interests matured, and this symbiotic process enabled me to reflect on my knowledge of teaching and to discover ways to act on my knowledge within and without my classroom. For example, the exploration of collaborative learning strategies that began for me in WAC faculty workshops led to more productive collaborations with students and among students in my classroom; collaborating with students and colleagues on classroom-based research projects helped me better understand various ways people learn in educational contexts; the more I understood how students worked together to generate knowledge and solve problems, the better I became at facilitating educational change within my department and on my campus. In my first twenty years in the profession, I learned how teaching is a collaborative rather than a solitary activity, is a knowledge-generating rather than a knowledge-dispensing activity. I've learned that the quality of social interaction with student and faculty colleagues, of mentoring and being mentored, creates the departmental environment and the professional values in which and by which we live.

Coda

Ann, our three daughters, and I have since moved to another small college town, one with dogwood trees, air-conditioned homes, and nationally televised football games. At times, as I'm sure you can tell, I'm nostalgic for Houghton, America, but most of the time I'm forward looking as I join with family and colleagues both to discover and to create the new (to me) sense of place that is Clemson, South Carolina. I've found another mentor in Dixie Goswami. I've been encouraged, supported, and rewarded by my department and my university to join with new colleagues like Chris Benson, Denise Boerckel, Beth Daniell, Susan Hilligoss, and Carl Lovitt, among others, in a variety of programmatic efforts: communication across the curriculum, outreach to the schools, a new master's degree in professional communication, general education assessment through portfolio assessment, joint teacher-researcher projects with faculty in engineering, business, science, and agriculture. I've taught new courses to new students, and I've learned more than I've taught, and while I no longer claim to be surprised that that should occur, I still have a continual sense of wonder at what it means to me to be an English teacher.

Works Cited

Fulwiler, Toby, and Art Young, eds. 1982. *Language Connections: Writing across the Curriculum.* Urbana, IL: National Council of Teachers of English.

Young, Art, and Toby Fulwiler, eds. 1986. *Writing across the Disciplines: Research into Practice.* Upper Montclair, NJ: Boynton/Cook.

3 Becoming a College English Teacher— More by Accident than Design

Donald C. Stewart
Late of Kansas State University

I suspect that a good many members of my extended family believe that my Aunt Alice, a high school and junior college English teacher, was mostly responsible for my choice of vocation. Not so. What she did was let my brother, sister and me roam freely over her small-but-fine library, reading whatever we found there that we liked. My first exposure to O. Henry's stories, Tolstoy's *Anna Karenina*, and Somerset Maugham's *Of Human Bondage*, for example, were a direct result of my browsing through her bookshelves looking for something interesting to read. And there were times when she entertained us with stories about the classroom. But if someone had said to me the evening of May 24, 1948, when I graduated from high school, that I would become a college English teacher, I would have thought that the wildest, most improbable thing I had ever heard. For good reason. At that time, I didn't know enough to even have such expectations.

I considered myself lucky to be going to college at all, much less to be aspiring to a faculty position. But I was not particularly happy about the college I was going to. The University of Wichita had offered me a music scholarship even though I had told them I had no intention of majoring in music. They just wanted me to play in the university and city symphony orchestras, and I was good enough to do that. I would major in . . . journalism? My high school journalism teacher had suggested that, and it seemed as good as anything to me, but I had no strong feelings about the subject. The problem was that I really wanted to go to the University of Kansas, the best college in our state, and I was bitterly disappointed that I hadn't been given a scholarship which would permit me to do that. So, I took what was offered and considered myself lucky to go to college at all.

For these reasons, William Stoskoof, my high school orchestra director, was, indirectly, the first person to put me on the road to becoming an English major and teacher. He was assisting in KU's summer music camp in 1948, and he told Russell Wiley, KU's orchestra and band director, about me. Would Mr. Wiley like to hear me play? He would. Mr. Stoskoof then came to my home in Kansas City and asked me if I would be interested in going to Lawrence to play for Mr. Wiley . . . if I were interested in going to KU, of course. I was ready to get into the car and head for Lawrence that minute.

Mr. Wiley liked what he heard. He offered me $100, more than enough to pay for one semester's fees then, and a job as orchestra librarian. Then we went to see the Dean of Men to find out why I hadn't been offered a place in Battenfeld Hall, at that time the only men's scholarship hall. A Residence Hall scholarship in 1948 was the second best thing KU had to offer; one could live in Battenfeld for half what it cost those living independently or in Greek houses. The Dean went to his files, pulled out a letter he had sent me, and said, "Well, we *were* interested in you, Donald. Why didn't you respond to our letter?"

The letter he referred to was one in which he had said that my high school record was fine and that I was certainly deserving, but that a few others had greater financial need than I and, thus, were given the available places in Battenfeld, but that I was to respond if rejection meant that I could not come to college.

At that point I gave the Dean a pointed lesson in communication. I told him that I could go to *college*. The University of Wichita had offered me a music scholarship. The Dean's blue eyes went vacant, and he blinked several times. He had *meant* that I was to reply if their rejection meant I couldn't go to *KU*. That's a problem some KU people still have; they think of themselves as the only real college in the state. As it turned out, I was given a place in a second men's hall that would open up during the second semester, but that never happened. I did well enough academically the first semester that the Dean put me into Battenfeld after all.

I tell this story in some detail because it was such a crucial event in my life. Everything that has happened to me since has happened as a result of me going to KU, not Wichita, and I came so perilously close to missing that opportunity.

Had I not gone to KU, I would never have had Ken Rothwell as a teacher, and it was Ken, not my Aunt Alice, who put me on the road to English teaching. He was my teacher for English 3, a required sophomore course, and I took it at a time when I was confused and uncertain about my own abilities and direction. The aptitude testers at KU had been no help at all; they said that I did well in so many things that I could choose any number of majors and vocations. But which one?

Ken asked me to come to his office one morning, and he got right to the point: "Mr. Stewart, I think you should major in English." That's what I had been waiting for: someone to say, "You're good at this stuff. Go for it." It should have been apparent to me all along. Although I play the violin well, I knew absolutely that a professional career in music was out of the question. It would spoil my enjoyment of my favorite leisure-time activity. The natural sciences were attractive, particularly geology, but what did one do with that stuff? Medicine, law, engineering, and business had no attraction for me at all. But reading and writing?—yes, that was what I did best. It was so obvious. I felt much better about the whole situation, but in less than two years, new problems cropped up.

The first question people ask one, as any English major knows, is "What can you *do* with that major?" Actually, there are a lot of things one can do with it, but the most obvious vocation is teaching. During my senior year, I confronted some unpleasant realities. I would soon be out of college, leaving the most congenial environment I had ever known. It was very pleasing to be surrounded by people who took learning seriously, who knew how to converse on a wide variety of subjects intelligently, who behaved toward one another with a kind of courtesy that, comparatively, made my high school experience seem like frontier life. I liked the life of a college campus more than anything I had ever experienced, and I was terribly reluctant to leave it. But next year I would be out of Battenfeld, and I would have to eat. I needed a job.

I talked with people in the School of Education and concluded immediately that there was no way that I could endure their program of study or high school teaching, for which they prepared students. So, what could I do? Fortunately, universities then had the same problem they do now: a shortage of people to teach freshman English. A person I can't even recall suggested to me that I apply for a teaching assistantship and admission into the graduate program. Why not, I thought. It would be a way of staying in the environment I loved; it would pay me enough to live on; and it would provide something to do during the months I was away from the really important activity in which I was now engaged: spending summers working for the National Park Service in Yellowstone.

But even as my life took this direction, I was not thinking beyond the end of the M.A. degree because I had been intimidated by

English Department faculty. The one option I was aware of, which was open to people who did not teach in high school, was college teaching. But that, of course, was out of the question because to teach in college, you had to "publish or perish." There it was, the first time I had ever heard the phrase, and it was, quite literally, chilling. We were made to feel that since we would, of course, be unable to publish, we would most certainly perish, and that conjured up images of pacing homeless through the streets of big cities during winter snowstorms, wondering where our next meal would come from, wasting away in general, all for lack of publishing. None of these "publish or perish" people ever took the trouble to point out the obvious: any college teacher worth her salt will discover areas of knowledge of special interest to her and will want to share what he or she found out about them. It makes as much sense to tell a college teacher that he must publish or perish as it does to tell an apprentice carpenter that he had better start building fences, cabinets, and houses or else perish. *What else would one trained for such work do?*

The publish or perish types were really saying to us: "We don't want you in the profession. You're extra competition and will make our jobs tougher. Get lost." The best way to scare off a potential college teacher who is insecure is to start the old "publish or perish" refrain. It's immoral. I've never done that to my graduate students.

In the fall of 1952, I taught my first freshman composition class. Again, I was in exactly the right place at the right time. KU's English Department had decided that they should get someone who had real expertise in composition teaching to run the program, and they could not have found a better person in the entire United States. Albert Kitzhaber, fresh from the experience of working under Porter Perrin and less than a year way from completing his doctoral dissertation, "Rhetoric in American Colleges: 1850–1900," was their choice.

Like most graduate students in English in that era, I assumed that literary analysis was the principal business of professionals in English. One taught composition to make a living while going through graduate school. My peers certainly thought so. I suspect that practically everyone in the country who began graduate work in English in 1952 was under the same delusion. But at KU, we had a little diversion. We had to take a course in composition teaching, taught by Mr. Kitzhaber, one evening a week. Much grumbling. Considerable sarcasm about demeaning ourselves intellectually for such pallid "stuff." Unlike a good number of my peers, however, I listened carefully to what Mr. Kitzhaber was telling us: that excessive concern for superficial mechanical correctness was a foolish and unproductive way to teach composition; that the Harvard people had established this pattern, making composition work demeaning and anyone who took an active interest in it inferior; that composition teaching was really the descendant of a noble intellectual tradition, rhetoric, and that in cutting itself off from its past, it had become shallow and superficial; that, as composition teachers, we were to conduct ourselves like professionals. He gave us great freedom to experiment in the classroom; he made constructive comments on our teaching; and, he liberated us (or, at least, me) from some very foolish notions about the legitimate work of a college English teacher.

In 1954, another of the incredible sequences of happenstances in my life occurred. I met my wife, and she had one thing in particular that I lacked at that time: direction. She knew what was required of one who wanted to teach in college: a Ph.D., and she was not about to get one at anything but a first-rate school. KU was a temporary stopover while she recovered from a year at Boulder, Colorado, where, in nine months she had earned her M.A.: twenty-four hours of course work, a language exam, comprehensive examinations, and a 140-page thesis. We had to go to Wisconsin, she told me, and I should get the M.A. immediately and head north.

Once again fate was kind to me. My major professor, who had stalled me for a year because he would not let me limit my M.A. thesis on Shelley in a reasonable manner, had a breakdown. I changed to Annette McCormick, and she helped me finish in two months. In the fall of 1955, my wife and I were in Madison, ready to begin our pursuit of the Ph.D.

Nothing goes the way one plans it, of course, and this is not the place to recall the difficult road we traveled in Madison, but I had one more extremely beneficial experience there. Since my wife and I were hired separately, we were both allowed to hold teaching assistantships the first year only. At the beginning of the second year, we had to give one up. I couldn't wait to get out of Wisconsin's freshman composition program—one efficiently administered, but philosophically and theoretically barren. Kitzhaber was light years ahead of these people, and I felt caged. But I was given a place on the composition staff of Wisconsin's Integrated Liberal Studies Program, directed by Robert C. Pooley, a former NCTE president and a man known in every department of English education from Maine to California and Washington to Florida. Mr. Pooley, while lacking Kitzhaber's expert knowledge of composition instruction in this country, was liberal and enlightened, and he gave us the freedom the regular program at Wisconsin denied assistants. Furthermore, he twice put me in charge of the composition staff when he was on leave. Without realizing it, I was being prepared for the direction my career would take.

The most attractive job offered to me in the year I was finishing my Ph.D. thesis was at the University of Illinois, which had decided that it could better monitor its composition program by dividing the 150 or so Ph.D. candidates and teaching assistants there into groups of sixteen to twenty and assigning these groups to assistant professors who would then meet with them, check their paper grading, visit their classes, and, in general, supervise their work. Since I had very little interest in explicating nineteenth-century English literary texts—a task I was presumably prepared for because I had done my thesis on George Meredith—but was very *much* interested in the reasons students wrote so poorly, this job appealed strongly to me.

In the fall of 1962, I burned my boats and decided that if I were to become the kind of college English teacher I wanted to be, I would have to find a place that rewarded me for composition teaching and research. I was pretty sure that, at crunch time, Illinois would not do that, but I would still take advantage of my years there to learn as much as I could. And the first thing I did was to get a copy of Kitzhaber's thesis because it was something I had been intending to read for some time.

Reading that thesis was one of the greatest professional experiences of my life. I began to remember what he had said to us ten years earlier; I took note of the way composition instruction evolved in the nineteenth century and the individuals who exerted greatest influence on that evolution; I got a refresher course on the paragraph, the forms of discourse, and a number of other concepts which were to take me back to that book time and time again. Most importantly I took note of the fact that Kitzhaber had identified Fred Newton Scott of Michigan as the solitary original thinker of his era. I would have to take a look at Mr. Scott's work some time.

I didn't do that nearly as soon as I thought I would because at Illinois I was too preoccupied with the daily requirements of my job, with trying to accumulate enough money to make a down payment on a house, and with learning how to be a father to two very cute little girls. And in 1965, the Illinois experience suddenly began to fall apart. The department head moved up to the deanship of arts and sciences; the search committee did not do a good job of screening candidates and suddenly found itself with a new head who, in the words of one colleague, started swinging a meat ax at all sorts of programs and courses in the department. The result was a politicized and fragmented department that lost a number of good people and that, unfortunately, began to jettison the program for which I had been hired. It was only a matter of time before I would have to look elsewhere.

As a matter of fact, Illinois's English Department hadn't been helping me very much anyway. I needed some of the summer grants given to young faculty members who were in the early development stages of their careers. These grants, I noticed, routinely went to people on the literature staff, people who were teaching in their special fields of literary expertise, and who, therefore, had time and motive for doing research in the areas they favored. But composition work was not considered worthy of such support. In 1966, when I put in a grant to do a study of duplication in freshman composition readers the following summer, I was told that this was "NCTE stuff," and I should seek help there. I had, asking NCTE's Research Foundation for $500 to supplement the $900 I was hoping to get from the department. When the department snuffed out the $900, I prepared to teach summer school and continued to wonder whether or not there really was a place for me in this profession. I also learned, from one of those who had received a summer grant from the department, that his subject, Andrew Marvell's imagery, had so excited him that he shivered all summer and accomplished nothing. Predictably, the department gave him another grant the next summer—for some more shivering I presume. But he was a Yale man, and one had to treat those fragile Ivy Leaguers gently. I did not have the luxury of time to shiver. I had a wife and two children to feed.

But once again, destiny intervened in my life. Sometime late in 1966, I received a letter from Richard Braddock of Iowa, a member of NCTE's Research Foundation and CCCC's Chair-Elect for 1967. He was interested in my proposal, but wanted me to come to Iowa City to talk with him about it, with a possible consideration of "upward revision" of the budget.

I was on the plane at the earliest opportunity. And that experience also proved to be another turning point in my professional career. Braddock just wanted to know, in more detail, what I was up to, and he satisfied himself on that score very quickly. Did I need more money though? I explained to him how I had planned to combine grants from the English Department and NCTE, but that the English Department had turned me down. How fortunate they had done that! Braddock gave me over $2000, enough money to cover my summer school salary and to pay two graduate assistants to do the secretarial work on the project.

It is impossible, even at this remove, to overestimate the benefits I received from my brief, but significant, encounter with Dick Braddock. He was the first person since Mr. Pooley to give me a solid sense that I belonged in the profession of English and that I was doing something of a value. Inadvertently, he introduced me to Gordon Rohman and Albert Wlecke's study on pre-writing. It was on the shelf of one of his offices at Iowa, and when he had to leave me there for a time, I began reading it and immediately realized that I was going to make some huge changes in the way I was teaching writing. Finally, Dick Braddock introduced me to Richard Lloyd-Jones, who later nominated me for membership on NCTE's Editorial Board and for the Assistant Chair's position in CCCC. Those are debts it is impossible to repay.

I returned to Champaign and wrote my department head one of the most satisfying letters I have ever composed, declining my summer school appointment to do research. In six months, despite working half of them in a primitive basement study which was not air conditioned—this in a part of the country that has hot, humid summers—I finished a 125-page report which went into the ERIC files and, abstracted from that, an article which was subsequently published in *Research in the Teaching of English* (1969). I had begun to get a toehold in the profession, but I still knew that I would have to leave Illinois if I were to develop and experience the kind of career I had in mind.

I was not too sorry about that because I didn't really like living in Champaign-Urbana. Illinois is a great university, but the country around the twin cities is flat, flat, flat. Geographical relief is at least fifty to sixty miles away. Having grown up in Kansas City, gone to college in Lawrence, Kansas, and Madison, Wisconsin, and spent my summers in the mountains of northwest Wyoming, I found Champaign-Urbana to be a severe depressant. I knew that I would have to get out of that place or go mad.

In the summer of 1968 we made our last move, to Kansas State University, back to a part of the country whose geography and people we knew well. My wife is from St. Joseph, Missouri; my parents were living at that time in Kansas City. Manhattan is, contrary to the notions that those with the Oz-complex have, a very beautiful, hilly, little city. I found a home here and a career. Duane Nichols, Freshman Composition Director at Kansas State, literally jerked me into immediate and intense involvement in the Kansas Association of Teachers of

English, one of NCTE's oldest state affiliates. Over the years, I was to become Associate Editor, then Editor of *Kansas English*, an almost continuous member of the organization's Executive Board, and one of its officers. As long as my health permitted me to serve the organization, I helped to rewrite the Constitution so that we developed a more rational and effective rotation of officers; put out membership lists on the computer; and lent support to the movement to create *Younger Kansas Writers*, a companion to *Young Kansas Writers* and one of our most popular magazines with students and teachers.

Even better, after four years I found myself working for a department head, Richard McGhee, who valued the work I was doing. Promotions and appropriate salary increases followed. My active involvement in NCTE and CCCC affairs began in 1972 when I was elected to the Executive Committee, increased in the fall of 1975 when I began serving on NCTE's Board of Publications, and reached its peak between 1981–84 when I was an officer of CCCC. The NCTE Editorial Board experience also gave new direction and importance to the scholarship which has preoccupied me for nearly twenty years now. In 1975 we were reviewing the manuscripts for Cooper and Odell's *Research on Composition: Points of Departure* (1978), and in Richard Young's essay, "Paradigms and Problems: Needed Research in Rhetorical Invention," I was reminded again that our discipline needed historical studies. The time to look at Fred Newton Scott's work had come. The following year, when Win Horner told me that Michigan had Scott's papers, I knew that I would be embarking on the defining scholarly project of my life. It is an enormous undertaking; I am still thoroughly immersed in it, but making steady progress; and each day I look back and think of that incredible route which has brought me to this school, this time, and this subject. And that is how I became the kind of college English teacher that I am, interested in the composing process, in voice, in the history of our discipline, and in the life and professional career of Fred Newton Scott.

I have reported this progress in considerable detail not only because I suspect a good many others have had similar experiences, but because I think it is a good way to find a career. There are some real advantages in not being cocksure, from the moment one goes to college, declares an English major, or even gets his or her Ph.D., about what one is going to do. A lot of valuable groping and help from the right people at the right time can help one, slowly but surely, define the career one wants. That has certainly been true in my case, and, as I look back on it, I realize that underlying all of the different kinds of work I have done is a single motive: a desire to reform the profession's attitude toward the study of rhetoric and composition. Progress has been made, but we have miles to go before we sleep. There are young people in our profession who believe that the battle between literature people and composition people is over, that enlightenment has spread to the corners of the country, but they will have a hard time convincing a number of my friends and colleagues who know that this is simply not so. My own department has made great progress, and there are signs of good attitudes among the younger people, but a number of older colleagues are still not comfortable with according rhetoric a respectable place in our program.

That takes me to the second part of this paper: what it means to be a college English teacher. In a nutshell, it means having the best job the human race ever invented. I cannot think of a single vocation that would have suited me so well, probably because I have come to believe, quite literally, what Fred Scott said in 1903 about the kind of dedication required of one who aspires to be an English teacher:

> The teacher who has not a passion and an aptitude for imparting instruction in English, who does not feel that it is the great thing in life to live for, and a thing, if necessary, to die for, who does not realize at every moment of his classroom work that he is performing the special function for which he was foreordained from the foundation of the world—such a teacher cannot profit greatly be any course of training, however ingeniously devised or however thoroughly applied. (Carpenter 1919, 306–7)

Why is what we do so important and our full commitment so necessary? Because the basic activities with which an English teacher is concerned are those which *define* a person: reading, writing, and speaking. Humans do physics, chemistry, biology, sociology, medicine, law, engineering, etc., but none of these goes as deeply into the heart of what we are as reading, writing, and speaking. I do not want, in this paper, to get into the argument of whether we are socially constructed or whether there is, in each human being, an identity beyond all the forces that socially construct us—that is a separate and large debate in itself—because in either case, the person is what his or her language is. The difference is between *being* and *doing*. Other vocations are about *doing*: we are about *being*. That is why what we do is so important.

Furthermore, we catch students at a time when most of life's important questions are, as yet, unanswered for them. They come out of high school apparently cocky, but really terribly insecure about who they are and what they will do. They do not know if they will marry or, if they do, whom they will marry. They do not know whether or not they will have children. They do not know, although some think they do, what vocations they will enter or where they will live. It is a terribly exhilarating time in a young person's life because the future is so full of possibilities. But because it is so undecided, it is a very unsettling time for them. As they try to define themselves, they seek the words to do so. As James Berlin has so beautifully pointed out in discussing one of the English teacher's major responsibilities, "regardless of one's approach to writing instruction, it is impossible to deny that in teaching students about the way they ought to use language we are teaching them something about how to conduct their lives." (1984, 92)

Being an English teacher also means being a sponge. Everything that happens, in politics, in business, in science, in art, is grist for our mill. All human activities begin with language, whether it is the inspiring poetry of Shakespeare's *Hamlet* or the prose of a manual telling us how to operate a personal computer. One's epistemological stance, language reports, and probes help create the multiple realities we live. Think about what can happen to any one of us in a single day. We might begin by trying to answer the question, "What does it mean to be a college English teacher?" It means taking time out to call to correct an error made by the accounting department of a medical laboratory doing blood tests on us; writing a letter to the state attorney general complaining about cable TV's forcing on us services we don't want; preparing a mid-term examination for a class in the short story; preparing a departmental memo describing a new rhetoric course and recommending its adoption by the department's curriculum committee; writing a consolatory letter to an aunt whose husband just died of a stroke; and spending several hours trying to decipher the occasionally illegible handwriting in Fred Newton Scott's diary. And in each instance we learn something about something else and about ourselves. Language is like the air we breathe; it permeates every aspect of our lives. And the greater command we have of it, the greater control we have of our lives. No wonder it is so important to help our students acquire an increasing mastery of their language skills.

Can we, however, measure the effectiveness of what we teach? No, we can't. Language skills defy quantification. I have seen college entrance examinations which tell a registrar that a student can spell, recognize departures from socially correct usage, and organize, very conventionally, a set piece on a subject of no interest to the student taking the test or the reader evaluating it. I have seen computer analyses of the style of student writing which, while they identified some editorial and syntactical problems, also examined a magnificent piece like Lincoln's Gettysburg Address and found its sentences too long and too monotonous; its vocabulary too abstract for modern readers; and its overall quality as a piece of writing questionable.

The problem is that the things we often do best are like delayed-action time bombs, little pieces and bits of things which students absorb almost unconsciously and then suddenly recover, two, three, four years later when a certain context and need suddenly make the latent knowledge relevant. We are often the last to discover the nature and extent of our influence on the young people we teach, some of whom write or come back five, ten, fifteen years later and say, "Now I understand what you were trying to do for us." So, there is rarely immediate satisfaction in this business. It comes later, often much later, when we are much older and our students have grown up.

So that is what it means to be a college English teacher: much hard work, total dedication to the profession in which we are engaged, low pay, and for the most part, delayed gratification. But these drawbacks in no way diminish the importance of what we do. As college English teachers, we have to believe that.

Works Cited

Berlin, James. 1984. *Writing Instruction in Nineteenth-Century American Colleges.* CCCC Studies in Writing and Rhetoric. Carbondale, IL: Southern Illinois University Press.

Carpenter, George R., Franklin Baker, and Fred Newton Scott. 1919. *The Teaching of English in the Elementary and the Secondary School.* New York: Longmans, Green, and Co.

Cooper, Charles R., and Lee Odell, eds. 1978. *Research on Composing: Point of Departure.* Urbana, IL: NCTE.

Maugham, W. Somerset. 1915. *Of Human Bondage.* New York: Modern Library.

Stewart, Donald C. 1969. "Essays, Analysis, and Better Writing." *Research in the Teaching of English* 3.1 (spring): 42–51.

Tolstoy, Leo. 1886. *Anna Karenina.* Reprint, New York: Random House, 1965.

Young, Richard. 1978. "Paradigms and Problems: Needed Research in Rhetorical Invention." *Research on Composing: Points of Departure,* ed. Charles R. Cooper and Lee Odell, 29–47. Urbana, IL: NCTE.

4 On (Not) Being Taken In

H. Thomas McCracken
Youngstown State University

I was a rebel in school. The reasons may become clear below. Later, I found a kindred spirit in Earl C. Kelley, who was a writer about schools and schooling, and I admired him for many reasons, not the least of which is his rejoinder to some false assumptions about education. In this chapter, using Kelley's assumptions, I offer my own rejoinder as a way of reflecting on who I have come to be as an English educator and how I came (not) to be taken in. Kelley wrote four books, three of which absorbed me in the 1950s as a reader, undergraduate English and education major, and as one thinking about my own schooling. I need to mention those books: *In Defense of Youth* (1962); *Education and the Nature of Man* (1952); *The Workshop Way of Learning* (1951); and his first, *Education for What is Real* (1947) with an introduction by John Dewey. I recently went back to recover the principles in his first book that caught me. My reflections are formed around "Some Common Assumptions of Education" (Kelley 1947, 13–23) that Kelley believes are wrong.

"1. We assume that the child goes to school to acquire knowledge, and that knowledge is something which has existed for a long time and is handed down on authority."

Dear Miss Eisele: Wherever you are now, I know you are beaming as you did every day I walked into our eighth-grade schoolroom. You were especially glad to see me because I *knew* some things others didn't. You bestowed expertise on me. "We'll ask our expert in history, Mr. McCracken," you'd say. Your yearlong class was my first recollection of "acquiring knowledge." That was a K–8 campus school, a place inhabited by college students preparing to be teachers and a place where chess was played in the hall and refugee children from war-devastated Europe came to better us at our own football and boxing and tell horrible stories that we didn't know how to believe. And it was a place where college students who were going to be teachers walked our halls from the other end of the building to teach some of our classes, to conduct case studies on us, and generally, boost our self-esteem by their comments and support. It was also a place where

I could read, win prizes for reading (the prizes were more books), learn chess, box, and play basketball. I also remember enjoying woodshop. Somehow the smell of woodshop, the forest, romantic adventure, reading, and creating forms with tools became connected in my outlook. One book prize I remember receiving was *The Black Spearman,* a story of a young Native American who had great courage and perseverance. One of my later goals was to work on what was known in the '50s as an "Indian Reservation." I never thought of those two things being connected until I just remembered the book. And I began a lifelong basketball career there, which is still going on. The combination of those elements—sports, woodworking, reading, writing, and good intellectual talks with Miss Eisele and the class—were what I now might call *connected knowledge.* I would like that phrase to mean a combination of physical, intellectual, and spiritual qualities that get translated into social abilities and action. I use it in a similar way to Belenky's in *Women's Ways of Knowing* (1986). The connected knowledge in Miss Eisele's room was made possible by her awareness that social activity gets other things done. I was able to work with most of the students in the class over a fairly short period of time on projects, sometimes encouraged by Miss Eisele, sometimes by our college observer-participants. Miss Eisele knew that when students were engaged with their own learning and were coaxed by someone who cared about bringing forth something in them, a classroom buzzed in the way it was intended. After eighth grade, when I was bused three miles to Oswego, New York (population 23,000) for high school, that connected knowledge simply stopped being honored.

Except for brief moments in algebra, history, and English, high school was not intellectually satisfying. Miss Eisele had been with us all day and we worked on most subjects together. When I got to high school, I was bewildered that connected knowledge wasn't revered as it had been in campus school. Instead, it was divided into forty-five minute chunks with a different teacher for each chunk and few links either among teachers or chunks of knowledge. Intellectual stimulation came from my reading (four to five books a week), from hours lived in the public library reading philosophy, travel, and adventure stories, and listening to Mozart, who was played every noon. I walked across the east bridge over the Oswego River to get to the library. No classes occurred during the noon hour, so I had about fifty minutes each day surrounded by books and music. One of the books I remember from 1950 in the travel section of that small public library had been a Book-of-the-Month-Club special and one of the best-selling nonfiction books for 1941 (800,000 copies): Osa Johnson's *I Married Adventure*. Osa was a sixteen-year-old young woman who married Martin Johnson in 1910, after he had sailed around the world with Jack London. From there, the couple filmed the "uncivilized" worlds of the Solomon Islands, Borneo, and Africa and brought their films back to Broadway. Intrepid explorers. Osa gave me a sense of worldwide possibilities and absolute bravery in the face of danger and loneliness.

I didn't blame my high school teachers for not stimulating me intellectually. It seemed, as I looked around, that it wasn't their purpose. They had other goals and didn't need me to get in their way. They had been supportive of me, in fact selecting me over most other students for special events, such as giving announcements in assemblies and performing little classroom duties, yet they had little time. And forty minutes or so a day, shared with twenty-five to thirty other students, meant that I couldn't really get to my teachers in any significant way. I concluded that if one wanted to read, if one wanted to explore, then one certainly should not expect to do it in an ordered bureaucracy. In my senior year, after the basketball season—a particularly good one for me—I took a full-time job in the local paper-making factory where I had started the summer before at the age of sixteen. I worked about sixty hours a week, sometimes around the clock while attending school fulltime. That forced me to make a decision within six weeks: school or work. School never stood a chance. I left school only weeks before I was to graduate. What my teachers were trying to teach me lacked the flesh and pace of the books I read daily on my own: *Tortilla Flat*, and *Cannery Row; Drums Along the Mohawk; Lorna Doone, Tobacco Road; The Young Manhood of Studs Lonigan;* and *The Naked and the Dead*. And I didn't appreciate being told how to read texts without any say in interpretation and without any concern for the only life I had to test interpretations by, although I did not put it that way then. I left high school in the spring of 1952, remembering Jessie Fleischman and Emerson. She was my English teacher in my junior year. One day she was reading Emerson's "The Rhodora." It was wintertime, old heat registers were gently clanging, my head was on a desk in the back, when I heard her reading aloud, "Tell them, dear, if eyes were made for seeing, then beauty is its own excuse for being."

That was a great moment of preparation for me which lay dormant for some time. Later during my M.A. in Literature from Middlebury College (1965), I rediscovered Emerson and extended some of the beliefs which had surfaced earlier. I also wish that I could go back in time and thank the late Jessie Fleischman. As I reflect now, however, I feel sure she knew how I felt about her. In addition to her love for poetry, she also affected me by what she said after I had performed well on the New York State Regents Examination in English: "You covered yourself with glory, Mr. McCracken." Shades of Miss Eisele. Despite momentary examples like this, I came to feel that high schools may be dangerous to the spirit of most of the young men who are forced to attend. They are too young or spirited or perhaps should not be "civilized" in the way that Huck meant—this schooling way. I saw too many for whom high school was a hostile place. Currently, I visit two or three high schools weekly in my duties as supervisor of student teachers in English and, in some cases, I see changes which may obviate my concern, but mainly I find myself siding with the students in the face of schooling (rules, regulations, and middle class mores). While I worked at the factory, I was singled out by a visiting engineer to become his assistant. He and the other older workers there told me to "return to school and stay there." I listened to them. I returned to high school in the spring of 1954, played the fragmented knowledge game perfectly, then entered the State University of New York at Oswego in the fall.

"2. We assume that subject matter taken on authority is educative in itself."

I found out later in college that a sizeable group of my peers chose the English major because they were rebels or at least somehow thought of themselves as independent thinkers. Most of them, though, were followers of The Word. Somebody's word. The professor's or the great and timeless author's (seldom female I later learned; it is interesting that a male has to *learn* that instead of *observe* it). And they used these authorities to establish a behavior of taste that would make them look good. I remember once serving on a panel with two of my professors (I think they chose me as the student rep because they liked people who argued with them), evaluating a book—it was James Gould Cozzens's *By Love Possessed* (1957)—and the title was the best thing about it. During the questioning period, one of my peers in the audience asked me a question intended to put me in my place and definitely to put himself above that place. He was a year ahead of me and I think he felt himself the darling of the English department and resented my usurpation. His opening move went something like, "As Faulkner has shown us in *Light in August* (1932), as Eliot describes in "The Tradition and Individual Talent" (1920), and as Wallace Stevens almost accomplished in 'Peter Quince at the Clavier' . . . (1923)" Well, you get it. I was faced again with a mimicking of the authority of reference as knowledge. I countered with, "Are you quite sure that Joe Christmas, in his final scene, demonstrates . . ." followed by, "Don't you think that Axel Heyst in Conrad's *Victory* (1921) is a better example of . . . ?" The smiles all around led me to understand that I had beaten the challenger. I was, after all, in the favored position, one of the lecturers for the evening, and I was not confrontational in my responses, so the mixed audience of students and professors took my side. I soon came to dislike the aftertaste of that and similar encounters: too much like fighting cocks. I had always played basketball and boxed to win, but the winning wasn't critical. What really mattered, my body told me, was playing, doing. My body also told me that school encounters where "winning" mattered were anti-intellectual. That included grading and prizes. Winning first trivialized, then obviated the act, the thought, the relationship. I echoed the cliché of the day, as you can tell I still hold with it, that how you play the game defines you. Connected knowledge, that combination of body, spirit, and mind, came to be the one constant for me. When high school tried to tear apart the connected knowledge that I had only begun to form, it didn't, I understood, mean anything personal. Instead of being asked to ape authorities, or being left alone to decide how to leap over the faults and fissures, I should have been asked to explore my own visions, my own roles, and my perceptions of others as avenues to understanding new concepts, new ways. But who had time for that? I was not rebelling against teachers so much as against a public arrangement that trapped us all, although, again, I would not have put it that way then. We were fragments of each other's lives in ways that were supposed to make "subject matter" the authority.

"3. We assume that the best way to set out subject matter is in unassociated fragments or parcels."

As long as subject matter is perceived as discrete knowledge, it will remain without power to affect lives. Today I think of code-words which suggest a predilection for such constructions of subject matter: "skills," "phonics," "basics," "basal readers," "eighteenth-century British literature." Colleges continue to act on anything beyond segments of knowledge as "interdisciplinary," a kind of connected knowledge that is generally not allowed in the system. Interdisciplinary has the flavor of extradisciplinary, a synthesis producing a new discipline, and sometimes it has the flavor of antidisciplinary. Both meanings of the word work against the system. Those meanings suggest *interdisciplinary* as rebellion. Segmentation works within disciplines very powerfully. Most students find that when the issue is whose interpretation of text has the most authority, the "segmented" teacher wins. Now my goal as a "connected" teacher is achieved when a class is studying a text and I happen to give my interpretation, to which someone responds, "Who asked you?" I would try to think of the student's growth and my own wherever I could, but our system isn't designed for it. We evaluate in terms of analytic and discrete approaches. Many teachers do integrate knowledge and people and movement, but they do so in spite of the system and are seldom rewarded for it.

The connected knowledge I had begun to learn as a youngster was too early separated out and placed in different venues: on the court, in unassociated classrooms. One of the things I learned was that adults I knew cared a great deal about me as long as I excelled in their segmented world. If I skipped across segmentations, whatever excellence was originally rewarded within segments became diffused. Disciplines and teachers seemed to work within segments, constantly protecting their positions by becoming more specialized at them or just better at them. Teachers become more comfortable as they gain expertise and support. I found that I no longer felt wary or defensive about my teaching and scholarship performances when I had become comfortable in the profession. That occurred for me by my fourth year of high school teaching and in other ways by my fifth year of college teaching.

"4. We assume that a fragment or parcel of subject matter is the same to the learner as to the teacher."

When I began teaching at a rural central school (K–12) in Adams Center, New York, in the fall of 1958, I took with me my beginning understanding of what English was and how I should share it with eighth and ninth graders. It was not yet connected knowledge, because it takes time to *produce* connected knowledge. I was, therefore, subject to most of the conventions already in place. The first thing I received was a four-page document from the superintendent, not the principal or a colleague. That document listed all the grammar I was to teach to my eighth graders. The profession had already produced research since the turn of the century showing that teaching grammar as a means of improving speech or writing was almost surely mistaken. Yet here it was: an order opposing what I thought I had understood in my studies. I taught those four pages and more, realizing only later that it was not much different from making sure that the American flag was hanging in front of my room every day. Cultural myths are stronger than fragmented knowledge (but are related). I remember too that when I had the seats rearranged in a circle, a student in the class came to me and said, "I told my aunt who teaches English in Adams [the next school down the road] that you had us seated this way and she said, "Don't worry. He'll be gone next year." Because I knew that method and subject are intertwined, I thought that students would see it too. Many just saw it as strange, although some were charmed. I stayed for four years, receiving tenure in a place I understood—rural America—but it was too small a world for me then.

Today when our English education students graduate from our program, my colleagues and I at Youngstown State University assume many things about what they do in their own classrooms. We can barely believe it when we occasionally find out two or three years later that a former student, now Teacher X, opposed or simply wasn't affected by our example in the English education program. What we had assumed was clear, irrefutable, and best, this teacher had simply ignored. How could that be? How could we, even now, not know that "a parcel of subject matter is not the same to the learner as to the teacher"? Beginning secondary teachers are often told by experienced teachers to forget what they have learned in college, particularly when it comes to making changes in texts, in seating arrangements, and in how much their students are encouraged to speak. Sometimes it is Teacher X again, the very person who denied her college program earlier. If change is to occur, it must come from the hearts and minds of students and citizens who have the fortitude to become the teachers and community members they originally envisioned.

A strong position in our profession is that the best we can do is model good teaching and learning for our students as a way of resisting bad examples and traditions. However, when I asked an English department colleague from an Ivy League university recently whether she thought she had responsibility to model good pedagogy for the preservice English teachers in her classes, she replied that she feels no such responsibility, nor for the requirements of any other particular vocational interest that her students may have. Such modeling is "required" in some cases for college accreditation, although her particular university doesn't belong to an accrediting agency. My colleague did not sign on to call attention to how she arranged learning for her students, as she argues. Her goals are to extend the goals of the learned societies in her field, in this case the Modern Language Association. Interest in pedagogy, let alone any serious study of it, is not an integral part of the enterprise of learned societies. Academic culture wants attention given to products and pedigrees, not to processes and pedagogy. Yet, for my colleague to deny the value of the very thing she does—teaching—seems somehow to be perverse or a bit blind. "But," she might say, "my own education without attention to pedagogy was good enough for me." Perhaps though, good pedagogy doesn't just happen. Good pedagogy is where the growth of the learner is at center stage and the teacher is well away from it. Within good pedagogy, parcels of subject matter, approached with an understanding that they are different for every learner, become diffused into a trinity: the learner, the teacher, and the subject. That makes a classroom learning-centered and not centered on any one of the three.

"5. We assume that education is supplementary to and preparatory to life, not life itself."

For college students the important world is supposed to begin afterwards. Commencement ceremonies seem to underscore the separation and irrelevance of what was just experienced. Life commences after graduation, students are told. Really? The best kind of future planning is to unleash the imagination of the learner. I think we are most alive (or feel the "real" world most) when we exercise our imaginations. From Plato's view, I can imagine, time "after" the use of imagination is a shadow world. And if we rid ourselves of the belief that learning is preparation for something else, we'll engage our students as never before. Tall order.

Connected knowledge does not grow well in a prerequisite system, the system colleges and schools have built. Harold Taylor, in a book called *How to Change Colleges: Notes on Radical Reform*, explained in 1971 that the lecture system (paying for instruction by offering classes through segments or departments) is the one thing that he does not believe can be changed. He may be right, but we can all at least examine what we're doing in this life, on this day in our classes. In my own methods class this quarter for twenty-eight students, who will be student teaching within the next two quarters then graduating, our emphasis is on what the student can learn about high school students in school settings and how language arts can make them come alive. That kind of knowledge is useful to legislators, community planners, almost anyone interested in adolescents and those who are interested in their own adolescence. But I also place emphasis upon undergraduates who are being. That is, the most obvious of vocational classes on the surface, the methods class, actually exists for anyone who wants to engage with people and ideas: the primary goal is for learners to talk to each other, to read and write to and for each other, and to respect each other. So whatever preparation qualities it may have are subordinated to the here and now. I am a facilitator in a workshop which has students working in groups to make portfolios and resource files for teaching. Their portfolios answer the fourteen questions established for the National Professional Board for Teaching Standards. Some of these are: "(1) I am systematically acquiring a sense of my students as individual language learners;" "(4) I try to create a caring, inclusive and challenging environment in which students actively learn;" and "(7) I am learning how to immerse students in the art of writing." So that's part of what I do.

"6. We assume that since education is not present living, it has no social aspects."

While collaborative learning has undergone a resurgence of popularity since the late 1970s, including multiple authors in dissertations and academic publications, it has not replaced classrooms which have familiar and apparently settling nineteenth-century characteristics. Seats are placed in rows; assignments are given and returned individually; grades are sought after and assigned competitively and, as Kelley says, "The one who pays the least attention to the fact that he is surrounded by other social beings is the one we value the most" (19). Although schools and colleges are the most social of places outside of classrooms, teachers and administrators often try to make places of learning asocial.

We have a whole system of competitive rewards which define academic endeavors and sort people out: merit, scholarships, and class ranking. Classrooms and classes will have to be built upon the belief that students learn socially if teachers are to become facilitators of learning instead of dispensers of it. That is especially true of college English classes, where the majority of instruction, occurring by example for the prospective teacher of English language arts, may affect values and attitudes about teaching more profoundly than courses in pedagogy. Such courses often model competition and transmission of fragmented knowledge, a subject of particular interest for me in the M.S. in English education degree I earned at SUNY Oswego in 1962. It was there that my rebellion began working toward more productive ways of integrating pedagogy and subjects, working toward producing connected knowledge for others rather than using it to defend myself from others.

"7. We assume that the teacher can and should furnish the purpose needed for the acquiring of knowledge."

What Kelley means here is that the teacher will decide what is taught and why it is learned. "The real world out there requires us to follow orders, write on specified topics, so freshman composition ought to reflect that world," a colleague of mine just said. Many college teachers regard determining what is to be taught as part of their jobs and would be either amused or angry to be told that some other arrangement might be more appropriate. They have been hired to teach nineteenth-century British Literature or even freshman composition and have been educated in what that subject is. It is, they might say, idle daydreaming, or, if taken more seriously, sheer romanticism to suggest that the learners have some decision in texts and procedures. The reality for me is that either students participate in decision-making or not much learning will take place. Nevertheless, our best students have become highly skilled at learning when someone else chooses their texts and even chooses the responses to those texts. When we make such changes—say choosing the texts together—(as I write I am preparing an English Education seminar for graduate students that will give them options in choosing texts and procedures)—those students are often the first to be wary. Change is not seen positively when one has been successful in the status quo. For me "acquiring knowledge" is making connections among texts to apply to my life and to other texts. Keeping knowledge separated and at sound-bite length, as in "Jeopardy" or "cultural literacy," is anti-intellectual. It doesn't require making connections consciously, but rather making connections through the synapses. It is done for you. Segmented knowledge suggests quick recall of isolated items. So we need to help students make decisions, especially when asked about what to study and how to go about it initially.

I was having lunch with a young colleague the other day. She is serious, hard-working, and a really good teacher, as our students say. We got to talking about a student in her class, an older man who had grown-up daughters, who was the breath of life in the class. He was verbally astute, cooperative, and something of a leader all at once. She enjoyed him and his work in the class, but he couldn't write and that would destroy his A in all of the rest of the class, perhaps even cause him to flunk. My colleague seemed to be looking for an answer, so I suggested having him compose on audiotape, edit it, then submit that as his "paper" to be graded, as I have occasionally done in my composition classes. "No. I don't think anyone should get by unless they can write." A gatekeeper in that respect. Composing seems less various to some instructors than to others.

"8. We assume that working on tasks devoid of purpose or interest is good discipline."

Of course, to some people everything English teachers do in interpreting texts ranges from evil to frivolous. The world excuses us a little if we teach grammar, written exposition, and other practical enterprises; independent, tough operations to get along in the world of business. Business leaders often see college teachers as the trainers for their own corporate purposes and in many ways, especially in enterprises like freshman composition, we comply, as Dick Ohmann made clear in *English in America: A Radical View of the Profession* (1976). Some argue that we succeed best where we undercut the business world by encouraging students to read critically and skeptically. But how students reconcile those oppositional values with the ones emanating from their eventual employers makes for interesting stories. Tasks which are devoid of purpose in education are those that I perceive as continuing to make people submissive. English educators came together formally by establishing NCTE's Conference on English Education in 1963 (an organization of which I was Chair from 1986–88) and by the time I completed my Ph.D. from the University of Illinois in 1970, which included two summers spent in Mississippi working on Head Start, I was on a mission to make changes. In the '60s though, others in the profession, and some English educators, were creating materials of hard "subject-bound" quality to show that English meant business in the United States. The Project English materials still remind me of the collusion with business interests. Our rattling the saber of high standards was just what corporate America wanted, winnowing out their leaders for them. So now, somewhat perversely, I associate calls for high standards with Marxist critiques of culture. Some of that rattling we did resulted in the attempt by the College Board to influence the definition of English in *Freedom and Discipline in English* in 1965, a work devoted, in major part, to the notion that hard facts discipline the mind. In 1966, The Dartmouth Conference helped turn the tide away from discrete knowledge (described in Herbert Muller's *The Uses of English* [1967] and more powerfully in John Dixon's *Growth Through English* [1967]). Those of us who still hold a sense of mission from those days can't help making these references repeatedly.

"9. We assume that the answer to the problem is more important than the process."

Most English and English education professors would agree that this seems true of science professors, but not of them. Teachers of creative writing courses also often exempt themselves from scientific, although not necessarily authoritarian, answers to problems. Teachers of college literature (I am one of those too) succumb to such conclusions when they dictate how a work will be read so that literate conclusions will not be muddied by the muck of students' lives. But many don't do that and find themselves unfairly lumped together in a stereotype. Often teachers are forced into being expert answer-givers by the culture around them, their students, and certainly those who fund colleges and universities. Kelley's greatest concern is that teachers may continue to use so many meaningless problems in order to focus on the answer that meaninglessness is what is learned. Still, I occasionally feel that something that appears to be meaningless has great power. Consider, for example, the mantras of Allen Ginsberg (or consider them as two examples).

"10. We assume that it is more important to measure what has been learned than it is to learn."

One of the great concerns of every generation of K–graduate school teachers is identifying the political climate in which they work, for that climate controls the temperature of assessment. It too often appears that we teach in order to measure. It takes time in harness for teachers to make significant strides in their teaching no matter what goal or standards are used, but the more intrepid start immediately. I remember a colleague, Barrett Mandell, then at Rutgers in the English department, who wrote a little book called *Literature and the English Department* (1970). It was very much appreciated by people in English education, but not very much by other English folk, a surprise to him then in his early career. He speaks of giving all As to those in his literature classes and being called in by the dean to account for his lack of discrimination. That dean, I am assuming, did not share Mandell's effort to rid the class of external judgments so it could attend to what was important—reading and responding to literature. And Peter Elbow has written of the grading dilemma in *Embracing Contraries: Explorations in Learning and Teaching* (1986). His notion is that if goals are set high, then the teacher and the students help each other reach them. It is the tension between the teacher's nurturing and judging behaviors that prompts much of the anguish in measuring student work. And we ourselves forget sometimes that we are not measuring students, but only their work. In my just completed methods class, in which the twenty-eight students spent each day in workshop, the grades were half As and half Bs, based upon a division of 40 percent portfolios; 20 percent resource files; 20 percent class writing; and 20 percent reports. Some might say that not enough discrimination is made among these preservice teachers, all of whom will be graduating with certification within the year. No bell curve here. My goal is to continue to help them *be,* as they think about teaching and integrating teaching and learning with their lives, not act as a gatekeeper for the profession on the basis of a few classes.

So, I still see Kelley as a rebel, one who continues to influence me because of his strong sense of mission for teaching and learning, and because of the compassion he had for his students. I am very pleased to be where I am now. I have long since been fully taken in, as I had been in eighth grade and some moments in high school, and it may be that rebellion, or not being taken in by orders and regulations, got me here. Where my students have made their voices stronger, have become more confident and able to do what will make their personal and professional lives close, rebellion seems vindicated.

Works Cited

Belenky, Mary, et al. 1986. *Women's Ways of Knowing: The Development of Self, Voice, and Mind.* New York: Basic Books.

Blackmore, R. D. (Richard Doddridge). 1869. *Lorna Doone.* Reprint, New York: E. P. Dutton, 1912.

Caldwell, Erskine. 1932. *Tobacco Road.* Reprint, New York: New American Library, 1956.

Commission on English. 1965. *Freedom and Discipline in English.* New York: College Entrance Examination Board.

Conrad, Joseph. 1921. *Victory.* New York: Modern Library.

Cozzens, James Gould. 1957. *By Love Possessed.* New York: Harcourt, Brace.

Dixon, John. 1967. *Growth Through English: A Report Based on the Dartmouth Seminar 1966.* Reading, England: National Association for the Teaching of English.

Edmonds, Walter. 1936. *Drums Along the Mohawk.* Boston: Little, Brown.

Elbow, Peter. 1986. *Embracing Contraries: Explorations in Learning and Teaching.* New York: Oxford University Press.

Eliot, T. S. 1920. "Tradition and the Individual Talent." *The Sacred Wood: Essays on Poetry and Criticism.* Reprint, London: Methuen, 1934.

Emerson, Ralph Waldo. 1839. "The Rhodora." Reprinted in *Poems of Ralph Waldo Emerson*. New York: Oxford University Press, 1914.

Farrell, James T. 1934. *The Young Manhood of Studs Lonigan*. Reprint, New York: The Modern Library, 1963.

Faulkner, William. 1932. *Light in August*. Reprint, New York: Modern Library, 1950.

Ginsberg, Allen. 1959. *Howl, and Other Poems*. San Francisco: City Lights Books.

Johnson, Osa. 1940. *I Married Adventure*. New York: J. B. Lippincott.

Kelley, Earl C. and Marie I. Rasey. 1952. *Education and the Nature of Man*. New York: Harper.

——. 1947. *Education for What is Real*. New York: Harper.

——. 1962. *In Defense of Youth*. Englewood Cliffs, NJ: Prentice-Hall.

——. 1951. *The Workshop Way of Learning*. New York: Harper.

Mailer, Norman. 1948. *The Naked and the Dead*. New York: Rinehart.

Mandel, Barrett John. 1970. *Literature and the English Department*. Champaign, IL: NCTE.

Muller, Herbert. 1967. *The Uses of English: Guidelines for the Teaching of English from the Anglo-American Conference at Dartmouth College*. New York: Holt, Rinehart and Winston.

Ohmann, Richard. 1976. *English in America: A Radical View of the Profession*, with a chapter by Wallace Douglas. New York: Oxford University Press.

Steinbeck, John. 1945. *Cannery Row*. New York: Viking Press.

——. 1947. *Tortilla Flat*, with seventeen paintings by Peggy Worthington. New York: Viking Press.

Stevens, Wallace. 1923. "Peter Quince at the Clavier." Reprinted in *Collected Poems*. New York: Knopf, 1955.

Taylor, Harold. 1971. *How to Change Colleges: Notes on Radical Reform*. New York: Holt, Rinehart and Winston.

II Going Along

The first step in the "patronage" style of advancement: I found faculty members who became my patrons and who made it possible for me to succeed.

David Bleich

5 How Do the Electrons Get Across the Two Plates of the Capacitor? Becoming a Writing Teacher

David Bleich
University of Rochester

No matter how many years go by, I always think back to my parents in reference to how I perceive the origins of my school and professional interests. Both started out as actors, and my father remained one outside the home for most of his adult life. My mother stopped professional acting at age twenty-six, when she and my father were married. Our home, our family gatherings, became a stage and our lives felt dramatic.

My mother was unusually articulate. Her identifying feature (to me and to many others) was the razor-like effect of her words. When she cut, you would bleed. She could find the right word, the right name, the right phrase, the right description, for almost anything. When she found these right terms, you could feel extraordinary sensations of affective understanding, as well as a moral, a message, a thought, a judgment, a complete perspective on things. She used this talent to survive in our family as well as to teach, indirectly, my brother and me her experiences in life. She was a fabulous name-caller—snot, dishrag, tightwad, or the frequently used adjective (in Yiddish, but translated), piggish or swinish. She used other names in Polish and in Yiddish that I just can't translate, but their very sound was uplifting. An unregenerate and mean-spirited person was a "cholera"; an insincere person and a scoundrel was called a "meshummed" (a traitor, a backstabber).

Once when I was eight (or so) and sitting in the kitchen watching her cook, as I often did, with perhaps her sister or someone else of the female persuasion there, I suddenly realized that my fly was open, and I quickly moved to close it. My mother, noticing this and having an audience, said, (in Yiddish, but here translated), "Don't worry, no one will grab anything away from you." This was in good humor and not meant to be mean, even if it was somewhat derisive. It was, as I must have learned much before that time, "Jewish teasing."

During the last four years of her life, my mother slowly lost her competence. Throughout this painful process, I now remember that at least once a day she seemed to retain that verbal acumen (mainly about things in immediate experience, since she could remember less and less). We were sitting outdoors at the nursing home in Rochester and I remarked to her, "You know, Mom, you are ninety-years-old." She looked at me, smiled, and said, "That's ridiculous."

There was a point when my mother's verbal talent and my father's commitment to acting "took" in my mind. I remember deciding (when I was about twenty) that I would enjoy teaching writing the rest of my life. At that time, I had learned how to write and had tasted actual teaching more than once at M.I.T. Yet I only began paying serious attention to the teaching of writing fifteen years or so ago, and as an expansion of my many years collecting and studying the responses people had to reading literature. As I got older and less occupied with securing a good role in the academy, I became less interested in "big pictures"—things that began with capital letters like Theory and Literature—and more interested in language use and everyday thinking. I began to value how important a small element of language use could be, a single word, or a single phrase given in a distinctive tone.

Rather than "The Text," "The Reader," and other stylish but conventional abstractions, I began to pay attention to the social and psychological details of reading, writing, and teaching: the habits of language use that sneak into our minds and make us into social beings. These habits, barely in our conscious sense of things, teach us who is to be loved, who feared, who admired, who rejected. They also tell us where we belong and affiliate us with others we may not even like or trust. Many of these habits are preserved in printed literature, appearing strange to us since we are unconscious of them to begin with. Once I learned the phrase "foolish prating knave," I understood this to be a translation of a piece of my own experience that I could not quite name before. But simply having the phrase identify my specific, remembered experience taught me its meaning. In graduate school it seemed to matter that I knew who wrote this phrase. Perhaps it still matters.

After many years of teaching, I have come to feel that there is less and less difference between what is written and what is spoken or said. If you can't read and can only listen to someone reading, it feels like that person is speaking, or better, telling us something. But it feels that way even if we can read. When we refer to a written text, sometimes we say "it says" and not "it reads." To "read" something is also to "interpret" it. In aircraft, "to read" means "to hear." "Do you read me?" I feel something like "language is one" with many different forms or manifestations. I think one important breakthrough for me is understanding the "oneness" of language, as well as a person's "oneness with" the language. From today's perspective—and I mean only this twenty-four-hour period—here is what I think happened to teach me this idea of language.

Until my third year in college, when I was eighteen, English was my worst subject. In the late '40s and early '50s, when I was ending my K–12 period, I excelled in science and math. I did not discern real value in being articulate, and although I frequently spoke up and out in school, I did not consider the meaning and value of becoming articulate. Since I was a good student anyway, I wrote well enough to be considered able, but not well enough to be distinguished, but that did not matter because math and science were what "really" mattered. During the above-mentioned period, the cold war was intensifying, and the transistor was just discovered. At the time, radios and television sets were made with vacuum tubes, almost an unknown item today. When I was eleven, my father's (and my) wishes overrode my mother's objections and we got a television set, an item of spectacular fascination for me at the time. In spite of my mother's constant urgings to read, I considered sports, science, and math (in that order) to be the activities for me. I played the piano and learned Hebrew after school; my parents said these were important. My best subject was French; I could outdo my brother.

In school (high school and college), I learned about vacuum tubes. At the "heart" of this item is/was a capacitor. It was depicted on the blackboard and in diagrams as two vertical parallel lines with a space in between. Its functions were explained through "circuit theory," a difficult and demanding subject. The key image in circuit theory for me was the "flow" of electrons, as if they were palpable "things" that obeyed laws vaguely analogous to, but decidedly different from, those describing the flow of water through pipes. One of these differences was that a capacitor may be part of a circuit. In other words, in spite of the gap of air (an insulator which did not conduct electricity) or emptiness between the parallel plates of the capacitor, this element functioned *as if* electricity "flowed" right through it. I must have asked dozens of times how this happened if either air or empty space ("vacuum" tubes) separated the plates of the capacitor. While the explanations seemed to honor my obvious desire to believe that electrons were just very small but solid "things," they did not finally admit that *no one really knew or understood just what happened — in the same sense as knowing the mechanics of billiard balls — inside the capacitor*. One of the occasions of my shifting to English in college was my discovery that experts knew only, and with certainty, how the capacitor will *behave* in an electric or electronic circuit. The mathematical descriptions of circuits, which did accurately predict how the circuits function, were the "understanding" that one had about circuits.

A related discovery of mine was this: when learning about quantum theory in college, I saw that, due to the work of Bohr and other early twentieth century scientists, statistical descriptions (as opposed to Newtonian mechanical descriptions—again, as are applied to billiard balls) were considered the real knowledge of subatomic phenomena. In other words, my learning that scientific descriptions in mathematics *could not correspond with verbal descriptions that presupposed mechanical palpability of phenomena* disillusioned me about science and persuaded me that it was a game I could not and did not want to play. To put it still another way: at first I thought that science—in my case, physics—really did "get to" the essence of "matter." I learned that this essence did not matter, but that what mattered was to get *enough* knowledge to be able to *predict* (pre-say) whatever it was that was studied. I now sometimes think, furthermore, that science tries to study *only* what will result in predictability. Understanding most scientific things, I learned, amounted to learning the mathematics that enabled us to predict and manipulate behavior.

There was no such thing, I came to believe, as just plain understanding, no such thing as the *veritas* that transcended the practical situations, that found its way onto so many misleading university seals. On the other hand, the use of language did not require a belief in a fixed, eternal, apodictic objective reality that was "higher" than the reality that we had come to accept through the use of verbal language. The scientists relied on a language to create their ideals. I learned that the ideology of science required the belief in the superiority of mathematical language to be suppressed. My perception of the oneness of language helped me toward the thought of the equivalence of different languages rather than their hierarchical arrangement.

During this same time in college, my perception that the verbally articulated symbolic family in *Death of a Salesman* actually explained something about my family, which also had two parents and two sons, seemed to be the kind of knowledge (postdiction, after-saying) that mattered to me, as well as the kind I could discover and announce with confidence. To this day I wonder if so many people really do want to know about electrons and about the origin of the universe, and if so few people consider what happens in families and classrooms as important as understanding physics. By reading and responding to literature, I understood that knowing *feels differently* than I thought it felt when I thought I knew science. In fact, in facing issues of language and literature, knowing *had* for me a *feeling of understanding* for the first time. Being able to relate this known experience to that known experience creates a new feeling; to know science had only the feeling of being able to perform certain exercises as well as others perform them. At the time that I felt I understood knowing, I also felt ready to be a teacher, and I did teach my peers a few times as an undergraduate, with the encouragement of my teachers.

However, there is a sense in which my involvement in teaching represented a differentiation from home in a way symmetrical to how my interest in language and literature represents an identification with home. Becoming a self-conscious teacher of language and literature seems now to have been associated in my history with gender identity and how it began to depart from its expected path of change in my life. At first, in my youth and young adulthood, my sense of gender identity was orthodox, but later in life, in my late thirties, it gradually changed as I began more satisfactorily, and to me more accurately, to identify the continuous drumbeat of discontent in my experience with the academic styles of prosecuting its missions of scholarship and teaching—styles that I had begun to see as socially masculine. Put another way, I came into university teaching because of the high value this profession had for men, especially insofar as it was a "search for truth" modeled by masculine scientists. Pursuing a masculine identity, was, in our society, synonymous with identifying outside the home. Both "inside" and "outside" of the home were gender identified.

My home felt "different" from other homes because Yiddish was my parents' native language and, as a result, English seemed like a "foreign" language. After a while, that I could speak English better than my parents posed a problem for me—it was as if I were an outsider at home. I was first able to identify with my father when, in my third year in college, I took his suggestion to read *Death of a Salesman*, received his indirect communication, and understood that his accent did not matter. My recognition of the value and worth of both my family and literature were mobilized by my achieving the traditional masculine gender identity. Also in my home, things happened which did not make sense and were sometimes unpleasant. But at school— the "outside"—everything seemed to make sense and the unpleasant things were still comprehensible. All these things considered, it took a long time for me to "understand" that my parents were immigrants, that they uprooted themselves and started over so that their children could have good lives, and that they endured my impatient judgments in this cause.

School first became a space of emancipation when I caught on to its public, nondomestic logic in the first grade. While taking pleasure in my ability to succeed, I was unconscious of the privileges the New York City School system gave to boys like me. The fifth grade, in particular, "masculinized" school when my one and only male teacher in elementary school introduced sports and science to the curriculum. These emphases further increased the good feeling that school had, and because I was myself male, school itself seemed vaguely to conceal the partiality of its gender emphasis. I say "vaguely" because it was obvious that the girls did not participate as I did, and I was not able to identify accurately the difference between their ways of participation and my own. I went to an all-male high school, a privileged one where you had to pass a test to be admitted, and to an all-male college, also privileged and selective. Why these were my opportunities, I did not know, but that they were opportunities was unmistakable. Nor did I know why my father and brother thought I should take these opportunities, but my mother thought that a more modest college choice was desirable. College seemed like utopia to me: everything was paid for, and my parents were not there to supervise my life. One could do whatever one wanted. I thought: high school and college were all male because both emphasized science, which is what men do. Real men understand the essence of capacitors.

College was good because even though the "humanities" teacher gave me a D minus on my first essay and read it aloud to give the class an example of "unintelligible" writing, he called me "Mr. Bleich," and not just "Bleich" as they did in high school. Furthermore, this teacher seemed interested in getting to know me, especially when he found out I knew Hebrew and could contribute something different to his "Bible as Literature" course the following year. On the other hand, this teacher had no truck with my including "current events"—in 1956, the British, French, and Americans invaded Egypt to protect the Suez Canal during the Israeli war with its Arab neighbors—in my essay on *Antigone*.

To give an idea of how far I was from learning to write for the academy, it took until about the end of my third year in college to write essays that stuck to the topic and adopted an analytical tone, thus producing "insight." This was about 1958, when one key to professional, academic success in literature was "insight." This word, in part, connected well to my interest in and experience of psychoanalysis, in which of course, Insight is what made you "get better." In one zone of the academy where my admired teacher, Leon Edel, worked, the ingroups of new criticism and psychoanalysis were united, and all the more influential, flying the common flag of "insight."

Insight got me through graduate school. In my senior year in college, while writing my bachelor's thesis on T. S. Eliot's plays, I learned how to write completely in Insight, to sustain sixty-four pages of analytical discussion without a single thought that I could believe in, but with dozens of insights about the plays and how they progressed toward their final state of what I today identify as maudlin religious syrup. The Rule of Insight urged me to take no account of the insufferably boring experience of reading Eliot's *The Elder Statesman*. When I finally got over Insight at the end of graduate school, the issues of androcentrism and Jew-hating became more prominent in my readings of Eliot. He appeared to me then, and increasingly now, to be a spokesman for the discontent of culture and not its enhancement. After recently rereading his two essays on culture and Christianity, the term "foolish prating knave" came to mind, in addition to the usual "pair of ragged claws / Scuttling across the floors of silent seas."

It took me three or four years of graduate school and I-forgot-whose review of Leslie Fiedler's *Love and Death in the American Novel* (1960) to understand the difference between insight and ideas. Fiedler's performance was the beginning of the end of Insight (I thought), and I moved on to things I thought would be permanently worthwhile—like understanding modern utopianism as a literary and cultural feature of collective psychology. However, just when I placed Insight in history and began teaching literary response seriously, Insight returned in its new Gallic packaging (theory, poststructuralism, postmodernism) as academics seemed to get drunk on a binge of new jobs and public respect during the late '60s and early '70s (Yes, this is when I got my first job). Even though contemporary feminism was emerging, it seemed to many academics, including some feminists, to be necessary to revive, with a vengeance, the thought and language styles that were used by the cozy club of male academics who were helping to create obfuscating cultural adornments for the captains of industry and the traditional ideologies of hierarchical social philosophy.

I was in graduate school just before the foregoing changes in the interests of the literary academy. What was the phenomenology of most of my classes in graduate school at New York University? I remember learning something very remarkable about "speaking up" in classes that had about ninety students in them and which were all lectures. Well of course, the teacher would recognize raised hands and thus, however inappropriate because of the large size, people would speak in class and comment on the lecture or the novel under discussion. Then I noticed that if I raised my hand and spoke in every meeting, the teacher would remember who I was, providing only that I *seemed* intelligently to enhance the topics of the lecture. I always did have something to say, and I *hated* to shut up and listen to expert lectures, but I did not know if it was "all right" to indulge these desires to participate in a conversation. When I saw that teachers welcomed contributions, I spoke up (in classes where I liked the teacher) and this helped me, in the long run, to enter the academy. I remember that it was perhaps only men who spoke up in large classes, and not many at that. But unconsciously, I learned how to "win" the competition for a limited amount of attention from the faculty. It helped me to enter the academy because it was the first step in the "patronage" style of advancement. I found faculty members who became my patrons and who made it possible for me to succeed. Because I had a father who respected my work because I had learned to respect his work, I knew how to become a good son (to a father) in the outside world of graduate school.

However, I was not such a good son to a mother. If I just went on the experience of my home, I would never have learned that women "feel silenced." Both my parents could "speak out" and did, at home and in public. My father could raise his voice and was good at telling the "truth." My mother did not raise her voice as much, but if she did, it was not necessarily in anger. Also, she did not revere the truth (*veritas*, again) as much as my father did. I always thought that if my mother did not speak, it was with consummate discreet calculation. If my parents argued, which they did at times, I invariably felt my mother would "kill" (verbally) my father. If my father would declare how things "would be" my mother would say "we'll see." She seemed so much more ominous to me than did my father's more histrionic behavior, because, I imagine, she was more restrained and calculating.

I feel certain that language styles in Jewish homes are different from those in Christian homes, particularly those Christian homes that are not Irish or Italian. I cannot remember any Jewish women who are not verbal and outspoken; I know there are such people. My knowledge of women feeling and being silenced comes mainly from observation in public scenes and knowledge of speech patterns in Protestant homes—for example, the dinner scene in *Annie Hall.* Nevertheless, Robin Lakoff, an internationally known academic Jewish woman, reports in her book *Talking Power* (1990) on her role in faculty committee meetings comprised mostly of men as: "But once I had spoken, the discourse would close over me like the ocean enveloping a pebble. It was as if I had not spoken—in fact did not exist" (149). She is referring to the endless arguing overwhelming her subdued contributions. In a not-so-obscure way, it now seems that what Lakoff reports about academic life does resemble what went on in my home; I just did not *perceive* my mother as "silenced."

Most people would think that my mother's language was rather harsh. Of course, I did too at the time, but as I grew older, I realized I learned to speak like her and from her. It took even longer for me to understand the profound irony of her speech, how utterly opposite of its tone and energy were the actual feelings behind her words. The fact is that my mother, because of her sense of what a woman's duty was, as well as her sense of inner despair about getting in return the devotion she routinely gave, periodically lashed out in quiet but deep anger over what sometimes seemed to be trivial provocations—arriving late for dinner, for example. She did not merely want acknowledgement that she was a superb cook—everyone always told her that—she hoped for the same regular, daily, monthly, yearly expenditure of involvement in her life by us three men at home that might match her involvement in ours, but was not forthcoming from any of us.

My mother sometimes would be silent for three days, trying to honor her own outrage (at one of us having presumed just too much), yet not wanting to fight. This too felt to me like "cruel and unusual punishment." But while it felt bad to me, I did not approach understanding of how badly she felt when she became aware, at these "small" instances of thoughtlessness we men routinely showed, of how unlikely it was that her own emotional and social needs would be met. One result of this situation is that I was unaware, until my thirties perhaps, that the political situation in my home was somewhat different than it appeared to me then: my father was free to work on one job, while my mother had to have two—home and her job as a dressmaker. Although my father was both ethical and generous, he too did not understand what my mother's needs really were, and recognized them, in part, only when he was in his fifties, as I am now also trying to "recognize" things earlier censored.

The language situation in my first home now seems to me to have been a political struggle. My father's was the "direct" language—the "truth"—of the established class; my mother's the "indirect" and angry language of the subordinate group. Being acculturated to identify with my father, I began to rely in college and graduate school on what seemed to me to be "direct" language even though I learned just as decisively the usefulness and pleasure of "indirect" language. Because my mother was so good at Yiddish, and because her anger relied on that, her "mother tongue," I also associated this "indirect" language with Jews as a minority. As a cultural figure, my mother was much more aware than my father of how Jews were opposed in society. My father was much less suspicious of the "outside world," and he was much more given to join in its various celebrations and enjoyments. He felt America was truly a liberating place to be. My mother also appreciated America (both were born in Poland and arrived here in 1921), but she did not accept the belief that in America the historic role of Jews in Christian societies had been revolutionized. My parents' perceptions of cultural roles and possibilities seemed definitely to have been closely connected with their gender identities, and I seem to have "inherited" some combination of these identities.

My perceptions since being in the university as a faculty member are that in ordinary mixed population classes, across racial and ethnic boundaries, women are *invariably* more polite and patient than men are. Men interrupt much more easily, "take" the floor, hold it longer, speak louder, make the point more than twice, and then allow very little time for (female) response. Male response happens when another male speaker interrupts and does the same thing as the first male speaker. Men, often myself included, are, seemingly involuntarily, taken up into a speaking "contest"; the arguing "tropism" seems to go into action all by itself. Here is what Lakoff says: "After a while I figured it out. My colleagues were playing by men's rules: what was important was to gain turf, control territory. That goal was achieved by spreading words around" (1990, 149). For a long time I had taken for granted the adversarial or "challenge" model of intellectual exploration, the technique of justifying one's own views by, as Karl Popper had explained, "falsifying" others: if someone makes a "competing" point that you may have some trouble accepting, find out how you can defeat it, show that your point is obviously better, and, naturally, *win.* The more you win, the more "respect" you get, including getting your work published, tenure, money, etc. The presupposition of discussion in my many classroom experiences as a student and then as a teacher has been conflict and dispute. I am having to learn, as a teacher, how to encourage a discussion in which the following items may appear in but do not define the experience: arguing, winning, scoring points with "evidence," loud voices, showing others up, agreeing with the teacher, remaining silent. Once these items are *not definitive,* it is easier for a classroom discussion to include many voices, to abide silence, to pose questions, to teach all members in all classrooms. Once the teacher's facts and opinions are equivalent in weight to those of the students', just what is to be understood as "true" also becomes less fixed, more open to collective determination. And if, in pursuit of a more generous and just classroom ideology, the received, traditional ways of teaching and learning are discredited and other ways are needed or included, school may become one of the principal sites for the transformation of collective values many of us have been hoping for for a long time.

Becoming a writing teacher took a circuitous route in my life because of the foregoing political considerations. When I was about to graduate college and finally made the Dean's List—that is, when I first received what was "received"—I decided I would be a writing teacher. It was an exhilarating feeling to know what I wanted to do with my life and to know what to do to get there. But as it turned out, I did not really face becoming a writing teacher until after two of my books were published and people in other universities read them. What happened?

Graduate school brought together the accumulating acculturation of the following: attending an all-male high school; leaving home to go to an all-male college and being treated with unquestioning respect by other men; committing myself to science, the "highest" possible calling; working among "the elite" in means and ability; living among others, in college, who believed that their work, science, and technology was the "foundation of Western Civilization," the title, ironically, of the first-year humanities course at M.I.T. in 1956 where my writing was "unintelligible"; competitive development of knowledge; the belief in the pursuit of "excellence" rather than benefit, understanding, or fairness; and the ability to "gain insight." These values helped to lead me away from writing toward what seemed the more attractive (and higher status) academic enterprises in English: literature, criticism, and literary theory. These fields required competition and promised, unambiguously, to bring tenure and recognition if one succeeded in them. Writing, in contrast, was still "freshman composition" associated with placement tests and academic hygiene, taught by graduate students, supervised by those who failed at our "real" business of literature and often by the "sad women in the basement." (Miller 1991).

With the help and encouragement of an extraordinary, progressive editor, Richard Ohmann, I published—in the late '60s and early '70s—several essays on literary response in *College English* (a comprehensive journal treating all phases in the college teaching of English). I knew these essays derived from the kinds of interests in language I described toward the beginning of this reflection—writing and language use in and out of literature. Nevertheless, my work was identified as literary theory. Also, I did not ask Jane Tompkins to use the narrow term "reader response" to bring my work and work related to it into public view. Yet, one could not waste time and effort disputing one's colleague's judgment when her effort was generous and helpful in a collective way that included all of our interests. Although the path I followed was rewarding (and in one sense was the one I *decided* to follow), my story suggests how intellectual interests are not always what we may individually consider them to be, but that they become collectively overtaken, molded, guided, and shifted by prevailing values, particularly those governed, underneath, by androcentric styles, goals, and interests. I also mean to say that I, like others who may not have consciously shared the overtaking values, are nevertheless implicated if we benefit from how the public translation of our work rewards us.

Today, perhaps twenty-five years after the "reader" became a legitimate critical category, the relation between criticism and writing as subjects in English has not changed very much, with one possible exception: While journals in composition, rhetoric, and the teaching of writing still have less influence with university tenure committees than journals in theory and criticism, now there are many more of the former kinds of journals. Both these and some zones in the critical community are, for the first time that I can remember, *sharing an interest in university teaching.* The Modern Language Association now has several divisions, study groups, special sessions, and forums devoted to teaching and to the teaching of writing. The Carnegie Commission study by Ernest Boyer, *Scholarship Reconsidered* (1990), emphasizes the need of Class I research universities to treat teaching activities with the same seriousness that research and scholarship has been treated traditionally. While the changes are slow and the outcomes uncertain, I think that issues of literary response, along with other movements in education—like the "whole language" interest—have helped bring criticism and theory, teaching, and writing more toward the concept of "language is one" that I discussed in a more subjective register at the beginning of this essay.

Speaking more personally, and for others like myself who consider themselves to belong to all zones of the "first language" profession—literature, theory, teaching, and writing: I feel that because of this multiple affiliation and resulting broad professional identity, I can more easily participate in the struggle of our profession to unite its different parts, more easily face political facts, more easily disclose my positions and perspectives, and more easily welcome people from other disciplines and other cultures to our work. I can more easily "read"—interpret, reconceive, rethink—the subject of English as "one's first language," and in this way include the literature, the speaking styles, the writings, the texts, the letters, indeed, all the genres, kinds, categories, and registers of language in my subject. At the same time, the "first language" need not be solely understood as one's native language, but can be thought of only as the *used* language, or the language of one of the major communities in our lives. This subject, language use and writing, more directly than the "English" I first entered, orients our profession toward the concerns of society at large, toward the subjects I first thought were mine when I first identified myself vocationally.

Thankfully, the truth of my story is hard to tell. From one perspective, I "decided what I wanted to be and went about doing it as anyone should"; in my case this would be "a college professor who studies and teaches language and literature." But from another perspective, I am the beneficiary of a spectacular run of good luck (for example, when young men were drafted to go to Vietnam, I became twenty-six) and good times (academic jobs were easiest to get just when I went on the market). From yet another perspective, I did what any *white man* could and would do: find a way to become something worthwhile in a society that made it easy for white men to do this. And so on with many more perspectives.

In any case, I urge those who are wondering about it to become writing teachers. Few things in our society are less alienating, less immobilized by competition and greed, more likely to bring us in contact with those from all parts of society, more likely to make it possible to participate in both individual and social growth, more involved in exchanging important thoughts and feelings with others, more relaxed and intense at once, and more joyful and less sad even in frustration and failure. I did not feel all of these things when I was twenty and thought I would become a writing teacher. I stopped worrying about how the electrons got through the capacitor because I learned that I liked to say things that mattered to people that mattered, and that school was the place to stay.

Works Cited

Annie Hall. 1977. Dir. Woody Allen. With Woody Allen and Diane Keaton.

Boyer, Ernest L. 1990. *Scholarship Reconsidered: Priorities of the Professoriate.* Princeton, NJ: Carnegie Foundation for the Advancement of Teaching.

Fiedler, Leslie. 1960. *Love and Death in the American Novel.* New York: Criterion Books.

Lakoff, Robin Tolmach. 1990. *Talking Power: The Politics of Language in Our Lives.* New York: Basic Books.

Miller, Arthur. 1958. *Death of a Salesman.* New York: Viking Press.

Miller, Susan. 1991. *Textual Carnivals: The Politics of Composition.* Carbondale, IL: Southern Illinois University Press.

6 Teaching as a Profession

Ann Shea Bayer
University of Hawaii

Teaching was not my first choice for a career, so it's ironic that I'm in this position of writing this manuscript about how my personal teaching philosophy developed. What happened?

I grew up in the forties and fifties resisting my older brother's advice that, as a girl, I should get an elementary teaching certificate as "something to fall back on." Even though the word "feminism" was not yet in my dictionary, I felt a secret stubbornness that led me to believe I could choose whatever profession I felt like choosing.

But while I majored in American History in college and dreamed of becoming a capitalist, my older brother's "voice" was with me. I decided to take the one-semester student teaching requirement to become certified to teach, should I need to do so.

Well, guess what? I needed to do so as soon as I graduated from college and discovered, that while there were plenty of capitalists, there was a shortage of teachers, and I needed a job. So in the early sixties, I entered the teaching profession.

I was twenty-one years old going on "eighteen." I had led a sheltered life, but now I was ready to have a good time away from parents and dorm supervisors. But I needed to support myself and my "good time" lifestyle, so I accepted a job teaching social studies and language arts at a junior high school in Connecticut. This was great! I shared an apartment with two other first-year teachers and we were ready to begin our adult life.

Of course, I forgot to think about what it was I would do exactly when I was in the classroom with twenty-five thirteen-year-olds. And since I was a new teacher, I was assigned one of the remedial or bottom-tracked social studies/language arts classes. The curriculum was ancient civilization. OK.

I didn't have a clue about how to go about teaching ancient civilization to seventh graders. As I remember, we left most of the ancient civilization back in Mesopotamia. Instead, I developed a curriculum that had more to do with the students' contemporary lives. We put on a class play. I can't recall the title, but I do remember we needed all these sound effects, so I had a room full of gadgets—like a vacuum cleaner and cymbals and other noise makers. I also remember having a headache, which interfered with my "good time" plans.

Other memories from that first year involve students working in small groups to argue the pros and cons about what appeared to be America's increasing involvement in Vietnam; and students working together to paint a mural on the back wall; and I remember George, who always came to class in the role of a car making loud engine noises like . . . whoom . . . whoom . . . whoom. . . . George acted out for the class his version of Lincoln dying after he had been shot. George used ketchup because he thought it made the dramatization more effective. George was right. His status among his peers increased.

As fate would have it, I was returning from lunch one day, with one of my classes, when we heard a noise from the school intercom. At first I thought it was the news about the World Series, but it was the announcement that President Kennedy had been shot. We were all pretty stunned . . . quiet. President Kennedy was a hero to many of these young people, and boys and girls alike began to cry. I comforted them as best as I could until school was dismissed for the day. We all retreated to our homes to watch and rewatch the burial.

It is an understatement to say that that event bonded our relationship for the rest of the year. We made it through. Although, I can still see the face of Danny with tears coming down his cheeks. To this day, I wonder where he is.

Well, that was my first year of teaching. I was pretty disorganized and I ended up the year exhausted. But there were seeds planted about setting up a community of learners. Something about having the students play an active role, and working together on problems that were complex, and something about the importance of relationships. All these concepts were, by the way, ideas supported by the school's administration. I was unaware at the time that I had the good fortune of starting my career by working in a school which fostered student creativity and complex problem-solving rather than the rigid and dull worksheet curriculum found in many public and private schools.

For my second teaching position, I had applied for an English position, but I was hired as the ninth-grade Remedial Reading teacher. Back to the drawing board! Could I read to these students? Could we read plays to each other? Maybe partners could work together to figure out meaning and unknown words. Looking back, I see I had returned to strategies which involved students working collaboratively on activities that had some meaning to them. I also observed my students more this time . . . what the Goodmans' call "kid watching." William, I discovered, needed glasses and he came to school cranky because he had to make breakfast for his younger brothers and sisters and get them ready for school. He was tired and couldn't see very well. I learned these things because I used to sit with William and talk to him. We had something of a relationship—as I did with the other fourteen boys in his class.

I was getting involved with teaching. Indeed, I had shifted out of "I need a job" into "maybe this is a career." But I was not yet viewing myself as a professional, so I returned to school to get a Master's Degree in Reading Education.

My graduate program in 1970 was probably fairly typical. It provided no explicit theoretical basis for reading methods that I can recall. I learned to break the reading process into small bits and teach the bits in sequence; eventually the students would put the bits together and comprehension would take care of itself. I was a good student. I graduated talking like my former language arts consultant. I had been enculturated into the status quo.

Unfortunately, my focus then shifted away from "kid watching" and collaborated learning and complex problem-solving tasks to individualized prescriptions for remediation that involved students working through a scope and sequence of skills taught in isolation. But now I viewed myself ready for "teaching as a career."

In the early seventies, I was hired as Chair of a middle school reading department in a suburban area on the West Coast. Duties as the chair took up half of my time, the other half I was teaching. And my first class was memorable. I was hired in the middle of the school year. One of my classes was labeled the "terminal" class, the "z" class, the "no substitutes will return" class. OK. My first day, I entered this classroom to discover *no* students. That's right. The students were in the neighborhood, but that was as close as they were coming to the classroom—voluntarily. With help, I coaxed and bribed the twelve to fourteen members of this eighth-grade class into the room.

I was desperate, and I resorted to extrinsic rewards to get some kind of control. I resorted to "food." I set up a plan for which a student would get points for showing up with a pencil; points for taking a seat; points for filling out worksheets. And finally, with enough points, I would take these students, in groups of three, in my Volkswagen, to

McDonald's for lunch. Eventually, all the students earned enough points to go to McDonald's. I ate a lot of cheeseburgers that year.

What I found so fascinating about these trips were the conversations I had with these students. They had failed "school" in every way possible. But they talked about science fiction; their fascination with car engines; shared some poetry; and discussed reasons for racial conflicts. I couldn't believe these were the same kids. We never had these kinds of conversations in class. I did wonder why these students came to life outside the classroom. I did wonder why they were so energetic and bright and interesting outside the classroom. It was finally dawning on me that "tracking" students according to some limited standardized test might be harmful rather than helpful. And I knew I had to do something different. But that first year, I was too reluctant to pay too much attention to my doubts because, after all, I had just been accepted into the school's "status quo" society, and with that acceptance came a little prestige.

Fortunately, I worked with more experienced colleagues. One day one of these colleagues came up to me. I was afraid of Margaret, who was smart and aggressive. Further, she didn't care if she was accepted into dominant culture or not. Margaret said, "I fail to see the purpose of testing students on syllabication. Why are you doing that to improve reading comprehension?" No one had ever asked me *why* I was doing what I was doing before. I thought about her question for several days and I realized I had no good answer. That may have been the first time I genuinely reflected on my teaching practices. Margaret continued to ask me *why* this and *why* that. She wore me down. And she made my own doubts come to the forefront.

I invited Margaret and the members of the reading faculty to meet and discuss the reasons *why* we were using our current teaching practices; to evaluate them; and to modify our program so that it reflected how individuals use reading in their everyday lives. We changed the reading program by radically eliminating ability grouping and skills taught in isolation. No more "z" classes. Instead we opted for heterogeneously grouped classes in which the students choose the books they wanted to read.

I worked with the program for seven years. The students read more. Parents told us they noticed their children reading more. Equally important, the diversity of students in each of our classes (the average size was thirty) turned out to be beneficial, as some avid readers become models for others; and as everyone pooled and shared their diverse interests, they read from a broader range of books. I also lost weight. Since I no longer relied on extrinsic rewards to motivate my students, I no longer had to spend my lunch hour at McDonald's.

This restructuring of our reading program was the beginning of our reading faculty's professional collaboration, which lasted for several years. It was the beginning of a school-site study group as our choice for professional development. It was the beginning, for me at least, of the shift from the "maybe this is a career" phase to the "teaching as a profession" phase.

The "teaching as a profession" meant, to me, that I could no longer view teaching as just a job to pay my bills nor could I "just go along" with the status quo in order to be accepted. It meant doing my part to figure out how to provide students with the best learning experience possible.

Thank you, thank you, Margaret!!! And thank you to the "McDonald's" groups. Because of these relationships, I found the courage and the support to face my doubts about traditional programs, examine them, and do something about them. Ironically, I had come full circle. I was returning to the intuitive teaching strategies I had abandoned. But this time, I was not alone.

Our study group submitted a proposal to our principal, the district language arts specialist, and the district superintendent to obtain release time so that we could meet one afternoon a month. We knew our teaching strategies and heterogenous classes were working, but we didn't know if there existed any theoretical rationale which would explain why they worked. We wanted to meet to read; to teach ourselves an alternative assessment technique called "miscue analysis"; and, if necessary, to organize a course that would be available for all faculty on issues that had to do with the new field of psycholinguistics and its relationship to the reading process.

Our principal supported the proposal; the district language arts specialist supported the proposal; and the district superintendent supported the proposal. Once again, I was fortunate to have worked in a public school district with administrators who were open and supportive of change. We were in business. Our study group did all of the above. At this point, I had come to realize the strength of collaboration with administrators as well as with fellow teachers and students. And through our work, I became conscious of the integration between theory and practice.

Attending the Bay Area Writing Summer Institute in 1978 changed how I viewed myself as a writer. It also provided an opportunity to seek connections between the reading and writing processes, and to understand how writing could be used as a tool for reference for learning. This institute reinforced my beliefs in the power of collaboration, the power of good teacher-student relationships, and the power of beginning with the students' frames of reference rather than the instructor's frame of reference. My first writing piece in the institute was not entitled the "Extrapolation of Theoretical Principles Underlying the Work of William Blake." No, indeed. My first piece was entitled "The Duckie."

"The Duckie" was a personal narrative from my life experience. I was scared to write and scared to share that narrative. At that point in my life, I had expertise in a number of areas, but, in truth, I was a novice author. The directors of the institute and my peers supported and guided the development of this piece, and then applauded (as we did for everyone) when I read aloud the final draft. I have been willing to tackle the often difficult task of writing ever since.

After thirteen years of teaching and learning, I decided to return to graduate school for a doctorate. By this time, the foundation of my teaching and learning in philosophy was pretty much in place, but, I continued to be curious about how other people thought about school, education, and the role that language played in all of this. I became particularly interested in Vygotsky's (1962; 1978) notion that learning is intrinsically social.

If learning is social, the role of talk is essential. And, of course, talk is what was occurring in both the peer collaboration and teacher/student collaboration that I had experienced. I wanted to know how individuals negotiated mutual understandings through talk. Then I wanted to integrate talk, writing, and reading as they all play roles in negotiating mutual understandings.

While I was in graduate school, I discovered personally the role of language within a particular social context. Because my graduate program in English education was interdisciplinary (I took courses in linguistics and cognitive psychology, for example), I became aware of how these different communities used language to shape meaning within their own disciplines. Members of each academic community had negotiated mutual understandings of certain ideas which an outsider might not get.

I remember my first term taking an advanced linguistics course on "Children's Language." What could possibly be that difficult about learning how children acquire language? As a novice, trying to enter into this new academic community, I had my everyday life experiences and my professional experiences to help me make sense of the class. I thought that would be enough background knowledge. Wrong!! I never heard anyone talk about children's language like my instructor did. Early in the semester she said something like, "Given sematic coherence, children's language repertoire excludes internal negative elements providing a way of looking inside inanimate propositions."

Well, eventually I caught on, and this unnecessarily frustrating personal experience reinforced my belief in the importance of starting from the students' frames of reference and working collaboratively to build on those frames. Let me make it clear, however, that I support interdisciplinary programs at all levels of schooling. I think they have the possibility of providing students with a more synthesized, cohesive, and broader view of concepts. The problem arises when the classroom communities do not provide avenues for students to enter into the conversations.

While I entered graduate school with various pieces of a framework, I exited with a belief that learning is social and that language plays a major role.

And so, I arrive at my current teaching–learning philosophy grounded in these life experiences. Those teaching strategies I used intuitively my first year served me pretty well. Those early ideas about setting up a community of learners in which students play an active role, working together on complex problem-solving tasks of some meaning to them, remain the core of my current philosophy. I've become more conscious of the need to begin from students' frames of reference to accommodate the diversity of life experiences and cultures we all bring to new situations.

I am also aware of the issues related to power that underlie a society's tendency to maintain a "status quo." Tracking, for example, I now view as a vehicle for "gatekeeping" in which students from backgrounds different from the mainstream are relegated to remedial tracks and, eventually, "out the door." I find it heartening that this practice, upon examination, has been found wanting, and that so many schools are moving to heterogeneous cores.

But how do I use my "grounded-teaching philosophy" in a Teacher Education Program? I turned in the final copy of my dissertation on a Tuesday. I got on a plane on Friday. On Monday, I faced my first group of college students. I was so tired, I'm sure I hung on to my desk for support. All I remember about my teaching that first semester is that it was busy, but I don't have a clue as to what we did.

Eventually, the fog parted and I became conscious of trying to model my college classes on the principles that underlie my teaching philosophy. I tried to think of ways to set up a community of learners; ways to start from the students' frames of references; ways to support active learning and peer collaboration; and ways to use language as a tool for learning.

I came to view my role as setting up a learning community in which a shared agenda exists. In other words, there are usually four to five concepts that I want my students to examine; and the students have their own questions that they want answered. But how to begin?

One day I received in the mail from one of my sisters a small black object. No note accompanied this object, and I didn't have a clue as to what it was. So, I tried to take it apart. I tried to think about what an object that size could be used for. I tried to think of past conversations with my sister that would have led her to send me this thing. Finally, I did remember a conversation we had had in which she told me of a magnetic car key holder she used to keep an extra set of car keys under her fender. Aha! I tried it, and sure enough, it was a magnetic car key holder. And since my social life wasn't all that great, I had time to reflect on the process I went through to figure this problem out. It occurred to me that I had tried to conjure up all my related prior knowledge to help me solve this problem. This might be a useful beginning activity, I thought, to illustrate how learners use their prior knowledge when faced with new situations, thus illustrating the importance of starting with students' frames of reference.

So I decided to start with concept in my language in education courses for education majors. I had two purposes in planning for this course. I wanted students to examine the theoretical constructs that learners have to make connections between new ideas and their prior knowledge; and that language and other people play an essential role in this process. Secondly, I wanted to set up my class so that my students would be experiencing these concepts themselves.

I structured a joint activity process that began with a freewriting question (about which I predicted all teacher education students would have some opinion), "How do individuals learn something new?"

Then I asked my students to begin to share their individual freewriting responses with their peers in groups of three, and to listen for similarities and differences. The small groups would then share with the whole class, and we could begin the process of making public what these students already knew and thought about this topic.

Next, I asked them to look for connections between their current ideas and the ideas which would evolve from the upcoming activity. At this point, I brought in the small black object and asked them to individually make a guess as to what it was. Typically, they would start talking with a neighbor about possibilities, and ten to fifteen different guesses would emerge. Then I asked them why there were so many different guesses for the same object. They would respond that each of them had different life experiences, which they used to make a guess.

In my role of instructor, I'd ask them to reflect on what they themselves had just illustrated. That is, that they had used individual prior knowledge, peer collaboration and language to problem-solve, and if this teaching-learning process worked for them, would they offer their students the same opportunities?

Well, this is the beginning of a teaching-learning process I now call Collaborative Apprenticeship Learning 2. I try to structure all my college courses using the same principle so that I can model, in the college classroom, what I would suggest future teachers might want to experiment with in their K–12 classrooms. If these principles provide comfortable communities of learning for these college students as "learners," then, I find, they are more willing to implement similar ideas in their own future classrooms.

And my own learning continues. I participate in the study groups to read, talk, and share in the same way I did in my first study group back in 1973. My students and peers teach me ways of seeing that have never occurred to me. Indeed one of my greatest pleasures about this "teaching profession" is that I expect to learn something new tomorrow.

Note

Parts of this narrative were first printed in *Collaborative-Apprentice Learning: Language and Thinking Across the Curriculum, K–12*, a book published by Mayfield Publishing Company and codistributed by Richard Owens, Inc. in 1990.

7 Going Back

Sally Hudson-Ross
Georgia State University

My students are all black. They are seniors. It is 1971, and many are angry. Within a month, so am I. We are in Ohio, but the impact of national civil rights events can be felt even here. I have worked for admitting minorities to my sorority, even traveling to the national convention to speak out. Vietnam flickers across screens in the background. And I am a student teacher.

On my first day, I walk down the dark, foreboding hall, and my "critic teacher" hands me her lesson plans—her college notes for British literature. I shudder—I have studied in England! I have read and come to live English literature with a passion. I know I can do far more than these notes to engage students. After a couple of weeks, she no longer visits, and I can experiment. The students begin to ask, "When are we going to get to the black writers?" For all my study, I never dreamed of that question. *Are* there any black English writers? None that I know of! My struggle leads to *Othello*—the only black person I can think of! But, of course, it isn't in the text. I'll check out a record from the university library.

During the fall quarter, all assemblies are canceled at our high school because of the fears of riots. During the winter I am there, we have to lock classroom doors in case fights break out in the halls during classes. This is both to keep combatants out and to keep our students in. An armed guard paces outside my window in the parking lot. During my planning period, I go to the school library for a record player—I've been told not to trust a student. I can have one, but only for a day at a time. I argue that I could lock it in my room, but no, students cannot be trusted. Finally, I get the record player to the room. It won't work. Neither will the next one, nor the third.

At my seminar that evening with student teachers from both my high school and the "other" (white) high school, our supervisor asks, "What creative uses are we finding for language labs and other media?"

"I can't get a record player to listen to *Othello*," I complain at my turn, "What can I do?" She won't hear of it; that's ridiculous, and she moves on to the next girl.

By March, I am as angry as my students with the world beyond our walls, and determined to act.

Why one moment stays and millions of others fade is beyond my comprehension. In becoming a teacher, I remember almost nothing of education courses, as you might guess from my recollection of seminar. British literature classes and a junior-year quarter in England inspired me to share the literature I loved. And I began. That seems to be all there was to it.

Yet somehow, moments of struggle—very unlike the training I received in New Criticism—shaped the teacher I would become. Somehow these critical moments led to this second-year teacher:

> *A Résumé, 1973.* I feel that education today must be an active experience with students and teacher interacting in the classroom, and with community and administration lending full support. Literature, as well as all other subjects, can and must be relevant to today's students, but they should also learn to appreciate all that has come before. I especially believe strongly in the use of the semester course [electives] approach (having helped to develop one and see it work), creative dramatics, individualized study, and extending classroom learning beyond the four walls and into the community. A class should be a group effort to search for, compile, and evaluate information and personal opinions.

This was me in 1973. I can see this sincere, passionate twenty-four-year-old as if she were standing beside me. She is full of dreams, believes fully in herself and in kids, has no qualms about approaching an administrator to take kids away from school, and recognizes when everything connects for a class. She thrives on these moments. Yet she is also guilt-ridden, privately fearful that she doesn't know enough (or anything), hesitant to speak out and in awe of others she perceives to be far more successful. She is insecure and often deeply hurt.

I've been seeing a lot of her lately. After five years of public school teaching, five years as a curriculum coordinator, three years of graduate school and now nine years as an English education professor, after seventeen years of being out of the classroom, I have made the big decision to return to high school teaching. Although it will only be for a year—in a job exchange with an exceptional local colleague—I find myself experiencing all of the pain and joys of my first years of teaching all over again. And I find myself in awe of that brave young woman I was in 1973.

And then I read Gloria Steinhem's *Revolution from Within* (1992). Much as I have been recalling my younger self, she remembers the Steinhem of the 1970s—young, determined, often bullheaded and misguided. She proposes a process of reparenting, observing, and finally confronting and consoling our younger selves, the ones full of hurts, dreams, misguided plans, and ways of living that we now see as sad and naive, but nonetheless heartfelt and our own.

In this piece, I would like to briefly revisit a few critical moments—other selves from my own elementary school years onward—that shaped the teacher I was seventeen years ago when I left teaching in 1976 with the lure of a county office position. I want to do this so that I might revisit and shape the new teacher I hope to be in 1993–94. "The art of life," Steinhem says, "is not controlling what happens to us, but using what happens to us" (1992, 22). This is what happened to me.

Becoming a Teacher: Getting to 1976

1960. It is sixth grade, Mrs. Reiser's class, and Robert sits next to me in the back row. He is dirty, taller even than I am, blond and sharply handsome under the grime and the faint smell. His dingy clothes are worn thin and gray. When he is here, Robert usually wraps his hairy arms over his head, asleep on his desk.

I am new to this school this fall and making friends is agonizing. Two girls invite me to ride bikes and, sitting at the hilltop park, explain that they are having a party next weekend, but "we're only inviting our friends." Later that afternoon, they steal my bike. I have been crying a lot, and I fear the wrath of loneliness.

One winter day, snow blows in gusts in the alley beside the school. Robert is absent again. The rest of us work quietly at our desks until the bell rings. A boy comes in late, and I hear him hitting the snow off his coat in the adjoining cloak room. Then he laughs, out loud. In disbelief, he walks in, a tennis shoe in his hand. "Look at this hole! Robert's got no bottom to his shoe!" he announces to all of us. Mrs. Reiser, plainly shaken, sits down with us and explains poverty.

When Robert returns, we stay our distance even more. One day in our shared back row, as Mrs. Reiser talks away in the distance, I watch him, head bowed, carve small block letters—ROBERT—in his arm with a small knife. I never saw him again after the rest of us moved on to the junior high.

There were many other peers I came to pity across many class-rooms, across silences more distant than geography. I never spoke to them for fear they would like me, a burden that I, in my own desperate attempts to be accepted, couldn't handle. At our twenty-fifth high school reunion, I was very conscious that these people did not appear.

1961. Mr. Sindlinger senses my painful shyness. In a creative gesture for the time, he has a new game to help us memorize our prepositions: We must carry our lists, copied from the grammar book, with us at *all* times so that we can memorize those useful prepositions. I'm called to the board; I've forgotten my list. As punishment, I must make a poster-sized sandwich board listing all my prepositions and wear it around the school for three days. All night I cry as I make it, horrified at the thought of being noticed. I survive, and in fact, grow stronger.

Years later, I wonder if Mr. Sindlinger's intention was more my self-respect than my knowledge of grammar, because during that year Mr. Sindlinger sets me free. On my own, at his recommendation, I'm reading *Frannie and Zooey, Wuthering Heights, A Tree Grows in Brooklyn.* I *am* all of these heroines. In class, Mr. Sindlinger reads aloud *A Child's Christmas in Wales*, and we read *A Christmas Carol.* I am enchanted by England, my family's ancestral home. He plays Dave Brubeck while we write, tells us about playing bass in a Greenwich Village jazz group, and we suspect he is a Beatnik. We all leave school for a morning to watch from Terry Mills' living room as John Glenn, an Ohioan like us, floats around the earth. Over and over and over, I am awestruck by the world.

By the end of the year, it is I who host the seventh-grade party for my class.

1967. Except for friends, high school has been bland. We moved my senior year, and I chose to become a recluse. I spent hours reading and writing pitiful poetry glumly alone in my windowed, sunporch bedroom.

But now it is September. The chill breeze flushes my cheeks and rattles leaves in the hundred-year-old oaks that shade the sidewalks. I smile at the crackle, of those that had already fallen, under my brown loafers. I stroll up the college hill, past old, red brick Myers Hall—where Mr. Sindlinger supposedly trapped a horse in the white copula at the top—on my way to the English building. It is freshman orientation week so few people are around yet. My head is full of the philosophy, history, science, and literature that we were required to read over the summer for freshman seminars this week.

Alone, climbing that hill, I firmly believe that I have arrived. All these years, I have been climbing for just this moment. This is my world. I knew it then. I know it now. School in fall. School in fall in an Ohio chill. A cardigan sweater, knee socks, and new books in my arms. The sharp, wooden smell of fresh, long, yellow pencils. The utter joy of crisp, untouched reams of notebook paper. So much to take in; so much to pour out. So much ahead. So much to learn.

1971. My first year of teaching, Lancaster, Ohio, second double session, teaching six classes straight through from noon to six P.M. Snow falls and darkness sets in by fourth period. Small town ninth and tenth graders are restless for dinner and slippery bus rides home in the Thursday blackness. The bell rings at six, and I'll have time for dinner before the 7:00 department meeting at my chair's house.

We gather there. Hippie-looking, long straight hair, blue jeans, Mahler on the stereo. Business settled early, we drink. Is it because of double sessions that we're all new teachers? Ed, our Department Chair, is the most experienced after three years. Most of us are just beginners. We have no curriculum, find whatever books attract us in the dark bookroom under the stairs, and we teach.

Tonight, someone has brought a copy of Hemingway. We pass the book, reading aloud in turn, dreaming of greatness as writers, musicians, lovers, and lifelong friends. By midnight, the idea emerges. We all call in sick—in a new school invention, we only have to leave a message on a tape, not talk to a human—and by dawn we are crossing into Michigan, seven of us in a car and George's pickup. We have warm clothes for the snow, Scotch, and a general sense of where north is. Our destination: The Big Two-Hearted River to read aloud on its banks, as it "should be done." And we do. Two nights and days tromping in knee-deep snow, drinking in the fine, warm bars of Grand Marais, piled into beds in front of burning hot electric heaters that blacken our socks.

By Monday noon, we stand in classrooms smiling, knowing, nodding silently to one another in the halls. We are amazing, and we know it.

1972. Many of my students come from the local children's home. They have parents, but not ones who can care for them at this time. Some children have been abused, some neglected. All experience lives I have never heard of before.

Yet, at open house we perform a play. The students themselves have written it, excerpting science fiction stories we've read to prove to the public that courses like science fiction shouldn't be abandoned.

They are serious about their goal and their performance—even when the principal yells at us for sitting on the floor to practice our lines, even when the props crash down on us, even on show night when a main actor chickens out and we grab a strange kid out of the hall to read his lines. The superintendent of schools comes to see us; more importantly, at least one parent for every child comes too.

Virginia is not from the children's home, but she often comes in bruised. I suffer over her sad face, love her warmth when I reach out to talk about stories we like together. Sometime after the play, she shares a beautiful pair of bell-bottom pants she has made in Home Ec.; the next day she is missing from school.

The next week I learn that her mother burned the pants— demonic, evil ornamentation when decent girls should wear skirts— in a pot on the kitchen stove. I am furious. The counselor tells me there is nothing to be done; calling the home and confronting the parent could only lead to harsher treatment. We don't have a case that will stand up in court.

1974. A visit to Atlanta for last spring's gorgeous Dogwood Festival weekend has brought me south. In rural Gwinnett County, Georgia, I am part of an era of electives, team teaching, role play, and population booms. I play a drug pusher for my roommate's social studies classes, all of whom have taken on roles and play an elaborate schoolwide game that ends up with my conviction in a student-run court. I'll never forget the terror of being trapped in the faculty rest room when the narcs figured out who I was.

I've imported courses from Ohio: Mass Media and Science Fiction. Together, the department develops a course simply called Books, Books, Books. The concept is that we simply let kids read all period and *do* something with what they read. They can talk with the teacher, with a peer group, do a project, share with another class. Because it's so manageable, the administration decides we can team-teach it in the leveled lecture hall: sixty kids, two teachers. We read.

All of these new courses allow us to mainstream kids from spe-cial education and not to group kids by ability. With small groups in our book room, I make cameras out of shoe boxes while my teammate takes the class. We see everything from *Singing in the Rain* to *Dr. Caligari's Cabinet*. Mass media classes go hear Marshall McLuhan talk at Georgia State. My sixth-period Speech class constructs Sesame Street puppets and goes on a tour of elementary schools for Thanksgiving, led by a shy Steve Whitmire who today is the new voice of the Muppets' Kermit the Frog. My lunch period Modern Poetry class teaches elementary kids to write poetry and gain insight into modern writers. Teaching is a joy, and planning means following the kids' leads. Within the year, I go to my first NCTE convention, and soon become Department Head.

Recrafting a New Teacher's Voice: Going Back

Does it take passing forty to stop moving and instead confront the issues that surround us? Perhaps that is the measure of wisdom. As we live a life, it is hard to see what we are learning. The clarity of the visions I recall is enhanced by the symbolism of the event and colored by all the other experiences that shape a life. Whether the memory is true or not is not the point. As Steinhem says, it is how we use it.

Placed together, today, these critical moments speak individually of great joy—the reason I came to teach—and of great pain—part of the reason I left. Next year, I'll walk back into the classroom with all of these younger selves by my side. This time, this teacher will have my age, my perspective, my eyes, my current knowledge. She will also have the benefit of a more informed time, when child abuse cannot be ignored, when poverty can be confronted, when some schools at least encourage the type of young teacher I was so bravely becoming. In going back, I hope to change some endings.

Although I couldn't at the time:

- I can finally reach across the abyss of those back-row school desks to touch the Roberts of the world and, luckily in these more insightful times, the Virginias as well. I can forgive my early self for a culture beyond her control, but never again avoid taking the next step, no matter how risky.

- I can comfort my seventh-grader self and listen to her loneliness, celebrate her friendships, reread her books with new eyes and remember her depths, amazing for her age. And with my newfound patience, I can listen again to a new generation and thereby help them find their voices.

- I can, and do, stand more often on college campuses, especially in the fall, and treasure the opportunity simply to be here again in September, a time of beginning. And I can put my arm around my freshman self—and many like her with whom I work—and let them know their dreams to be educators are worthy.

- I can applaud the young student teacher who tried within a stifling canon to find literature and activities that would enhance students' connections with English. And I can continue to help her fight for equality, mutual understanding, and multicultural enrichment of all curriculum.

- I can listen to the driven young teacher and let her know that her dreams were possible, that she and her peers were on right paths, even though some would be sidelined due to political and administrative trends. And I can incite the next generation of teachers to create support networks and to read on the shores of the Big Two-Hearted River of their own generation.

- I can admire the emerging teacher and department head who fought for elective courses and helped colleagues design them, who team taught and mainstreamed, and interacted in schoolwide role plays. She was one damn fine teacher. If all students couldn't read, at least many of them have warm memories of schooling. Perhaps the next generation will find reason and invitations to literacy that were unavailable then.

In every teacher, there is a need to revisit our stories, to see ourselves as persons of growing power. To forgive ourselves for what we could not have known or done at the time so that we can move into ourselves today. Our blessing as teacher is that as we relive our past selves, we not only rebuild our own self-esteem (it is, after all, okay to be me), but unlike many others, we have the chance to recast these insights the "next time" in the lives of new groups of young people as well.

In his popular romance, *The Bridges of Madison County* (1992), Robert Waller has come up with a quote for my generation: "The old dreams were good dreams; they didn't work out, but I'm glad I had them." Maybe my dreams of teaching and changing the world didn't work out, but I'm not sure they still can't. So I'm going back, as surely as I can envision those young women who preceded me to this point, I can envision starting again. With a renewed fervor, a renewed sense of self, a renewed vision, and this time, I pray, with the power and magic to confront the questions that still haunt me.

Postscript: August 19, 1994

Recrafting the Teacher Educator's View

Once again, the first day of a new school year rolls round. Last year at this time, I was just meeting Kenta, Jamie, Shondra, Natasha, Brian, Merideth, Jason, and Corey—the kids of my "going back" year. Perhaps, more importantly, I was about to really meet myself, or more appropriately, my selves, again as well.

Going back, for me, was truly an experience of self-discovery as person and as educator. I had known pain and joy, but I once again came to feel them. How it hurt to recognize that in this "enlightened" time, abuse, abandonment, cruelty, and poverty infect children's lives more than ever. Of course, as a teacher educator, I knew that. But now the horror once again carries the names of those I love. How it hurt to realize that even renewed vision and passion often aren't enough to touch them all. I reached out, reexperienced the loneliness of adolescence, rediscovered the utter joy of collegiality, renegotiated curriculum, recreated exciting worlds, remembered, relived. And what did I learn?

- Maturity, perspective, and knowledge just bring realities into high relief. The naiveté of youth may be a blessing.
- Some endings can't be changed; lives are lived no matter what you do.
- Some questions can't be answered, and confronting those questions in particular is painful.
- I hope I am willing now to forgive myself for all I still don't know.
- My résumé vision in 1973 remains intact. I was on to something. It is that sound and fervent vision, if not the perfect enactment of it, that allows me to continue as a teacher and to encourage others to do the same.

I was also on to something as I described that college campus of 1971. I love the fall in the air as I walk across campus, the opportunity to learn and reflect, read and grow, to think deeply alone and with others. I've learned, most importantly, that I belong here. I am a teacher educator—one with many new stories, opinions, understandings, experiences, and concerns. The wisdom of teacher education comes, not from decontextualized research in a rarefied setting, but from knowing—in reality and with self-conscious honesty—what teachers need so that together we can keep our visions alive, so that as a profession we never stop going back, hanging on to what we believe, and having faith in "next time. . . ."

Works Cited

Brontë, Emily. 1847. *Wuthering Heights.* Reprint, Oxford: Clarendon Press, 1976.

Dickens, Charles. 1843. *A Christmas Carol.* Reprint, New York: Oxford University Press, 1976.

Salinger, J. D. 1961. *Franny and Zooey.* Boston: Little, Brown.

Singin' in the Rain. 1952. Writers: Adolph Green and Betty Compton. Metro–Goldwyn–Mayer.

Smith, Betty. 1943. *A Tree Grows in Brooklyn.* Reprint, Boston: G. K. Hall, 1982.

Steinem, Gloria. 1992. *Revolution from Within.* Boston: Little, Brown.

Thomas, Dylan. 1954. *A Child's Christmas in Wales.* Reprint, New York: Holiday House, 1985.

Waller, Robert. 1992. *The Bridges of Madison County.* New York: Warner Books.

8 I Did It My Way . . . With a Little Help From My Friends

Peter Smagorinsky
University of Oklahoma

Exploring how I came to be the teacher I am today is quite a fascinating challenge. I suspect that most contributors to this volume could write lengthy treatises—their own *Emile* or *Lives on the Boundary*—to address the topic. In many ways the writing I have done since the mid-1980s has been an effort to explore what I think is involved in good teaching, or at least good teaching as it has appeared through the various lenses I have tried. To produce a short essay on my development as a teacher, then, requires me to boil a lot of thinking down to a few succinct points.

I think if I were to identify two general rules that currently guide my thinking about teaching, they would be:

1. Learning is social and active.
2. People learn by making things that are important, useful, and meaningful to them.

I believe that these two principles have guided my thinking about teaching since 1976, when I first began my M.A.T. at the University of Chicago and taught in the Upward Bound/Pilot Enrichment Program for inner city teenagers; through my high school teaching in Westmont, Barrington, and Oak Park-River Forest (IL) High Schools; and finally in my work in the English Education program at the University of Oklahoma. I will next try to trace some of the experiences that help me recognize these principles as important.

One of my favorite tidbits from educational research comes from a study conducted by Csikszentmihalyi, Rathunde, and Whalen (1993). They were trying to understand how learners felt at different points during the day: how engaged they were, how they responded affectively, and how they otherwise felt when involved in different pursuits. In one high school honors history class, the teacher was lecturing to the students about Genghis Khan's invasion of China. When asked to describe their levels of attention, affect, and engagement during the lecture, only two of the twenty-seven students in the class reported that they were thinking about anything remotely related to the lecture; and of those two, one was thinking about Chinese food and the other was wondering why Chinese men wear their hair in ponytails.

My own experiences as a student, as a professional attending conference presentations, and as an educator have impressed on me why most of the students in that honors history class were drifting off into another world as the teacher imparted important knowledge about the Khan's invasion. Learning, as Vygotsky (1962) argues, comes about through social engagement. I first learned the importance of this concept as a graduate student in George Hillocks's M.A.T. program in English Education. George stressed, among other things, the importance of using small groups as a vehicle for promoting learning, and the importance of developing instructional activities to engage students in learning processes. Both involve students in *activity* to keep them engaged in learning.

In my subsequent teaching, I was fortunate to work in a stimulating environment at Barrington High School through the departmental leadership of Dale Griffith. Many teachers I have met over the years have said that they would love to engage students in active learning, but that they are discouraged from doing so by administrators who are disturbed by loud classrooms that deviate from the straight-and-narrow path. During the formative years of my teaching I was given (along with the rest of my colleagues) a great deal of latitude to develop activities and conduct extremely noisy classrooms. Dale saw my teaching as being in the process of development and encouraged me to explore and take risks, even when what I was trying appeared to be off the wall. In retrospect, I think that Dale was really urging us to engage in a continual process of teacher research; he urged us to throw out "the curriculum" and maintain notebooks in which we would inquire into our own practice and reflect on the relationship between our teaching and our students' learning. I would say that working in an environment that encouraged adventuresome teaching was a critical factor in helping to foster the way I learned to think about teaching and learning. My own learning flourished during those years because of the level of creative activity in the department as a whole, the enthusiasm that we generated among ourselves over teaching and learning, and the interrogation I routinely conducted into the processes of my classrooms.

After six years of full-time teaching, I took a year off to begin working on a doctoral program. After I completed my doctoral course work, I returned to teach full time at Barrington High School. By that point, the department had developed a new speech program in which every sophomore in the school would devote one semester to an untracked course that required participation in public speaking, oral interpretation, improvisation, role playing, and other activities involving oral communication. At that time, I taught juniors and wanted to make sure that students followed up their learning from the sophomore speech program in their subsequent learning. With released time provided by my supervision of a student teacher, I was able to observe a number of speech classes, discuss their purpose with the teachers, and plan appropriate instruction for the students when I would teach them as juniors.

My incorporation of the speech activities into the junior curriculum brought about changes that profoundly affected my approach to teaching. My classes had always been activity oriented, but my exposure to the activities in the speech classes opened up new possibilities to me. The students brought a tremendous amount of imagination to their oral work and had become acclimated to an environment in which spoken and acted texts were valued just as much as written ones. When I encouraged students to develop literary interpretations through oral speech activities, they would bring a wide range of resources to the projects, often providing musical accompaniment, elaborate sets, costumes, and even special effects: One group dramatizing the satanic side of Puritan literature provided a spectacular (if dangerous and probably illegal) effect by, first of all, simulating a boiling cauldron by using dry ice (fogging an entire wing of the high school in the process), and then darkening the room and striking a lighter beneath the jet from an aerosol can to shoot flames across the set as part of a nocturnal ritual.

Exhibitions such as this—though I subsequently insisted on a few restrictions to bring the activities in accordance with fire regulations—created an atmosphere that valued different ways of constructing meaning as legitimate. In the following years, in addition to the core of writing I required, I increasingly encouraged students to represent their understanding of literature through unconventional types of texts. My rationale for doing so was that the students were, almost without exception, highly engaged in the projects they would undertake, far more so than they were when being evaluated through conventional writing. In particular, students who were low achievers—including many students whose patterns of communication at home were dissonant with the conventional genres of interaction and evaluation in school—were often among the most enthusiastic and productive workers on these projects. Students who were loath to turn in simple homework assignments would spend all weekend producing elaborate video productions dramatizing their interpretations of literary relationships. Above all, the students, besides being engaged, were clearly demonstrating an understanding of literature in ways not accessible through their writing. Not only were they active, they were learning in the process.

My interest in students' artistic production of texts led to my reading of Howard Gardner's *Frames of Mind* (1993) and the development of a research program investigating students' composition of artistic interpretations of literature. It also led me back to a reexamination of my attitudes about writing. If writing is as valuable a tool as teachers of writing insist it is, then students should find it to be as engaging a mode of production as they do making films, producing sculpture, and fashioning other types of texts. I found that when my students produced their nonwritten interpretive texts, they were learning a great deal *through the process of creating the texts*, because the films and other unconventional productions that they developed were interesting, important, and useful to them. Could I say the same of all the writing that my students were doing?

My question was driven home to me one year when I was teaching at Oak Park-River Forest High School and was participating in a Teacher Evaluation and Student Achievement (TESA) program through which I observed a number of other classes around the school. One day I was observing a driver's education class that included several students who were enrolled in my "basic" sophomore English class. The driver's education class was conducted in the "simulation room," which was a large room with twenty-five or so simulated car cabs complete with dash board, steering wheel, brakes, and other accessories for driving. The students would sit in the simulated cabs while in front of them, on a large screen taking up the front of the classroom, they viewed a film that provided a view of the road from out of a car's windshield; I felt myself in an odd time warp as I viewed the same grainy driver's education films that I had seen as a high school student in the sixties as the cinematic car, fins and all, negotiated contrived traffic situations. The students, without the benefit of my sense of anachronism, felt as though they were actually driving their simulated cars: they would turn on their signals when the film slowed for them to make a turn, hit the brakes when a car pulled out in front of them, and otherwise "operate" their cars in response to the conditions presented by the film.

At one point, the film was speeding smoothly along at about sixty miles per hour when suddenly a car swerved onto the screen in the path of the "drivers," seeming to come from out of nowhere. At that point, I was watching one of my "basic" English students, who was so engrossed in his driving that he spun his steering wheel violently and then actually fell out of his seat from the momentum of the turn. Fortunately, he was wearing his seat belt or he might have flown out of his cab entirely and crashed into the student in the next lane. Many other students in the class had the same reaction, and there was much embarrassed laughter among the students over the incident. My own thought immediately was: How could I make that happen in my class? How can I make the activities so real to students that they actually fall out of their chairs from involvement?

The answer, of course, is that it is hard to motivate basic students to read and write to the extent that they are motivated to drive a car. Yet, the question has haunted me ever since and forced me to think how useful my class is to students. Are they truly engaged in activities that absorb them in meaningful ways? Is the process of writing (or the process of creating other kinds of texts) an activity so real to them that they believe in it even in the "simulator" of a classroom desk?

Unfortunately, just as I was beginning to explore those important questions, I made a career move to a university setting. I have since had the opportunity to explore those questions—at least as they apply to adolescents—through research, though not so much through my own teaching. Yet the questions have still influenced my thinking as I teach my undergraduate courses in language development and methods of teaching English, and my various graduate courses in the teaching of writing, the teaching of literature, the study of language, and other aspects of language arts instruction.

At the undergraduate level, students are preparing for a career, and should enter the workplace with as many tools as possible to help them perform effectively, especially during that first overwhelming year. In my view, the most useful tool my students can have when they begin their first jobs is the ability to plan units of instruction. Our undergraduate teaching methods class, then, is built around teaching preservice teachers how to conceive of instruction in related blocks of study, primarily in the form of thematic units of literature. The class is structured as a workshop so that students spend time both in and out of class working collaboratively on the design of teaching units. No one has yet fallen out of a chair, but the students do create units of instruction that they often use during their student teaching and then subsequently in their permanent teaching jobs.

At the graduate level, I've learned that people go to school for a number of reasons, and I feel that my duty as a professor and graduate advisor is to help teachers use their education to serve the needs they sought to satisfy when they decided to return to school. For some practicing teachers, the most productive way to use their course time is to rethink courses they are already teaching, or plan courses they will teach in the future. Other graduate students want to try to break into publishing and, therefore, want to use their course work to learn how to write for publication, develop conference presentations, and otherwise enter the public side of professional life. In all cases, I encourage students to use their course work to help them learn how to create products that are useful, interesting, and important to them, and that enable them to learn through the process of creation. I have been very happy to see some of these students influence the curricula of the schools they teach in, present their course projects at state and national conferences, and, in some cases, publish their ideas in journals. For a graduate student, that is possibly the closest we can come to my high school student's driver's education car crash.

In my own work I have also found that my learning has taken place through the creation of useful products, originally in the form of classroom activities I developed for my high school students, and more recently in the form of books and articles I have written about teaching. In many cases my learning has been highly social, starting with my early collaboration with Tom McCann and Steve Kern on a series of workshops and a TRIP book for NCTE, and progressing through a number of other collaborations with colleagues and graduate students. By writing about the issues I am interested in, I learn more about them; and by sharing my writing, I engage in conversations that help me learn further. The composing process I go through in writing and talking about education is vital to my continued growth as a professional. I hope I never reach the stage where I think I'm an expert with nothing more to learn; if I ever do, please lock me in an empty classroom and leave me there to enlighten the four walls, who will listen about as attentively as would a room full of people.

Works Cited

Csikszentmihalyi, Mihaly, Kevin Rathunde, and Samuel Whalen, with
    contributions by Maria Wong. 1993. *Talented Teenagers: The Roots of
    Success and Failure.* New York: Cambridge University Press.

Gardner, Howard. 1993. *Frames of Mind: The Theory of Multiple Intelligences.*
    New York: Basic Books.

Rose, Michael. 1990. *Lives on the Boundary.* New York: Penguin.

Rousseau, Jean Jacques. 1762. *Emile.* Reprint, London: J. M. Dent and Sons,
    1911.

Vygotsky, L. S. 1962. *Thought and Language.* Cambridge, MA: MIT Press.

III Finding Rewards

Many of our "best" students may be paying too high a price in their compliance. . . . And many of our "worst" students, our refuseniks, might be potentially some of our best.

Peter Elbow

9 Illiteracy at Oxford and Harvard: Reflections on the Inability to Write

Peter Elbow
University of Massachusetts at Amherst

What got me interested in writing was being unable to write. First at Oxford, then at Harvard. First, I will tell the story straight—as I experienced it—and see what we can learn. But I've rethought this story—reexperienced it really—and now I also want to go on to *retell* it, crooked perhaps, and draw more reflections. But this is not just an exercise in story telling; I will be working for insights about writing, teaching, and learning. In the end, I'll have two versions of the story and five ruminations. Thus my structure is a kind of collage—a collage in which I am also trying to show that there need be no conflict between academic writing and personal writing.

First Version

I enjoyed writing in the last few years of school. Because my older sister and brother left home for college and I was lonely by myself, because I wanted to ski and was stuck in New Jersey, and because my grandmother had left money for our education, I went away to boarding school for three years. Proctor Academy was then an undistinguished school in New Hampshire. My English teacher, Bob Fisher, was just beginning his career as a teacher. He was excited about reading and writing and learning, and he had us writing about Dostoevsky and truth and the meaning of life—and writing fairy tales too. I loved writing and I decided I wanted to become a high school English teacher like him.

In college, my experience of writing was the experience of being knocked down, but then stubbornly picking myself up, dusting myself off, and finally succeeding. On my third essay for freshman English, my teacher wrote, "Mr. Elbow, you continue your far from headlong rise upward"—and the grade was D. The teachers I met in 1953 at Williams College were sophisticated and I was naive. But I was eager to do well and I worked hard at it—and by the end of my first year had begun to do so. Indeed, I gradually found myself wanting to enter their world and be like them—a college professor, not just a teacher. I wanted to be a learned, ironic, tweedy, pipe-smoking, professor of literature.

As for writing, I took no particular pleasure in it. I wrote when assigned. I no longer experienced any imaginative element in the writing I did; it was all critical. I found it difficult, but I sometimes got excited working out a train of thought of my own. Toward the end of my four years, however, I began to notice out of the corner of my consciousness, an increase in the "ordeal" dimension of writing papers: more all-nighters; more of them the night *after* the paper was due; more not-quite-acknowledged fear. But still I got those As.

And with them, a scholarship from Williams to go to Oxford. I wish I'd been as smart as my predecessor from Williams, Price Zimmerman: smart enough to study a *different* subject at Oxford from what I planned to study in graduate school. But I was too earnest and chose English. My Oxford tutor was another teacher in his first year of teaching: Jonathan Wordsworth, the grand nephew of the poet. My experience with him was, in a way, like the one I had at college, but more so. He played harder. Again I was knocked down—but it felt like I was knocked out and when I gradually staggered to my feet, the grogginess wouldn't go away. I thought I'd become sophisticated and critical at college, but this experience showed me I was still the same old tender, naive boy who wanted to be liked and praised. I thought I'd learned a lot about irony from my college professors, but Jonathan brewed a tougher English strain. (Interesting that I eventually wrote my Ph.D. dissertation on double and triple irony and the relinquishing of irony in Chaucer.)

Tutorials were conducted in the tutor's rooms. Once a week, I'd knock on the oak door and come in and read my essay to him, and be instructed, and then at the end he'd say something like, "Why don't you go off and read Dryden and write me something interesting." My first essay was on Chaucer and he was pretty condescendingly devastating. ("What are we going to do with these Americans they send us?" Interesting again that Chaucer was my Ph.D. topic.) During one tutorial, he cleaned his rifle as I read my essay to him. On another occasion I quoted Marvell. As I pronounced the title of the poem in my broad-vowelled American accent, "On a Drohp of Doo," he broke in with his clipped Oxford accent, "On a Drup of Djyew," and remarked, "Maybe that's why you don't understand poetry, Elbow. You don't know what it sounds like." Before the end of the fall term, I was coming in every week saying, "I don't have an essay for you. I tried as hard as I could, but I couldn't write it." And I really had tried hard, spending the whole week writing initial sentences, paragraphs, and pages and throwing them all away.

Eventually, I changed tutors and limped through my second year. I took a lot of Valium as exams approached. For in fact, it turned out that the Oxford degree didn't depend at all on any of these essays written for tutors over two years. They were nothing but practice for the nine three-hour exams you took during your last four-and-a-half days. I was terrified, but it turns out that the exams didn't throw me as much as the essays had done: in each exam there were only three hours for at least three essays and there wasn't time to agonize—even to revise. I survived with acceptable results (an "undistinguished second")—and very grateful too. "Pretty much what we expected," was Jonathan's comment on the card on which he mailed me my results.

With all that education, you'd think I'd have learned a few simple things—for instance that I needed a break from school. And in fact, I spent the last weeks in August looking for a teaching job in schools. But none turned up and, ever earnest, I started on my Ph.D. in English at Harvard. I still wanted to become a professor, and people kept telling me to "just get the degree out of the way"—like having a tooth pulled or an injection before going on a trip. But, of course, in our American system, the graduate seminar papers count for everything. I had a terrible time getting my first semester papers written at all, and they were graded unsatisfactory. I could have stayed if I'd done well the next semester, but after only a few weeks I could see things were getting worse rather than better. I quit before being kicked out.

My sense of failure was total. It wouldn't have been so bad if I had been less invested or hadn't tried so hard. But I'd long announced my career commitment to my family and relatives, my friends, and my teachers—and I'd tried my damndest. I'd defined and staked my identity on this business of getting a Ph.D. to become a college professor. And I'd also defined myself—to others and to myself—as "successful," particularly at school. So when I quit, I felt ruined. I felt I never wanted to have anything to do with the world of books and teaching again.

First Reflection: On the Experience of Failure

I realize now that much of the texture of my academic career has been based in an oddly positive way on this experience of complete shame and failure. In the end, failing led me to have the following powerful but tacit feeling: "There's nothing else they can do to me. They can't make me feel any worse than they've already done. I tried as hard as I could to be the way they wanted me to be, and I couldn't do it. I really wanted to be good, and I was bad." These feelings created an oddly solid grounding for my future conduct in the academic world. They made it easier for me to take my own path and say whatever I wanted.

In subsequent years, I've noticed that lots of people's behavior in schools and colleges is driven by the opposite feelings—sometimes unconscious: "Uh-oh. They could really hurt me. I *must* do this or I'll fail. I *couldn't* say that or they'd kick me out. To fail or be kicked out is unthinkable." When you live with these feelings—as I had certainly done through all the years before I failed—you sometimes notice a faint impulse to say or do something unacceptable (for example, to skip an assignment, or to do it in a way that the teacher would find unacceptable, or to stand up to the teacher with some kind of basic disagreement or refusal). But you scarcely notice this impulse because acting on it would be unimaginable; insupportable. I realize now that the most unsuccessful students are often the most adventuresome or brave or mentally creative. They operate from the feeling of, "They can't hurt me any worse. What the hell!" That feeling can be empowering. In truth, the most successful students are often the most timid and fearful. They have the most at stake in getting approval. They do the most cheating in school; they have the most suicides.

On with the First Story

Do I seem to celebrate failure here? Am I sounding smug? ("Look at me. They couldn't kill me.") Am I implying a kind of tough-guy Darwinism? ("It's good to fail students; it toughens 'em up.") I don't mean that. I went back and succeeded because I was stubborn and hungry, yes, but I probably wouldn't have been able to overcome my experience of failure without a foundation of privilege (good schools and lots of support I could take for granted) and *luck*. And in fact, it was the old-boy network that got me into the academic pond again by way of a job I never would have sought: an instructorship at M.I.T. They needed bodies in the middle of July because of a departmental feud and a bunch of resignations—and an old college teacher of mine was doing the hiring. (And instructorships were much easier to get in 1960 than they are now.)

I was terrified to take this job, but I needed work. I stayed scared as I started teaching Homer, Aeschylus, Thucydides, and Plato with these M.I.T. first-year students, but I gradually woke up to the fact that I was having a good time. I gradually realized that teaching was much more fun than being a student. I *liked* to read and talk about books when it wasn't for the sake of taking tests or writing papers. I loved the change of agenda that teaching brings. No longer, "Do I understand well enough for *them*?" but rather, "Can I find something to do with this book that students will find worthwhile?" No longer, "Do I love this book enough and in the right way?" but rather, "We're stuck with this book; how can we make it useful in our lives?"

Second Reflection

Since that time in my life, I've often reflected on a curious fact: If you can't write, you can't be a student. But the inability to write doesn't get in the way of teaching at all. Of course, I couldn't have gotten tenure without writing, but my teaching went well. I was an excited teacher and learner. If I'd taught in the schools or at some college, like Evergreen, that doesn't require publication, no one would have ever thought to define my nonwriting as a problem.

I don't know what to make of this asymmetry between being a student and a teacher. On the one hand, I think it's dumb to require people to publish if they want to teach—at least as publication is presently defined. On the other hand, it's sad to define teachers as people who read, not as people who write. (This asymmetry between being a student and a teacher recalls another one: Teachers can't teach without students, but students can learn perfectly well without teachers.)

Finishing the First Story

After three years at M.I.T., I joined the founding faculty at Franconia College, an experimental college in New Hampshire. This was 1963. My three years at M.I.T. gave me more college teaching experience than anyone else on the faculty—all five of us. My M.I.T. years had been, in a sense, about the rehabilitation of reading for me. These next two years at Franconia were the beginnings of a rehabilitation of writing. For I discovered that I enjoyed writing when I was no longer writing as a student. It was no longer, "Here is my writing. Is it acceptable?" Now it was, "I have some ideas about Socrates that excite me and I think I can make them useful to you in your teaching."

I remember writing into the night—long memos on purple dittos—writing out of an excited connection with the material and with my colleagues, who were all teaching the same course.

After this total of five years' teaching, I was hit with two strong reasons to re-enter graduate school. First, it looked as though Franconia might fold in its second year, and I found I couldn't get another job without a Ph.D. Second, my experience of moving from highly successful students at M.I.T. to highly unsuccessful students at Franconia convinced me that something was deeply wrong with how education worked. For it became clear to us that these students whom everyone defined as failures were very smart, and they did good work when given good learning conditions. I wanted to speak out about higher education, but I realized that unless I got a Ph.D., people would say, "You just don't like it because you couldn't do it."

My first impulse was to get my degree in psychology or education—the two subjects that really interested me at this point. But I discovered that I could get my degree much more quickly if I stuck with English. So I climbed up on the same horse I'd fallen off of five years earlier. I wasn't worried that I had no commitment to literature, indeed, I found it enormously enabling as a student to have a completely pragmatic motivation. Instead of worrying, "Am I committed enough to literature?" (a question I had worried about in my first go round), I felt, "I don't care whether I like it or it makes sense. I'll do whatever damn thing you ask. I just want a degree." Under the protection of this psychological umbrella, I gradually discovered how much I loved literature.

But I *was* worried. About writing. Would I get stuck again when I tried to do school writing? I was *so* scared that I set myself a personal deadline for every paper. I forced myself to have a full draft for myself a full week before every real deadline. No matter how bad the writing was, I had to produce the requisite number of pages that I could hold in my hand. Then I had a week to try to improve it. This regime forced me to do something I'd never been able to do before, namely, to write out sentences and paragraphs and pages I knew were no good, to write garbage, and to say, "What the hell." The key was my crassly pragmatic frame of mind.

In addition, I encouraged myself to write little notes to myself about what was happening as I wrote. In particular I wrote notes at stuck points ("How did I get into this swamp?"). And when I finally got my writing or thinking functioning again, I tried to remember to stop for a few moments to explore how I'd managed to do so. Often these were just scrawled notes on little scraps of paper, but I put them all in one folder. After I finally got myself employed again (back at M.I.T.), and I'd finished my dissertation on Chaucer (and even revised it for publication), I did what I'd been wanting to do for a couple of years: pull out that folder of notes to myself and see what I could figure out about writing. I knew there were ideas there that I wanted to figure out. This resulted in *Writing Without Teachers* in 1973. But it wasn't until I had written *Writing with Power* in 1981 that I would call writing "my field."

Retelling the Central Story

A number of years after it happened, I began to think again about this story of my inability to write: not just because I was beginning to have a professional interest in the writing process, but also because my life was coming apart. My first marriage was breaking up. This difficulty led me to a lot of writing in a diary and talking in therapy. So, in fact, I didn't just *think about* my writing difficulty; in this writing and talking I would sometimes touch on these earlier events and feelings and begin in a sense to reexperience. I've always enjoyed watching cows and other ruminants with two stomachs chew their cud—somehow attracted to the idea of re-chewing one's food at leisure afterwards. That's what I started doing.

In my first chewing for my first stomach—that is, during my original experience of struggle and inability with writing—I experienced myself trying as hard as I could to do what I was supposed to do, but failing. In retrospect a number of years later, however—as this experience of struggle passed on to my second chewing for my second stomach—I gradually got hints of a different story. In my diary writing and talking therapy during this later period of struggle in my life, I began to get whiffs of an under-feeling: a feeling that maybe I didn't *really* want to give those teachers the papers they were asking for. Maybe I *didn't* want to be such an earnest, diligent, compliant student. What I originally experienced as an inability, I now began to sense as perhaps resistance; in fact, *refusal*.

I'd always been so obedient. I'd never been able to understand my friends who goofed off or didn't do what they were supposed to do. I'd always experienced myself as simply *wanting* to do what I was supposed to do. I never felt any gap between my duty and my desire. I suppose you'd say that in my formative years I'd badly wanted praise and affirmation and learned that school was a good place to get it. And I'd become skilled at it, become hooked on that role, if you wish. I was the paradigm good student—just what you'd want in your class. For I wasn't just a fawning yes-man; I engaged in sophisticated independent thinking of my own. After all, that's what my best teachers wanted and I wanted to do what they wanted me to do. But now I began to sense an underside to the story.

The essays I wrote in college were often ambitious and thoughtful, but they were almost always muddy and unclear. Teachers were always writing comments to me or telling me straight out: "Why don't you just *say* directly what you mean? Why do you wander and digress and beat around the bush so much? Why so tangled?" But I was struggling as hard as I could to say what I meant—to be clear. If they had described me to a third party, they probably would have said, "He's a smart kid, but when he writes he ties himself in knots." And tying myself in knots is literally what I was doing, according to this second hypothesis.

That is, in retrospect, I think I was playing a game with those teachers: they thought they were putting me to the test, but really I was putting them to the test—the following test: "I'm smart. I'm terrific. If you can understand my paper and see through my paper to how good I am, you pass the test. If you can't, you fail. It's my job to write the paper, but it's your job to recognize my brilliance." It strikes me now that maybe I didn't *want* my meaning to be so clear.

Third Reflection: Language to Convey, Language to Disguise

There emerges here a curious and pregnant fact: that language can be used not only to convey meaning, but to disguise it. We characteristically articulate our meaning in words so people will understand us; but sometimes we do it so that they *won't*—or at least so some of them won't. This may seem perverse. And perverse is what I was being— "contrary" with my teachers. And I get mad when I feel others using language this way—such as when professionals and academics write not just to communicate their meaning, but to exclude the unwashed.

Yet this "game" of using language to convey-but-also-to-disguise was explicitly celebrated in medieval theology and criticism as a model for poetry. According to this theory, the poem consists of a tough *husk* that hides and protects, and a sweet and tender *kernel* inside. (Petrarch cites Gregory and Augustine in saying that if it is appropriate for scriptural wisdom to be veiled, how much more appropriate for poetry [See

Robertson 1963, 62ff].) The function of a good poem is to convey the kernel of wisdom or sweetness—but only to those worthy of it; and to hide it from the unworthy.

This wasn't just a theory spun by intellectuals and theoreticians. Christ proclaimed it openly in his parables—talking about his very use of parables, and from the Gospels, it became common currency. Here is Matthew's version:

> Then the disciples went up to him and asked, "Why do you talk to them in parables?" "Because," he replied, "the mysteries of the kingdom of heaven are revealed to you but they are not revealed to them. For anyone who has will be given more, and he will have more than enough; but from anyone who has not, even what he has will be taken away. The reason I talk to them in parables is that they look without seeing and listen without hearing or understanding." (Matthew 13:10–14, Jerusalem Bible)

He goes on to say this is the fulfillment of a passage in Isaiah (6:9–10).

This is a hard saying, but he makes it even harder in Mark 4:11–12. " 'The secret . . . is given to you, but to those who are outside everything comes in parables, so that they may see and see again, but not perceive; may hear and hear again, but not understand; otherwise they might be converted and be forgiven.' "

When Christ said that the rich will get richer and the poor poorer, he wasn't so much trying to preach Reagan economics (though he did seem to mean it in all its economic astringency). He was really using money as an analogy or metaphor for his *main* message—which was about the conveyance of meaning through language (see Kermode 1979, 33ff). It's a disturbingly elitist point whether it's about money or meaning, but there is no denying an element of truthful empiricism too: The best way to make money is to have a fund of previously accumulated money to work with. (See Matthew 25:14ff for the passage where Christ bawls out people who don't invest their money to make more, but instead settle for mere saving—timidly "burying their talents.") And the best way to understand hard words or ideas is to have a fund of prior understanding or wisdom to build on.

We see this approach to conveying meaning in many mystical traditions. The master purposely makes something hard to understand so that learners have to go through the right process of *nonunderstanding* struggle to get it. Without that nonunderstanding and struggle, they won't "really" get it. A clear conveyance of the "mere meaning" leads to a kind of superficial cognitive understanding that, in fact, functions as a filter against the deeper understanding or full digestion we need. The common theme here is a purposeful use of language to conceal, not just to reveal.

Helen Fox (1994) points out that many traditional, non-Western cultures value this indirect, and often metaphorical, way of conveying meaning and scorn the modern Western value of being direct and literal. Here is an account by Deborah Fredo (1995) of the difference between traditional and modern ways of conveying knowledge in Senegal:

> The [traditional] kind of knowledge that is sought after is that kind which can come from 'minds that bleed best' [the wisest minds]. . . . [I]ndirect thought . . . is more valued than direct thought because what can be attained through direct thought is said to be the kind of knowledge you don't have to work for, the kind that is given to you. Riddles are used as a kind of intelligence test to see if the mind is open enough to 'bleed.'
>
> Being modern, on the other hand, is associated with being direct, a decidedly inferior attribute of the mind. Being true to traditional form means being able to speak in ways which require a listener to decode what you are saying and analyze your meaning. Making meaning, in such a process, always involves some inquiry and analysis but it is the qualities of the person seeking to understand meaning or knowledge that guarantee its acquisition. (66–67)

This approach to language and learning can't be too crazy or we teachers wouldn't use it so much. For we often give the best and the fullest explanations of things to students who already understand a lot—and give far less to students who don't understand.

So even though I resent this use of language (which I now think I engaged in with my college teachers) and dislike this parable about parables, I must recognize that language-to-convey-and-to-disguise is not only a venerable tradition but a perennial human impulse. It lies behind much spontaneous and unsophisticated word play. And isn't much, or even most, poetry an attempt, in a way, to slow down comprehension? (The poet Richard Hugo famously remarked, "If I wanted to communicate, I'd pick up the telephone.") Almost everyone loves riddles, which are a central art form in most oral cultures. In short, humans naturally use language to make their meaning more clear and striking; but they also like to use language to make their meaning *less* clear—to use language as a kind of filter or puzzle or game to distinguish among receivers.

So, although I'm not wanting to defend the tangled quality of those old papers of mine, it strikes me that perhaps we shouldn't be so single-minded in our pursuit of clarity. Perhaps Richard Lanham and Winston Weathers are right in resisting the assumption that good writing always means clear writing. Perhaps students would write better and learn quicker if we were more appreciative of their impulse to write things that we *don't* understand.

Back to the Story

This test I was putting my teachers to—this game I was playing with language: I sense it wasn't just an arrogant game, but an angry one. I think I was mad because they weren't willing to try to build my education on who I was. They felt that the only way to educate me was to strip me down; get rid of all my naivete and wrong feelings. *Learning* wasn't enough for them; I had to be made to *unlearn* and then be built up from scratch. They wouldn't accept or respect me unless I stopped being the kind of person I was. I seem to be implying that I was blaming them—and the taste in my second stomach *is* the taste of anger and blame. Yet, there was no taste of blame at the time, and they would be astonished to hear any talk of blame because I so deeply *wanted* to be like them. Perhaps that's why I was mad—and I guess I still am: it wasn't just my behavior that was dancing on their strings, but my very desires.

   In knocking on my *tutor's* door week after week with *no* paper at all, I was being a tacit refuser, an objector. I didn't experience myself as mad at those Williams College teachers (even though I now suspect anger might have been lurking hidden); I kept giving them their papers. But I *knew* I was mad at Jonathan. Still, I couldn't openly refuse. My inability to write was the closest I could come to giving him the finger. I hid my refusal not only from him, but from myself. Thus, I experienced myself as weak and helpless and trying as hard as I could to be compliant—but now I suspect I was actually angry and stubborn and (in a sense) shrewd. (See Alice Miller on the anger of the "good child.")

Fourth Reflection: Being Wrong about One's Own Feelings?

Of course all this is just hypothesis. I started by telling events; then I told feelings I was having; and now I'm suggesting that I was having different feelings from what I thought I was feeling. One of my published essays ("The Pedagogy of the Bamboozled") is about how

I loved these college teachers that I am now saying I was mad at; how I wanted to be like them; and how falling in love with teachers is such an efficient way to learn because it solves all motivation problems. It seems a kind of absurdity to say, "I thought I was feeling X, but really I was feeling Y." What else does the concept *feeling* mean, after all, but "what we are feeling"? Yet there is this perplexing and troublesome fact: we can be mistaken about our own feelings.

"So what else is new?" the sophisticates will answer: "You've never heard of Freud and the unconscious? And how he was only reminding us of what every nursemaid and mother knows."

Yet surely, we must allow people to be the final authority for what they are feeling. I certainly get mad when a psychoanalyst tries to tell me what I *really* feel, or a Marxist tells me I have "false consciousness"—just as mad as the toddler whose mother brushes aside what he just said with, "Oooh, poor dear. You're just tired [or hungry or wet]." When my son wanted to drop the cello because he said he hated practicing, I made no headway at all by saying, "No you don't. You actually like it. When you practice, I hear enthusiastic verve and cheerful singing." Lots of luck, Dad. But the troublesome fact is, we *can* be wrong about our feelings.

What if a wise and deeply trusted friend had come to me back then and said, "Peter, do you think maybe you don't *want* to give them those essays?" Would I have gotten an inkling of those feelings I wasn't feeling? Who knows? Or did I need some play therapy, perhaps with clay? It might have saved a lot of pain if (the Reagans are everywhere) I'd just said no.

Fifth Reflection: Writing as Giving In

My story seems to be about the movement from compliance to resistance. As a good student I had been expert at compliance, at doing what my teachers wanted me to do, but too much compliance got me in trouble. I was so unable to notice or experience any resistance or refusal or anger—so mistaken about my feelings, so unable to find a path for these feelings—that they found their own underground path to short circuit my entire ability to write or even be a student. My story seems to be about the need to learn fruitful or healthy ways to resist rather than ways that undermine oneself.

This is a familiar theme in studies of the learning process (see, for example, Brooke, Felman, Fox, Jonsberg, Lu, Street, Tobin *Writing Relationships*). These commentators emphasize not only how learning leads inevitably to resistance, but also that we can't learn well without resistance. It seems clear that an important goal for teachers is to help students find fruitful or healthy ways to resist. This became my theme too in most of my subsequent writing about writing: I have been a celebrator of writing without teachers, writing that is free, writing that ignores audience.

But at this stage in my autobiographical reflections, I'm noticing something different in the story. Yes, it's about ineffective resistance, but now I'm struck with how it's also about ineffective compliance. When I couldn't write my papers at all, I may not have been resisting very effectively, but I certainly was resisting. What I wasn't doing at all was complying. During the earlier stages of writing this paper, I was noticing my gift for compliance; now I'm noticing my *problem* with compliance. Something tugs at me now to learn more about this side of the authority relationship of a student to a teacher.

Once I open this door, I'm struck at how many ways writing involves complying or giving in. The need for compliance is most obvious in the case of writing in school and college. There is always a teacher and an assignment and criteria to be met. Someone other than the writer is in charge. The writing has to conform to the teacher's criteria or it's not acceptable (Cleary gives us good pictures of this in her interviews with students). But even when scholars write for learned journals, there is often a strong sense of the need to conform to someone else's criteria. The constraints can be even stronger with a supervisor or employer—sometimes, in fact, the obligation to say exactly what the person in charge wants you to say. Thus in many, or even most, writing situations, there is a subtle, or not so subtle, pressure to give in. When we send writing to journals, publishers, and teachers, what is the verb we use? We "submit."

But now I've come to see in writing for *any* audience a subtle but powerful requirement to give in. Babies and toddlers get to say things however they want, to speak the words and ideas as they come—and parents feel it is their job as audience to interpret no matter how garbled the language. But when we write, we can't be like babies and toddlers. That is, in the very act of writing itself—at least if we want to be understood—we have to give in to the code or the conventions. The conventions. To write is to be conventional.

Look at writers who resist the conventions and refuse to give in. There has always been a small but powerful tradition of writers who feel that accepting conventions means losing their integrity. The most obvious cases are avant garde writers who violate the conventions of meaning, structure, syntax, and orthography: Emily Dickinson, James Joyce, and William Blake are now-hallowed examples. To notice the dimension of resistance in their writing—or in the writing of more recent avant garde writers—helps us notice the unspoken but inherent pressure to comply that they are reacting against. Such writers write the way they want or the way they think best; they push aside the needs of readers. They may lose readers, yet a few are so skilled as to win wide readership. James Joyce managed to persuade readers to do the interpretive work that we usually only do for our own children. (He allegedly said that the only thing he wanted from readers was for them to devote their lives to trying to understand his words—what every baby and toddler simply deserves, but a writer has to earn.) French feminists like Kristeva directly link the conventions of language and writing with the oppressive structures of society and culture (the "law of the fathers").

This pressure from writing to make us give in shows itself in a humble but naked way if we consider the process of copy-editing. Good copy-editing is difficult for all of us who are not real editors, and especially for many students, but I'm not talking about ability, I'm talking about compliance. What interests me here is the common phenomenon of people *not* copy-editing—or copy-editing much less than they are capable of. Copy-editing is such a drudgery; we are never done; we always miss mistakes that we *could* find if we just went through it one more time or read it out loud. Is there not a universal tendency to feel, at some level, "I want you to accept my writing just the way it is—just the way I put it down. I don't want to have to exert myself to clean it up just to make it easy for you." (I found an embarrassing number of surface mistakes in a previous draft of this paper that I had, in fact, shared with friends and colleagues.) I now think that a lot of the mistakes we see in student writing are really the result of a reluctance or even a refusal to change their "natural product." "Take me as I am!" If our only hypothesis for bad copy-editing is laziness, we are forgetting to notice an interesting flavor behind the laziness.

We can also notice the pressure to give in if we notice the release from that pressure when we *don't* have to give in—that is, when we write completely privately, perhaps in a diary or in freewriting. Or we notice this release *if* we can permit it—if we can allow ourselves to turn off that pressure from conventions and readers that most of us have internalized. It's not so easy. I've become pretty good at it, yet sometimes I find myself fixing the spelling of words I've written down, even when I know this is a throwaway draft that no one will read—even when it is just a venting that I won't even read *myself*. (Haswell 1991 studied freewriting and was struck at how *obedient* to conventions it tends to be.) But those who can put aside the pressure to comply almost invariably experience a significant relief.

The very act of *giving* itself exerts a pressure to give in. We smile at the child who gives his mother a bag of gummy candy for her birthday. Gradually, we learn that we're supposed to figure out what the recipient would like—not what we would like.

Am I being one-sided here and neglecting the importance of resistance? I don't want to do that. After all, perhaps it was my resistance in quitting school (odd as it was—being experienced as shameful failure rather than as resistance) that eventually allowed me to comply. But if I make this case for resistance, I am also acknowledging that the function of the resistance was to help me comply. The implication is that students need resistance for the sake of healthy learning because learning so deeply requires giving in. Even if there is no healthy learning or writing without resistance, the fact remains that there is *no learning or writing at all* without a crucial element of compliance or giving in.

It's a little frightening to stick up for compliance. Compliance is what repressive schools and teachers have been emphasizing all along: "What kids need to learn is how to go along, to follow directions, to give in, to obey!" My reflex is the opposite: "What kids need to learn is how to resist and maintain their autonomy." But it's not an either/or matter. It *feels* either/or because that's how we tend to experience it: "Will I fight the dirty bastards or cave in?" But we need *both* resistance and compliance. Nothing I say about the importance of compliance diminishes the need also for resistance: we clearly need resistance if we want to do our own thinking and be our own person— to go against the grain, to hang on to our autonomy, integrity, agency.

In short, we have fetched up against a familiar binary pattern— an opposition between necessary but conflicting elements. I think this pattern helps us understand better the complexities of the teaching and learning process—helps us look at the rich variety of students' strengths and weaknesses around us and notice the spectrum of methods students have developed to deal with this conflict between the inherent need in learning both to resist and also to give in. Some methods are more successful than others, but none feel very comfortable or ideal, for in the last analysis the two needs are—though necessary and complementary and perhaps even potentially reinforcing—nevertheless, at odds with each other.

- At one extreme are the compliant students. I was expert at compliance; I wanted to do what my teachers wanted me to do. There is a long tradition of learning by imitation and copying. Probably the most psychically efficient way to learn a lot is to fall in love with your teachers—as I tended to do (see my "Bamboozled," p. 96–98). Many feminists see girls as traditionally socialized to comply. Girls and women seem to go along more with teachers—to give less back-talk or other kinds of resistance. (See, for example, Gilligan; see Bolker on the "patient Griselda" syndrome in writing. It's worth noting that the word *buxom* originally meant obedient.)

- At the other extreme are the highly resistant students. They fight and sabotage the teacher, they sometimes walk out, and the only thing they give is the finger. Boys and men seem to fall more often into this relation to teacher authority than women do (see Connors; Tobin's "Car Wrecks"). We don't have to be essentialists to see that women often have a harder time with resistance and men have a harder time with compliance. But this is slippery ground: there are plenty of women who resist and plenty of men like me who seem to love doing what their teachers want them to do (not to mention the complexities of complying-but-not-really-complying and resisting-but-not-really-resisting).

- In between these two extremes we can look for the various ways that students try to serve *both* goals—to negotiate the competing pressures to give in and to resist. Some make a compromise and are sort of resistant and sort of compliant. These are not the excellent students, but rather the middling or passable or mediocre ones. You can't do a very good job if you only sort of go along with the assignment and conventions and needs of readers—and only sort of fight your way to your own thoughts and point of view.

- True excellence is rare because it consists of something paradoxical and hard to explain: the ability to be *extremely* assertive or even resistant while at the same time managing to comply *very well* with the requirements of conventions, teachers, assignments, and readers. David Bartholomae points to this paradox in saying that a writer learns "by learning to write *within* and *against* the powerful writing that precedes him, that haunts him, and that threatens to engulf him" (1985, "Against" 27, emphasis added). In writing an essay about his own writing process, he emphasizes resistance and titles it "Against the Grain." And yet, he emphasizes how important it was for him not just to be influenced by strong teachers and writers, but in fact to imitate them and even to *copy over by hand* extended passages of their writing.

■ And then there is dysfunction. That is, some students feel these conflicting pressures to comply and to resist so strongly that they get tied up in knots and can't write. (Perhaps this is what stopped me when I had to quit graduate school.) Or they struggle but don't turn out much or any work—or it's very bad and they feel terrible about it.[1]

Surely these competing needs to comply and to resist are not just school issues but rather play out in many areas of life—especially in growing up. What I'm exploring here is related to the Piagetian concepts of assimilation and accommodation. I wonder whether eating disorders might not sometimes be about the dilemma of giving in and refusing.

What follows for us as teachers from this way of looking at writing and learning? For one thing, we might look with new eyes at the unclear writing we get. We might consider the possibility that some of it—perhaps much of it—represents not so much a lack of skill as a way of resisting us as readers and wielders of authority. Much of the tangled quality of my writing in college was really a disguised form of resistance and resentment. Instruction in syntax and organization did me very little good. I had good teachers, they worked hard, and so did I. And still my prose stayed tangled. The problem was that I didn't fully *want* to give those teachers my meaning. My syntax never got clearer until I was finally wholehearted in my desire to *give* myself and my meaning to my readers. Sadly enough, this never happened until I stopped writing for teachers.

This way of looking at unclear student writing doesn't make it clear. But it helps me say to myself, "Maybe lack of skill is not the main problem here; maybe he or she doesn't really *want* to be clear to me. Maybe this is part of the 'writing process' considered from a wider angle." That doesn't make me want to reward unclear writing when it's supposed to be clear, but it does help me say, "this is very unclear to me" with better grace, more charity—and less discouragement. I find I can sometimes look *through* that unclear writing to unused capacities for clarity and force. Most of all, it helps me ask myself, "Am I giving my students enough occasions where the writing can be as unclear or problematic as can be?"

I think my teaching benefits when I recognize that I am faced with conflicting goals: helping students find ways to comply, yet still maintain their independence and autonomy; and ways to resist, yet still be productive. We can't remove the conflict, but we can at least understand it. Thus, I believe it helps our teaching to realize that it is possible ideally for resistance and compliance somehow to reinforce each other. Resistance gives us our own thinking and the ownership over ourselves that permit us to do the giving in we need for learning; compliance fuels resistance and gives us the skills we need for better resistance.

But I believe we should also recognize how difficult and paradoxical this trick is—how neither we, nor our students, can expect to pull it off consistently. We can acknowledge that students are, in fact, doing very well if they manage to career back and forth a bit between complying and resisting—and not stay stuck in one mode. (I make a similar analysis of the dialectical relationship in the writing process between generating and criticizing, being credulous and skeptical [see my *Power*].)

Finally, I want to suggest some concrete teaching practices that have become even more important to me because they seem to help with this paradox about resistance and compliance. The main thing is the helpful contrast between high-stakes and low-stakes assignments. High-stakes assignments foster compliance: When we raise the amount of credit that an essay carries, we raise the pressure on students to comply. Low-stakes assignments allow more space for resistance or rebellion: When we assign work but structure it so it doesn't count for so much, we make it easier for students to resist or refuse— for example, by writing what they know we hate, or writing in a way that we hate.

But now I want to complicate this picture somewhat. In particular, I'm struck with how low-stakes writing helps with compliance too—not just resistance:

- *Private writing.* Look at the interesting mixture of occasions for compliance and resistance. When I assign private journal writing I am asking for a certain minimum but real compliance with the demands of the teacher: to produce writing at a certain time or lose credit. But since neither I nor any other outside reader sees it, there is no need to comply in any other respect. The writing doesn't have to conform to *any* criteria. I just ask students to flip the pages for me. Thus students can even cheat on this if they want to badly enough. When we do private writing in class, a few students sometimes just sit there not writing. I used to try to pressure them in some way, but it's hard when I won't even see it. Now I don't fight them—seeing it as an important occasion for saying no—as long as they don't disrupt others.

What I hadn't figured out until now is that private writing doesn't just make it easier for students to resist by making it easier for them to give the finger to conventions or standards or my preferences, it also makes it easier for them to comply. Students can decide to *give in* without anyone seeing it— without a shred of teacher-pleasing or caving in to institutional pressure.

- *Writing merely to share.* I assign a good amount of writing that I ask students only share with each other—no feedback, and which I read but do not respond to or grade. Because this writing is shared, most students feel more pressure from audience and conventions than they do with private writing. But because there is no response to or grading of this writing, students are freer to resist any of these quiet but perhaps powerful pressures, and to frustrate or even annoy readers with no explicit penalty.

  But here too I am now realizing the low stakes that come from mere-sharing-no-response can help with compliance too—not just resistance. It's sometimes easier to comply with conventions or readers' desires when one doesn't have to comply.

- We see this same dynamic with the *extensive publication of student writing.* (At UMass Amherst, every teacher in the first year course publishes a class magazine four or five times a semester—paid for with a ten dollar lab fee.) Students can thumb their nose at readers; or go along with reader needs. The fact of publication—seeing all your classmates holding in their hands a copy of a class magazine that contains your writing—increases the pressure from peer readers. But by the same token, it helps put teacher standards into more perspective. It helps students think a bit more explicitly about the question, "Are the teacher standards the ones I really care most about?"

- *A grading contract.* I now tend to use a contract for grading. I promise students a B if they comply with an extensive set of requirements. (e.g., they must have consistent attendance, take major assignments through two genuine revisions, copyedit final drafts well, give and receive thoughtful feedback from each other, write process notes for every main assignment, keep a journal, and so forth. Sometimes I have additional clauses for an A, see my "Grading.") A contract shakes up the normal resistance/compliance dynamic of the writing classroom—or rather clarifies it. The contract makes the pressure to comply more concrete and explicit: my "demand" that they "do what I want them to do" is more naked than with conventional grading. This in itself is a relief—compared to the indirectness of conventional grading. But what is perhaps more important is how the contract asks for things that are so clear and external—rather than things that are a matter of quality and interpretation. My request for compliance is not an attempt to reach inside their head—or to get them to fit themselves into what's inside my head. It's not that I've given up trying to affect the insides of their heads—their standards or desires. For, of course, I often give them extensive feedback on their writing—often giving my reactions and values. But, in fact, I think I can have a bigger effect on my students with the contract than with conventional grading by letting my reactions be personal and insulating them from having any effect on the grade. Thus the contract makes it easier for students to resist; even on major assignments they can write what they know I will hate or write in a style they know I don't like—with no penalty. But in the end, I think the contract makes it easier to comply because they don't have to. They are not caving in; they have more choice.[2]

If writing is an act of giving in, it seems to me that one of the most practical goals for us as teachers is to help students fall in love with their own ideas and their writing. Then they are stuck with the compliance problem in a productive way instead of a destructive way. Yes, they still have to give in to conventions and to audience—that's hard and it can hurt—but it is easier to put the resentment to one side and get yourself to give in because you love what you've created and you want others to get it, understand it, and appreciate it. It helps if *we* also love what our students write (see my "Ranking, Judging, and Liking"). The trouble with most school writing is that students have to comply not only to the conventions of written language, good thinking, and reader needs; they usually feel most strongly of all the need to comply with the teacher, the assignment, and the authority of the institution. This raises the stakes of compliance and makes it harder to give in. For students in this situation, giving in carries a higher price.

I've been describing this difficulty from our point of view as teachers. But it's fruitful to reframe it from the students' blunt point of view: "How can I be a good student without 'sucking up' or being a 'brown-nose?'" (Anyone who resists a psychoanalytic view need only reflect on the ubiquity of these metaphors among students.) Sadly, for many students the dilemma seems impossible. But let's turn the question around and use it as a framework for structuring our teaching: How can *we* conduct our teaching to maximize the opportunities for students to be good without experiencing themselves as "teacher pleasers?" Again, it's not easy. We need new thinking and shrewd suggestions.

Researchers have begun to think about this general issue as it is faced by adult nonliterates and by students coming from a culture that identifies away from school: how to learn without giving up one's identity or one's culture. Researchers have begun to notice better the inevitable *loss* that goes along with any learning.[3]

Let me conclude with a brief thought about the relationship of my whole story with issues of race, class, gender, and sexual orientation. I imagine someone reading what I have written here and muttering, "What a whiner! A privileged and successful white boy is making such a big drama out of his struggles with the system. Shit, man! It's *his* system."

What if I were a different color or culture or gender or class? How much harder I would find it to negotiate a fruitful and productive way to comply with a culture that I see as devaluing or even destroying my culture! Given who I am, perhaps I should just laugh at my struggles and brush off my resentments since they seem so minor in comparison.

Yet my struggles and resentments were real—and they may be instructive. There's something to be learned from seeing how a culture tries to prepare people in privileged institutions. When looking from the outside at the fit between me and these elite institutions, one is apt to notice how much I seemed to *belong* because of my comfortable mainstream background. But when looking from the inside—from the point of view of my experience at the time—what strikes me most is my completely opposite feeling: my sense that I *didn't* belong and didn't fit in at Williams, Oxford, or Harvard. But, perhaps more important, how badly I *wanted* to belong—how deeply undermining it felt not to be "right"—and thus how high a price I was willing to pay to get that precious feeling of belonging. In a genuine sense it was "my system"—but it seems as though the way my system functions (except perhaps for deeply secure people) is to make it feel as though it *isn't* my system unless I give up on part of what is central to me and go along with it. Perhaps this is how structures of power and elitism function.

It's true that Oxford and Harvard and other elite institutions are, in significant ways, more tolerant of resistance and idiosyncrasy than less elite schools are (at least for those students with unflappable confidence). But in other ways, elite institutions exact the *most* compliance and elicit the most "buying in." If we doubt that, we need only look at how such institutions react to the possibilities of significant change in the educational process—or look at their alumni magazines to see how much graduates have "bought in."

On the one hand, I was the *best* kind of student: just the kind you'd want in your classroom. But I was also the worst: a failure who couldn't do the work and quit and never wanted to have anything to do with books and learning again. My goal in this essay is to complicate our notions of best and worst student. Many of our "best" students may be paying too high a price in their compliance and preventing themselves from doing lasting good work—or complying but not complying and sabotaging themselves. And many of our "worst" students, our refuseniks, might potentially be some of our best, but they are in the same dilemma: we haven't managed to help them find fruitful or productive ways to comply.

Notes

1. Edward White writes: "Those who have learned to succeed [on multiple choice tests] do so not by asking which answer is correct in the world or under various circumstances, but by choosing the one the *test makers* are likely to have chosen to fit the needs of the test. The multiple-choice test thus examines—along with its 'content'—the degree to which the student can adapt reality to the needs of authority. This indeed may be the reason that many such scores correlate well with success in college. The required submission to the world of that kind of test may also suggest reasons why minority groups score less well on these so-called 'objective' tests than they do on writing tests" (1995, 34–45).

2. Bruce Bashford of SUNY Stony Brook points out that many teachers learn to shape assignments in such a way that the emphasis is on the "demand encountered within the activity" itself, in the problem—rather than on the demand to conform to a teacher's authority. "[A] task can have an integrity of its own, can contain its own criteria of success—what John Dewey had in mind when he said the solution is in the problem" (correspondence 3/9/95). Related here is the recent growth of interest in public service activities in writing courses. Students aren't just writing for the teacher but for outside tasks and people.

3. Arlene Fingeret writes of how "Illiterate adults . . . identify a risk connected to learning to read and write"—a risk of having to "separate themselves from their communities" and social networks (1983, 144). She speaks of the "findings of other researchers that nonreading adults would like to know how to read but that they have been unwilling to tolerate the profoundly disrespectful environment of most educational programs" (1989, 13). Mary Savage speaks of the need to learn to *mourn* "for the way schools teach us how to separate the 'us' from the 'them' " (1990, 25); for "how the academy rearranged people and knowledge in hierarchies and isolated us in agonistic relations" (1990, 27); and for "students who disappeared and relationships

which ended and families which became strained and distant" (1990, 36). These are all costs of giving in.

Works Cited

Bartholomae, David. 1985. "Inventing the University." *When a Writer Can't Write,* ed. Mike Rose. New York: Guilford Press, 134–65.

———. "Against the Grain." 1985. *Writers on Writing,* ed. Tom Waldrep. New York: Random House, 19–30.

Bolker, Joan. 1979. "Teaching Griselda to Write." *College English* 40.8 (April): 906–8.

Brooke, Robert. 1987. "Lacan, Transference, and Writing Instruction." *College English* 49.6 (October): 679–91.

———. 1991. *Writing and Sense of Self: Identity Negotiation in Writing Workshops.* Urbana, IL: NCTE.

Cleary, Linda Miller. 1991. *From the Other Side of the Desk: Students Speak Out about Writing.* Portsmouth, NH: Boynton/Cook Heinemann.

Connors, Robert J. 1996. "Teaching and Learning as a Man." *College English* 58.2 (February): 137–57.

Elbow, Peter. 1987. "Closing my Eyes as I Speak: An Argument for Ignoring Audience." *College English* 49.1 (January): 50–69.

———. "Getting Along without Grades—and Getting Along with Them Too." *Theory and Practice of Grading Writing: Problems and Possibilities,* ed. Chris Weaver and Fran Zak. Albany, NY: SUNY Albany Press.

———. 1986. "The Pedagogy of the Bamboozled." *Embracing Contraries: Explorations in Learning and Teaching.* New York: Oxford University Press, 87–98.

———. 1993. "Ranking, Evaluating, and Liking: Sorting out Three Forms of Judgment." *College English* 55.2 (February): 187–206.

———. 1993. "The Uses of Binary Thinking." *Journal of Advanced Composition.* 13.1 (winter): 51–78.

———. 1981. *Writing with Power: Techniques for Mastering the Writing Process.* New York: Oxford University Press.

Felman, Shoshana. 1982. "Psychoanalysis and Education: Teaching Terminable and Interminable." *Yale French Studies* 63: 21–44.

Fingaret, Arlene. 1983. "Social Network: A New Perspective on Independence and Illiterate Adults." *Adult Education Quarterly* 33.3 (spring): 133–46.

———. 1989. "The Social and Historical Context of Participatory Literacy Education." *Participatory Literacy Education,* ed. A. Fingeret and P. Jurmo. New Directions for Continuing Education, no 42. San Francisco: Jossey-Bass. (summer).

Fox, Helen. 1994. *Listening to the World: Cultural Issues in Academic Writing.* Urbana, IL: NCTE.

Fredo, Deborah. 1995. *Women's Literacy, Indigenous Form and Authentic Co-Learning: A Research Approach to Participatory Training for National Language Literacy in Rural Senegal.* Diss., U Mass Amherst.

Gilligan, Carol. 1991. "Joining the Resistance: Psychology, Politics, Girls and Women." *The Female Body: Figures, Styles, Speculations,* ed. Laurence Goldstein. Ann Arbor: University of Michigan Press, 12–47.

Haswell, Richard H. 1991. "Bound Forms in Freewriting: The Issue of Organization." *Nothing Begins with N: New Investigations of Freewriting,* ed. Pat Belanoff, Sheryl Fontaine, and Peter Elbow. Carbondale, IL: Southern Illinois University Press, 32–69.

Jonsberg, Sara Dalmas. 1990. "Learning Requires Resistance." *PRE/TEXT* 11.1–2, (spring/summer): 41–45.

Kermode, Frank. 1979. *The Genesis of Secrecy: On the Interpretation of Narrative.* Cambridge: Harvard University Press.

Lanham, Richard A. 1974. *Style: An Anti-Textbook.* New Haven: Yale University Press.

Lu, Min-Zhan. 1987. "From Silence to Words: Writing as Struggle." *College English* 49 (April): 437–48.

Miller, Alice. 1981. *The Drama of the Gifted Child.* Trans. Ruth Ward. New York: Basic Books.

Murphy, Ann. 1989. "Transference and Resistance in the Basic Writing Classroom: Problematics and Praxis." *College Composition and Communication* 40 (May): 175–87.

Robertson, D. W. 1963. *A Preface to Chaucer.* Princeton University Press.

Savage, Mary C. 1990. "Mourning into Dancing." *PRE/TEXT* 11.1–2 (spring/summer): 23–38.

Street, Brian. 1985. *Literacy in Theory and Practice.* New York: Cambridge University Press.

Tobin, Lad. 1996. "Car Wrecks, Baseball Caps, and Man-to-Man Defense: The Personal Narratives of Adolescent Males." *College English* 58.2 (February): 158–75.

——. 1993. *Writing Relationships: What Really Happens in the Composition Class.* Portsmouth, NH: Boynton-Cook Heinemann.

Weathers, Winston. 1980. *An Alternate Style: Options in Composition.* Rochelle Park, NJ: Hayden Book Co.

——. 1976. "The Grammars of Style: New Options in Composition." *Freshman English News.* (winter).

White, Edward M. 1995. "An Apologia for the Timed Impromptu Essay Test." College Composition and Comunication 46.1 (February): 30–45.

10 Disrupting the Transmission Cycle in College Teaching

Gordon M. Pradl
New York University

From 1986 to 1992, I served as Director of Staff Development for our university's Expository Writing Program. Putatively, I was responsible for helping one hundred instructors improve their classroom teaching strategies, which might include everything from conducting class discussions to grading student papers. Most of these instructors, however, came from graduate programs in the Arts and Sciences, where "education talk" is a foreign tongue, or at best some substandard dialect. Phrases such as "active student learning" or "writing to learn" held no meaning for such instructors; indeed, they seemed to point to some alien progressive vision of what should be happening in the classroom. Working with these instructors, I came to realize that the approaches I was asking them to consider as being representative of *enlightened* writing instruction could not be divorced from their contrary beliefs about how their own disciplines—from American History and English Literature to Media Ecology and Cinema Studies—might be best taught and learned. In short, I found myself faced with a contrasting version of academic socialization, one that disrupted what I thought I valued in teaching. Together, we would need to reflect on our conflicting understanding of how students might go about learning.

I wanted to open up for their consideration how learning involves a student being *transactionally* engaged with the issues at hand. In large part, I saw this as a matter of getting these instructors in conscious touch with the magic and joy of those occasions when they felt they were most actively involved as learners. What might they do in their own teaching to spark similar encounters for their students? How might they view themselves as other than budding scholars, intent on accumulating

I wish to thank Barbara Danish, Darlene Forrest, Jane Douglas, and Julia Kasdorf for conversing with me in ways that made this essay possible.

more information to pass along to their students? Inevitably, such a concern brought me back to issues of expertise, power, authority, and control—and raised some disturbing questions about my own teaching. In
the following meditations, I see these issues as centering on the nature
of the relationship that teachers foster with students. In our writing program, we continue to work in collaborative ways toward what Barbara
Danish, the Director of our Writing Center, has accurately labeled a
"pedagogy of listening," a pedagogy that focuses on *the discourse of possibility*, rather than *the discourse of certainty*. To my chagrin, I discovered
that in attempting to break down patterns of "transmission" in the
teaching of these instructors, I had to face up to my own very real limitations as a teacher/listener.

When I consciously stand aside, listen, or attend, I actively focus
on the student's agency rather than my own. I hold back and acknowledge the student's self-expression instead of emphasizing my own
power. Yet in doing this, I realize, there is always something of myself
I am holding back—an idea, an opinion, an action—and so how I am
present in the classroom represents a choice. How aware, how responsible, am I as a teacher when these choices arise?

Whose agenda am I taking up when I help a student? How do
I resist intruding on a student's prerogatives? When I hold back
information from students, am I in danger of disenfranchising them?
I have attempted to get beyond merely imposing or "transmitting"
information, especially information that is seen exclusively from my
point of view. Yet relinquishing the position of "expert" forces me to
consider a new picture of myself as a teacher and brings with it a
new set of anxieties and crosscurrents to be examined in my teaching
behavior: Why, in my silences, do students not always perceive me
as listening? How can I best establish the kind of student autonomy
necessary for acquiring knowledge? Learning viewed from the perspective of the learner creates many dilemmas for me because I'm
never sure exactly how, as teacher and student, we get to pursue at
the same time our mutual needs for attention and growth. For
instance, I'm never sure how to work with students who are clearly
brighter than I am.

Conventionally, teachers get to choose what and how knowledge is defined—schools thrive on maintaining strict boundaries,
around both people and academic subjects. But if knowing more than
my students is what characterizes my chief advantage as teacher, of
what do I know more? I'm not always sure; it's certainly not always
easy to tell, and this may prove to be the first instance of a reversal, an

invitation for me to learn from my students, and thus, legitimize *their presence* in my conception of teaching. When I see my *presence* in partnership with the *presence* of the students, I begin to acknowledge my limitations, for suddenly my failures appear productive, maybe even a necessary part of my students' and my own learning.

To begin with, how do students read my actions in the classroom? How should I adjust when I find out what students are thinking; what they'd like to know? How do students interpret the "quieting of my voice" when I try backing off from the traditional role as lecturer? Here is Chris, a student in one of my graduate courses on the teaching of writing, interpreting my "manipulation" of the position of teacher:

> My first reaction when I entered this classroom was that this course would be really dreary because it didn't seem that I would be able to have decent discussions given the unmovable furniture, which seemed to reflect the immobility, dare I say reification of the university. That is, social relations are masked so that *students are seen as merely an audience for the Truth* which supposedly will emanate from the head of the class body.
>
> [Gordon] attempted to dismantle this apparatus by giving students a chance to discuss issues. He did this, not by launching off in the direction of some self-proclaimed politics of liberation with wonderful claims to radicalness, but by beginning or rather *initially seeming to operate within the status quo*. He also played an interesting *game of near and far*, that is he played with distance. Furniture which seemed to lend itself to magnifying *the distance of the teacher from the students* was used in what initially appeared to be a liberal humanist call for authentic communication between students.
>
> This was deceiving, however, because the teacher was only *faking the role of facilitator*. He was more a persona or mask than the "genuine" human being necessitated by empathetic theories. Especially toward the beginning of the course there was a sense when he moved by the furniture to sit in on different groups that he was *not revealing himself*. One had the sense that he had a particular *script* that he had planned for the encounter. It's hard to describe, but I think some of us felt that we only got glimmers now and then of *what Gordon was really thinking*. Although at first it seemed *manipulative*, it struck me that he was *playing a neat balancing act* between the *role of facilitator* and the *role of lecturer*. I began to see that the distance that he maintained even in so-called "human" encounters was a way to *get us off guard* so we could begin to *critique or reflect on power relations in the classroom*. Actually, I think he was constantly oscillating between facilitator and lecturer.

> When he lectured, he didn't use his position as a soapbox
> for his own opinions about the texts we were reading. I think
> he was *faking* the role of lecturer by seeming to lecture to us
> and yet keeping the discussion *open*. In the beginning it seemed
> that he was not giving us the "truth" about the texts and that
> some [students] seemed disappointed by the lack of commen-
> tary. [my italics]

I found Chris's words exposed certain of my deliberate teaching
moves as I tried to force the students to "critique or reflect on power
relations in the classroom." I wanted these students, who themselves
were instructors in the University's Expository Writing Program, to
recognize that they're following some "script" when they're teaching
and that this script always involves choice. They might see their role
as "invisible" or "natural" and just proceed blindly, or they might
decide consciously to monitor and adjust their roles as teacher. In any
case *they* are the ones responsible for these options, and their choices
have consequences that help determine the nature of learning in their
own classrooms.

But for this lesson to be understood, I felt that the student/
instructors had to experience the varying boundaries of a teacher's
role at some felt affective level. I couldn't just tell them; they had to
feel it for themselves. But how does a teacher disrupt what students
normally expect to find in a graduate class, especially one held in a
large amphitheater with fixed seats all facing down toward the dais?
Here the architecture was sending a pretty clear message about lecturing and expertise, about knowledge flowing in one direction only. But
the obvious solution, abandon center stage, I believed, would too easily have been discredited. As Chris had recognized, it could be written
off as an anomaly, a simple refusal to follow the predicted rules of the
academy. Therefore, it would have failed to problematize the "lecture"
itself and the "transmission of knowledge" metaphor it embodies.
Accordingly, I tried to improvise a teaching script that, in a seemingly
contradictory fashion, played with the boundaries of teacher authority
and thus provoked fruitful student bewilderment. The challenge was
finding ways to balance commentary with distance and silence.

In both emphasizing my *presence* ("seeming to lecture" and outlining all the assignments) and refusing to be a source of answers ("not
revealing himself"), I hoped to call attention to the students' role in
constructing knowledge—how they are finally responsible for putting
together and going beyond the information and opinions they are listening to and reading. Might they question their own roles as teachers

by experiencing a reversal of the conventional patterns by which they related to a teacher who held the power of assessment over them? When I failed to give direct answers or deflected one question with another, I became aware of the students gradually becoming frustrated, even angry, and so I realized that as the convening teacher I could never completely withhold information or my own convictions. In short, I began to see my task as raising discontent to a level where students could begin to enter the learning arena with some of their own interests and concerns. Then I could be more forthcoming with my own stories and ideas. It seems my "manipulations" *were* catching a number of these instructors "off guard": In the reflective teaching journals they kept throughout the semester, they wrote about trying to approach their own students differently by actually listening to what they had to say.

But listening begins with oneself. Until I construct some point of correspondence between my own perspective and that of the person talking to me, their words lie dormant and a conversation never develops. Wishing to tap the inner awareness of these instructors, I have found a "writer's autobiography" to offer a fresh start. "Just give me the story of how you came to be able to write, what turned you on or turned you off, and how you actually go about writing in the real world that you value, not some dummy run for a professor." A simple enough directive, but I find resistance everywhere—this seems to be too personal a request for many budding scholars, too much vulnerability on the line here. Then I cajole and insist: Know thyself! And almost universally they come to invest this piece of writing with a seriousness of purpose that combines emotion with penetrating analysis. In the process they discover, or rediscover, parts of themselves that are more like freshmen than the "grown-up" academics they're openly striving to become. My secret dream is that these stories, multiplied many fold, will validate alternative ways of *being* in the university.

Outside of the large class setting, I have been trying for a long time to improve my capacity as a listener during graduate student conferences. One sign of progress, I felt, was my ability to stay silent for fairly extended periods of time in conversations with students. Lately, however, I've begun to discover that students understand quite differently this particular way of holding back—it is not always appreciated and is sometimes even seen as aggressive behavior. One student finally spilled the beans: apparently I was failing to send back signals to students about just how I'd heard them. So this kind of standing back that I had been judging as successful, namely that the student had been allowed to talk a lot, was not seen in kind by the student. Further, given that most of my graduate students are women, my stance of silence was ignoring the importance they placed on establishing interpersonal connections among participants in a conversation. Thus in our exchanges, they were often more interested in elaborating the narrative thread of what they were pondering, while my predilection was for impersonal abstraction that incorporated explanations and solutions.

As Deborah Tannen has pointed out, our conversational strategies are only successful to the extent that they are appropriately interpreted by our interlocutors. Mere silence, without checking how the student is perceiving it, may not always be accomplishing my objectives. Intending that my silence would provide a space of importance for the student, I neglected to see that it could also be read as the withholding of approval and intimacy. Despite my goal of collaboration, too many students were construing the situation in competitive terms and, accordingly, ended up feeling quite uncomfortable—a surprising conclusion for me to suddenly discover. By acknowledging the validity of these student perceptions, I came to see that I needed to find ways of encouraging each learner to articulate just how my attempts to be tentative in the teaching/learning situation actually appeared to them:

I'm having difficulty with your silences.

I'm terrified of getting this wrong.

I'm having trouble with this idea.

I'm afraid you don't understand my position.

I'm not getting any direction here.

I'm sorry I can't seem to write this up.

I'm nervous about these procedures.

I'm wondering what you're thinking.

I'm worried about how this project will end.

I'm anxious that this isn't working.

I'm troubled that people don't take me seriously.

I'm distressed not to have written all semester.

I'm concerned about the results.

I'm happy you're finally listening.

Trying to shift out of the role of expert is not easy because to do so means I must begin to see my "understandings" as contingent, not absolute. While acknowledging that others need to talk—to actively produce some language of their own—I may grudgingly remain silent, but am I really listening? Sometimes my silence is viewed as condescension—I seem to be sending a message to the student that what they're saying is inferior to what I would be saying if only I weren't being so polite and self-righteous in shutting up. An obvious, but difficult, first step toward clarifying these mixed signals of communication is to stop and actually check how the students are perceiving their learning situation.

Thinking I really do have superior knowledge is a sure way of failing in my attempts to forge new teaching relationships with students. Within the dialogue silently being woven in my head during a period of listening, I might still think and act as though I controlled the situation—the silence of superiority can be worse than direct imposition. Students are adept at reading such silences as judgmental, and this can quickly poison any trust that may be developing between us.

Dispensing knowledge makes me feel confident and self-possessed, but trying to live with uncertainty and error can make me feel insecure, even stupid. Quickly, I can find myself becoming defensive, for what will the stance of my students be toward me if I expose the insecurities, the indeterminacies, out of which I work? Facing these fundamentally unresolved questions about what I'm doing in the classroom disturbs me, and yet it keeps pushing me deeper into my teaching. As a teacher, how do I view my paradoxical responsibility to provoke even as I get out of the way, to appear even as I disappear? How can I contribute to students' learning, realizing that my success will be measured by their ability to perform independently of me?

Holding back can be misinterpreted as coolness, as aloofness. And learners may be accurate in this perception if I fail to inquire into how they are construing the revised conditions and consequences of my *presence*. And yet, sometimes when I have talked at length, I realize I've actually proven to be absent for the student. I've been *present* only in the content of my talk and ignored my responsibility for attending to the teaching/learning (self/other) relationship that exists between me and the student. Everything depends finally on when and how silence and talk occur—their interweaving patterns and rhythms. After a give-and-take relationship with the student has been developed, I find I am able to talk more because the student now feels confident about being able to take or leave what I am saying.

It keeps occurring to me, however, that there is no set way of determining when exactly I should talk about my teaching intentions and actions with students. The broad contours of a course, assessment demands, what might be expected of teacher and student: none of these things are secrets. There is no need to be secretive about this information, though students will not always hear it, especially if it is contrary to their expectations. Sometimes, for instance, I might tell a group of students beforehand, "You're going to notice long silences as I start to talk about this poem. I won't be stepping in any more at those points when no one is speaking up, no matter how awkward this makes us feel." Other times, when I'm making things up as I go along, I certainly don't know exactly what will happen next, what moves I will make, but it may be useful to reflect with students about what is happening. Of course, explicit talk about my procedures is not, in every case, appropriate—sometimes it may only confuse students or undercut what we are trying to accomplish together.

On those occasions when I've started feeling comfortable with silence and mistakes, I've found my *presence* in the classroom is marked by collaboration and genuine listening. I'm deliberately monitoring my contributions, invitationally giving space to others, modifying my talk so it hooks up with what others are saying. I actively listen, even invite the learner to comment directly on the conditions of learning, on feelings and understandings. When this occurs, however, I see the irony of my own position: what I initially thought I was withholding now becomes transformed into a new kind of contribution. Taking the perspective of the other person allows me to recognize the collaborative nature of a group's learning together. Understanding that there are many sides to the student/teacher relationship, I keep trying to acknowledge that they often see this relationship in ways quite different from me.

Kierkegaard encourages me to reconsider the spirit in which I would like to approach my students, however well-intentioned I may consider myself:

> [T]he helper must first humble himself under him he would help, and therewith must understand that to help does not mean to be a sovereign but to be a servant, that to help does not mean to be ambitious but to be patient, that to help means to endure for the time being the imputation that one is in the wrong and does not understand what the other understands. (Kierkegaard 1962, 27–28)

Often adult students have an inferior status instilled in them from years of schooling. "Humiliation" may seem a strong word, but, as long as I continue to collude in such power relationships that work against a student's interests, then nothing short of humiliation seems sufficient to change the direction of my teaching and replace looking down with looking across. When I "lower" myself to become more of an equal in the classroom, then other people and *their* questions, rather than my presumptions about what might be good for them, become the medium of exchange.

To experience this shift, however, is also to feel that somehow my education is regressing, that I know less today than I knew yesterday. Lacking a clear sense of my limitations as a teacher, I don't find it surprising at how resistant I am to practicing "humiliation" in my teaching. When I stand apart, or stand above, I limit the range of learning/teaching relationships that are possible in the classroom.

Being *present* for a student involves my paying deliberate attention to the social transaction that surrounds learning. This means I need to modify my behavior at many junctures, anticipating how my actions will affect others. While it might seem sensible to look before I leap or think before I speak, when I ignore the other, there seems little motivation to look ahead and ask questions. Stepping back, I'm able to reflect about consequences before opening my mouth. Teaching, which attends to the personhood of the learner, comfortably takes soundings all the time. A voice in my head constantly tries to review my intentions, my actions, and how I am being received—"OK, it's going this way," or "I seem to be having this effect," or "I'm not saying this thing right; they're not getting it"—then I consciously readjust, or pick myself up when I stumble, and try to begin again. To monitor my *presence* in this way requires me to make *choices*, choices informed by how I value the "other" in my teaching.

Yet, in an age that flaunts the most greedy expressions of individualism and commands us to only honor our "true" selves, it's not popular to actually take responsibility for the various scripts I have at my disposal in any given social situation. Some might label as "manipulative" the kind of control I'm speaking of. But, as Raymond Queneau argues, I can be misguided by a false sense of freedom and self-expression, one that fails to include how my intentions are always entwined with social constraints:

> . . . inspiration, which consists in blindly obeying every impulse, is in fact slavery. The classical author who wrote his tragedy observing a certain number of known rules is freer than the poet who writes down whatever comes into his head and is slave to other rules of which he knows nothing. (Calvino 1988, 123)

This suggests that my students often benefit when I selectively encourage them to hold still and concentrate on a question, on listening to the voice of a text, and not immediately be filled with their own responses and interpretations. This stillness of repetition within a world of acknowledged rules prevents the learner from rushing past an opportunity for engagement and reflection.

An incident in a writing workshop led me to consider how I might use such repetition as a strategy of *presence*. Angela brought in a poem and after she'd read it once and the other students appeared ready to jump in with their analysis and commentary, I paused and asked her to read it again. Another pause, as I tried to suspend this "silence" of listening over the student responses struggling to get out. Why not have Lisa, the class's "storyteller/performer" also read it twice? And so I requested this and then in turn I asked for additional volunteers and eventually about five others read it over and over again—maybe about twelve readings were done in all—as the class began to listen to the poem rather than move to interpret or judge it. The students thought me slightly deranged at this point, but I said to Angela, "What did you hear?" and she said that the readings actually presented her with different understandings of the poem and, while she was slightly embarrassed by the repetitions, insistently inviting the poem into everyone's head with all those readings made for a more pleasurable, and finally more immediate, experience of the poem.

By the time discussion arose, the class was less prone to leave the poem behind—its language and cadences still rang in their ears. The class had withheld its commentary so as to stay with the poem. This allowed them to more completely experience its chant. By holding back their own assembled voices, the students were better able to hear the voice of the poem *itself*. Maybe we can't ever get a poem enough into our ears, and thus mere repetition, which allows for continued reflection on the direction and the resonances of the language of the poem, is probably an important but neglected ritual of celebration. Hearing the words of the "text" deeply and thoroughly before these words were diffused by everyone's clamor to say something in response allowed me to wonder about how strategies of *presence* involved more than holding myself back from contributing my teacherly knowledge during class discussions.

In fact, I now want to see the flow of my participation and control during that three-week writing workshop as exhibiting a continual experiment in what it means to be *present* with students, *present* in ways that avoid simply transmitting my own prearranged agenda. Mostly I felt that I went too far in acting out my tendency to withdraw; I worry about being seen as aloof, as seemingly uncommitted in style and manner, when inside I often feel shy or inadequate. Without intending to be enigmatic, I was distancing myself from overt class-room management in ways that I hoped would force the students into taking more control of the work in the class—after all, it was supposed to be a writing workshop. At the end of our time together, the students wanted to discuss this dynamic of the class and how they saw me modeling an alternative pedagogy that may be easy to talk about but hard to enact. Further, they remarked that they saw my contributions as exhibiting different kinds of *presence* as the course progressed; they'd especially noticed me talking more during the last week and wondered what that meant. Had I lost patience with them? Yet they also admitted appreciating my silences and my honoring of their own judgments. Once again as this discussion proceeded, I was struck with how important it is for students to participate in articulating and ana-lyzing the learning environment. They were learning by hearing a teacher talk about teaching intentions just as they were helping me understand better the effect of my deliberate orchestration of how I was *present* with them. Of course in this instance, what might appear deliberate retrospectively was not always clear in advance, so while it might be better to have such a talk at the beginning of the course, it may not always be possible.

Ironically, it seems, I've come to find that teaching/learning works best when teachers and students manage not to get in each other's way—a discovery that breathes fresh air into any collective learning endeavor. Even as I say "getting out of each other's way," I wonder how adequately current talk about teaching captures the rich-ness of conflicting purposes and relationships that make up the lives filling any classroom. I believe that the landscape of our collective *pres-ence* in the learning space of the classroom will best be charted by teachers and learners sharing stories and paying close attention to the learning relationships we have with each other. There will have to be new metaphors, such as teaching is listening. In consciously stepping back as a teacher, I've realized that *listening* and *presence* have brought me closer to collaborating with those writing instructors who had ini-tially arrived filled with skepticism and ready to isolate themselves in their authority as discipline experts. A matter of trust, of humiliation, in endless conversation we keep challenging the complacency of our separate positions.

Works Cited

Calvino, Italo. 1988. *Six Memos for the Next Millennium.* Cambridge, MA: Harvard University Press.

Kierkegaard, Soren. 1962. *The Point of View for My Work as an Author: A Report to History.* New York: Harper Torchbooks.

Tannen, Deborah. 1984. *Conversational Style: Analyzing Talk among Friends.* Norwood, NJ: Ablex Publishing Corporation.

11 Out and About in English Education: How It Was!

Robert E. Shafer
Late of Arizona State University

The Early Days

In Wisconsin the winters are cold and long. Transferring to a new school can be an exciting event. Somehow things hadn't worked out for me at Cunningham School. Although the building was new and kindergarten had been exciting, things in first, second, and third grades seemed to go from bad to worse. Whatever was happening was not very rewarding. The years have blotted out much from that time, but I do remember the warmth of my kindergarten teacher's personality and the good feelings that were always in her classroom. Whatever Miss Bromlington said or did thoroughly captivated me. I was deeply in love with her and would have followed her anywhere. Kindergarten started off well. I liked all the other children too. That was to change. In first grade the physical appearance and demeanor of some of my fellow pupils became clear. I soon concluded that they had come straight from hell! Recess consisted of one fight after another. And after school a group of kids chased me almost every afternoon calling me horrible names. Academically, I started off well, but my grades soon tailed off since I began to be afraid to go to school at all. This continued in second grade and reached a high point during the end of the school year. Then my parents contacted the school and everyone began to piece together what was happening. It all had to do with reading. I was able to read long before I went to school and almost immediately read all of the stories in the Dick and Jane book before the end of the first week of the first grade. The teachers knew this and were able to find other books to give me to read. Of course, they set me apart from the rest of the class with their compliments and always called on me to read when other kids could not. I was proud to show off my reading ability and lorded it over some of my fellow pupils. Somehow, I didn't make the connection that my treatment on the playground and after school was largely a result of my attitude about my reading successes in the classes. Clearly, I was not headed for social success! By the end of third grade, I had developed a rather serious stammer and my parents had had enough of the situation at Cunningham School. They complained and asked for me to be transferred to Gaston Elementary School, which was located in a different part of the city altogether. The only problem was that I now had to walk two miles to Gaston instead of one mile to Cunningham. Although I lived about two miles from the school, I enjoyed my new fourth-grade class there immensely. The teacher seemed much more interested in me than my other teachers had been. The children were generally friendly. There were even some good readers and writers among them, which drew us together immediately. Some of those good readers and writers in that fourth grade class are still close friends to this day. Al Hoover lived one mile from my house, along the route to Gaston School. He soon discovered that I walked past his house each morning. On those cold, winter days when the temperature was ten to twenty degrees below zero, the Hoover family would invite me in to stand beside the stove and warm up before Al and I took off to walk the remaining mile to Gaston. We became good friends along the way and I will always remember those walks with him through the cold, wintry mornings. Later, at the end of the seventh grade (our first year at Lincoln Junior High School) at a special assembly, I was given an award for not missing a day of school for the first seven years of schooling. But praise be to the classmates and teachers of that fourth-grade class, and to the Hoover family. They were a big help along the way.

In junior high, I continued my life as an avid reader. I had discovered the Carnegie Library in Beloit, which became my second home. There I discovered *Robinson Crusoe, Hans Brinker and the Silver Skates* and other less well-known novels and collections of short stories, which were favorites I read at night with a flashlight under the covers. English and history classes at Lincoln Junior High were the most exciting places of my existence. Our eighth-grade English teacher allowed us to work in groups to make up ads for mythical products. Some of my classmates and I went even further. We wrote a play based on the further adventures of Frankenstein's monster. Displaying our exposure to various horror films of the time, we embedded elements of "The Hunchback of Notre Dame" and "The Phantom of the Opera." We suddenly found ourselves performing the play before a school assembly. The play lead to instant fame although in looking back, I am not so sure that it was our acting ability or our writing ability that made us famous rather than the complete abandon with which we made fools of ourselves on stage. My classmates, whether amused or bored, tolerated my continuing involvement in reading, writing, drama, and speech activities, as well as my film criticism throughout my junior and senior high school days. To the very day of this writing, I have met no one from my high school class who has expressed any surprise that I became a teacher of English or a teacher of English teachers.

What High School Had to Offer

Beloit High School in the early 1940s reflected the problems and prospects of many American communities. Still isolated from the concerns of what appeared to be a limited war in a far off Europe and a remote Asia, life was centered on dates, sports, social activities, after school work programs, and even at times, classes. My hero was my sophomore World History teacher. Playing the *Overture of 1812* and describing the ill-fated attempt of Napoleon's armies to capture the vast Russian empire made for dramatic ways to symbolize and forecast events taking place in our own time. Hitler's armies were to suffer the same fate in Soviet Russia as did Napoleon's, but in the fall of 1940 we could not yet foresee the future that clearly. Nor could we sense then the precise meaning of Santayana's words, "Those who do not know history will live to repeat it." But I was hooked on history anyway and plunged into a host of historical novels; indeed, it was fiction that captivated me. So I read on, to the delight of my English teachers.

The circumstances of my life in those depression years dictated that even during my sophomore year in high school, I needed to go to work as soon as I legally could do so. Therefore, I started to work that year at the Rex Theater in Beloit as an usher. During those high school days, I worked from 7:00 to 10:00 P.M. every evening but one. In the dead of winter, I was climbing on ladders and changing the signs on the theater marquee every night in wind, rain, and the freezing weather of the Wisconsin winters.

Although the job brought in spending money, I have since realized that it seriously detracted from my studies and my "social life" became virtually nonexistent. In the summer of 1942, my mother died and circumstances dictated that I move in with my older sister and brother-in-law. They became my surrogate parents for several years.

Marguerite Shafer Warren was an elementary teacher in Riverview School in South Beloit, Illinois. During the war years, she became principal of that school. She was a powerful woman, completely dedicated to teaching and devoted to her school and community. It was from my observations of her and my conversations with her that I began to sense the significance of the teacher's influence both in the classroom and in the lives of individual children. I also began to understand the power of the public school in an American community. When she died in 1972, she had taught more than fifty years in that school district and had served three generations of citizens in that community. She has always been my personal inspiration and role model, both as a person of character and as a professional educator in an American community. Although I did not realize it at the time, she was clearly also a model for "feminism," as she combined the role of "careerist" and "homemaker" so successfully and naturally in her life that it was never a subject of envy, comment, or wonder by those who knew her well. Her husband, my brother-in-law Elliot Warren, was devoted to her. He was a father figure for me in many ways. An engineer who understood mechanical things in a way that I never could, he was a kindly, sensitive man, a World War I veteran, who could move in an instant from lively humor to philosophical reflection.

World War II

"I don't understand why all the boys have to leave to go off to this war," said one of my classmates as we sat in Walt's Little Bungalow on West Grand Avenue in Beloit, eating hamburgers in late May of 1943. She was the only one I knew who spoke thusly, as everyone else in my surroundings seemed committed to a total war effort. Almost all of us 1943 high school graduates left on June 24, ten days after high school graduation. I and one other were the only two destined for the United States Marine Corps at the time. I spent most of the war in California, the South Pacific, and ultimately in China, returning in April of 1946, luckily scarred only with malaria that remained off and on for the next four years. Although much can be said of military service as "an educative experience," for me, it was a vast exercise in drama as I was required to play the role of Marine, a role I knew I would not continue after the war. The long days and nights of boredom spent in various camps gave me considerable opportunity to continue my reading. My senior English teacher at Beloit High School had introduced me to the literature of England. Somehow, in the base library at El Toro Marine

Air Station, near Santa Ana, California, I ran across the Armed Forces edition of *From Beowulf to Thomas Hardy*, edited, I noted with surprise, by one Robert Shafer, a Professor of English at the University of Cincinnati. The book was used by thousands of young men and women in the Armed Forces taking a survey course in English literature during those times. I read in it searching out not only what Keats and Shelley had written, but what Robert Shafer had said about what they had written. I remain curious about that Robert Shafer to this day. Were we somehow related? I still have not found the answer even after a rainy day spent in the spring of 1992, asking questions at the English Department of the University of Cincinnati. I know little of him other than that he was a distinguished scholar, who for many years edited a learned literary journal. That we have the same name and have traveled similar paths seems a remarkable coincidence.

University Days

My readings in English literature were to help launch my career in English studies at the University of Wisconsin. The fall of 1946 found me in a freshman English class in Madison, taught by a fascinating young woman who held rather strong views on higher education. "Most of you won't last," she said on the first day. "Most of you shouldn't even be here." Somehow that same day she turned to literature. Although I do not remember the context, I most certainly remember her question, "Could anyone possibly know who said, 'In Xanadu, a stately pleasure dome did Kubla Kahn decree?'" Remembering the difficulties encountered in the first grade, I tentatively put up my hand. "Yes," she said. "Samuel Taylor Coleridge wrote that," I said confidently. "Good heavens," she snapped. "I've been wrong about at least one of you!" Off to such a good start, I did well in that English class.

One other event occurred in that same class which stands out now as having significance for my career as an English educator. One day, a visitor came to the class. He was a white-haired, middle-aged man, of medium height. I was impressed by what was happening in the class. Instinctively, I knew he was there to "inspect" the class. (Of course, I had read of Matthew Arnold's role as a school inspector and I knew that Marguerite had to visit teachers' classes to evaluate them in her role as principal). Although I couldn't have imagined it at the time, I was to meet Robert Pooley (our class visitor) years later in his role as president of the National Council of Teachers of English. He and I were to become friends and serve together on the important Committee on the Structure of the NCTE from 1970–72, chaired by another past NCTE president, Albert C. Marckwardt, of the University of Michigan and Princeton.

My successes in freshman English propelled me directly into an English major, which also turned into an American Institutions major since I could not forget nor ignore my interest in historical studies. The University of Wisconsin had outstanding departments in both areas. My adviser, a distinguished historian who also taught me American Diplomatic History, and who was ultimately to become president of the University, told me to "take plenty of English and history courses," which I did. I became intrigued with both English and American literature. Minority literature, as we know it today, and feminist literature and criticism were not yet a part of that English major. European History and American History were the "frosting on the cake," along with the education courses in the junior year which I did not at all dread, but rather liked. I had committed myself to becoming a teacher and personal contacts with my instructors, who were also committed to teaching and to making me a teacher, were valued. But the most fascinating person I met during those years was Francis Shoemaker. Francis taught *Methods of Teaching English* and ultimately supervised my student teaching at Wisconsin High School and West High in Madison. In Francis Shoemaker's Methods class there were three men and twenty-eight women. The three men were Edward Fagan, Robert Johnson, and myself. We were all to follow Francis to Teachers College Columbia University and finish doctorates with him in English education. In that early class, Francis introduced us to the concept of English as a part of the humanities and the "Communication Arts," a new view of the subject for all of us. The study of media seemed at the time, 1949, as exceptionally important in a postwar society. It seemed important in the sense that the first glimmerings of television were to be seen. We were clearly in a technological revolution—the computer was not yet very much in evidence—but we needed to understand what was happening and to prepare our students for it—especially as critical readers.

It was, indeed, a new view of the humanities that the three of us carried from that Methods class at Wisconsin into our graduate study at Teachers College Columbia University, where we had followed Francis Shoemaker. His views of English were not popular in the English Department at Wisconsin, although many of his colleagues within the School of Education thought him to be a most creative and imaginative scholar and teacher. He was considered an "academic adventurer" by his English Department senior colleagues and happily returned to Columbia in 1952, when the call came from his former mentor, Lennox Grey.

My teaching career in Wisconsin was short-lived. After beginning the year in a small, Wisconsin, rural community, I was recalled in the United States Marine Corps during the Korean War and was ultimately stationed in Washington, D.C. I met teachers from the Arlington, Virginia public schools and began my real teaching career at Washington-Lee High School there in 1951. There I met Charles Weingartner who was to become a colleague, close friend, and fellow student at Columbia. He is perhaps best known as the co-author (with Neil Postman) of *Teaching as a Subversive Activity*, which every teacher and prospective teacher should read even though it was written in 1969. Our attempts to "reform" the English Program at Washington-Lee High School were largely unsuccessful, although we enlisted many other colleagues in attempts to rid the Program of formal grammar studies and an overload of classical literature and inject it with Hayakawa's General Semantics and studies of popular culture.

On to Columbia

After two years of teaching at Washington-Lee, I left for Columbia where Shoemaker and Grey had arranged a teaching assistantship. I took with me my bride, Susanne Mueller, an Arlington Junior High teacher of Social Studies and English who I had met through colleagues at Washington-Lee. Fortunately, Sue was able to obtain a teaching position in the New York area which bore the cost of part of my graduate study and our living expenses for two years, since my assistantship paid next to nothing. Her parents in Scarsdale, New York, provided us with more moral and material support, as well as a refuge from the city and the rigors of graduate study during those years.

As I have written in a recent article in the *Encyclopedia of English Studies and Language Arts* (1994), we were to conceive of school English as made up of art, music, literature, language, dance, drama and film. The symbolic process was at the center of it all. Lennox Grey (1944) first proposed that all of the "processes and media, social, psychological, artistic and linguistic, which are at work in the exchange of information, ideas, and common feeling on which the health and moral stamina of any community depends" as a new center for the humanities. He proposed that the interdisciplinary study of communication and the

"Communication Arts" were to lead to a "new view" of the humanities and especially to a new view of English as a school subject. Shoemaker and Grey further proposed that their broadened concept of humanities and the Communication Arts become important within English studies in high school and college. They used as a foundation the studies of Susanne Langer (1942), in her book *Philosophy in a New Key* and those of Marshall McLuhan (1951), who first proposed the study of media of communication in his book *The Mechanical Bride* and later exemplified it in his other writings. I was intrigued by these ideas.

In later years, I became a student of Marshall McLuhan's and later a colleague on several projects while I was at Wayne State University. McLuhan used to take the train from Toronto to Windsor, Ontario. I would pick him up at the little train station in Windsor. We would drive across the border and have steak and eggs for breakfast before we went to work at the university. Grey and Shoemaker and others who were spokespersons for Media Study at the time are no longer active. Few have emerged to take their place among the leadership of the profession. There is an active assembly on Media Study within NCTE and an active NCTE Commission on Media, but the leadership of the Council itself appears to have other priorities. Given the current interest in standards projects linked with assessment and accountability, which are essentially reductionist in nature, it is possible that Media Study will be reduced out of whatever emerges in an English curriculum for the twenty-first century.

I have come to realize the extent to which I was influenced by not only the program at Teachers College and the faculty, but by my fellow graduate students—a truly remarkable group of people, most of whom I have continued to keep in close touch with over the years and to work with on many projects, usually through the National Council of Teachers of English. To attempt to delineate their separate influences on me would be both impossible and unproductive; suffice it to say that after two years of intensive study with them, I was both better informed and wiser in many ways. Although I cannot indicate in this short paper what their influences were, I should mention them and how much I gained from their fellowship. I have already mentioned Edward Fagan, who was to become Professor of English Education at Pennsylvania State University and Robert Johnson, who was to become a leader in NCTE. Some of the other graduate students were Ken Macrorie, one of the early contributors to the national revolution in teaching writing; Neil Postman, who was to found his own Department of Media Ecology at New York University; William Hoth, who was to become my colleague at Wayne State University; Robert Wright, who was already a professor at Michigan State University; Father Daniel Fogarty, S.J., whose doctoral study became the book *Roots For A New Rhetoric* (1968); and many others.

The California Experience

Those who have known me best throughout my professional life will not be surprised by my acknowledgment of the influence of those colleagues and friends in central California, who developed and still maintain the Asilomar Conferences as central figures in my philosophy of teaching and learning. Many of the founders and leaders of that Conference saw to it that I was involved in that unique professional group when I arrived in California to work at San Francisco State University in 1955. They have continued to encourage me to return each year to enjoy and profit from it, as I take part in the ebb and flow of the discussion groups which are a unique feature of that Conference beside the Pacific. That the National Writing Project (clearly the most significant development in English Education in our time) found its roots in such a group was not at all surprising to me. I continue to value that Conference format as central to my own philosophy of interaction, sharing, group process, and professional dedication to self-improvement, goals to which I have always committed myself in English Education.

I owe another large debt to those many former students of Professor Dora V. Smith of the University of Minnesota, whose graduates essentially established the field of English Education at many American universities. I have become particularly close to former graduates and faculty members from the Florida State University, especially William Ojala, who became my colleague at Arizona State University, and Dwight Burton, former *English Journal* editor, as well as John S. Simmons, with whom I have worked closely over the years on a variety of projects. My colleagues and students at Wayne State University, San Francisco State University, Teachers College Columbia University, and Arizona State University contributed much to my understanding of literacy, language, literature, and the learning process. I continue to learn from many of my former graduate students who have now become teachers. For example, from Geneva Smitherman, then a student of mine at Wayne State University, now a distinguished professor of English at Michigan State University, I learned what it is like to be a young, black woman and single parent in a large American city and how perseverance, sheer determination, and innate ability, all of which she possesses in large quantities, can overcome most adversities. From her later writings and presentations at conferences, I learned much about the black idiom and the historical development of that idiom in African-American culture. I must mention (at least in a footnote)[1] those young women who made a special contribution to my understanding of the struggles women have in our contemporary society when they take on the roles of graduate student and professional practitioner in English Education while often maintaining the traditional female roles of marriage partner and parent. They were graduate students over the years at several institutions. I am told by the editors that two have made contributions to this volume; I would have been surprised if it were otherwise. I am convinced that the others are being heard from in other quarters. Of course, I had male graduate students too. They were all outstanding and have gone on to significant careers. Two, I remember from my professor days at Columbia, are Hal Hamilton and Stan Bank. But I mention the women graduate students because they made me aware of the struggles and tensions surrounding the role of women in society. Most of them never thought that they would be a candidate for or receive a graduate degree. Many of them, as they started out, conceived of their professional lives as being devoted to the high school classroom and ending there. Most of them are today outstanding college teachers.

To be honored on two occasions by the Arizona English Teachers Association demonstrates to me the closeness I have always felt to classroom teachers of English at all levels and I salute them again in these pages, acknowledging the critical nature of their role as teachers of the mother tongue in our society. If I could salute all of the student teachers I have worked with by name over the years, I would do so happily. One of the most fascinating aspects of work with student teachers is to see young people taking on the role of teacher in our society. I have enjoyed making contributions to that process in whatever small measure.

---

[1]Deane Hargrave, Nancy Thompson, Linda Shadiow, Lynn Meeks, Maybeth Mason, Jean Johnson, Pam Davenport, Deborah Wells, Nyla Ahrens, Karen Smith, Karen L. Hess, Iris McIntyre, Maria Schantz, Martha Davis, Claire Staab, Geneva Smitherman, Margaret Ferry, Brenda Bruno, Elizabeth Simpson, Kathy Bell, Marty Townsend, Kris Gutierrez and Pat O'Friel.

International Studies

From my wife, Susanne M. Shafer, Professor of Comparative Education, I have learned many things, among them an abiding interest in other countries and their educational systems. As I began to attend international conferences on the teaching of English—first at York, England in 1971 and later at Sydney, Australia; Ottawa, Canada; and Auckland, New Zealand—I developed a strong interest in the teaching of English in other English-speaking countries—including other countries like South Africa and India, where the English language is either an official language or has an important historical place in the country's history. Fortunately, I had an opportunity during the 1970s and 1980s to visit most of these countries and to make notes about what was happening in English teaching in them. It became clear to me that there were very few recent accounts of the teaching of English in many of these countries. I began to write about developments in these countries and when Ken Watson came to Arizona in 1984–85 I asked him if he would join me in doing a book which would describe some important aspects of teaching English in a number of these countries. He agreed and we decided to approach Jimmy Britton to join us as a co-editor. We three met at the Ottawa Conference and signed up a number of chapter authors at that Conference. Others I found on my trip around the world in 1987. The result was *Teaching And Learning English Worldwide,* which was published in 1990 and reviewed by Courtney Cazden at the International Conference on the teaching of English at Auckland in August of 1990. It is, as far as I know, the only book that gives historical accounts of the teaching of English in thirteen countries where English is either the mother tongue or a significant second language.

I have a continuing interest in the acquisition of language and the development of new "Englishes" as English changes in various parts of the world. But my work in reading acquisition and language acquisition is another story for which there is no time or space in this account. There are also other parts of my story which must be left out of this account altogether. These will be told elsewhere at another time and place. Until then, let it be known that I have no professional regrets, only continuing good memories and feelings of what Don Graves has called "the joy of watching children and young people learn," learn to speak, write, read, think, study, create and become teachers, critical readers, graduate students, and yes—English educators!

Works Cited

Britton, James, Robert E. Shafer, and Ken Watson, eds. 1990. *Teaching and Learning English Worldwide*. Clevedon, England: Multilingual Matters, Ltd.

Fogarty, Daniel. 1968. *Roots for a New Rhetoric*. New York: Russell and Russell.

Grey, Lennox. 1944. *What Communication Means Today*. Chicago: NCTE.

Langer, Susanne K. 1957. *Philosophy in a New Key*. 3d ed. Cambridge: Harvard University Press.

McLuhan, Marshall. 1951. *The Mechanical Bride*. Boston: Beacon Press.

Shafer, Robert, ed. 1924. *From Beowulf to Thomas Hardy*. Garden City, NY: Doubleday, Page and Co.

Shafer, Robert E. 1994. "Communication Arts/Skills." In *Encyclopedia of English Studies and Language Arts*, vol. 1, ed. Alan C. Purves. New York: Scholastic, 216–17.

12 Beyond the Obvious: Connoisseurs and Critics in the Classroom

Virginia R. Monseau
Youngstown State University

Gwen slipped quietly into the room, taking the last available seat around the large rectangular table that occupied most of the conference room where we held our weekly seminar for student teachers. The room buzzed with talk and occasional laughter as the students shared their teaching experiences with one another—some complaining about discipline problems, others basking in the glow of a successful teaching day. Gwen, however, did not join in. Instead, she sat with downcast eyes, fiddling with a pencil stub, doodling on a sheet of notebook paper.

As we began our discussion, and one of the students asked for suggestions of a good short story he might teach with Robert Cormier's *The Chocolate War*, the group was startled when Gwen slammed her pencil down, looked at me, and declared, "That's all we ever talk about—short stories, novels, poetry! Why don't you tell us what it's *really* like out there? Why don't you prepare us for the *real* world of teaching, where other teachers try to intimidate you and even make fun of you for doing your job? Why don't you tell us how to deal with people who don't like the kids they teach and don't care whether they learn or not? I had the worst experience of my life today, and I feel like a fool because I know I didn't handle it well. I didn't know what to do. You never taught us what to do in situations like this."

After some prodding from the others, Gwen told us her story. She had gone to the teachers' lounge during her free period to run some dittos on which she had typed several poems that she felt would enhance her poetry lesson, when her cooperating teacher, sipping coffee in the corner, confronted her. "Don't you ever use the textbook?" he asked.

"Why do you go to all that trouble typing those handouts? The kids don't appreciate them. They just throw them away. I teach from the book, and if the kids don't get it—tough! You're so naive, but you'll learn soon enough," he laughed. Gwen was so taken aback and so humiliated at being laughed at in front of the other teachers in the lounge that she couldn't reply. Instead, she hurried from the room, close to tears.

Her comments upset me, not so much because she challenged my teaching, but because she had touched a nerve. For quite some time I had been feeling hypocritical about encouraging students to enter a profession populated partly by jaded teachers, ineffective administrators, and difficult students. Knowing the problems they would encounter, I still trained them to enter this field where the tangible rewards are few and the hours long. I've wondered, "Am I doing them a disservice by not emphasizing these negatives enough?" But hearing Gwen's story, the larger questions, for me, were, "Why did this teacher's behavior come as such a shock to her? Didn't she notice his attitude toward his students when she observed his class prior to beginning her student teaching?"

As I mulled this experience over the following day, I remembered two concepts that I had learned from reading Elliot Eisner years before as a doctoral student: educational connoisseurship and criticism. Eisner defines these as a keen awareness of classroom life that looks beyond the obvious, resulting in description, analysis, and public disclosure of what the connoisseur sees (1997, 352). Eisner's theory is designed to provide an alternative to the type of scientific educational research commonly practiced, as he emphasizes the descriptive nature of this phenomenological research, but he points out that "connoisseurship . . . goes well beyond the use of awakened sensibility" to a recognition of how and why certain classroom phenomena occur. According to Eisner, connoisseurship is the art of appreciation, while criticism is the art of disclosure, making connoisseurship a private endeavor and criticism a "public art" (1977, 347–48). Thinking about this, I realized that though I saw great value in Eisner's ideas, I had never exposed my students to them. I guess I needed someone like Gwen to bring me up short—to, in effect, make me a connoisseur/critic of my own teaching. I thought further. If Gwen had been trained as an "educational connoisseur," how might she have reacted to her cooperating teacher's classroom behavior? What might have been her assessment? How might she have dealt with his confrontational attitude? What valuable information did she overlook for lack of a trained eye? I made my decision. At the next seminar meeting I would introduce

Eisner's concepts, then give the students scenarios to consider through the eyes of an "educational connoisseur."

When we met the following week, I began by inviting each student to tell us one important thing he or she observed about the class and/or the cooperating teacher in the early weeks of student teaching. Laura began with this story.

> Today I ate lunch with a bunch of male teachers in the shop teacher's office. I'm sure that I was out of place there, with the pin-up girls glaring down at me from the cork board—not to mention the conversation, which centered around their past experiences in strip joints/bars and how much money the girls made at their glamorous careers. Personally, this type of conversation disgusts me. If it had not been my first day—well, let's just say that they didn't even consider that they were in the company of a lady. You need not guess what my first impression of them was. They proceeded to try to persuade me that I should change my career if I was interested in making money. I felt very uncomfortable. I thought that someone would respond by saying that there was a lady in the room, and I looked to my cooperating teacher for some sympathy, but there was no acknowledgement of the offensiveness in the conversation.

As Laura finished, there was immediate response from the group. "What jerks!" one woman cried. "Why didn't you tell them off?" asked another. I interrupted. "What really happened in that room that day?" I asked. "What conclusions might we draw about these teachers as professionals by observing their behavior in this situation?" "Well, they're sexist for one thing, and they're guilty of gender stereotyping," answered Laura. "Sure, that's pretty obvious," I said, "but what else is going on here?" Their silence gave me a chance to introduce Eisner's concepts, after which I invited them to think of Laura's experience again. I was pleased to hear Gwen pipe up with, "I see a group of grown men who think they're professionals acting like adolescents. They were using Laura to vent their own frustrations about teaching and to show off their 'maleness.' It's no wonder teachers don't get respect if they behave this way in front of people outside the profession. I don't want these people representing me to the general public! Why did they become teachers in the first place?"

Gwen's response was certainly that of a connoisseur. Not only was she aware of the teachers' sexist attitudes, she also recognized the motivation behind their behavior and the possible impact of that behavior on the public's perception of teachers. She made these observations as an educational connoisseur, disclosing them as a critic.

Encouraged, I proceeded with my plan, giving the students copies of two scenarios that they were to read and respond to.

Scenario #1. He saunters into the classroom and surveys his ninth-grade students, casting a friendly smile in his student teacher's direction. The students are oblivious to his entrance—too busy catching up on weekend news and passing along the latest gossip to notice that his smile is slowly changing to a scowl. "That's it, people! Didn't you hear that bell ring?" he bellows over the din. Things quiet down, except for two talkative students huddled together at the back of the room, sharing pictures of last week's prom. The teacher grabs a stub of chalk from the tray and writes "Mackey" and "D'Amico" on the chalkboard in a stabbing gesture so fierce that the chalk breaks in two. "Oh, no," moan the accused in unison. "What's that for?" questions D'Amico. "We didn't do anything," Mackey whines. The teacher picks up another piece of chalk and places a check mark next to each name. The two talkers slump in their desks, defeated. No use arguing with a teacher who uses discipline points as a weapon. They've just lost the ten points they worked so hard last week to gain.

"OK. Turn to page 98 in your literature books," he orders. "Let's answer the questions about 'The Secret Life of Walter Mitty.' Who wants to take number one?" Silence. "Frank, what about you?" Silence. Frank squirms and examines his fingernails. The other students, fearful of being called on, find interesting things to look at on the floor.

Scenario #2. A fifty-ish woman, bifocals hanging from a fashionable cord around her neck, regards her tenth-grade honor students with quiet skepticism. "Are you going to read to us today?" asks a long-haired fellow sitting in a front desk. The noise begins to diminish. She smiles wryly, eyeing the rest of the group. "Of course," she replies as she picks up the worn paperback and walks to the lectern, glasses perched on the end of her nose. "Do you remember where we left off?" "Yeah," pipes another fellow sitting off by himself near the windows. "The White Witch just tricked Edmund into betraying his brother and sisters. She tempted him with that stuff called Turkish Delight." "Right-O," she says, and begins the next chapter of *The Lion, the Witch, and the Wardrobe.* As she becomes each of the characters, her voice rising and falling, her arms gesticulating, her face alive with expression, the students listen in rapt attention. When she finishes the chapter, and they beg her to go on, she puts the book away, leaving them hungry for more. She said she would read *one chapter a day.*

I had witnessed these two scenes on separate occasions as I was observing two of my student teachers. It was early in the quarter, and in both cases the cooperating teacher and the student teacher were working collaboratively. I offered these bits of information to my students, then let them take control of the discussion. Kurt began:

> In the first classroom, I saw a friendly teacher and a group of animated students. Yet the energy-charged classroom atmosphere quickly disintegrated into a tense, hostile environment. And it was at this point that the teacher expected the students to learn something.

Gwen chimed in:

> This teacher's emphasis on discipline was really counter productive. Striking fear into the hearts of students, then expecting them to voluntarily cooperate is unreasonable. Maybe some of those students really wanted to discuss "The Secret Life of Walter Mitty," but how could they risk going against their peers after the teacher had drawn the battle lines? This teacher's really cheating his students and himself because he has made it impossible for his students to learn—or for himself to teach.

"But don't you think a certain amount of discipline is necessary and important in the classroom?" I asked. "Sure," replied Kurt, "but it shouldn't be tied to academic work. That can get a teacher in trouble because once the system's in place, the teacher has to use it, even if it defeats his or her purpose on any given day. That's exactly what happened to this teacher." "OK, then what would you suggest as an alternative?" I asked them. The usually quiet Stephan offered this suggestion:

> This teacher might have found a way to assert his authority without silencing his students. Maybe he could have quietly approached the two talkers as the class was settling down and asked them to put the pictures away. Or, he could have called on one of them to begin the discussion of "Walter Mitty." The students were obviously in a talkative mood. Maybe he could have put them in small groups and focused their discussion on the story. I don't think those two kids were being deliberately nasty. I think the teacher overreacted, and the whole class had to suffer.

Pleased to see that the group was taking my invitation to look beyond the obvious seriously, I suggested we take a look at the second scenario as educational connoisseurs. "I notice right away that this teacher is in control of her class," said Gwen. She went on:

> She doesn't need to raise her voice or threaten her students to get them to quiet down. She's smart because she uses course

content to control their behavior. I would never have thought of reading a children's story to tenth graders, but why not? Her students seem to love it. They're obviously paying attention since they remember where she left off the day before and seem very interested in the plot. Even if they think they're leading her off the subject of their regular work, they're still learning without realizing it.

"Right," said Kurt. "She makes them *want* to behave; she doesn't *force* them to do it. And since she's so dramatic in her reading, they're learning something about oral interpretation too."

Gwen, Kurt, Laura, and Stephan were beginning to get the idea. By examining these classroom scenarios as connoisseurs/critics, they were prompted not only to describe what they saw, but to speculate on its significance in their disclosure. As a result, they discovered how much they really knew about teaching and how alternative teaching methods might be useful in certain situations. As Eisner points out, "the critic's task . . . is to provide a vivid rendering so that others might learn to see what transpires in that beehive of activity called the classroom. . . . In this task the educational critic does far more than describe behavior" (1977, 352).

Proud of my students' insight into these two situations, I asked them how useful Eisner's theories might be to them in their own teaching observations. Would/could they take the time, for example, to think beyond what they're actually seeing and speculate on its significance? Though they were all enthusiastic about the idea and certainly saw the value of being a connoisseur/critic in the classroom, several of them did express apprehension at the thought of negatively criticizing a cooperating teacher, and a few cited the lack of time available for such sustained analysis. All agreed, however, that they would be better prepared to handle a situation such as Gwen experienced if they approached their initial observations as connoisseurs/critics.

Kurt had an additional comment. "Once we're experienced teachers, this kind of thing will come naturally to us. If you teach long enough, you're bound to become a connoisseur." He had a point. We're all observers to some extent, and we all develop some degree of connoisseurship in our profession. But Eisner offers several reasons why the deliberate development of connoisseurship is necessary:

> In the first place, connoisseurship, like any art, is capable of refinement. . . . Unfortunately, one of the consequences of familiarity is the development of obliviousness. We learn not to see, [and] we turn off what we have become accustomed to. . . . Being oblivious to a large portion of their environment [teach-

ers] are in no position to bring about change, to rectify educational ills they cannot see, or to alter their own behavior. What is even worse, the conditions and qualities they do see they might believe to be natural rather than artifactual. We often come to believe, because of habit reinforced by convention, that the way things are is the way they *must* be.

In the second place connoisseurship when developed to a high degree provides a level of consciousness that makes intellectual clarity possible. . . . Many teachers have developed sufficient connoisseurship to feel that something is awry but have insufficient connoisseurship to provide a more adequate conceptualization of just what it is. (1977, 350–51)

The preparation of teachers is such an important business, especially as we try to reconcile academic life with the real world. Most of us who do this work feel a total commitment to our students and to our goal of helping them become valuable, contributing members of the profession. But every once in a while we need students like Gwen to shake us out of our idealistic mindset and nudge (or push) us toward a reassessment of our role as teacher educators. Stepping back and looking at my own class from the perspective of the connoisseur/critic, I am convinced of the value of teaching Eisner's concepts, both before and during the student teaching experience. Watching this group of student teachers move beyond superficial observation to a deeper understanding of classroom life gives me comfort in my angst about presenting to them the real world of teaching. It also gives me pause to reflect on my own teaching more often, a beneficial activity no matter how long the teaching career. I am sharpening my own vision as I better equip my students to be lifelong connoisseurs and critics of their profession.

Works Cited

Cormier, Robert. 1974. *The Chocolate War.* New York: Pantheon.

Eisner, Elliot. 1977. "On the Uses of Educational Connoisseurship and Criticism for Evaluating Classroom Life." *Teachers College Record* 78.3 (February): 347–48, 352.

IV How We See Ourselves

It has always irritated me whenever somone talks about "teachers" as though I am not one. I wonder when I crossed that invisible line between "university" and teacher, when what I did ceased to be teaching and became something less worthy or well-defined.

Susan Hynds

13 My English Education

Susan Hynds
Syracuse University

My English Education

I didn't always want to be a teacher. The idea came to me by happenstance rather than design. Growing up in the days between Sputnik and Vietnam, I wished for chemistry sets and doctor kits, not chalkboards and erasers. I spent summers playing baseball and gang war with my neighborhood pals. Teaching never entered my mind.

I did love school though, and all the memories that went with it: the smell of crayon wax melting down the radiator on cold Illinois mornings, the aphrodisiac odor of duplicating fluid on the teacher's handouts, the excitement of spelling bees and recess, the new pencil box every September. I must have loved language from the very start. I remember standing at the blackboard in Miss Schulte's first grade class and spelling the word "transportation" by sounding it out and copying each letter in my cramped, crooked printing. Miss Schulte kept us in rows according to our reading ability. In those days, I thought that reading well meant reading fast. I sped through the words of my Dick and Jane reader, and earned a permanent seat in the "first row" next to the window.

But my real love affair with books probably began in the fourth grade, when I enrolled in the local library club. There was a special pleasure in the smell and size of a good book, especially one I'd taken out with my very own library card. Sometimes my father and I would talk about the books I read. His favorite author was John Steinbeck. Mine was Charles Dickens. By this time I no longer measured my reading ability by speed, but by the size and weight of the books. There was such a sense of accomplishment in finishing one of those ponderous books, and a certain sadness too at having to leave the world that Dickens had created just for me. Books enticed me into worlds of wonder and possibility. They saved me from the plainness of my small town life. Sometimes when my parents went out of town and I would stay with my grandmother, she would go down to the

---

This essay is dedicated to Mom, Dad, Ray, and Bob.

musty cellar and bring back an ancient, stiff-backed book that had belonged to my father when he was a boy. I would curl up on the carpet, lost in the world of *Tom Swift and his Big Dirigible, The Bobbsey Twins,* or my father's favorite, *The Wizard of Oz* by L. Frank Baum.

School

I don't know when it was that I started to know the difference between reading and writing for school and for self. Maybe it was in junior high school, when the post-Sputnik push toward standardized testing and homogeneous grouping suddenly segregated neighborhood pals into different classes on the basis of intelligence and aptitude. I remember each term when the principal would arrive in my seventh grade homeroom to announce the names of the lucky students who would be moving to a higher track. Triumphant, they would gather up their books and leave for the classroom across the hall. Then with great pomp and sobriety, the principal would announce the names of those few unlucky souls who would be moving to a lower track. I lived in dreaded fear that I would be one of the unlucky few. It was about this same time that I became a discipline problem, much to my mother's horror. I was sent out of the room so often by my homeroom teacher that by the middle of the fall term, he had installed my desk permanently in the cloak room. I made it into the higher track by the eighth grade, and my discipline problems ceased.

Then came high school. I was in "honors" English my first year, but I remember very little about the class. We were supposed to find a Shakespearean play to read on our own. I chose *A Comedy of Errors,* partly because it was one of the few remaining Shakespearean texts on the library shelves, and partly because I thought it would be funny. I was disappointed on the last count. The language was alien, the plot was confusing and convoluted. I had no one to guide me through the labyrinth of meaning, and no idea of what my teacher wanted in the paper I was supposed to write afterward.

To make matters worse, I was no more than four feet tall, and had a locker on the third floor at the far end of the building, away from all of my classes. I carried a stack of books as tall as I was, and had the habit of spilling them onto the floor of my English teacher's classroom as I hurried in each day. At the end of the year, my teacher announced that she was going to recommend that I be dropped from the honors program. She seemed more displeased with what she called my "immaturity" (as evidenced by all the book dropping) than she did any intellectual inadequacies on my part. I talked her into giving me one more try, but she promised to write to my sophomore English teacher and tell him that I was on probation.

The Teachers

To this day, I don't know if Ray Brolley ever got that note. If he did, I can only imagine it made him like me all the more. Brolley was one of those English teachers who was either adored or despised by his students. He had a passion for good fiction and an intolerance for adolescent indifference. When we'd wiggle in our seats or whisper to each other, as sixteen-year-olds are likely to do, he'd roar: "You swine! Why don't you go up there and spit on the flag!" He kept me in fits of laughter. I remember how he used to flex his long fingers together like a spider on a mirror whenever he became pensive or struggled to choose just the right word to make a point.

The back wall of Ray Brolley's classroom was papered with colorful covers from *The New Yorker* magazine. Every Friday, he'd read aloud to us, leaning back precariously in his swivel chair, his feet propped up on the desk. On days when he'd been up with his teething baby the night before, he'd fall asleep in the middle of a sentence. We had to stifle our giggles as he'd jerk awake a few minutes later and start again, a page ahead of where he'd just left off. We met a whole cast of literary figures in Ray Brolley's classroom: Roald Dahl, E.B. White, John Ciardi. We studied *The Elements of Style* and learned to trim the fat out of our writing. We spent a grudging week on grammar, since it was part of the required curriculum, and sped through *Silas Marner*, or "Silly Ass Marner," as Brolley called the dreadful book. What a refreshing change his class was from freshman English! Once, when I was sick for a week, my classmates sent me a get well letter. Brolley had penned the return address: "Nobel Prize Committee, Ocean View Drive, Depue, Illinois."

To me, Ray Brolley was a sorcerer of words. I felt as though I had been invited into a special literary society. He had standards for our writing and for the published writing he shared with us. He taught us to capture the passion and the power of language, and helped me to become a writer, as my father and my grandmother had helped me to become a reader so many years before. There would be many teachers in my life that would revive or threaten to extinguish this passion, but none quite as influential as Ray Brolley. Many years later, as I would find myself sitting on the edge of a desk, cracking jokes with a group of high school students, or reading a poignant story with a catch in my voice, I would remember this remarkable man and the imprint he made upon my life.

And then there was Robert Manahan, my music teacher. In 1963, "Mr. M," as we called him, wore a crew cut and drove a red Chevy convertible. He was the heartthrob of every adolescent girl. Twice a year, he brought a touch of Broadway to our small town. I remember being in his music class the day that John Kennedy was shot. When the final news came over the radio, Bob Manahan walked over to his desk, put down his head, and wept. It was the first time I had ever seen a teacher—a man, at that—cry openly in front of his students. A few minutes later, he walked to the front of the room, raised his baton, and announced to the members of the sophomore chorus: "Ladies and Gentlemen. In honor of our beloved president, John F. Kennedy, we will now sing 'The Hallelujah Chorus.'"

Like Brolley's passion for language, Manahan's love of music was contagious. Over and over again, I tried out for leading roles in the school musicals; but each time, my voice would freeze in my throat and I would be cast in the chorus once again. Bob Manahan taught me perseverance. Miraculously, on what must have been my tenth tryout, I landed the role of the mother abbess in *The Sound of Music.* The next year, I played Fanny Brice in *Funny Girl.* I had broken the barriers of my own adolescent insecurity, and had begun to come into my own as a performer.

Many years later, in the rare moments when I would manage to create a sort of classroom family with a group of my own students, I'd remember my days in summer stock, the cast parties by the river, and the bus trips to Chicago twice a year to see a musical at the Shubert Theatre. I'd remember the special family that Mr. Manahan had created for so many of us. I still try to keep in touch whenever I go home for a visit. It's interesting that toward the end of his teaching career, he became an English teacher, no doubt mesmerizing his students with the lines of Shakespeare as he had mesmerized us so many years ago with the music of Rodgers and Hammerstein.

I remember reading somewhere that when people are asked about memorable teachers, they almost always mention an English teacher. Maybe this is because English teachers put us in touch with the great issues and themes of all time. They give us the tools with which to live our lives. We read and develop an empathy for others, an understanding of human nature, and a wealth of vicarious experience with which to understand our own. We write silently, and give voice to our inner struggles. We write to and with others, and we feel less isolated, more connected. I became a teacher, I suppose, because I wanted to bring to others some of the gifts that Ray Brolley and Bob Manahan had given to me. I wasn't always so sure of the wisdom of this career choice though.

Teaching?

I didn't decide to be a teacher right away. I suppose the initial decision wasn't even mine. In the mid-sixties, it didn't seem as though small-town children of blue-collar parents thought very deliberately about whether or where they would go to college. Ever since I was a little girl and took my first trip to the Field Museum of Natural History in Chicago, I had envisioned myself an archaeologist on a dusty African plain, collecting and cleaning the fossilized bones and clay pots of another civilization. Later, I'd begun to think I might like to try acting or singing, or maybe writing for a newspaper.

I was taken off guard when my mother suggested that I become an English teacher. After all, I'd have my summers off and I'd have a nice fall-back career in case I didn't get married. Archaeology didn't seem like a career for women. Acting, singing, and journalism were for starving artists. I should be an English teacher, my mother reasoned, because they would always be in demand. This idea took me a bit by surprise. I had to agree that getting married seemed like the least likely event in my near future, but being a teacher seemed like a rather uninspiring choice.

I put my mother's idea aside for several months. But by the time I was ready to go away to college, I began to see some merit in it. I'd managed to catch enough of Ray Brolley's passion for writing and literature to make teaching high school students and having summers off seem a bit more appealing than it had at first glance. I decided to give it a try. I could always do something else if it didn't work out.

I wonder today how many women went into teaching because they thought that it would be a fall-back career, a fail-safe against a broken marriage or an unfortunate life of spinsterhood. How many of my women friends have alternately entered and left teaching as they stopped to have their babies or moved for their husbands' careers? Of course there are some rare individuals who, from their earliest days, see teaching as a lifetime vocation. In fact, lately I'm meeting more and more young people who are leaving careers in business or journalism or law to begin a life of teaching. I am heartened by these eager newcomers. But

I wonder how many people see teaching only in terms of its tenure, its pension, and its summer vacation. And I wonder if this is why our profession is still invested with so little status or reward in a world where the education of our youth should be our greatest hope.

Learning to Teach

My English courses at the university were supposed to comprise my "content area" preparation for teaching. The question was, who decided the content, and what kind of preparation were those "today-is-Tuesday-it-must-be-Chaucer" courses for the real world of the high school or the junior high school classroom? I needed something more than a knowledge of literature and of writing, though I wasn't able to grasp exactly what that was at the time. After my undergraduate education courses and most of my English requirements had been completed, I was ready to student teach. I should say I was placed into student teaching because, as it turned out, I wasn't ready at all. My placement was in a ninth-grade classroom in a school on the outskirts of Champaign, Illinois. The students were fairly typical ninth graders—an unruly mix of professors' kids and those of more blue-collar parents.

I approached the business of learning to teach rather like the business of writing essays in my university composition courses. I started out by trying to model myself after my cooperating teacher. That was my first mistake. "Jack Smith," my cooperating teacher, was convinced that the university was putting out student teachers who knew nothing about the great literary works. He was probably right. I'd relied on my careful notes and my professor's lectures to teach me all I needed to know about Hawthorne and Blake, the Brontës, Dickens, and Dickenson. I picked up on Jack's cynicism about my lack of literary knowledge, and wished for a chance to start over again. I imagined myself this time reading and remembering every detail about each selection in my anthologies. But it was too late now.

I spent my first few weeks of student teaching imitating someone I hardly admired. The students picked up on my deception immediately. Jack was a disciplinarian; I wasn't. Besides, I wasn't even confident about knowing more about literature than my ninth-grade students. To top it off, I didn't remember learning anything useful about how to plan a real lesson, how to manage a discussion, or how to get respect from junior high school boys who were taller than I was.

Ninth-grade language arts classes were an hour and twenty minutes long. My first lesson plan was a series of "compelling" questions designed to get my students to explore the great issues and themes of *To Kill a Mockingbird.* Typical of a new teacher, I was terrified by the silence that followed each question. I must have answered most of them myself and skipped over the rest because the lesson lasted only twenty minutes. I had enough sense, at least, not to run out of the room in tears. I asked my students to take out their books and read silently for the rest of the hour.

After that first mortifying day, I began staying up far into the night trying to plan enough for eighty minutes, and arriving fifteen minutes early each day so I could sit in the parking lot and cry. There were very few successes in my student teaching experience, a fact that appalled me. I had been a "good student." I had done assignments on time and managed to graduate magna cum laude. Why, I wondered, was I so easily overwhelmed by a class of twenty-five junior high school students?

I've heard it said that we learn to teach by the way we were taught. By the time I was a senior in college, my memories of Ray Brolley and Bob Manahan had begun to fade a bit. My university teachers, having little or no formal preparation in teaching, were hardly models for emulation. Today, as I work with preservice teachers, I wonder if I could have been better prepared for the emotional and physical endurance test called student teaching. My literary training as an undergraduate was so removed from anything I'd ever teach in my ninth-grade classroom. Most of my literature courses seemed to be designed for students planning to enter a graduate program in English. I needed a different kind of expertise.

I needed mentors with a wealth of knowledge about literature, language, and writing; and a wealth of experiential knowledge about what it means to teach those subjects to someone else. I wouldn't develop what Lee Shulman (1987) calls "pedagogical content knowledge" until much later, after I'd taught English for several years and then gone back to graduate school to discover and develop the theories to explain my classroom experiences. This special blend of knowledge, I would someday learn, was what defined the field of English education and set it apart from the liberal arts.

When I graduated with my bachelor's degree, I was technically certified to teach, but I had no vocabulary to describe what I needed. I just knew that I hadn't gotten it. I vaguely remember my last day of student teaching. That morning I carpooled with a friend of mine, another student teacher. She was a graduate student, who probably had enough seasoning and maturity to enjoy her rambunctious junior high school students. That day, her students gave her a going-away party. I simply walked out the door with my plan book under my arm, vowing never to teach again.

I kept on walking and ended up a few weeks later in the office of the Speech Department at the University of Illinois. I had decided that I couldn't possibly think about looking for a high school teaching job. Going to graduate school seemed like a way to buy more time before deciding on my career. That spring, I was accepted to the degree program in Rhetoric and Public Address; but there was still the problem of how I was going to finance the degree. In an ironic twist of fate, I received a graduate teaching assistantship. To my delight, my master's degree would be completely financed; to my horror, I would have to teach two sections of undergraduate public speaking! In two short weeks, I would find myself back in the classroom again, but this time, on my own terms.

University Teaching

Monday, January 19, 1970
It is the morning of my afternoon . . .
Just finished my Speech 101 final . . .
The kids were in good spirits . . .
I think they rather enjoyed the class . . .

I had started this journal in graduate school. It was in the university classroom that I discovered I "rather enjoyed" teaching. In the fall of 1969, I gathered up my courage and managed to get through my first Speech 101 class. I had to sit beside the desk to stop my knees from buckling and my notes from spilling onto the floor. Gradually, my own anxiety managed to fade into the background as I took my students through their first public speeches—one to inform, another to persuade, and so on. Ironically, I had never taken a university level course in public speaking. But it didn't take long to learn the system. The speeches required the same attention to form that I'd learned in my writing courses. Each one consisted of an introduction, followed by an overview, three major points supported with evidence or example, a summary, and a conclusion.

In my third week of classes, I assigned a demonstration speech. When one of my students placed two large jars on the desk and announced that he was going to demonstrate how a snake devours a rat, I lost my whole class in ten seconds flat and had to herd them back in from the hallway. I think it was the first time that I let my guard down enough to laugh with my students. At the end of that first term, they gave me a gift—a poem, written on a brown paper bag. Today, I can't recall the actual significance of this gesture; I can only remember how proud I felt. They liked me! I had passed! I had become a teacher.

Being a graduate student was another kind of growth experience. I had rather naively thought that a degree from the Speech Department might have something to do with giving speeches. Instead, I spent hours in the rare book room, where I checked my indelible pen like a weapon at the door. Armed only with a pencil, I pored over the works of Aristotle, Bacon, Descartes, John Locke, and David Hume. I suddenly found myself in touch with theories about the origin of ideas, the nature of subjectivity and objectivity, deduction and induction, and the roots of scientific empiricism. At the same time, I had to admit that I still wasn't sure I knew what the word "rhetoric" meant, or how it related to what went on in my Speech 101 classroom.

In the spring of 1970, I was in the midst of writing a series of analytical papers on Eric Hoffer's theories of mass movements. In my journal, I scribbled:

> Man is most frustrated . . . not when he is oppressed, but when limitless possibilities lie before him.

It was only later that I would realize the significance of those words in terms of what was happening across college campuses at the dawn of the seventies. Gradually, almost imperceptibly, the campus had changed its appearance. Chino pants, oxford shirts, and Florsheim wing tips were being replaced by faded denim jeans, blue workshirts, and navy pea jackets from military surplus stores. By this time, I had learned to play the guitar and was just beginning to perform in campus coffee houses. By some accident, I found myself in October of 1969 on a makeshift stage with Eartha Kitt, leading nearly 10,000 of my fellow students in song during what came to be known as "The Moratorium."

At the dawning of the seventies, I was coming to terms with the first glimmerings of feminism. I wrote a paper on the life and rhetoric of Emmeline G. Pankhurst for a professor who gave me my first taste of gender discrimination. Toward the end of that spring semester, after assigning and turning back several papers, he had failed to assign any grades. One day, I walked into his dusty book-filled cave of an office to ask about my grade. His remark took me totally off-guard: "I thought I'd give you a B. After all, you'll be getting married soon and leaving academia. You won't need an A."

I hated to admit that any part of this man's theory might be true. Defensively, I countered that I had been offered a graduate assistantship to pursue a doctorate in rhetoric and public address at the University of Southern California that next fall. That part was true. It earned me an A in the course. But he was right about one thing—I was engaged to be married. I never took the assistantship. That fall, I moved with my husband to Nashville, Tennessee, where he took a position at George Peabody College for Teachers, and I was to begin my career as a high school English teacher.

I've thought many times about Robert Frost's poem "The Road Not Taken" (1960). I wouldn't resume my university career until some ten years later, and when I did, it would not be in rhetoric and public address, but in English education. And "that," as Robert Frost said, "has made all the difference."

High School Teaching

I began my high school teaching career as an imposter. My first position was as a part-time teacher in a private women's academy in Nashville, Tennessee, where I taught public speaking and coached the forensics and debate team. Before I took the job, I had never heard of a "forensics" team and I had never even seen a debate! I learned a great many things in those few short months, though most of it by accident. Then, in the spring of 1972, I took a position as a speech and English teacher at McGavock Comprehensive High School in Nashville, Tennessee, leaving the small world of a private academy to teach in the largest high school in the metropolitan area.

A brand new facility and part of a pilot program, McGavock had over three thousand students in three grade levels. The school had an English faculty large enough to offer some twenty different elective courses on a rotating basis from year to year. I taught courses such as public speaking, advanced speech, debate, oral interpretation, readers' theater, and introduction to theater, as well as more traditional offerings in English. I coached the speech and debate team (by now, I'd seen a debate). In those days, students could take any elective in English as part of their requirements to graduate. My speech and oral interpretation courses attracted two kinds of students: verbally proficient students with an interest in the performing arts, and more limited students who had failed out of the more traditional English offerings and needed the credit to graduate.

My life as a high school teacher was never dull. In the course of any school day, I might find myself collecting money from candy sales, arranging rides across town for an after-school meet, figuring out how I could transport the set for a one-act play to another high school, slipping into the office to make motel reservations, and trying to remember what I was teaching in fourth period. My biggest challenge was finding ways to teach my odd mix of verbally-proficient and verbally-impoverished students in the same classroom and with equal success.

The Students

I seldom remember the straight A students. I'm more apt to remember those who tugged at my heartstrings or tried my patience. Some of them might have never realized how special they were. There was always at least one student in my classroom who came from juvenile detention facilities or foster care, or who was the victim of parental neglect, drug abuse, or any other of the tragedies that can befall vulnerable adolescents. There was a reason these kids could be so disruptive—they were the natural leaders. They had street smarts and a sort of hard-core charisma with the other students. I could either fight them or get them on my side.

There was Ricky, whom I called every morning at 6:30 to make sure that he (and his copy of *The Old Man and the Sea*) made it to the school bus on time. There was J. B., who stayed up all Friday night after work, then walked five miles to meet the speech team on Saturday mornings because his family didn't own an alarm clock or a car. And there was Rhonda, who came to my class from "Juvenile" in the middle of one semester, and one day astounded me with a book of poetry she'd been writing over the years.

I've often thought that no other profession would have allowed me to rub elbows with the future novelists, brain surgeons, politicians, actors, and musicians of the world—the best and the brightest—who, for a few brief moments, stop in their young charmed lives to learn something from you, and teach you something in the bargain. There was Mark, who had honed his considerable acting talents by making up elaborate schemes to hide his rather decadent lifestyle from his fundamentalist parents. And there were others. Nina was a concert pianist, Becky a modern-day impressionist, Amy a recording artist. There was Melody, who was elected president of Girls Nation in her senior year. And there was Ann, who sent manuscripts to *The Saturday*

Review and *Seventeen*, breaking the world's record for rejection letters by her eighteenth birthday.

It's somewhat ironic that just as I'd begun to hit my stride as a teacher, I made the decision to leave the high school classroom. In many ways, I enjoyed my career far beyond any expectations I had had at the end of my disastrous student teaching experience. And I didn't want to be like so many of my talented colleagues whom I had watched leave the profession. Over the years, one had become a production assistant in Hollywood; another a professional photographer; another a lawyer. As each of them made their decision to leave teaching, I felt a tug at my heart. They were the best and the brightest. They had given the kinds of gifts to their students that Ray Brolley and Bob Manahan had given to me.

By the time I was ready to change my own career path, I knew I didn't want to give up teaching. It had already given so much to me. In my last year at McGavock, I figured that I had taught over fifteen hundred students. I wanted to try a different way of reaching them— through their teachers. I had been doing a few inservice workshops for the district, and had been teaching a methods course for George Peabody College. I decided to become a teacher educator.

Nearly a decade earlier, I had gone to graduate school to escape a career in teaching. This time I would be going back to learn more about it. I needed labels and terms to describe what I did. I needed to learn the theories behind what worked and what didn't in my classroom. That spring, I went to Elizabeth Burgess, the supervisor of language arts for the Metropolitan Nashville School System, and asked her for a leave of absence. Then I went to Robert Whitman, a long-time friend who would become my advisor in the English Education program at George Peabody College For Teachers. The time to pursue my doctorate had finally come.

Looking Back

Someone once said that we choose careers because they give us a chance to work out our most perplexing and challenging life issues. Is it odd that I spent nearly every day of my seventh-grade year in the hall for detention, and became a teacher myself in later life? Is it coincidental that I almost failed student teaching and am now a teacher of teachers? I don't think so. I believe that I teach because teaching always invites me to change. The changes have rarely been easy. Often they've been fraught with false starts and struggles. Sometimes I thought I'd never survive them. But I see the world in a different way as a result of my years in the classroom. And that gift has been worth all of the struggle, the lack of status, the low pay, and the meager social reward. I have a certain kind of knowledge that enriches my life.

Here's what I know today: I know that every young person needs to be recognized as special by at least one important adult in his or her lifetime. That doesn't need to happen all the time—just once—but it must happen. I know that teaching English is really teaching life, and anyone who doesn't recognize that is not an English teacher, but a technician. I know that all teaching decisions must begin, not with the general objectives of a curriculum plan, but with an intimate understanding of a particular group of students, their particular abilities, needs, and potential. To begin anywhere else is a waste of time.

I know that passion is contagious, and the best way to create readers and writers is to love reading and writing yourself. I know that there is no denying the art in the language arts. There is poetry in music, and story in painting, and a legacy of human experience in words enacted on a stage. I know that learning isn't always easy or entertaining. Sometimes our best decisions are the result of accident and our shining moments are borne out of pain and struggle.

I know that good teachers are never liked by all students. They are often blamed by those who seek mediocrity. Good teachers demand almost too much. I know that teaching is more than method, and that no student has ever been seriously hurt by a caring teacher with an outdated method. I know that the student with the most potential is usually the one who looks the least like the student with the most potential.

How did I learn these things? I've learned from my teachers, many of whom were my students at one time. I thank those people:

Miss Schulte, who sent me to the board to spell my first word.

My father, for his love of books.

My grandmother, for the books in her cellar.

My mother, for recognizing my career before I did.

Ray Brolley, who taught me to love words.

Bob Manahan, who taught me to bring them to life on the stage.

Ricky, who graduated.

J. B., who, I hear, led a student protest at Tennessee State University over the despicable condition of the dorms.

Rhonda, for her poetry.

Mark, for his brilliance.

Ann, whose first novel brought me to tears.

Amy, whose records make my heart dance.

Melody, who is sure to be the first woman president.

Afterthought

It has always irritated me whenever someone talks about "teachers" as though I am not one. I wonder when I crossed that invisible line between "university person" and teacher, when what I did ceased to be teaching and became something less worthy or well-defined. I have always been a teacher, and I am today. Because I teach adults and not children, or because I teach about teaching, or because my classroom is in a university and not in a high school doesn't mean that I've ceased to be a teacher.

A few years ago, a young woman gave me a parting gift as she was about to leave for college. In the gift was a note. It said, "Please, when you speak of me in the future, do not refer to me as a 'former student.' In this world we are all learners and teachers."

I'd have to agree.

Works Cited

Frost, Robert. 1960. "The Road Not Taken." Reprinted in *The Poetry of Robert Frost: The Collected Poems, Complete and Unabridged,* ed. E. C. Latham. New York: Holt, Rinehart, and Winston, 1979.

Shulman, L. S. 1987. "Knowledge and Teaching: Foundations of the New Reform. *Harvard Educational Review* 57.1 (February): 1–22.

14 From Reading to Writing, from Elementary to Graduate Students

Sandra Stotsky
Harvard University

Although I have devoted more of my professional energy to research and scholarly writing than to teaching, I have always subscribed to the widely held notion that teaching and research or scholarship ideally inform each other, especially if one's scholarly work is in a pedagogical discipline. It is as desirable for teachers to be scholars, constantly seeking to understand and evaluate the worth of their practices, as it is for scholars and researchers, in pedagogical disciplines especially, to be teachers. Pedagogical theory or research not grounded regularly in classroom practice may easily result in inaccessible, if not irrelevant or erroneous, abstractions. Practice critically reflected on, evaluated, and constantly modified keeps theory honest and relevant.

My first reflections on practice took place soon after I began my professional career in education, not as a teacher of English or composition but as a third grade teacher. I had long recognized how intellectually important and personally meaningful reading was to me. I quickly learned again—this time from a teacher's perspective—how central reading was to success in school, and I was deeply puzzled by why it seemed to be so easy for some children to learn and yet so difficult for many others. An observant and pragmatic teacher could do much for most students, regardless of ability, but every year there were some who did not progress as well as I expected them to, and it was not at all clear why.

My intellectual curiosity about the nature of reading as a language process and about the most successful methods for reading instruction remained after I stopped teaching full time to raise a family.

I avidly followed the controversies about reading instruction as they were reported in the popular press. Rudolph Flesch's *Why Johnny Can't Read and What You Can Do About It* had appeared in 1955, beginning an unnecessarily polarized battle between those advocating a sight word approach and those arguing for systematic phonics instruction that has continued uninterrupted to this day (although with somewhat different labels for the antagonists over the years). In 1967 appeared the most famous book of all about the controversy over approaches to reading instruction—Jeanne Chall's *Learning to Read: The Great Debate.* I read it eagerly and experienced a minor epiphany. It was the first account of the issues in reading instruction that made sense to me in light of my own teaching experience. And it wasn't filled with opinions, dogma, or cant; it was a careful, clear, and systematic presentation of research evidence by someone who seemed to know what children and classrooms were like. This was somebody I wanted to study with. I applied and was admitted to the Harvard Graduate School of Education (HGSE), with the intention now of examining the pieces of the reading puzzle from a research perspective.

My entry into graduate school in 1970 brought me immediately in touch with all the major currents of academic thinking about the teaching of reading. The tenets of transformational grammar dominated reading research, and a "psycholinguistic" approach to reading (the term for the sight word approach at that point in time) was being hailed by some as *the* only method of instruction and *the* answer to the failures of our urban schools, despite the substantial evidence (then and now) supporting systematic phonics instruction, especially for low-income children. But with professional roots in that not forgotten third grade classroom, I regularly applied practical criteria to every new theory or pedagogical implication generated by academic research and found them all wanting.

I first began to sense that writing had a distinctive—perhaps crucial—role to play in the entire educational process as well as in learning how to read when I read Vygotsky's *Thought and Language* (1971) in 1971 (a second minor epiphany for me), particularly his passages on the role of grammar and writing in intellectual development. However, at the time, there was no intellectual context at HGSE for developing this idea. No one had, as yet, tried to make any connections between what was taught in English education departments and reading departments, that is, the connections between the teaching of reading and the teaching of writing. These pedagogical focuses were the responsibilities of two different departments with differently trained scholars and researchers. And since HGSE no longer had an English Education program, cross-disciplinary contacts could not take place within the school.

Two years after reading Vygotsky's work, I stumbled onto the sentence-combining research literature (at that time, people in reading research paid almost no attention to writing or language arts research) and some of the pieces of the puzzle finally began to fit together, so it seemed. I searched for anything that related grammar, writing, and reading to each other, and I was amazed to discover that, at the time, there wasn't even an index card on the psychology of writing in the Union Catalogue at Widener Library. The results of my research and thinking—an evaluative review of the research on sentence-combining and its effects on reading comprehension—became my qualifying paper for a dissertation and my first publication. However, because, on practical grounds, I was in no position to carry out an experiment on sentence-combining and had to focus on a topic related to the teaching of reading, not writing, I decided to explore some theoretical issues in vocabulary instruction for my dissertation, picking up on an interest that went all the way back to my high school Latin courses. Little did I suspect that the esoteric lexical phenomenon I chose to restrict my research to—the prefixed words used in reading instructional materials—would lead me right back to the psychology of writing again. Moreover, the very act of writing a dissertation at this point in my thinking occasioned a good deal of introspection about the role of writing in the development of my thinking. It became obvious to me that I wasn't just expressing my thoughts as I wrote my dissertation, but literally working them out.

For part of my dissertation research, I tallied the frequency, in reading instructional texts for grades one to six, of words with "living" prefixes, i.e., words such as *transatlantic, pro-labor,* and *pseudo-intellectual,* whose prefixes can be removed (as opposed to etymologically prefixed words such as *transpire, propose,* and *pseudonym* whose prefixes cannot be removed because what remains cannot stand alone as independent words in the sense required). The skewed distribution of words with living prefixes in different types of reading material and their increasing number as reading material became progressively more difficult seemed to point to linguistic differences between expository and narrative writing. More words with living prefixes appeared in expository than narrative texts, possibly, I speculated, because of the more learned, Latin- and Greek-based character of the vocabulary of exposition, especially academic exposition, and the constant word-coining that had accompanied the growth of scientific discourse in post-Reformation England (as in ancient Greece itself). These linguistic differences, in turn, pointed to differences in the cognitive demands of each. Yet, the overwhelming emphasis on narrative selections in all instructional readers for the elementary grades meant that, unintentionally, reading skills were being developed for one kind of reading only. As relevant as the differences between narrative and expository writing were for the teaching of reading, I couldn't think of a course, seminar, or research presentation at HGSE in the six years I had been there that had ever alluded to the stylistic differences between them and to the possible cognitive consequences of these differences. Nor had I ever heard anyone even inquire whether a skewed emphasis on narrative selections might negatively influence reading development. Further, as I thought about why the use of words with living prefixes might well be more characteristic of succinct expository writing than narrative or literary writing, it seemed reasonable to view active prefixation as a more deliberate than spontaneous linguistic choice and hence more likely to take place while writing or revising than while speaking. I concluded that active prefixation was probably a phenomenon that characterized written more than spoken language.

I couldn't believe that I had come across questions that no one else had ever thought about. So I spent a few days looking through the entire Harvard catalogue, hoping that what I was looking for was not unknown to other scholars, simply unknown to me and the field of reading. I finally found one course description (and that was all) that sounded a little like what I was looking for—Morton Bloomfield's course on stylistics. He was the Boylston Professor of Rhetoric, a subject about which I knew very little formally. I took his course as a postdoctoral student and, through it, discovered what those in the field of reading had rarely, if ever, discussed—the teaching of rhetoric, questions of style, the theoretical issues engaging those concerned with the teaching of composition, and more broadly the teaching of English. My reading, of necessity, expanded to encompass several disciplines that I had barely known existed in the previous six years.

At the same time, I obtained a position as the coordinator of the Elementary Education Program at Curry College, a small liberal arts college in Milton, Massachusetts. My professional experiences at Curry College were instrumental in accelerating my transition to becoming a teacher of teachers of writing rather than a teacher of teachers of reading. I was by now convinced that writing was the chief instrument for developing thinking. While reading was still essential for intellectual development, and while I had always seen writing as highly dependent on reading (and still do), writing was (or at least could be, I now believed) the more powerful activity. It required more active, more precise, and more strenuous thinking than reading did. Thus, in the reading and language arts courses I created at Curry College, I incorporated a variety of writing activities designed to enhance my students' reading, thinking, and learning. I also found myself relying on the pedagogical principles I had evolved when teaching third grade years before. Although most of my students were not highly skilled readers or writers (especially because Curry College admitted large numbers of dyslexic students for whom it had a special support program), they were willing to work on their reading and writing assignments in the context of a highly individualized, structured, and supportive pedagogical approach.

The responses of my students reinforced my belief that a lot of writing and different kinds of writing were instrumental to learning. But more influential on my evolving professional interests was my work with the Boston Public Schools. I became director of Curry College's partnership with the William M. Trotter School in Roxbury, one of many state-funded collaborations between the Boston Public Schools and surrounding institutions of higher education that had been designed to improve education in the Boston schools in the aftermath of the court's school desegregation decision. Not surprisingly, I discovered that little writing was being taught in Boston's elementary schools, not only in the sense of how often students were being asked to draft and revise their work but also with respect to how much writing students were asked to do altogether. Many students could barely write anything intelligible even by sixth grade. With the cooperation of the teachers, I developed the beginnings of a writing program at the Trotter school and then, with further funding from the Boston Public Schools, went on to organize and direct a week-long, city-wide writing institute in 1979 for about seventy selected teachers, administrators, and parents—the first of its kind in Boston. It was clear to me from these projects that teachers were the ones who needed to be reached most if student writing was to improve. After the institute, I decided to create a graduate course for teachers on the pedagogy of writing. I worked out a detailed syllabus for such a course and was gratified that the Director of the Harvard Summer School immediately saw its value. Thus, the path I followed to become a teacher of writing paralleled the evolution of my interests as a scholar/researcher, from reading to writing, and from the education of young children to the education of professionals.

Writing institutes and projects were just being developed all over the country, but there was nothing available yet in the Boston area. The course I began teaching at the Harvard Summer School in 1980 drew on my ideas about what good teaching in general should be and on what I judged participants should learn about writing theory, research, and pedagogy, regardless of whether they taught first grade or college freshmen, served as English language arts curriculum coordinators in the schools, or administered writing programs at the college level. Entitled Teaching Writing Across the Curriculum, my course differed in its content from other writing projects chiefly in the way in which my ideas always were at odds with those of most advocates of the writing process.

First, I wanted participants to see some value in giving students a principled sequence of assignments. I therefore asked participants to respond to a cognitively based series of writing assignments that went from several kinds of experience-based informal writing, an experience-based formal essay, and a critical essay about two self-selected readings to a formal curriculum project or term paper shaped for the eyes of a potentially relevent and self-chosen audience in addition to those of the instructor. These assignments were all in addition to regular academic journal writing and a self-chosen piece of writing for a class anthology. I designed this sequence of assignments because I deplored the seemingly singular emphasis on the process of writing, on narrative writing, and on experience-based or personal writing by writing process advocates. My many years of activity in a variety of civic organizations in my home community had consistently pointed to the ultimate importance, for effective public writing, of the final text (i.e., the importance of the product as well as the process), of nonnarrative informational writing, and of the need to be able to incorporate ideas and information beyond one's experience and to see one's experiences within a broader perspective or as instances of more general phenomena (see Stotsky, 1995a for an evaluation of the research and pedagogical literature on the uses of personal writing). I wanted participants to be able to judge for themselves whether a coherent organization of their writing experiences might provide cumulative learning just as a coherent organization of content did in other subjects, and to see that good teaching in any area entailed planning and a thought-out pedagogical structure for all classroom work.

Second, I wanted participants to know about all the different schools of thought on writing instruction. Thus, the ideas presented in the course as well as the required readings were as far-ranging and as eclectic as could be. Participants were exposed to a variety of theoretical and practical views on writing instruction, writing development, program construction, and the uses of writing for thinking and learning from kindergarten through college (for example, the writings of James Moffett, Nancy Atwell, George Hillocks, E. D. Hirsch Jr., Mina Shaughnessy, and Lawrence Behrens). Based on my own teaching experiences, which had spanned all educational levels, I knew that individual differences among students in any one classroom anywhere (even in urban schools) traversed a developmental spectrum that required individualized teaching and precluded dogma and ideology; no one school of thought ever had all the answers. Moreover, I felt that the participants had a right to know what the competing schools of thought on composition pedagogy and theory were from the best words of their proponents as well as from my own description of them. The required readings in the course were many in number for yet another reason; my own research and scholarship had consistently underscored the role of reading in writing development, and, to the extent possible, I wanted the participants to have that experience too.

Third, I wanted participants, as a group, to look at and critique many different examples of student writing, in addition to discussions and critiques of their own writing. Teachers needed to analyze the strengths and limitations of these compositions and to practice teacher response in a group (something they rarely, if ever, did in their schools or other coursework in education) so they could get a better sense of the variations in the response teachers bring to the same piece of writing and learn from each other. I had them examine samples of student writing from content area classes as well as English language arts classes, and from the full range of writing ability at all educational levels, so that those with teaching responsibilities at either end of the educational spectrum could better appreciate the general kinds of changes that took place as writers developed.

With respect to pedagogical structure, I wanted as much active and inductive learning to take place as possible. To accomplish this, I regularly alternated small-group work and short lectures, devising learning activities for part of the lectures or the small-group work that would enable participants to experience for themselves whatever the focus of the class session was. In this way, they would gain their own insights into both the positive and less positive features of the pedagogical model I was discussing. I also wanted participants to experience as much variety as possible in learning activities. I therefore created a different pedagogical structure for each class session. Working this out was the greatest challenge for me when devising the course, but I wanted to emphasize that good teaching can be as creative as good scholarship and, in many ways, more of a challenge.

With respect to pedagogical process, my course differed little from national writing project models except possibly for its major requirement. In addition to many short pieces of writing, I required the working out of a term paper or formal curriculum project in draft stages, supported by substantive instructor and peer response at every stage. This was the crucial learning experience of the course. My purpose for this assignment was to show participants the limitations inherent in the traditional practice of having students submit major research papers at the end of a semester without formative feedback from the teacher or peers to stimulate rethinking and revising. Even though the writing process for this assignment required a great deal of organization on my part and, frequently, an even larger investment of time (after the course was officially over, I often helped participants complete a document that was indeed going to be read by others for professional purposes), I believed strongly in its value. I had come to recognize how significant my thesis readers' critiques of my own writing were for the development of my ideas at the time I was writing my dissertation. Since then I have continued to be grateful for and stimulated by tough-minded cogent critiques from colleagues or editors.

Every year, my writing course changed a little to keep abreast of developments in the field, to reflect my own assessment of what seemed to work well or not work, and to respond to the candid comments of participants on their course evaluations. I learned, among other things, how useful it was for students (even at the graduate level) to understand why they were being asked to do a particular assignment and what the instructor's goals were. I also found out how much they valued receiving specific, focused comments to help them address the problems a reader sensed in their writings. Hopefully, they would engage in these practices with their own students. On the other side of the ledger, most found it difficult not to receive a graded evaluation of their writings as they were completed throughout the course. I gave a grade only at the end of the course primarily because I wanted participants to experience something that is frequently recommended in the field so that they could judge the psychology of it from their own experience. Perhaps the most telling comment frequently made to me in person or on course evaluations was how rarely, if ever, they had experienced any of the elements of the pedagogical model the course was demonstrating in all their years of precollege, undergraduate, and graduate education.

Since I first developed that course, my own research interests have continued to evolve in tandem with the growing emphasis on the social contexts for literacy. They now encompass the functions and audiences for public writing, whether in the classroom or the community (see, for example, Stotsky 1987; Stotsky 1991a; and Stotsky 1995b), as well as the moral and civic dimensions of writing, whether assigned in the classroom or engaged in by scholars and researchers themselves (see, for example, Stotsky 1991b; Stotsky 1992a; and Stotsky 1992b). My research interests have extended as well to the teaching of reading as it has traditionally been considered by English teachers, that is, literary reading (see, for example, Stotsky 1991–92; Stotsky 1994; Stotsky 1995b; Stotsky 1996a; and Stotsky 1996b).

My pedagogical interests and experiences have also continued to evolve. During the 1980s, I began to think more concretely about how reading and writing, whether in the classroom or in the community, whether literary or academic, whether in the English class or the history class, could be used to help our schools fulfill their essential civic purpose—the development of active and responsible citizens who appreciate the civic culture they have inherited and who seek to extend the right and responsibility to participate in it not only to those who have not been able to participate fully in it, but also to new and future generations of Americans. In 1987, I developed a one-week institute on writing, reading, and civic education with support from the Lincoln and Therese Filene Foundation, and have been planning and directing it at HGSE ever since. Designed chiefly for teachers and administrators of secondary school English, humanities, social studies, and history courses, this institute integrates most of my many professional and personal interests to address what I believe to be the most challenging task confronting educators today—the shaping of reading and writing programs to reflect our nation's extraordinary ethnic, religious, and racial pluralism and at the same time to foster individual intellectual and moral growth within the broader framework of our civic communities at the local, state, and national level.

In 1992, I stopped teaching my summer course on writing across the curriculum in order to devote more time to this institute and to a new and unusually challenging teaching experience. Also in 1992, I became a member of a team of educators from the Mershon Center at the Ohio State University that began working with the Polish Ministry of National Education and with a group of teachers and administrators under the direction of the national director of teacher training to develop a civics curriculum for the Polish schools. My particular role in this cross-cultural project—which the Ministry designated as its first priority for educational reform—was to suggest how teachers can use writing, in civics courses or in other subject areas, for fostering active academic learning and active democratic citizens. As the Polish project moved from the Ministry into a newly formed (and less government-controlled) Center for Citizenship Education, the Mershon Center began a similar project in 1994 with Lithuanian educators. As part of these two undertakings, I have added an entirely new dimension to my professional life—from America to Eastern Europe. I see my work in these two projects as perhaps the most challenging task I have faced in the evolution of my work as a teacher of writing: to help teachers in Eastern Europe create democratic citizens in countries filled with appalling reminders of what ethnic and religious hatred can lead to, and burdened in the last century by abusive dictatorships on both the Right and the Left, with few democratic precedents or institutions in their history.

In reflecting on my work with the Polish teachers in what will be the first book on the issues in developing democratic civic education in Eastern Europe (Stotsky 1996c), I realized how impressed I was by their eagerness to learn how they could develop in their students a commitment to individual rights and an understanding of the concept of individual responsibility that they knew underlay a real republican form of government. While they knew they couldn't adopt for their own country exactly what our own public schools have done over the past two hundred years to help develop the civic character of our citizens despite the diversity of their origins, they wanted to know about whatever might contribute to the development of a genuine participatory democracy in Poland. They were particularly interested in understanding where the dividing line is between the kind of instruction that is little more than a crass political manipulation of the student's mind and the kind of instruction that teaches students how to think for themselves. For forty-five years, they were expected to do the former, but they knew that it was possible to do the latter even though they could not officially do so. I am grateful to these teachers, most, if not all, of whom were members of the Solidarity Movement, for demonstrating to me by their very presence that we are never so thoroughly shaped by our social contexts that we cannot see beyond them and learn how to think for ourselves. I am particularly grateful that I had the opportunity to suggest to them how writing instruction could facilitate that goal.

Works Cited

Chall, Jeanne. 1967. *Learning to Read: The Great Debate.* New York: McGraw-Hill.

Flesch, Rudolph. 1955. *Why Johnny Can't Read and What You Can Do About It.* New York: Harper.

Stotsky, Sandra. 1987. *Civic Writing in the Classroom.* Bloomington, IN: Social Studies Development Center, Indiana University, in association with the ERIC Clearinghouse on Social Studies and Social Science Education and the ERIC Clearinghouse on Reading and Communication Skills.

——. 1991a. "Participatory Writing: What Citizens Can Write." *CIVITAS: A Framework for Civic Education,* ed. Charles Bahmueller. Project of the Council for the Advancement of Citizenship and the Center for Civic Education. Calabasas, CA: Center for Civic Education, 83–88.

——. 1991b. *Connecting Civic Education and Language Education: The Contemporary Challenge.* New York: Teachers College Press.

——. 1991–92. "Whose Literature? America's!" *Educational Leadership* 49 (December/January): 53–57.

——. 1992a. "Ethical Guidelines for Writing Assignments." *Social Issues in the English Classroom,* ed. C. M. Hurlbert and S. Totten. Urbana, IL: NCTE, 283–303.

——. 1992b. "Conceptualizing Academic Writing as Moral and Civic Thinking." *College English* 54 (November): 794–808.

——. 1994. "Academic Guidelines for Selecting Multiethnic and Multicultural Literature." *English Journal* 83 (February): 27–34.

——. 1995a. "The Uses and Limitations of Personal or Personalized Writing in Writing Theory, Research, and Instruction." *Reading Research Quarterly* 30.4: 758–76.

——. 1995b. "Changes in America's Secondary School Literature Programs: Good News and Bad." *Phi Delta Kappan* 76 (April): 605–13.

——. 1996a. "Multicultural Literature and Civic Education: A Problematic Relationship with Possibilities." *Public Education in a Multicultural Society,* ed. Robert Fullinwider. New York: Cambridge University Press.

——. 1996b. "Participatory Writing: Literacy for Civic Purposes." *Nonacademic Writing: Social Theory and Technology,* ed. A. H. Duin and C. J. Hansen. Mahwah, NJ: Lawrence Erlbaum Associates.

——. 1996c. "Reflections on the Poland Project." *Building Civic Education for Democracy in Poland,* ed. Richard C. Remy and Jacek Strzemieczny. Bloomington, IN: National Council for the Social Studies: ERIC Clearinghouse for Social Studies/Social Science Education.

15 Living with Tension: Doing English and Talking Pedagogy

Joseph Milner
Wake Forest University

Teaching English is difficult, but delightful; teaching English teachers is also delightful, but more difficult. While the recent *Handbook of Research on the Teaching of English Language Arts* (Flood 1991) and what Jim Raths calls "pedagogical content" give English educators confidence that there is a science as well as an art to what we know about teaching our discipline; we confront some stubborn dilemmas in trying to do our jobs. Over my twenty-plus years as an English educator, I have taught a variety of methods courses, have worked with teachers in hundreds of continuing education programs, and have directed a writing project, so I have approached the difficulties involved in helping people learn more about teaching English in a number of different ways.

I would like to approach how I teach my English Methods class via four routes: offering some candid snapshots of how I teach that course, briefly tracing my life story to explain how I came to teach in that particular way, exploring two special field-based methods classes, and then discussing the tensions which operate in those special settings, as well as in most methods courses.

Snapshots

I would like to describe, as straightforwardly as I can, a sample early lesson in my English Methods course. I walk into my methods class on the second day of the semester and ask my students to consider three classroom scenarios. I briefly describe three lessons, and ask them to consider which of the three seems most central to their vision of English instruction and which is most peripheral. We then begin to enact the three prototypes as if we were a tenth-grade English class.

In Scenario I, I ask my newly minted tenth graders to think of a highly controversial social issue. We list their suggestions and then select one that seems clearly provocative (like the validity of Dr. Kevorkian's assistance on suicide). I ask for the tallest student to take a seat in one of four chairs in the middle of the room. We then select three companions to join the first to create as diverse a group as possible. The remaining students sit in a circle surrounding these four. I ask the four in the "fishbowl" to respond to one another and to carry on as natural a conversation as possible. I initiate that conversation by asking one of the four to respond to a definitive statement such as: "No one has the right to help people end their lives." The encircling students are asked to listen carefully to the conversation of their four friends. After five to eight minutes when the conversation has just about played out, I create a grid on the chalkboard at the top of which I list the four student's names horizontally and four statements drawn from the positions of the four discussants vertically one under another (e.g., Every citizen has the right to control his or her life.) For each of the four statements, I ask the listeners to decide what the response of a particular conversationalist would be: strongly agree (5); mildly agree (4); uncertain (3); mildly disagree (2); strongly disagree (1). In this manner they fill up the chart, a number representing each of the conversationalist's responses to the four statements. When each of the fishbowlers enters four numbers that represent their true response, the fishbowl watchers can measure the acuity of their listening numerically by measuring the difference between their numbers and those of the conversationalists. That's Scenario I: an activity in a classroom that my students must compare with two others to determine which is more central and which is more peripheral to their vision of the English classroom.

Scenario II is different in content and form. I write a sentence on the board: "Who cares if the shooting of the Apaches is terrible." As their tenth-grade teacher, I ask my students to put a symbol for the part of speech over each of the words in the sentence and then to diagram it. After they have begun, I pick out three of the most diverse diagrams and ask those students to put these schematics on the board for the rest of the class to review. My students are a bit reluctant and let me know that they never had to diagram sentences or that it was too long ago to remember. They are even uneasy about designating the parts of speech. When the three diagrams are on the board, I ask other students which schematic is correct. After we stumble and falter over that, I ask them to label each word's part of speech. I quickly draw the curtain on Scenario II and most are relieved to get away from it.

Scenario III has really begun when I ask a resilient student working on a diagram of the Apache sentence to leave the room and prepare for a four minute beginning lesson on the *adverb*. While that student prepares for this teaching role with the *adverb*, I tell my students what I have assigned their classmate, but that our class goal is quite a different one. We will actually study body language and so we will attempt to keep the *adverb* teacher off balance enough by our irritating mannerisms, poor questions, and downright bad behavior to provoke her frustrated body language. They are asked to note how the *adverb* teacher uses her arms and hands, what her face tells us, where she moves, how she postures her body, etc. Shortly after our unsuspecting teacher comes in and begins, usually with an expository lecture, the other students and I begin to interrupt her flow of thought, distract her from her teaching plans, and generally disrupt the classroom. They particularly enjoy seeing me bedevil the teacher and relish even more her strong discipline of me. I stop the lesson after about three minutes and apologize to our victim, and explain that we were studying her body language and not her *adverb* wisdom. In groups of three, the harassing students compare their notes and we, as an entire class, try to come up with three pretty solid generalizations about body language. This ends Scenario III.

I ask my students to think about these snapshots of three different kinds of classes and try to say what is the nature of each of the lessons (what is their meaning and intent with regard to English language arts). Then I repeat my original question: which of the three is most central to their vision of English and which is most peripheral? I, of course, have some strong beliefs about the three scenarios and which should be most central to an English language arts class. I like the participation, the interaction, the unrehearsed language and the layered consciousness of fishbowlers as they infer the meanings of the conversationalists in Scenario I. Such a class is in touch with the world around it and taps the feelings and beliefs of the participants. The language about language, the three-steps-removed diagram that is imposed in Scenario II on the grammar that is, in turn, imposed on the Apache sentence separates metalanguage from real utterances about as drastically as one can imagine. The clever arrangement of baselines, slants, and perforated lines has its appeal, but its usefulness is doubtful. The third scenario is appealing because it allows sanctioned mischief for a brief time and because it is well grounded in the world of human communication. If diagramming is effete, reading body language is vital and full of efficacy. It is not a dry, narrow English drill, but a very broad view of language. That is its problem for me, if there is one. We need to open the gates and expand the paradigm, but are there limits to what we can do in English? This may be a once- or twice-a-year activity, but it would not be a staple of my classroom as would the lively talk of Scenario I.

Tracings

How did I come to be this kind of methods teacher? What gave me my style, my preferred posture? I can look back at my life and see the ineluctable formation of my style, my self as a methods teacher. I grew up in an extended family which was rich in argumentative, rather than narrative, conversation. My two older brothers as graduate students, their friends, my aunt, a slew of aggressive cousins, and my parents were weekly Sunday evening dinner participants. Politics, economics, and religion were the staple of those conversations. From early boyhood through college, I listened and thought things through. Despite my silence, those energized, contentious evenings were the happy climax of every week. My high school and early college English teachers, probably a typical well-intended group who were told never to let politics, economics, and religion enter the classroom, almost killed any hope that a sports-loving, high-energy, reluctant reader could care about English. But incredibly English became my college major when a fastidious, gateway math teacher took away all the mystery, exploration, and joy of the subject and I had to chose a new major by default. Still, college English courses only now and again captured my soul and left me with only a bookish knowledge to show for my years at Davidson College.

Meeting Lucy, my wife, put me on track; talking about texts with her brought life and meaning to a subject that previously had too little of that for me. After a tour of duty in the army, I returned to my native city where I had a strong reputation as a basketball player and was offered a job that I didn't deserve; I became a high school coach and English teacher. Both I did, and not too poorly, but the tension of trying to do both jobs well made me put aside coaching to work on a graduate degree in English at Chapel Hill. It was a straight English program that I entered—I was naive about other options. In less than a year, I was married and soon began to think as much about Lucy's high school English teaching as I did my own graduate English studies. Watching and sorting out with her, refashioning what I was studying in pedagogical as well as academic terms, made my engagement in English all the stronger and provoked me to think about teaching in a way I never did in my first two years in the classroom. I was so taken by the idea of returning to the public schools that I interviewed with two very different school systems, rural and urban, along with the traditional college and university English departments. So, when on a campus visit to Wake Forest I heard the Chair drop a final "would you, perchance, be interested in teaching our methods course?" I was ecstatic. The other offers immediately lost their luster.

I accepted Wake Forest's invitation, returned to Chapel Hill and asked Sterling Hennis what one book I must read to begin my journey as a methods teacher. His immediate response was Moffett's *Student Centered Language Arts* (1976). With Moffett's charge, I began to grow and change, and my methods course began to shape all of my teaching. As a result, I fit less comfortably in the college English world. That same pedagogical impetus led to my being asked to become editor of the state affiliate's journal. I was drawn into that organization and quickly into NCTE. Soon, I was working wholly in the Education Department and was offered a reaearch leave for graduate work at Harvard. I was drawn there by Lawrence Kohlberg's theories of moral development, but left as a broad-based developmentalist. The next twenty years were spent writing for *English Journal*; learning from Denny Wolfe, Bob Reising, and Collett Dilworth and others in North Carolina; serving as Chair of the Education Department at Wake Forest; working for the Writing Project; teaching for the National Faculty; writing *Bridging English* (1993); serving as Chair of CEE; and serving on NCTE's Executive Committee. All of this history has made me much more a listener and participator in Scenario I than a prescriptive grammarian who dotes on the exactitude of diagrammed sentences. And, I am just enough infected by my study of language in an English graduate program to be unwilling to lend the passionate attention to signs and gestures that I devote to language acts (words) and just enough of a social constructivist to feel a real need to develop students expressive side and their ability to transact with language. So, my pedagogical dispositions have clearly been shaped by my story.

Integrated Formats

In the midst of these two decades of work, two special, integrated settings made my path arc in a little different trajectory. In the regular methods course, I work out of a two-level structure: doing English language arts and then moving to metatalk. At this second level, my students and I consider the range of pedagogy that would be appropriate and effective for the particular activity at hand. The steady use of work at two levels—doing English and talking about pedagogy—has been central to the success of my methods course, and to any other, I would think. I cannot imagine teaching such a course for prospective English teachers without giving serious attention to both. But I have taught experienced teachers in a field setting that, in a sense, effectively brings the two levels together. That unusual format has altered my sense of what a methods course should be. I taught for three summers at the Whittenberger Institute in Idaho, a program that focused on sixty bright and talented secondary English students who studied together for two weeks with four master teachers. Each of the master teachers taught a special dimension of their chosen discipline: writing, the essay, film, and contemporary literature. What was peculiar to this format was the fact that four secondary teachers sat alongside the fifteen outstanding, rising seniors in each of my four sections of contemporary literature. All nineteen students read the literature and engaged in class activities. The students were fully engaged in an exploration of the texts we considered without much, if any, consciousness of the pedagogy employed. The teachers, in contrast, had the difficult task of immersing themselves wholly in the study of the text alongside the students, while at the same time putting a part of their minds to work on the pedagogy at hand. Because the texts were challenging and new to them, and the high school students were quite bright, the teachers were stretched to the limit as they explored the text at the first level. But because they were select participants attending the institute to develop their skills as teachers, they were keenly aware of the pedagogy used in our classroom. We did not discuss pedagogy during this class each day, but created informal sessions and engaged in dinner conversation throughout the two weeks where we discussed the effectiveness of the various methods I used to shape their classroom experience. The Idaho teachers were working at both levels, but were involved fully in the study of the text before any articulation or critique of the pedagogy was considered.

Since then, a course I taught in adolescent literature provided a further variation on the two-level theme of active study of texts mixed with a period of pedagogical investigation. In this course, my Wake Forest students explored a set of twelve young-adult novels over the course of fourteen weeks; selected secondary teachers were also a part of the class. Each week I used a very different pedagogical approach to the novel we were reading. The secondary teachers read the text assigned for the students and were, in addition, assigned an article or a chapter excerpted from a book that explained the particular pedagogy I was using to explore the novel during that class period. After class concluded for the undergraduates, the teachers and I would reassemble to talk about the concept they had studied and its effectiveness in our classroom that day. Here, in contrast to the Idaho experience, the teachers had a prior articulation of the pedagogy to be employed and could watch it play out with half a mind, while the other half was engaged in exploring the text alongside my undergraduate students.

Tensions

In both teaching formats, two levels of engagement and understanding were alive in my classroom, though not in exactly the same fashion. Each format has its strengths and each has a special appropriateness for the students and teachers for which it was designed. Different though they are, however, both formats have tensions at work, some continuously, some intermittently, all created by contending desires:

- exploring philosophy and doing methodology

- talking pedagogy and doing English

- understanding broad concepts and examining specific methods

- practicing specific techniques and defining multiple methods.

The initial tension I confront flows from my desire to help my students think philosophically about such questions as what English is, what it means to teach English, what language is and how it changes shape over time. My students are curious about these matters, but their interest is overrun by their anxieties about teaching and uncertainties about themselves. They want to arm themselves with things to do; they want to know how to teach literature and composition, and these philosophical matters seem a luxury they cannot afford. So in my regular methods class, we quickly move from philosophical engagement to consideration of questions about the sequence of activities, what improvisations might improve the lesson, how genuine response might be better elicited by a different structure, or how to evaluate an entire lesson in terms of its place in a larger unit, its depth of inquiry, its capacity to help secondary students engage in a concept, explore it and extend it into their lives. The prospective teacher's impatience with philosophical speculation is not endemic to experienced teachers. These veterans are more immediately interested in examining philosophical matters they have been considering for years as they reflect on their teaching. In the Idaho and adolescent literature class settings where doing preceded reflection, the philosophical and linguistic dimensions arose, but always informally, as adjunctive comment on the lessons just completed. For these experienced teachers, the transition from philosophy to methodology is smooth and continuous.

When my methods class has moved out of the early philosophical segment of the syllabus and we begin to do microteaching, a second kind of tension arises. We can become immersed in a very stimulating exploration of Frost's "The Lockless Door" (1923), so attracted to that collaborative exploration of the text that we grow quite hesitant to relinquish our hold on our new interpretation. I know that our achievements are in large part due to the structure of the exploration, that it has allowed a number of rich, new understandings of the poem to be constructed. So I have to prompt them to shift their attention from the *what* of the poem to the *how* of the methodology in order to see the relationship between methodology and achievement. With bright, creative students engaging a text, it is easy to become energized by the uncovering process, to lose my methodological footing. But I need to recognize the misdirection and tug us back to the realities of the teaching task at hand. We must talk about the sequence of activities, the invitation to exploration prompted by small learning groups, the timing of the switch from that intimacy to a whole class discussion and the use of narrow or broad questions in generating that discussion. Their knowledge of the poem, of poetry, and of Frost is essential, but it is of slight value without full attention to the methodology to be employed.

The experienced teachers are aware of the fundamental place of method, so, both in Idaho and in my adolescent literature class, they can fully engage in doing the Frost poem during regular class time and find time afterward to reflect on the beauty of a certain methodological shift or comment on a misstep in raising questions in the whole class discussion, though something may be lost in the waiting period.

The question of understanding broad pedagogical concepts rather than examining specific methods is a third tension point. Prospective teachers are sometimes so anxious to deal with specific methods that they grow impatient with or overlook the conceptual framework which holds specific techniques together in a meaningful pattern. When I have explained the broad conceptual framework of a developmental approach to writing, the aspiring teachers and experienced ones as well will hear me out. But after participating in the specific writing activities that illustrate the framework, they tend to lay the framework aside and remember only the classroom activities. Experienced teachers will come up to me three or more years later and refer to the effectiveness of an activity I had used illustratively, but will have totally put aside the broad concept from which it was drawn. I know the truth of the retort to Dewey's idea that there is nothing so practical as a good theory: there's nothing so theoretical as good practice. Theory and practice are inextricably linked, so I am pleased that the practice is solid and may inversely yield good theory. Still, I am needled and want to whisper: do you have an inkling of the theory?

The final tension is that between using precious class time to master a few methods or racing through an array of theories, broad concepts, methods and activities so that an awareness of a variety of possibilities may be gained by my students. In the two integrated courses where we are doing literature and methodology, I always give the nod to depth rather that exposure, uncovering rather that covering. But with prospective teachers, I have a greater sense of the need to engage the whole landscape. We encounter some methods in a thorough way because I demonstrate them. But while a large portion of class time is devoted to these in-depth exposures, I always feel a need to present a number of other possibilities to my students. It comes down to a philosophical split between teacher education and teacher training. I realize we are engaged in preparing professionals, not merely offering another liberal arts course, but I side with the idea of educating teachers as leaders and decision makers, not training them as technicians or mechanics. So I expose them to a multiplicity of contending ideas that I believe will endure after a few well-practiced procedures fade. A single technique may work well repeatedly, but a compelling concept can generate an infinite set of effective teaching activities.

Conclusion

This survey of my practice, my personal and professional experiences which gave rise to it, and the tensions that animate it, still ends inconclusively. Perhaps that is the best final demonstration of the dynamics of my fundamental teaching chore in English education. I am ever at work absorbing and adapting and trying to re-vision what will best prepare us all for the challenges of the English classroom.

Works Cited

Flood, James, ed. 1991. *Handbook of Research on Teaching the English Language Arts.* New York: Maxwell Macmillan.

Frost, Robert. 1923. "The Lockless Door." Reprinted in *Complete Poems of Robert Frost 1949.* New York: Henry Holt, 1959.

Milner, Joseph O'Bierne, and Lucy Floyd Morcock Milner. 1993. *Bridging English.* New York: Maxwell Macmillan.

Moffett, James, and Betty Jane Wagner. 1976. *Student-Centered Language Arts and Reading, K–13: A Handbook for Teachers.* 2d ed. New York: Houghton Mifflin.

V Telling Different Kinds of Stories

[In telling stories about teaching] I especially want to learn how to rouse people who are "different" from each other.

Mary C. Savage

16 What's a Story?

Mary C. Savage
Hofstra University

I began teaching in college in 1968 while I was still in graduate school, and, while I teach only part time now, for almost fifteen years I worked at a small liberal arts college where I taught writing, literature, and education; directed interdisciplinary programs; and sometimes chaired the English department. I probably should have become a storyteller sooner than I did, but I ignored messages to that effect, more or less successfully (I took a Ph.D. in Medieval Narrative, for example), until I met Laura Simms and she scared me nearly to death.

Vasilisa the Beautiful

Laura Simms is one of the people responsible for the renaissance of professional storytelling in the United States. I met her the year I was forgetting how to teach literature. I had agreed to direct a reading group for teachers, but, since teachers joined the group to expand their own reading and not to learn from me, I was perplexed about my role. I learned to pay careful attention to what they did with the literature they read and by October, when one of the teachers asked me to attend a storytelling event, I had forgotten how to teach literature. As it turned out, it was just as well.

At the event, Laura told the Russian tale "Vasilisa the Beautiful." In this story, while Vasilisa's father is away, her jealous stepmother sends Vasilisa into the forest to get fire from the witch Babi Yaga. Few who go into the forest return, but the girl goes on her way and finally comes to the witch's house which is fenced around by a structure of human skulls and bones. At night, light shines in each of the skulls. Babi Yaga takes the girl inside the house and sets her impossible tasks that the girl is able to accomplish with the help of a doll that her dying mother gave with her blessing. When Babi Yaga discovers the girl has a mother's blessing, she thrusts her out of the house and hands her a skull containing the fire for which she had come. The girl is horrified by her burden, the flame burning in the dead eyes, and she hesitates several times on the journey back. Once she considers just burying the dreadful thing. But she returns and when she does, her stepmother and stepsisters are fascinated by the fire that finally consumes both them and their house. Vasilisa goes to live with a poor old woman and learns to make shirts so beautiful that they are wanted by the King, whom the girl finally marries.

Laura's Babi Yaga is terrible—crude, raw, and powerful beyond the human. I couldn't sleep that night after the performance. For the next two weeks, the scenes of Vasilisa's hesitation with her dreadful burden returned to me unbidden. I was dizzy, sick to my stomach. Finally, I signed up to take a storytelling class with Laura.

Laura thinks fairy tales like this one are an opportunity to encounter the awesome face of natural power, that which gives and sustains life, but also destroys it. As Vasilisa travels to and from Babi Yaga's house, members of the audience are invited to face both the untamed power of the natural world and the private daemons that are its inner counterpart; they are invited, like the hero, to return with burning knowledge capable of transforming the world around them. From the first, I knew what terrified me about "Vasilisa." When I was nine and my mother died, I learned about death and change, but I have been stuck in the middle of the journey. "Vasilisa" encouraged me to move along. Even though when I tell the story my Babi Yaga is not nearly as terrible as Laura's, adults often caution that my telling might be too frightening for children. It isn't, but the story does frighten big folks like me who are reluctant to budge from some stuck spot. Children, by contrast, mostly want to know what happened to Babi Yaga. I tell them the truth: she is still in the forest.

"Vasilisa the Beautiful" was the first lesson storytelling gave to my teaching: literature is mostly about transformation. Performance and publication are now at the center of courses I teach in Language Arts. I structure them to have something of the proportions represented in the diagram included in the appendix. Even in literature courses I think I would stress performance, reading aloud, and "sustained silent reading." Storytelling showed me how stunted the process of publication was in my classes. What keeps me telling stories is that I can sense the transformation happening in an audience almost as it happens. When I tell a story, they laugh (or not), sit on the edge of their chairs (or not), hold their breath (or not), sigh in relief or contentment (or not), or linger silently after the story is over (or not). Novice writers miss this relationship. If students are lucky, they have peer groups or other audiences who read or listen to their drafts. If they are lucky, they publish their pieces for the class or other school-based audiences. If not, they hand it to a teacher who gives it a grade.

Storytelling is teaching me to rely on publishing student work for actual audiences.

This has required some ingenuity. Colleges are not structured to facilitate the drafting, editing, illustrating, laying out, printing, reading, responding, partying, and general carrying on of the process of publication. College classrooms give the impression that literature and knowledge are discussed here, but made somewhere else. Then there is the problem of genres. I know it is a weakness in me, but I am weary of the traditional student genres. I know all the arguments about enabling students to get through the requirements, to handle these culturally powerful genres, and to overturn the system once they master it. I just don't want to do it any more. Storytelling has made me want to explore with students genres that will affect the people actually present in our class, college, or community.

On the occasions when we do have discussions and arguments, I try to pay as much attention to how literature affects our lives as to how we interpret texts. I've learned to focus on material things: how we find and keep books and pay for them; how we restructure our lives to fit reading in; how we create communities to support our literary lives; and how literature affects our relationships with others. In every class there are things to think about: a teacher who started reading poetry to her six-year-old only to find her teenager and her husband joining in; a woman in her forties who renewed a romance by reading aloud to her partner, and two who read themselves right out of their relationships. After all, as I once heard Shirley Brice Heath say, "Literature isn't information; it's a chance to change your life."

Hospital Dolls

I changed my teaching practices to accord more with "process"-oriented theories of composition only after many years of teaching traditional composition. It was the students who convinced me. The college where I worked was so small I could huff down to the Registrar's Office to find out who taught Freshman Composition to the obviously deficient students now in my Advanced Literature Seminar. It turned out to have been me. Honest, I worked very hard in Freshman Composition. So did the students, but their academic gains were not very long lasting. I decided to adopt a Catholic Worker slogan for my composition course. Next year I would find an easier way to be good. My second lesson from storytelling is that knowledge—and culture generally—emerges from people actually present to each other.

Now that I have been telling stories to audiences for several years, I realize I was scared away from my own classroom. In my first full-time job, I had 125 students spread across four classes of Freshman Composition. My own writing was a mess—collapsing under the weight of a dissertation—and I had very little academic preparation to teach writing. After several years, I was allowed to teach a literature course or two and things seemed much better. Actually they were worse; I just didn't know it. As I look back, it was the literature classes I had when I was a student that encouraged what Mary Daly in *Pure Lust* (1984) calls the absence of presence and the presence of absence. When I was an undergraduate, I was pretty impervious to courses which seemed empty. My literature courses, by contrast, seemed to be what school really should be: profound, sophisticated, esoteric. So when I finally got to teach some literature courses, I felt I knew what I was doing. My college courses predisposed me to the "prepare" and "deliver" school of education. I "prepared" before class and "delivered" the stuff when I got there. Storytelling has made me very suspicious of all these things which are "already known."

One day early in my career, the elderly chair of our Speech and Drama Department stopped me just as I finished my literature class and said, kindly, "Dear, do you know you don't have to project so much?" I didn't know. As a result of her caution, however, I noticed I was actually looking over the heads of the students, not at them, and that I was loud.

The lesson from my storytelling is be present, relate, let culture emerge. Knowledge is made by us together in this place; it is like recognizing someone by their laugh, getting the punch line of a joke, or breathing together to become the audience for a story.

In education classes I have begun to call this way of teaching Culture-Based Teaching. Under the influence of Culture-Based Teaching my educational questions have become very simple: Who are you? Who am I? What can we do together? A community already exists in (and around) the classroom; Culture-Based Teaching is a matter of uncovering it and discovering together the work to be done. Culture-Based Teaching is reorganizing my classrooms, but I cannot yet fully describe just how. I do know we look at each other more and it is quieter.

My apprenticeship in Culture-Based Teaching has not been in college classrooms; it has been in the Henry Street Storytelling Workshops where I practice listening to the stories parents have to tell. At the start of the Workshops last year, Sharon (Cookie)

Kennedy told through her tears the story of how her daughter Gail died when she was eighteen as a result of having had cerebral palsy. Over the several weeks it took her to make a book of this story, her courage helped other mothers with children in Special Education to talk about them. Finally, the storytelling group "adopted" a Special Education class and each of ten mothers told or wrote a story for the class about someone who was special to her: a ten-year-old son who was his mother's support when the family lived in a shelter; a brother who took two weeks off from work to help his sister when each of her four children was born; an aunt who had attention for children when their mother was burdened by work. The children wrote stories for us in return. Near the end of the year, the parents and children wrote a book together about things they enjoyed playing. One day while the parents were busy working on this book, Cookie came into the room and said she wanted to tell the story of *The Hospital Dolls*. Here is a shortened version of what she said:

> Every time my daughter Gail went to the hospital, they had a doll for her. She had about twelve dolls and each doll represented her sickness. Whatever was wrong with Gail, the people in the hospital had a doll with the same problem. I really appreciated that the nurses made these dolls because the dolls gave her some strength. She would look over at the doll and the doll would have an IV just like hers. I remember when they had operated on her back, the doll had stitches down her back and the same cast and everything. The doll would just lay there like Gail would.
>
> Gail had a skinny doll when she lost weight. The doll was very skinny because after her transplant, Gail went down to around fourteen pounds. She was two years old. She needed the transplant because she was draining all the water from her body. And the skinny doll stood up there and had the band aid on her stomach where they put her new kidney in. And the doll had two IV bottles.
>
> One of the dolls she would play with. She would sleep with that doll and take a bath with that doll. That doll sat at the table with her. Wherever she went, that doll went. Even if she went to the hospital and they made up a new doll, that doll still went with her. Her name was Cindy Lou. She just loved that doll. When Gail died, that doll went with her. Cindy Lou went with her. So now the dolls are all packed away. But I miss Cindy Lou. I miss her.
>
> So that's the story of Gail and her dolls. We went through a lot with those dolls. I don't think I could look at them just now.

Jeptha's Daughter

Laura says stories find storytellers more than storytellers find stories. I came to storytelling after years of doing liberatory education so I should not have been surprised when stories with liberatory work to do found me. The liberatory traditions I follow have been articulated by Paulo Freiere, Alma Flor Ada, Gustavo Gutierrez, Letty Russell, Margaret Farley, and others. Their theories proceed from the obligation people have to free ourselves from the consequence of the terribly unbalanced way our society is arranged. Among poor and oppressed people, the consequences are death, too often, too early.

In New York City where I work, the consequences are punishingly obvious. Boys growing up in my Harlem neighborhood would have a greater life expectancy if they moved to Bangladesh. Parents in the Parent Storytelling Workshops are visited by death often. Friends and family members die from asthma, cancer, AIDS, poor and unresponsive medical care, drug-related violence, or adolescent rage. But it is not just the poor. Even the lives of people who are not poor are touched daily by the consequences of imbalance. Liberation requires that we find ways to respond to the unbalanced, quickly changing nature of our lives, ways, at least, to create the public space we need to mourn those we have lost to changing family patterns, to downward or upward mobility, to economic instability, to moving, to depression, addiction, war, or poverty.

The journey for most people involves breaking identification with the present order and realigning with those most harmed by it. Middle-class and professional people who go on this journey often get stuck right after they face up to Babi Yaga. Fear and guilt grip them. But until they can face the consequences of our unbalanced society, they cannot change it. Unless they allow their guilt to transform into grief, they are stuck, the skull frozen in their hands, its fire lighting only the dead eye sockets.

"Jeptha's Daughter" found me years before I became a storyteller. It was one of a series of public lectures given by the scripture scholar Phyllis Trible at Yale Divinity school while I was still a college teacher trying to figure out how to make our academic disciplines more responsive to the world around us. The series was based on Trible's analysis of Old Testament stories about women and was later published as the book, *Texts of Terror*. "Jeptha's Daughter" is the story of a young woman burned alive in fulfillment of a vow her father had made. Trible built up the terror of the story in a patient, academic way, carefully quoting its language and describing its rhetorical devices. At the end of the lecture, however, she shifted genres and read a lament she had composed for the heretofore unsung Jeptha.

The audience was mostly women, many from traditions, such as Roman Catholicism, which denied them recognition and access to official ministry. They wept openly. So did I. Grief, long held, half-known, welled up from me. Grief for my friends excluded from ministry, for the Maryknoll missionaries recently raped and murdered in El Salvador, for my grandmother's sacrifices in keeping her household going, for my mother, dead before she was thirty, and for countless other women whose lives spilled out heedlessly in harsh and unjust circumstances.

I forgot this story until it found me again at the end of a Storytelling Residence Laura held in a retreat house nuzzled in the hills of northern California. We were all coming back to the house along a trail from the Redwood Forest. I was holding a large stone, recently fallen from the hill on our right. It hung down from my left hand like the bowling ball of a southpaw. Actually the image I had was of the man who repairs the stone wall in Frost's poem: "like an old stone Savage, armed." Frost wrote "savage," not "Savage," but that's how I felt, a member of the Savage clan armed with the ancient stony weight of our separating and protecting grief. Long-buried sorrow over my mother's death moved to the surface. I swung my arm out over the stream to the left and let the rock go on the course it would naturally have taken from hill to stream had I not picked it up. I knew then that I would have to tell "Jeptha's Daughter" (Judges 11, The Bible).

Here is a summary I wrote as I prepared to tell "Jeptha" at a conference of English teachers:

> In the time of the Judges the people of Israel were happy and prosperous when they obeyed the Lord their God and cared for the poor and the aliens who dwelled in their midst, but when they forgot God armies rose up against them. When God raised the Ammonites against Israel, the elders turned to Jeptha who had gathered a strong band of ruffians in the land of Tob where he lived in exile because the men of Israel had driven him away saying his mother was a harlot.
>
> Jeptha did not trust the elders and made them swear they would accept his victory as a sign God had chosen him to be their ruler. The spirit of the Lord came upon Jeptha and he raised an army. The night before the battle he became afraid he could not lead the people. Then he made a vow before the Lord saying, "If you will give into my hand these Ammonites, then

whatever comes from the door of my house when I return victorious, that I will offer up to the Lord as a burnt offering." Jeptha crossed over to the Ammonites, subduing them in their cities, making a great slaughter, and taking much spoil.

In Jeptha's house, his daughter awaited her father's return. From the time she was a child she had heard how Miriam raised her tambourine and sang and danced as Israel crossed the Red Sea. The daughter of Jeptha bathed and perfumed herself and put on her best robe. She heard her father's footsteps in the courtyard and burst out of the doorway, the tambourine high above her head, her voice raised in the song of praise.

Jeptha saw her and rent his garments saying she had brought him very low because he had vowed a vow to the Lord to sacrifice the first thing he saw on his return and the vow could not be taken back. His daughter lowered the tambourine and said he must do what he had sworn since he had sworn before the Lord. She asked only that she and her women companions go away to the mountains for two months to lament her virginity; that she would never know a man; that she would never have a child; that her name would be cut off from among the people of Israel. So they went to the mountains, Jeptha's daughter and her female companions, and they stayed there comforting her and each other until the time came for their return. In their absence the men of Israel had built an altar. Jeptha's daughter returned to her father and there on the altar he did to her what he had vowed.

Jeptha ruled the people for six more years and he is known as a great judge in Israel. Of his daughter we know nothing more, except that it became a custom in Israel that every year for four days the women go apart to mourn her passing.

Telling this story allows me to help people transmute horror and guilt to grief, and telling it (and others which have liberatory work to do) has helped me move along on my own journey, both personal and professional. As a college teacher, I had begun to feel preoccupied by institutional issues, taken over by already polemical conversations about education: competing paradigms for interpretation; the struggle of writing versus literature; the need to convince people that whole language is more sensible than education based on basal readers; and the efforts to stop standardized testing, at least in the lower grades. I know these issues are as much a reflection of the unbalanced society as are hunger and homelessness, but I have needed to shift my gaze so these issues are more background than focus. I was enormously relieved, therefore, to find liberatory work which I can do in the outside world. Actually, as I said, this work found me. Other liberatory work is likely to find other people to do it.

What's a Story

Because I am convinced that multicultural relations will be the predominant reality in schools, colleges, and communities for many years to come, I still have much I want to learn from storytelling about teaching. I especially want to learn how to rouse people who are "different" from each other, and often in unfriendly relationships, to tell stories and sing songs that will recreate culture in more balanced and just ways. Laura said she once asked a particularly wise and practiced storyteller and teacher, "What's a story?" Slowly he said, "It depends on who hears it."

Works Cited

Daly, Mary. 1984. *Pure Lust: Elemental Feminist Philosophy.* Boston: Beacon Press.

Trible, Phyllis. 1984. *Texts of Terror: Literary-Feminist Readings of Biblical Narratives.* Philadelphia: Fortress Press.

Vasilisa the Beautiful. 1970. Trans. from the Russian by Thomas P. Whitney. New York: Macmillan.

17 Two *Women's Ways of Knowing* Teaching Writing

Rhonda C. Grego
Benedict College

Nancy S. Thompson
University of South Carolina

The mental processes that are involved in considering the abstract and the impersonal have been labelled "thinking" and are attributed primarily to men, while those that deal with the personal and interpersonal fall under the rubric of "emotions" and are largely relegated to women.

Women's Ways of Knowing

Two teachers whose professional paths have merged, we have formed a team that permeates our work, and a friendship that enhances our lives. After becoming teacher-colleagues in our English Department, we recognized parallel lines of research in our work: Rhonda's on memory as the repository of unfinished stories that comprise our image of ourselves and others, and Nancy's on imagery, or imaging, as the basis for understanding an internal representation system through which we become aware of our memories and our selves. Early on, we realized that we were drawn together because both lines of research reach inside the mind; they are ways of exploring our own minds to know ourselves better, as well as teaching techniques to reach into our students' minds so that we might know them, and that they might know and develop their own mental powers.

Rhonda's interest began when an undergraduate history professor commented on the ways in which the defining strength of southern cultural memory keeps the South alive as a "region." She began to pay attention to the ways in which the South is recollected by Southern and non-Southern writers and thinkers. In graduate school, she explored the ways that ideas about memory informed classical rhetorical theory. And now, after returning to her Southeastern homeland where she teaches writing, she wonders: How are our memories composed and what influence do they have on our composing?

Nancy's work took the direction of imaging-as-internal-representation after a leisurely week spent reading *Seeing with the Mind's Eye* by Mike and Nancy Samuels (1975) while camping at the beach. Her own mind was filled with the sensory images of that tropical beach context. If we can "see in the mind's eye," she wondered, couldn't we also hear in the mind's ear, such as a song playing over and over in the mind all day? Or feel . . . either the physical feeling, for instance, of walking out of your front door this morning or the emotional feeling of re-experiencing an embarrassment? Or smell . . . ? Or taste . . . ?" She taps the common knowledge we have of our visual imagery as a defining example of the more inclusive phenomenon of imaging, to make the distinction that—like the visual—all different kinds of sensory images emerge as images in the flow of thought, culminating in an "internal representation system."

These were important beginning moments for interests that both of us, independently, had developed into separate teaching practices and inquiries. Once we came together as collaborators on a curriculum-change project, however, we began to see how strongly our interests were connected. To trace those connections, we engaged in collaborative inquiry—in-depth interviews—and analyzed what we found to uncover the connections we sensed.

In the next two sections, we will elaborate on our individual teaching stories, showing how personal realizations influenced our professional work with student-writers. Then we will share the results of our collaborative inquiry, showing how it led us to a current research interest in emotion and writing.

Nancy's Teaching Story

I began from the premise that understanding visual imagery is the entryway to recognizing the play of all-sensory imaging as the internal representations we are aware of in conscious thought. In the same way that meaning arises for a reader through arousal of prior experiences stored as images, the writer also must access these internal representations. They are the shadowy prefigurations hovering around a topic from which the writer works to generate language that will arouse similar images in a reader. My research led me to Sylvia Ashton-Warner's concept of the Key Vocabulary: using children's highly charged emotional images—and the words that name them—

as the initial material for learning to read. How could student *writers*, then, be led to tap into and develop such a powerful inner resource? I am interested in how the mind works, especially the role of this internal representation system as the medium through which we experience the past as memory; the future of what we plan as mental projection; and the present, momentary flow of thought that we are conscious of at any time.

For five years, I conducted reflective-teaching inquiry to discover how students can become more conscious of and learn to purposefully use their elusive mental processes. At the beginning of each semester, I used an "Imaging Questionnaire" to elicit students' awareness of visual imagery so they could, in turn, build on that awareness as a basis for understanding the larger sensory system of internal representations in their thought processes. The Questionnaire asks for a "yes" or "no" answer to whether or not they experience visual, hearing, feeling, smelling, and tasting as internal image-representations, and to give an example or explanation. The Questionnaire then leads students to apply their knowledge of internal representations to literacy learning by asking *how* they experience internal imaging as they read and write, and further directs them to give an example of how they have learned to use their minds to accomplish school or learning tasks of any kind.

This Questionnaire at the beginning of the semester is the impetus for the immediate assignment of the "final exam" paper, to be worked on all semester: a "Mental Process Essay" asking students to discuss their mental processes as they read and write and think throughout the semester, in general terms, as well as specifically, how they experience and use internal representations. To generate material for that final essay, students handed in each week a "Mental Process Journal" entry commenting on the mental processes that they were able to observe in themselves as they completed coursework during that week. These assignments constituted an "overlay" focus on mental processes throughout the semester, to produce metaknowledge of their reading and writing for class assignments.

As the "data" for this reflective-teaching inquiry, I compiled from the Questionnaires and the Mental Process Essays a fascinating set of examples from the students, corresponding to the topics raised by the Questionnaire. From the study of more than five hundred Questionnaires and Essays, I supported my theory that, indeed, imaging/internal representation is a universal phenomenon that students can and do use in reading and writing and other thought actions, and, concomitantly, helped students become more aware of and consciously use what were, at the beginning, very elusive thinking processes. One example from the study shows various sensory representations operating in an integrated thought structure:

> . . . the second mystery of my writing process concerns its power over my mind. When I give in, the emerging idea moves into my conscious mind and dominates my thoughts. The inner dialogue that is almost always present in my mind begins to focus on the subject of the writing. In addition, I begin to see, and believe in, the purpose of the writing. I envision an audience and a response. I hear myself talking to the audience. And I begin to get wrapped up in the feeling of producing something that will have some kind of effect somewhere, even though I haven't started producing it. This stage of my writing process is very much like a fantasy, or a focused daydream. The entire writing situation is quite vivid in my mind; my mind becomes a theater with scenery, actors, voices, motives, actions, even applause and music. (Mental Process Essay No. 1)

Thus, I used my initial insight about imaging to move it into a teaching inquiry for studying the internal representation system, at the same time introducing to my students a way to "get a handle on" elusive mental processes so that they might wield their mental powers to greater advantage in the academy and in life in general.

Rhonda's Teaching Story

Our memories are, as Patricia Hampl would say, "warehouses of unfinished stories"—characters, events, plot lines, scenes, social/cultural motifs, myths, etc. What writers do when they "invent" is tap into that warehouse and try to construct a collection or recollection of those social and interpersonal memories. For years I have been asking students for what I call a "writing autobiography" in the first week of classes. Here is one most recent version of that assignment:

Your "Writing Autobiography"

Start by reviewing/remembering/thinking about your reading and writing history, as far back as you can remember. Then, after selecting and organizing your thoughts, write an essay about the reading and writing you've done, with any angle (thesis, focus, point) you choose—but don't organize it chronologically! Your purpose is not to tell me everything you've ever read or written, but to choose what things to say, what details to include to illustrate or illuminate your experiences, your main point. I want more than a simple list of what

> you did when. I want you to make some sense and meaning out
> of your experiences. It is likely that everyone will write a very
> different essay.

Despite that last claim, I have seen a common (though not universal) story running through *many* student-writing histories: Students speak of writing/language experiences in elementary school and at home as "fun" and free-form, practicing in many genres, including drawings with their writings, publishing their work on bulletin boards and in school hallways. But, once students hit junior high/high school where English classes turned into grammar exercises, reading books assigned by the teacher, and writing about them in critical/academic essays or mimicking forms required on basic skills or AP exams, they describe writing as hard and begin at this point to comment on their interpersonal relationships with their teachers. They feel that some teachers liked them and their style, and that some liked neither. Many of these student-writing histories tell about the significant difference that a "caring" someone—a teacher, peer, or parent—made in their writing experience.

I have always felt that students have difficulty making connections between the everyday cares and concerns which moor and motivate their lives and the "abstracted" terminology which writing courses present to them. And in these student-writing histories, the gap between academic language and their "other" life seems manifested in the marked *absence* of much "teacher talk" about the quality of their writing products or about their writing processes. What seems to matter most to many students is that, even in their academic writing, they are composing a self that their teachers and peers will either like or not like.

It is not that I want to change students' perception of the importance of these interpersonal relationships—indeed, I see this as a vital connection to be further explored. Their stories are just "incomplete" or, as Hampl would say, "unfinished," but I know that there are fragments of the "rest of the story" within their warehouse of experiences and observations. What I tried in fall of 1991 was a pedagogy based on what feminist recollective researchers have called "memory-work":

> Memory-work was developed by the German feminist and
> scholar Frigga Haug (1987). The strength of her method is that
> it is integral to her theory of socialization, of how persons
> become selves and the part persons themselves play in that con-
> struction. The underlying theory is that subjectively significant
> events, events which are remembered, and the way they are
> subsequently constructed, play an important part in the con-

struction of self. Because self is socially constructed through
reflection, Haug's theory dictates memory-work as method.
The initial data of the method, memory-work, are memories,
which are reappraised collectively to uncover and document
the social nature of their production. (Crawford, et al. 37)

I designed assignments that I hoped would encourage the "collective
analysis" of student memories about themselves as writers, hoping
that in sharing the observations and experiences that didn't fit the first
version of their writing history, they might, together, begin to discuss
the broader bases of and influences on people's behavior in academic
contexts like English classes.

Students engaged in the following sequence of assignments:
Interview with a Writer, Extended Writing Autobiography, and
Exploring Yourself as a Reader. The first project, Interview with a Writer,
came directly from a suggested assignment in Elbow and Belanoff's
text, *A Community of Writers* (1989). The second project, an extended
Writing Autobiography, incorporated several mini-writing and reading
assignments designed to expose them to different perspectives (from
both peer and professional writers) on past writing experiences. And
the third project, Exploring Yourself as a Reader, asked students to read
Richard Rodriguez's *Hunger of Memory* (1982) while stopping to
freewrite for one-half page after reading every twenty pages or so of
that book. Then they traded freewriting pages (almost twenty pages
each) with a classmate and read and categorized the particular kinds of
responses that they saw their classmates giving to that book.

I know from class discussion and conferencing that the most
important change occurred in the kinds of questions my students
began to ask. Their questions about writing, even about very specific
writing issues and decisions, changed from questions wanting an
answer for a specific moment in their completion of an assignment to
questions asking about the way of thinking that lay behind answers
they'd been given in the past. For example, the typical question about
"Can I use 'I' in this paper?" became "Why do some teachers say you
can't use 'I' in your writing?" There were similar differences in questions about paragraph boundaries, shape, and topic sentences, about
thesis sentences, conclusions, outlining, etc.

I worked hard to give answers that were not cut and dried,
answers that did not blame individuals, but that presented different
"socially-situated" ways of reconstructing those particular past
experiences in learning to write. I told students about the relevant
history of teaching writing, history of rhetoric, history of English

studies, history of educational institutions like our university, and about upper administration decision making in our state, particularly where such items were connected with recent news stories of which they were aware or with which they had had experience. When discussing administrative or institutional decisions and actions and reasoning, I worked to talk about such decision making in terms of the difficulties and conflicts faced by the people who occupied those positions, as I did when discussing their teacher's actions and rules. Students became interested in the interaction between personal and social motivations which they began to see at work in their own past writing experiences and in the reasoning behind the actions of the other people involved in that past. By the end of the course, they were asking questions about the actions of their other college professors in other classes, about why they taught as they did, about the kinds of research they did, and about the career choices and requirements for those people in those jobs. They were beginning to make connections between the intellectual and the personal aspects of people's academic lives.

Collaborative Inquiry: Exploring Underlying Connections between Our Stories

At the beach and in an undergraduate history class . . . even though we could each identify those earlier moments as starting points for the development of our interests in memory and in imaging/internal representation, what both of us knew from our teaching inquiries was that such "magical" focal points are themselves rooted in other influences and confluences of our past and present lives, that there was much more to our stories. So, on the basis of this intuition, we decided to use in-depth interviewing as a collaborative exercise for tracing our interests to those other less tangible, and perhaps more intrinsic, connections between not only our past and present, but also between our personal/professional lives as well.

We met regularly at a time when we were fresh and excited about ideas, walking to the sidewalk cafe first for a strong cup of coffee to start the ritual. We decided to dig back systematically into our personal histories to understand who and what we were that caused these particular stories to spring into being. We audiotaped the interviews, beginning with exploratory questions used in *Women's Ways of Knowing* (Belenky et al. 1986). Beginning was difficult: We were excited and nervous, expectant, tongue-tied at the thought of spinning into our selves with an audience of another and a tape recorder. After plunging in, the difficulty of articulating unformed ideas persisted; the unformedness itself was uncomfortable. But we pushed forward. The trust in our friendship produced a safe and stimulating environment, with the open hours of those precious mornings stretching out before the duties of the teaching day set in. Gently we pushed each other, poking in prying questions wherever a chink presented itself.

When we first began the interviews, we felt ourselves "swimming" in the seas of our respective past lives: In listening to our tapes, we caught several metaphors related to swimming, or swirling, usually when one was justifying a question (talking about what the question was trying to get at and why) or trying to force out an answer to a hard, unthought-of-before question about possible connections. Rhonda had a very physical sense at times of a "swirling" in her head, a feeling of not being able to focus her mind on any one thought or idea, a sensation like one might get watching passenger train cars whiz by while trying to search the windows for one particular face, while all is a blur. We were literally lost in our "warehouse of unfinished stories," busy trying to recollect as complete and honest a narrative of ourselves as teachers and researchers as possible. Or, as Nancy might say, we had gone through the tunnel into the larger internal representation system and were struggling to articulate what we saw there.

What the interviews revealed is a complex layering, a dense web of connections among our research, our teaching, our friendship. More specifically, a dense web of relationships, where the two—and for us *simultaneous*—meanings of relationship are very important: First, we mean the traditional academic sense of relationships between ideas, relationships such as cause and effect, consequence, and other of the commonplaces for inventive thought. And second, we mean "relationships" like that between the two of us as friends, between ourselves and our students, between our past and present lives, the social, "peopled" contexts of our being and thinking and writing, what we will term here "interpersonal relationships." Our interviews also revealed that those interpersonal relationships were transformative. For both of us, "changes" or "transformations" (in the sense of "crossing" or "traversing" boundaries) were important, key episodes in our lives, transformations which both caused and were caused by a greater self-awareness. We came to see that we both believe that change/transformation underlies learning; that for us and for our students, the idea of transformation is inherent in our work through memory and internal representation. Both are ways of encouraging writers/thinkers to look into their lives, into themselves, as agents for learning.

Through the interviews, we could see how we both looked for ways to use these learning-changes in ourselves as the basis for helping others—our students—learn to trust themselves as writers and transform their attitudes towards writing. What had led us, first, to the desire for change was some sense of emotional unfulfillment that supplied the motivation to find the ways of achieving this necessary change or "tranformation." Thus, central to learning is the emotion to drive the desire. *Attitude* is another way of seeing emotion: The attitude we observe in ourselves and in our students (for us, seeing negative attitudes towards writing in our students) is the outward manifestation of an internal emotion. What this exploration showed us is that the interpersonal relationships are the roots from which spring the academic *relationships* we discover *between ideas*. Even the abstract, research-oriented ideas of a field of study or academic discipline are much closer to these everyday, emotional roots than we traditionally like to believe.

Out of the interviews came connected realizations about our ways of knowing as women, our ways of knowing teaching, and our ways of knowing teaching writing.

1. Our ways of knowing: "Knowing" means, for us, self-awareness that is most intense in times of transformation: Transformation of ourselves as women from existing stereotypes about what/who women should be, to a recognition—through images, memories, and internal representation of self—of those elements of our lives not privileged by the master narrative. Increasingly the term "master narrative" is used (without citation) in feminist scholarship to refer generally to an often invisible and unquestioned, yet powerful, patriarchal representation of life and work which governs how we see and talk about our life and work. In *Breaking the Sequence: Women's Experimental Fiction* (Friedman, Fuchs 1989, 45n), Ellen G. Friedman and Miriam Fuchs define the term and its origins as it is used by Alice Jardine in *Gynesis: Configurations of Women and Modernity* (1985):

> "Master narrative" as used by Jardine in *Gynesis* is the discourse of Western culture that encodes its philosophy, history, central truths, and values. The "questioning or turning back" of this discourse involves a "reincorporation and reconceptualization" of what master narratives have omitted, and in France this is conceived as a "space" of some kind (over which the narrative has lost control), and this space has been coded as *feminine*, as *woman*. (Jardine 1985, 25)

2. Our ways of knowing teaching: Through our interviews, we saw the value of moving into this alternative space with an active, challenging, and supportive listener to lend a hand. We realized that we had each been constructing our own alternative narratives, and that over the years we had each come to identify what Jardine calls "reincorporation and reconceptualization" with the mental processes that we knew as "memory" and "imaging." Through our teacher-researches and our work with writing assessment and instruction, we had each used our growing understanding of those processes to restructure writing courses, finding ways to introduce these processes to our student writers. As teachers, we work to create a space within our classrooms where students come into contact with memories or images (whether their own or others') which have been omitted or neglected by traditional institutional practices or understandings. Though the space has been "coded" by Alice Jardine and others as feminine, as woman, we know that here too lie issues of race, class, sexuality, etc.

What we realized from our interviews is that emotions often live in this "feminine" space, that they are a part of any environment which seeks 1) to pursue those alternative narratives, and/or 2) to understand the effects of current master narratives on language use. Emotions can, thus, be instructive for both teachers and students as they engage with each other's mental processes within the kind of interpersonal relationships that we work to foster in our writing classrooms. Unfortunately, as an institutional site for the organization and licensing of socially acceptable "thinking" (the mental processes involved in considering the abstract and the impersonal), American higher education, by and large, denies that educating students means being in an interpersonal relationship with them: Compositionists, for example, are asked to find ways to generalize and stereotype student writing and its development in order to handle large numbers of students.

3. Our ways of knowing teaching writing: A further problem is that the master narrative of academia *omits* students from the label "writer" in many material and systematic ways. In order to change institutional attitudes towards student writers, we must find a way to incorporate, as part of an acceptable academic definition of what a writer is, the broader range of experience-as-writers that our students bring to their work; the definition of writer useful to composition teachers and researchers cannot be limited by a traditional English department canon (writers are those studied in English courses) or the publishing world (writers are those published and sold) or by typical

delimitations of "thought" (and the accompanying institutional devaluing of our work with student-writers).

We have come to realize that we are all writers, "writing" our lives in various degrees around or away from pre-existing master narratives. In this way, we would define every human being as a writer in what amounts to a challenge—to our students, to ourselves as teachers, to ourselves as researchers, and to the University—to change essential attitudes about what writing is and who writers are. Thus, we work to create an alternative learning narrative within our classrooms by valuing student-writers in the ways that we outlined previously through our work with memory and imaging.

Conclusion

To conclude, we'd like to return to the epigrammatic quote from *Women's Ways of Knowing* with which we began this admittedly brief exploration of our work as teachers of writing:

> The mental processes that are involved in considering the abstract and the impersonal have been labelled "thinking" and are attributed primarily to men, while those that deal with the *personal and interpersonal* fall under the rubric of *"emotions"* and are largely relegated to *women.* (Belenky et al. 1986, 7, emphasis ours)

What is significant to us about this passage is that Belenky, Clinchy, Goldberger, and Tarule define "emotions" not as we commonly think of them—individual emotions and moments of, say, anger or fear or happiness. Instead, they lead us to consider "emotion" as a holistic event with spiritual significance, hinting at some set of underlying experiences which vitally inform our ways of knowing. These knowledges may be excluded or ignored as "unintellectual" or even "unprofessional" by current definitions of "thinking" and the institutional realities that those definitions support. However, as teachers of writing we *must* be concerned with how our language for dealing with these alternative ways of knowing either does or does not do justice to their value. Belenky, Clinchy, Goldberger, and Tarule thus provide us with an understanding of the political function that the concept of "emotion" serves within the academy. We as teacher-researchers believe that composition needs to pursue this territory even further than we have here in this initial attempt to reinscribe the mental processes that deal with personal and interpersonal relationships as a part of both thinking and writing, and certainly as vital to the teaching of writing.

From our collaborative-inquiry interviews with each other, we have come to the conclusion that our way of knowing teaching writing begins with a holistic, intuitive feeling, a feeling like that which initially attracted us to work together as collaborators, a feeling that we struggle to listen to in ourselves and that we want our students to listen to in themselves. That feeling—fueled by the energy of all that is excluded from typical definitions of "thinking" in academic life—provides the impetus for trying to trace and articulate the social and interpersonal background of our ideas about writing and the teaching of writing.

For this investigation, we used our interviews to dig back. From this archaeology of intuition, we have struggled here with initial articulations of the social and emotional ways of knowing that emerge in our professional work and inform our everyday lives. Through thus intellectually pursuing the feelings and intuitions that ground our collaborative efforts, we have come to know a direction for our studies. The joy of friendship and the excitement of ideas engender our continuing work.

Works Cited

Ashton-Warner, Sylvia. 1963. *Teacher.* New York: Simon and Schuster.

Belenky, Mary Field, Blythe McVicker Clinchy, Nancy Rule Goldberger, and Jill Mattuck Tarule. 1986. *Women's Ways of Knowing.* New York: Basic Books.

Crawford, June, et al. 1992. *Emotion and Gender: Constructing Meaning from Memory.* London: Sage.

Elbow, Peter, and Pat Belanoff. 1989. *A Community of Writers.* New York: Random House.

Friedman, Ellen G., and Miriam Fuchs, eds. 1989. *Breaking the Sequence: Women's Experimental Fiction.* Princeton, NJ: Princeton University Press.

Hampl, Patricia. 1986. "Memory and Imagination." *The Dolphin Reader,* ed. Douglas Hunt. Boston: Houghton Mifflin.

Jardine, Alice. 1985. *Gynesis: Configurations of Woman and Modernity.* Ithaca, NY: Cornell University Press.

Rodriguez, Richard. 1982. *Hunger of Memory.* Boston: D. R. Godine.

Samuels, Nancy, and Mike Samuels. 1975. *Seeing with the Mind's Eye: The History, Techniques, and Uses of Visualization.* New York: Random House.

Vasilisa the Beautiful. 1970. Trans. from the Russian by Thomas P. Whitney. New York: Macmillan.

18 The Teaching and Learning of English in the College Classroom: Creating a Unified Whole

Brenda M. Greene
Medgar Evers College

Woman, African American, teacher, student of English, researcher—a contradiction in terms, a parcelling of the self, a resistance to harmony: I attempt to weave my way toward a unified whole. I look for a balance among competing epistemologies, classroom environments, and diverse cultures. I negotiate the conflicts that emanate from different world views, discourse communities, and peoples. I confront the struggles of being an African American teacher/scholar in a field that is dominated by the "other": by either white Anglo-Saxon males or white privileged women, women who could go to school full time, take a teaching fellowship, and travel to Oxford in the summer. The story of how I endeavored to find my place among such worlds is an evolving one, as I attempt to find a center.

I began the teaching of English parcelled among the roles of student, teacher, mother, and wife. Faced with negotiating among these roles, I looked within for inner strength. Additionally, I realized that because I had chosen to be in a field that was dominated by the "other," I had become in the mind of the "others" who dominated my field the representative symbol, the collective voice of all African American teachers/scholars in my profession.

Having obtained undergraduate and graduate degrees in English education, I had been made aware of the importance of informing my instruction with a theoretical base and of examining the teaching and learning of English from the perspective of the student rather than from the perspective of the discipline. Believing that students' needs were paramount, I operated on the principle that I could not teach English without first establishing a relationship with my students and grounding my instruction in language-related theory. Finding a way to accomplish this posed many challenges.

As I now reflect on my years of teaching, I can recall an incident which intuitively underscored for me the importance of creating a student-centered classroom environment that is informed by an awareness of the theoretical constructs of language learning and that symbolizes what John Mayher (1990) calls uncommon sense, rather than a common sense approach to teaching. This incident, which predates my teaching of college English, was a turning point in my English teaching and learning.

After teaching middle school and elementary school children for six years, I realized that I desperately wanted an opportunity to work with adults. My own children were young and teaching primary age school children felt particularly draining and left me with little energy to devote to my own children. I resented the fact that I had no time for my own children and, although I enjoyed teaching children, I began to feel both unrewarded and unfulfilled at home and in school. At this point, I knew it was time to rethink my career choice and I subsequently made a decision to resign from the teaching of primary school children. Having made a difficult but necessary decision, I began to explore the possibilities of working with college students.

Little did I realize that my desire to teach adults would be fulfilled so soon. While at a social gathering, I met a college administrator who learned that I had experience in the teaching of English and reading. Although I had no experience in adult education, she took a chance and offered me a job as a writing instructor in the College's Department of Continuing Education. I was ecstatic; my dreams would be realized; I would be "one of the chosen"; I would work with adults in a college setting.

This administrator informed me that these adult students lacked grammar skills and needed practice at them. Taking her word literally and using what Mayher calls a common sense approach to teaching, I reflected on my undergraduate education and remembered that I had been required to purchase a college writing handbook as a reference book and had referred to it whenever I was not sure about addressing writing problems related to punctuation and mechanics. I attributed the fact that I had not been required to complete exercises from this book to my status as an English major. In my view, only those students who had writing problems used a book like this extensively, and thus, in my common sense way, I concluded that this text would be an excellent one for the adult students I would encounter.

My students, a combination of working class adults and immigrants from a wide range of ethnic groups and cultures, appeared surprised to see an African American instructor. I sensed that many of them had never had a black instructor, and they were cautious but willing to accept me as their instructor. They gave me a chance.

Structuring my classroom around the grammar text, I proceeded by reviewing the parts of speech and the rules for the creation of good sentences and for the avoidance of errors with verbs and pronouns. Each lesson consisted of reviewing a rule and then completing exercises which demonstrated whether students understood the rule. The only writing students did was to create simple paragraphs. I had been told that these students needed grammar and I strongly believed that my focus on grammar would enable them to improve their writing. Ironically, I did not consciously know many of the grammar rules I was teaching and believed that the learning of grammar was tedious and boring; as a result, I constantly referred to my grammar text and often wondered how my students would remember these rules when I could not. By the end of that semester, I was totally bored and the students were more bored than I. They stopped completing all the assignments and began dropping out.

It was difficult for me to accept the possibility that my common sense approach to teaching was not working, that I could be the cause of this ennui in my classroom. From an intellectual and common sense perspective, I had given my students the tools to become better writers; however, from an intuitive perspective, I believed I had failed, not only as a teacher, but as an African American woman. My self-esteem was shaken. In my view, I had failed myself, failed my race, failed to meet the expectations of the administrator who had given me a chance, and failed to make that connection with my students, to place my students at the center of my teaching and to draw on their knowledge and experiences as a way to bring them into the world of academia.

When I left that teaching/learning situation, I thought about giving up on my desire to work with adults, but a part of me slowly began to realize that my failure was more the result of my assumptions about the learning processes for adults who had not mastered the conventions of standard written English (SWE) than it was a result of my performance as a teacher. I had had success with elementary and middle school children, and that success had been predicated on the fact that I had applied what I had learned about a student-centered English curriculum to my classroom. Moffett's text on this concept had provided many illustrations of ways to engage students in creative writing, in sustained reading, and in the active participation in their learning. I had managed to find a balance between teaching "reading and writing skills" and teaching reading and writing. My failure in that first adult basic writing situation was in assuming that the principles I had learned about teaching and learning would not apply in my adult classroom of inexperienced writers. The value of using an uncommon sense rather than a common sense approach to the teaching and learning of English had not yet been embraced and internalized by me.

Despite the fact that this traumatizing experience in adult basic writing instruction shattered my self-confidence and made me question my ability to work with adult students, I eventually became a full-time instructor in a small urban college. I have been teaching at this college for the last sixteen years and my teaching and professional experiences have been catalysts in helping me to create a unified whole of an African American woman/mother, teacher/researcher.

My students are, and traditionally have been, first generation college students who have decided to return to school after spending a period of time in the "adult world." Their average age is twenty-five, and they are predominantly of Caribbean and African American descent. They are generally the students who have resisted the system for a variety of reasons. After going through twelve years of schooling, they have come away with few skills in the reading and writing of SWE. Hence, traditional schooling has either turned these students off or failed them.

Having recently immigrated or having dropped out of high school, my students quickly find out that they are limited by how far they can go without a high school diploma. Disillusioned by the prospect of a future that promises little chance for upward mobility, they are now motivated and, for them, college represents a way out. My students need much more than an education. They need nurturing, support, and guidance. They need to be in learning situations which present challenges, foster warmth and caring attitudes, and help them to develop self-esteem and a sense of their capacity for success. They need teachers who can instill self-confidence and provide them with ways to negotiate the alienating culture of academic life. My awareness of the needs of my students has made me aware of my responsibility as a teacher and role model, and as I continue to work with them, I find that the process of searching, examining, analyzing, and revisiting ways of teaching and learning is neverending.

Upon initially entering the college teaching situation, I was faced with teaching a basic writing course before I had begun to study composition pedagogy and theory. I had learned from my experience with the adult basic writing course that I could not structure my entire course around a grammar text. However, as the following illustrates, I still had a great amount to learn.

My approach to the teaching of these students was initially a common sense one, as it had been in my adult basic writing course. Upon examining the kinds of writing problems my students manifested, I decided to "teach" my students the rules for writing SWE along with the formulas and models for constructing well-formed essays. Thus, my teaching paradigm expanded to include rhetorical models and the rhetoric text used by the English Department.

My students readily connected to me: a young, accessible, black, female college professor. Like many of them, I had children. I knew what it was like to sacrifice and to negotiate among school, work, and home. They believed in me, believed that I could show them the way in, and they eagerly accepted my guidance and tried to draw on and learn from whatever I offered. I have often reflected on the fact that, given a different mindset, I could have been one of these students. I have family members who fit the patterns of these students. However, having been imbued with the desire to go to college and to teach from a very young age, I have "made it," and I am committed to finding a way to bring my students into the circle.

As I began to take courses in language learning and composition theory, I began to reflect on why my students had such difficulty with reading and writing the language of academia and why they produced the kinds of texts they did. I became interested in exploring and trying to determine the cognitive processes they used as they composed, revised, and edited their texts. Vygotsky's (1962) and Flower's (1981) theories on inner speech and writer-based prose made sense to me and provided me with a context for explaining my students' difficulties with writing. Because they had not had experience in moving along the continuum from private to public discourse, they did not utilize the strategies that more experienced writers used. They created sentences which represented what Shaughnessy called a "mismanagement of complexity." They were not able to create enough distance from the text in order to do what Bartlett characterizes as "inhibiting their privileged information." Thus, the texts they produced revealed those ideas and thoughts which were closest and understandable to them. Rather than reader-based prose, they created writing that reflected that they did not have a sense of audience awareness.

My traditional common sense approach to composition instruction did not appear to be helpful to my students' understanding of the processes that they needed to use in order to improve their writing. Consequently, there emerged a situation in which I was using a traditional formulaic approach to writing instruction although I was becoming increasingly aware that this approach appeared to hinder my students' ability to be aware of the relationship between themselves and the readers of their texts and to produce fluent, coherent, and error-free essays. In other words, this type of instruction was not providing my students with the opportunity to transfer what they learned in grammar and prose books into real writing and to engage them in the writing that illustrated their competence in using their voices to produce clear, sustained narratives or arguments.

My awareness of the contradictions and inconsistencies inherent in my approach to composition and grammar instruction was amplified by my knowledge that a good writing program was language-based and provided for students' right to their own language. The program which I emulated in my rhetoric and grammar textbooks did not provide a way to incorporate students' right to their own language.

The concept of students' right to their own language was and has been problematic for me. I have encountered many students who have never received formal instruction about the structure of the language. In my view, these students have been victims of a misinterpretation of the concept of students' right to their own language. Their ultraliberal teachers, in attempting to ensure that they do not negatively interfere with a student's dialect, have decided not to provide them with any knowledge of the formal structure of the English language. Thus, these students have gone through twelve years of the school system without formally learning the language necessary for competence in SWE. They have been victims of miseducation.

Students' right to their own language meant, for me, that in teaching students about the structure of SWE, I had a responsibility to validate both SWE and students' own language/dialect. The dilemma posed by the issues associated with incorporating the concept of students' right to their own language was addressed for me when I began to participate in the Medgar Evers College Language Symposia. These symposia offered theory, research, and pedagogy for language instruction and were a turning point for me with respect to English Studies.

The Medgar Evers Language Symposia were based on the premise that students in our college came from linguistically and culturally diverse backgrounds, and that a language instruction program should build on these diverse backgrounds. Therefore, the symposia provided opportunities for educators and researchers from applied linguistics, sociolinguistics, pyscholinguistics, reading, ESL, and composition to come together in order to discuss theory and pedagogy for addressing the needs of linguistically diverse students. A corollary to the symposia was the development of an English as a Standard Dialect Program (ESD) at Medgar Evers. The ESD Program was based on the premise that SWE should be taught as a second dialect. During my second year of teaching, I was given an ESD class. The class met for nine hours per week and using a text designed for ESL instruction, along with various readings and contrastive analysis techniques, I established a learning environment where my students and I could engage in the study of the processes of reading, writing, listening, and speaking. This approach to language instruction and my growing awareness of the need to continually create meaningful reading and writing situations helped me revitalize my approach to teaching English Studies. I began to resolve the contradictions between what I intuitively knew about language learning and how and what I taught my students. I began to teach only those rules which would assist students in understanding that they were acquiring a second dialect and that the purpose of the acquisition of a second dialect was to provide them with the language competencies that would enable them to manipulate the language system.

My students began to develop an awareness of language. They read excerpts from Malcolm X's autobiography, Frederick Douglass's *Narrative of the Life of a Slave* (1968), and Alice Walker's *The Color Purple* (1982). They listened to tapes about the need to acquire two dialects. They read essays on the nature of literacy, language, and ESD. They role-played and switched dialects. They began to listen to and analyze their dialects and to create skits, narratives, and expository essays which incorporated their range of dialects. My students became a community of language learners who began to develop an ear for how they used language and who shared their writing and critiqued their peers' texts. Many have come back to me over the years and have commented on how they have become more aware of their own dialect as well as of the dialects of their family members and peers.

Although the dilemma posed by the problem of how to incorporate students' right to their own language was addressed as a result of my experiences in the symposia and in the ESD course, I was still faced with the dilemma of how to maintain the balance between process and product; that is, how to negotiate between students' right to their own language and students' need to draw upon their knowledge about the structure of English in order to become competent writers of SWE. My concerns with my ESD course, basic writing and composition courses, and College English course lay in ensuring that my teaching created a balance which respected students' dialects, engaged them in the writing process, and provided them with strategies for resolving syntactical and grammatical problems in their writing. I wanted to encourage students in all my courses to continue to take risks and to experiment with ways to manipulate language, but I was anxious about the possibility that very few of my students would satisfy their exit writing requirements (students' writing errors were counted and points were deducted for specific kinds of errors). I was using a language-based writing program which drew from my students' experiences and backgrounds, but my students were evaluated by a skills-based program which was imposed upon them. Added to this was the silent pressure that, as an African American teacher, I was expected to accomplish for my students what white teachers had failed to do. I pondered how I could continue to create exciting language-based classrooms and still ensure that my students exited their courses. I had not yet reached the point where I was confident that my student-centered language approaches to learning were working.

George Kelly (1963) posits that as active participants in this society, we face situations which require us to take certain kinds of risks. There are those who take elaborative risks and those who take restrictive risks, risks which are safe. As I continued to search for ways to resolve the conflicts I found myself faced with, I began taking elaborative risks. I wanted change and I realized that change would not occur unless I set up a situation that would ensure major change or risk-taking. Thus, increasingly confident that growth only occurs with risks, the first big risk I took involved a decision to omit a grammar text in my classroom.

Rather than use a traditional text that included grammar and student models of writing, I chose to use Ken Macrorie's *Telling Writing* (1980), and I supplemented this text with excerpts from Peter Elbow's *Writing without Teachers* (1973). This experiment, another turning point in my teaching odyssey, helped me to realize that my students could improve their writing if they were treated like writers and were provided with strategies that would enable them to focus on their ideas rather than on isolated workbook exercises that emphasized the correcting of grammatical and syntactical errors. I realized that I did not have to be bound to a grammar text, and that I could individualize writing instruction and teach students grammar by providing them with techniques derived from transformational grammar and second language acquisition.

The second risk I took was more of a challenge than a risk. The English faculty in my department were committed to using an evaluation scheme that was the antithesis of a holistic approach to language study. I dramatized the inappropriateness of this evaluation scheme by asking the English faculty to grade several essays using this evaluation scheme. The result was that there was a wide range of scores for each paper. Consequently, the faculty agreed to constitute a committee that would redesign the evaluation criteria used to exit students from their English courses. We developed a writing evaluation scale that was based on primary trait scoring. This change in writing assessment, along with the change with respect to grammar instruction, helped me to bridge the gap between theory and pedagogy in my English classes. These changes were another step for me in the creation of a unified whole.

My odyssey towards the creation of a unified whole of which I am the center ends with my use of an uncommon sense approach in my College English classroom. After serving as a discussion leader at an NCTE Summer Institute for Teachers of Literature, I was motivated to use Joseph Conrad's *Heart of Darkness* (1920), a text on the reading list of the institute. I decided to use this text in my second-level College English class and to present students with an historical and sociological framework for reading it. The selection of this text was particularly problematic for me, for I was disturbed by the racist language and the depiction of the Africans, and I expected that my students would have similar reactions; however, my experience at the institute had provided me with an opportunity to read Chinua Achebe's critical essay (1990), which adequately expressed my sentiments about the novel and offered me a way to teach the novel from the perspective of the "other." During my undergraduate education, I had studied the novel from a Western perspective and although I was angry at what I saw as blatant examples of racism, I had not been able to articulate this, nor had I been encouraged to express my views.

Given my reading experiences and sentiments about *Heart of Darkness*, my embarkation on the teaching of this "controversial" novel to my African American and Caribbean students was guarded.

As I suspected, my students initially questioned the assigning of a novel which depicted so many negative images of Africans. In addressing this issue, we discussed the literary qualities of the novel and the historical and sociological factors that contribute to the issue of canonization. We also discussed censorship and the importance of providing multiple perspectives for reading and interpreting fictional and nonfictional texts.

My classroom came alive as students worked in groups to share responses, formulate interpretations, and debate their support of various critiques of the novel. Most indicated that they had found the text difficult and offensive, but after reading, critiquing, and arguing their views, they found the experience very challenging. Surprisingly, most believed it was important to read the novel because it presented a powerful illustration of how a writer could use language to mesmerize his readers and to depict the cruelties of colonialism and racism. In addition to reading the novel, students viewed the film *Apocalypse Now* (1979), a modern interpretation of *Heart of Darkness.*

The reading of the novel and the viewing of the film engaged my students and helped them to understand the value of reading and rereading, of reading "closely with a vengeance" (a term used by Steve Lynn to characterize the reading of the deconstructive critics). My students revised aspects of the novel and rewrote parts of the plot from the perspectives of the least privileged characters. They created skits which highlighted the themes suggested in the novel, and they analyzed the ways in which the colonialism depicted in *Heart of Darkness* and the imperialism depicted in *Apocalypse Now* were related. My students' readings revealed that literature not only afforded them the opportunity to critique colonialism, expose racism, and reveal humankind's capacity for evil, but illustrated the factors that set these forces in motion. The teaching of this novel resolved another dilemma for me: how to include literature which was regarded as classic but offensive to those who were objects rather than subjects of the text. Moreover, the study of this novel from a non-Western perspective afforded students the opportunity to become more critical readers of this text and various other texts.

Since that semester, I have continued to teach the text to various groups of students: homogeneous white working-class groups and multiethnic groups. In these cases, I have often been the minority in a class predominantly composed of Italian and Irish students. Unlike my African American and Caribbean students, these students have not tended to be offended by the racism inherent in the text and have complained only about Conrad's style and vocabulary. Their inability to see the racism has prevented them from questioning why I would use this novel in an English class. However, upon reading the critical essays and engaging in thorough discussions of the text, they have become more sensitive to the issues of race in the novel and have approached the study of it with a purpose. They have learned to read the text closely and to analyze their responses to it. This experience has reflected for me what teaching and learning should strive for: providing students with opportunities to acquire knowledge in an active, productive, and critical way.

What has emerged for me as I have engaged in the teaching of English Studies over the last two decades is the tacit knowledge that the hurdles, obstacles, and journeys along my path have been my strengths rather than my weaknesses, for they have enabled me to see that the teaching/learning process is an evolving one, is a continual search for creating knowledge and finding a unified whole. To be fortified with the realization that I am in a position to symbolize many collective voices of the African American teacher/scholar, that I am a role model, that I view the teaching/learning process as representative of what one of my professional organizations refers to as Language Educators Applying Reflective Action Now (LEARN) has affirmed the importance of sharing my experiences as a teacher/scholar of English. To this end, I have presented papers and published articles related to my pedagogy and research on the teaching of English. Unfortunately, I have found a disproportion between the number of students of color and the number of teachers of color (Surprise). As in graduate school, at professional conferences I find myself representing the small minority of people of color in English Studies, and I find that many want to hear how I have addressed the educational needs of students of color, students whose numbers have rapidly increased across college campuses.

As an African American woman, mother, teacher, and researcher, I am in a position to serve both as a voice and role model for African American and non–African American students. I am always learning, always reading, and always writing, and I must continually search for ways in which my students can do the same. My experiences as a mother have constantly reminded me that young people and students can teach you much, that learning is a two-way process. I have used this knowledge to draw and learn from my experiences and the experiences of my students, to engage students in conflicts and stimulating discussion, to encourage students to examine their own and others' texts from different perspectives, and to take elaborative risks. This process has given me self-confidence and helped me to find a center and to connect those parcelled aspects of myself into a unified whole.

Works Cited

Achebe, Chinua. 1990. "An Image of Africa." *Joseph Conrad: Third World Perspectives,* ed. Robert D. Hamner. Washington: Three Continents Press: 119–29.

Apocalypse Now. 1979. Writer: John Milius. Director: Francis Ford Coppola. United Artists.

Bartlett, E. J. 1982. "Learning to Revise: Some Component Processes." *What Writers Know,* ed. Nystrand. New York: Academic Press: 345–63.

Conrad, Joseph. 1920. *Heart of Darkness,* ed. Robert Kimbrough. Reprint, New York: Norton. 1971.

Douglass, Frederick. 1845. *Narrative of the Life of Frederick Douglass, An American Slave.* Reprint, New York: New American Library, 1968.

Elbow, Peter. 1973. *Writing Without Teachers.* New York: Oxford University Press.

Flower, Linda. 1981. *Problem-Solving Strategies for Writing.* New York: Harcourt Brace Jovanovich.

Kelly, George A. 1963. *A Theory of Personality: The Psychology of Personal Constructs.* New York: Norton.

Lynn, Steven. 1990. "A Passage Into Critical Theory." *College English* 52 (March): 258–71.

Macrorie, Ken. 1980. *Telling Writing.* 3d ed. Hasbrouck Heights, NJ: Hayden Book Co.

Mayher, John. 1990. *Uncommon Sense: Theoretical Practice in Language Education.* Portsmouth, NH: Boynton/Cook.

Moffett, James, and Betty Jane Wagner. 1976. *Student-Centered Language Arts and Reading, K–13.* 2d ed. Boston: Houghton Mifflin.

Shaughnessy, Mina. 1977. *Errors and Expectations: A Guide for the Teacher of Basic Writing.* New York: Oxford University Press.

"Students' Right to Their Own Language." 1974. *College Composition and Communication* 35 (fall).

Vygotsky, L. S. 1962. *Thought and Language.* Cambridge, MA: MIT Press.

Walker, Alice. 1982. *The Color Purple.* New York: Harcourt Brace Jovanovich.

X, Malcolm, with the assistance of Alex Haley. 1965. *The Autobiography of Malcolm X.* New York: Ballantine.

19 On English Teaching as Poetry, *or*, Samuel T., You'll Never Know What Organic Unity Did for Me

Michael L. Angelotti
University of Oklahoma

I would guess that at least half of the members of NCTE might begin a retrospective essay with "the last thing on my mind in college was becoming an English teacher." Nevertheless, that was the case with me. I mean, there was not one thought. I was *not* driven by a family teaching tradition or a charismatic high school English teacher or college professor who imbued me with a passion to save the youth of America through inspired literature, language, and composition teaching. It was more subtle than that. It happened in a way so deeply unconscious that I could not fight it, *could not* make a choice not to make English my life's work. I was an English teacher before I knew it. Oddly, although the inevitability of it began almost at birth, the fact of it happened overnight. Literally.

Being second generation Italian American had something to do with it. My mother insisted that I master American English and, to this day, I think that spoken Italian was forbidden within the walls of our home to ensure that I learned English well. It was foregone that I would go to college to become a doctor like Uncle Jinks or an engineer like Uncle Vic.

I liked to write stories as a child, so the family soon found room in our upstairs flat for a Royal portable typewriter, a small desk, a Webster's dictionary, and a world globe with raised topography—scarce dollars spent for precious gifts whose progeny continue to be the staples of my home office. Those gifts and a considerable appetite for reading and adventuring by slipping away to the Pennsylvania woods, the Erie public docks, or anywhere that had a high fence around it, compose the largest part of my childhood quilt.

High school, for the most part, is very fuzzy, although I do remember that the Kuder Preferential Inventory advised that I think seriously about a career as a forest ranger; that I never could get the damn doorbell to work on that first General Shop project; and that I really liked Miss Necci's radio commercial English project where the group of us invented Mother Murgatroid's Moisturized Meatballs and Sophocles Saturated Sopping Slop Spaghetti Sauce. I seldom made an "A" in English, although I was very good at helping others achieve that outcome.

College became an exercise in exploring majors while taking electives in creative writing, literature, and classical studies for relief. Finally, after four years I had more hours in English than anything else, finished my undergraduate work at Florida State with a B.A. in English and minors in business and psychology. Post facto, I decided that this whimsical mix might be an appealing combination to Miami corporations seeking a bright, young executive trainee bent on earning his first million by age twenty-five.

While I was deep into group insurance, I came upon an advertisement for an English teaching position at a local military academy— only requirement, a degree in English. On a Friday I interviewed and was offered the job on the spot. Stunned, my first thoughts were: 1) I have a wife and a baby, 2) this has to be better than sales, and 3) how hard could teaching be anyway?

On the following Monday, I taught (fought?) my first four ninth-grade English classes. I discovered how hard teaching could be. There was no mentor, no introduction, just me and them. My teaching resources were the olive brown U.S. Military Academy (USMA) *manual* on grammar and a Harcourt Brace *Adventures in Literature* anthology. The texts really did not matter because there was not one doubt in my mind that I could teach.

I approached the teaching problem logically. The textbooks were the curriculum: two days USMA, three days Harcourt Brace. My strategy was to stay at least a page ahead of the students. We started with page one, did all the exercises, and worked as much of each book as we could by the middle of May. My job was to help them understand text. We didn't finish either book. We did finish the year together. I finally learned school grammar and the differences between tone, mood, and atmosphere. I want to think that I did not injure them too badly, that they learned something as well.

Actually, my recollection is that mutual survival motivated us to work to some mutually beneficial end. We had good conversations about grammar and literature, probably a function of learning text together and my own natural curiosity about kids. On the other side, I am sure that I have repressed the ugly moments, when I learned through painful trial and error. In any event, my sense is that we did learn together. Intuitively, I did do some things right.

I mainly remember what that year did for me. I found that I was comfortable in the classroom with all kinds of kids, that teaching was learning on both sides of the desk, and that it was a tough, gut-wrenching, unpredictable, frustrating, euphoric business. By the time the year ended, I was thinking seriously about English teaching as a career. And so it was that in the summer of 1963, my wife, infant daughter, and I journeyed back to Florida State so that Dad could go after a master's degree in English education.

The first thing that Dwight Burton, Roy O'Donnell, John Simmons and a host of doctoral students made me aware of was how much I needed an education in methodology. I came to know that intuition can only take you so far in teaching. Florida State University was exactly the right place for me to be at that time of need: The Dartmouth aftermath was exploding, a weird guy named James Moffett was talking about a "universe of discourse" (1968), Noam Chomsky (1957) was catching fire, reader response was reigniting, and adolescent literature was smoldering throughout the *Swiftwater* (Annixter 1950) underbrush. I learned T-units from Kellogg Hunt (1965) and the effectiveness of writer response groups from James McCrimmon (1963). Also, the campus laboratory school was in need of a secondary English teacher. Clearly, I was a pawn of the Fates—a willing pawn, had I known what they had in mind.

With all that has come to be the seminal underpinning of constructivism swirling about me, the most important learning for me may have come in the graduate classes of one of my English department professors, James Goodman; for it was there that I stumbled into romanticism, into Wordsworth's "Preface" to his *Lyrical Ballads* (1802), into Coleridge's *Biographia Literaria* (1817), into the romantic theory of organic unity. That theory of universal holism helped me realize what unconsciously I believed. There is harmony in even the most discordant elements. The harmony exists naturally. It is the human being who must reconcile the apparent opposites. It pulled together crawling through a wild blackberry thicket as a ten-year-old to follow a rabbit trail and hunting and pecking on my first typewriter to discover story after story. It allowed me to make sense of Noam Chomsky's transformational grammar, Louise Rosenblatt's transactionalism (1938), John Dixon's processes of language (1967), and Dwight Burton's imaginative entry (1970). The wanderlust of youth continued into adulthood, only the landscape had changed. My growth from seed to flower was inevitable.

Further, given this experiential dynamic, this life dynamic, I was able to understand without translation what came later: Kenneth Goodman's (1980) psycholinguistic approach to understanding reading as process, everyone's schema theories, and process writing—as though these holistic innovations were natural extensions of my own romantic thought. Indeed, I embraced them because they agreed with *me.* After all, at base, holism and organic unity are the same. In Chomsky/Goodman/Dixon/Rosenblattian terms, I was able to bring meaning to those transformational, psycholinguistic, experiential, transactional, and constructivistic texts because of relevant prior experiences (including acquisition of appropriate transformational rules needed to effectively interpret uttered and written surface structures, of course).

Out of all this evolved a kind of professional identity linked to young adult literature and writing. My dissertation explored relationships between literary response and characteristics of literature read, leading me to my first university faculty position in 1976 teaching English education and secondary reading courses at Texas Tech. Now I was able to translate my life experience, twelve years of teaching young adults, and my graduate work into a profession. I looked forward to a life of teaching, writing articles and books, and the ultimate paid employment: tenured full professor. Then, I thought, with my pipe and elbow-patched corduroy sport jacket, I would write the great American methods book and have the power to spend three or four years doing it. I didn't count on spending an evening with Stephen Dunning at the 1977 Conference on English Education in Knoxville.

I wandered into a reading session hosted by Steve in his suite for any conference member interested in sharing poetry. As I described it in the fall 1989 issue of *Oregon English*, it went something like this:

> About ten people showed up, including Malcom Glass the poet. I, on impulse, decided it was time to come out of the closet and go public with my poetry. I was quiet through the other readings, unsure of what to say, maybe hoping that they would go easier on me if I did not comment on their work. My time came and I was shaky, dry of mouth, classically anxious. My first poem was one about my grandmother, and I buried my eyes in the text, mumbling throughout. Steve made the first

comment, something positive about the last line, then said he would like to hear it again, but read a bit louder this time. I recognized the cue, caught myself doing all of the negative things I tried to teach my students not to do when oral reading. I read a little better. The group nurtured me through a third and fourth reading, praising word choices, suggesting alternatives. In the end I knew that I had not presented well and had not written very good poems, but I was confident that I could make them better and felt good about the experience. My sense is that it was the nurturing that did it. (37)

Here, in retrospect, do I notice how the seemingly insignificant becomes the significant, and the significant, relatively insignificant. That small poetry experience in Knoxville would connect to a highway blink called Junction, Texas, and my right brain would light up like a hill country dance hall. I did the professional things well: taught, published, served (I also bought several sport coats and had the elbows patched, but I never could get the hang of pipe smoking). Tenure and full professor came on time. At the risk of banishment for blasphemy, I now classify these accomplishments "relatively insignificant," for even then there existed the slight uneasiness, the faint shadow of dissatisfaction, the hue of incompleteness enveloping this professional success. The wanderlust I would not recognize remained, only gently nudging, but always there.

And so it was that during the late seventies when my professional eye was focused on tenure and promotion, I agreed to teach a graduate reading course at the Texas Tech Junction campus, frankly, to earn summer money. And the first afternoon there I was awestruck and became complete. You have to understand something about Junction. It is primarily a biological research center carved out of the Texas Hill Country near San Antonio. It also provides graduate work in the fine arts for Texas teachers. In summer it is mainly populated by water colorists, photographers, jewelry makers, and potters: artsy types. The campus itself, divided by a branch of the Llano River, is one-half developed, one-half natural. My first afternoon there I was drawn to the woods. Alone in a small clearing, as I absorbed the natural beauty of the place, I had the sensation of time collapsing, taking me back to my boyhood in the Pennsylvania woods. Those childhood eyes became my eyes. I supposed that I had experienced something like an epiphany, that for a moment I had been with Wordsworth, Shelley, and Keats. I knew then what was missing. I had not been writing, not real writing. The writing passion of my youth, suppressed by too much wrong-brained activity, returned.

Also in the summer of 1979, the Rotary Club of Junction invited me to lunch to give a talk on reading. I was flattered, not thinking that a town of two thousand or so might soon get desperate for a luncheon speaker every week. Nevertheless, like a good speaker I researched my audience and discovered that they mainly were ranchers experiencing a drought and frustrated by apple trees dying by the orchard. Intuition told me that a talk on psycholinguistics and reading wouldn't sit too well with those folks. The night before the talk I pondered late what to do. Just when I nearly convinced myself to graciously bow out of the engagement, inspiration struck. I mean it. Inspiration. All that I had seen and felt about the natural wonder of that place poured out, non-stop, page after page, straight Whitmanesque poetry. I choked up, tears dampened the yellow legal pad. I was moved by my own writing. It was good. I was saved. I would talk to them about themselves. But would they respond to poetry? Ranchers?

When I walked in the next day, I tried to be professorial, poet-like. Ranchers eyeballed me, whispered things. I overheard one say (this is the truth, I swear it), "I hope this guy don't read any of those poems, like that last professor. I about went to sleep." But once again, the Fates and the Muses were on my side. For some reason I clicked with the ranchers. I was introduced (I never told the guy I was going to read poetry). A lively repartee followed the introduction. Honest laughs. Then it was time. The Junction Rotary Club still expected a professional talk on reading. I told the ranchers I was going to read a *piece*. That word substituted for "poem" in my brain a split second before I spoke it, and I knew why it did. I told them I had written it especially for them. I spoke my title "Reading the Hill Country Around Junction, Texas." I noticed a few wry smiles. Heard a chuckle or two. Some suspected that they were being had. I read the poem and nearly choked up again in places. They could tell. They were dead silent. Moved. Transfixed. I ended. They gave me a standing ovation. I told them about my trick. They laughed.

The editor of the *Junction Eagle* was there and asked if he could publish my "piece" in the next edition of his weekly. So there it was, what an experience. My first public reading and a standing ovation. My first real poem and a publication (yes, it *is* on my resume and it *did* count for tenure).

Poetry, it turned out, was my natural form. I experienced, understood Wordsworth's sense of poem as emotion recollected in tranquility. Ultimately, I became the Junction campus writer in residence, and my annual Junction writing workshop and Rotary talk became the peak experiences of the year for me during those Texas Tech years. Poetry became part of my publications trail and creative writing a part of my professional repertoire. The Knoxville experience translated into the first "Fountain of the Muse" at the 1979 Kansas City NCTE and I have been chairing the session ever since. Erie, Pennsylvania connected to Knoxville, Tennessee connected to Junction, Texas. I finally had a completed circuit. If only my old shop teacher could have been there to hear it ring.

And now that the pieces are in place for the moment, that I am whole, that I have laid bare the professional influences on my life to date and my philosophy as an English educator, what effects on teaching? On professional writing?

On teaching, I think of my undergraduate methods course, as example. Students begin the semester with a read-response of Natalie Goldberg's *Writing Down the Bones* (1986), working and commenting on the personal writing exercises through the semester. I would describe *Bones* as a conversation between a successful writer and her readers about how to find the writer within, how to move writing from inside out, how to get words on the page and feel good about both process and product. Without proselytizing, Goldberg freely interplays writing theory and Buddhist philosophy. The result is romantic, holistic, and organic—a perfect book, in my view, for blossoming English teachers who often are intimidated by their own perceptions that they are expected to leave an English education initial certification program as powerful writers and teachers. In truth, they often have little sense of themselves as writers and, typically, little confidence in their abilities to teach writing. One piece of my course attempts to address these issues.

We begin the semester writing, finding a sense of authorship, discovering personal writing processes, exploring possibilities for teaching writing as personal expression and exploration as well as communication. In practice is an old adage, "know thyself," to which I add, "before you teach others." This process of discovering, knowing, translating to schooling, spills over into literature and response, language and use, whatever at the moment makes up the thing we call English teaching. I see it as a nurturing, growing, inside-out approach to becoming aware of oneself as learner and practitioner, then teacher. During the semester come classroom teachers who talk, listen, interact, and model; safe fieldwork with kids to test theory, mettle; experiences with current articles and books on teaching English; and wrestling matches with traditional and innovative practice. I throw out the challenges, facilitate, guide, inform, organize, evaluate, learn, and grade. To my mind, the whole process is organic, poetic—nurturing growth, always seeking passionate teachers for whom the blooms are unending as they reinvent themselves, seed to bloom to seed, each time the same, yet different. Always new.

And so, I am back to poetry. If I have succeeded in this narrative thus far, how poetry and life and teaching and my particular bent on the profession interplay, at once separable and whole, is evident. Striving for the poetic, philosophically, is all there is. It encompasses everything. More literally, writing poems keeps me sane, whole. It keeps me in touch with others who strive to write, particularly students reaching for poems, and the craft of composing poems. We wear each other's shoes and share the comfort and pain that goes with the wearing. In short, writing poems informs me of a catalog of moves to make when I sit down with a kid and his writing. In the broadest, maybe most enigmatic sense, writing poems is my window to life as poem, to English teaching as poem. It drives whatever I might do—even now, composing the thoughts behind these words. This essay as poem. It represents to me my life as the fundamental romantic metaphor of the seed and the flower—apparently discordant elements organically reconciled. The image returns of the little kid on hands and knees underneath the blackberry briar ignoring the pains of salty perspiration in thorn-inflicted scratches just to see what was there. Now I can see in that little piece the story of my life. The unity of it all makes perfect sense.

As with everyone, the person I have become, in part, goes back to how I lived my childhood. Somehow that childhood established the romantic ideal as basic to my persona—most particularly, the experiencing, the wanderlust, the love of nature, the wonderfully human abilities to soak it all in and continuously create marvelous cognitive concoctions. But I, and people like me, maybe all people in some way, *must* as children run off to the woods. There is not a choice for us. And no one takes us. No mother. No father. We run off. That is the thing. Having that impulse and making freedom and doing it. Where the push comes from I do not know. But it is there. Waiting. Always ready for the next blackberry patch.

Work Cited

Annixter, Paul. 1950. *Swiftwater.* New York: Wyn.

Burton, Dwight L. 1970. *Literature Study in the High School,* 3d ed. New York: Holt, Rinehart, and Winston.

Chomsky, Noam. 1957. *Syntactic Structures.* Gravenhage: Mouton.

Coleridge, Samuel Taylor. 1817. *Biographia Literaria.* Reprint, London: J. M. Dent, 1910.

Dixon, John. 1967. *Growth Through English: A Report Based on the Dartmouth Seminar 1966.* Reading, England: National Association for the Teaching of English.

Goldberg, Natalie. 1986. *Writing Down the Bones.* Boston: Random House.

Goodman, Kenneth S. 1980. *Linguistics, Psycholinguistics and the Teaching of Reading: An Annotated Bibliography.* 3d ed. Newark, DE: International Reading Association.

Hunt, Kellogg. 1965. *Grammatical Structures Written at Three Grade Levels.* Champaign, IL: NCTE.

McCrimmon, James McNab. 1963. *Writing With a Purpose,* 3d ed. Boston: Houghton Mifflin.

Moffett, James. 1968. *Teaching the Universe of Discourse.* Boston: Houghton Mifflin.

Rosenblatt, Louise. 1938. *Literature As Exploration.* New York: Appleton-Century.

Wordsworth, William. 1802. "Preface to *Lyrical Ballads.*" Reprint, ed. W. J. B. Owens. Copenhagen: Rosenkilde and Bagger, 1957.

VI Professional Relationships

Often my brightest students are told by certain members of the English department that they are too bright to become teachers.

Hal Foster

20 Learning to Love Being a Second-Class Citizen

W. Ross Winterowd
University of Southern California

Notes on (or in) the Margin

My marginalized position within my own department and within the establishment (e.g., MLA) comes about through what I call "English-department humanities": the attitudes, values, practices, and epistemology that resulted in the exaltation of the "imaginative" and the degradation of the "nonimaginative," that is, the exaltation of poems, narrative fictions, and drama and the degradation of narrative nonfiction (autobiographies, biographies, and histories) and the marginalization of essays; the concomitant exaltation of "creative" writing and the degradation of composition; the exaltation of what I call "literary technology" and the degradation of such humane endeavors as scholarship that probes the uses of literature among your nonacademic friends and mine or that concerns itself with teaching; and the high value placed on theory and the degradation of practice. With an image, I want to illustrate what I mean by the paradox of English-department humanities. It is the week between Christmas and New Year's Eve. In a hotel (the Americana in New York, the Palmer House in Chicago, and the Hilton in San Francisco), the year's work in English-department humanities culminates. Scholars solemnly (and somnolently) read papers; audiences nod (affirmatively or soporifically); the lobby bubbles with literary talk; the publishers pour, and the conventioneers libate. But, then, you know the scene as well as I do. The convention ends. And, paradoxically, nothing that your neighbors or mine would find important or interesting has transpired. We realize that the work *most* valued by literary scholars has little or no bearing on the human condition.

And, sadly, any work that purported to have "uses" would be devalued—because two roads diverged in an agora many centuries ago. As M. H. Abrams, among others, has pointed out, Aristotle took one road and Plato the other. The empirical tradition, to which I belong, goes back to Aristotle: the materials of art are "out there," and art imitates, reproduces, mirrors. The transcendental tradition of English-department humanities stems from Plato through Plotinus, Coleridge, Shelley, Emerson, Richards, Krieger, and others: the objects of art are "Ideas or forms which are perhaps approachable by way of the world of sense, but are ultimately transempirical, maintaining an independent existence in their own ideal space, and available only to the eye of the [sensitive] mind [of the person with good taste]" (1953, 36).

The end of the Platonic road is the almost unbearably sad Nietzschean world, in which the *Übermensch* looks disgustedly at the agora, now populated by poseurs and noxious flies.

> Where solitude ceases, there the market-place begins; and where the market-place begins, the uproar of the great actors and the buzzing of the poisonous flies. . . . The people have little idea of greatness, that is to say: creativeness. . . . A truth that penetrates only sensitive ears [the actor, the poseur] calls a lie and a thing of nothing. Truly, he believes only in gods who make a great noise in the world. (1896, 78)

Before the late seventeenth and early eighteenth centuries, the rhetorician-humanist conversed in the agora and spoke in the Senate; after this period, the humanist (for *he* was no longer a rhetorician) pondered alone, withdrawing from the parlor to his upstairs retreat (leaving the dirty dishes, the soiled linen, and the sooty stoves to Mary and Sarah and Dorothy).

The dichotomies "creative writing–composition," "imaginative literature–nonfiction prose," and "literary theory–any application (e.g., pedagogy)" result from (a) a destructive epistemology, (b) institutional rigidity, and (c) political atavism; I am necessarily a second-class citizen in *my* English Department and *the* English Department, for the foundational English-department epistemology is Romantic, sometimes alembicated and attenuated, but often idealistically pure. From Coleridge to Krieger, the Romantic project has attempted to create and maintain, removed from the agora, a special place for literature, the sensitive plant protected by English-department minions from the hobnails and tank-treads of rhetoric.

A rhetorician, of course, takes literature to be a robust growth, able to flourish in the suburbs and the ghetto; a rhetorician believes that literature is good for people and thus concerns him- or herself with its uses in the schools and among "common readers." With

Kenneth Burke, a rhetorician is quite likely to view literature as equipment for living.

However, institutions are rigid, and none more so than the English department and the literary establishment. Paradoxically, the "rebels" (e.g., Terry Eagleton and Gerald Graff) with their manifestoes (e.g., *Literary Theory* and *Professing Literature*) simply stoke the fires that burn so merrily in the Palmer House, the Americana, or the Hilton between December 25 and January 1 and flicker out on the last day of the convention. Controversy (even subversion) only provides more fuel for the panels and more fodder for the insatiable "literary" journals, without affecting the institution. It is as if Marx only gave the czar's council something new to argue about.

Why, after all, should the institution change since in its atavism it is invulnerable? As every university president and every member of every board of trustees knows, you can't have a great university without at least a respectable English department, and the *institutional* measure of an English department finally comes down to these questions: How many pages of literary scholarship does the faculty produce? On how many scholarly panels do faculty members appear as *speakers*, to *read* the papers and chapters of books before publication? Within the establishment, no English department gains credit because its faculty brought the experience (and the presumed salubrious effects) of literature to a nonliterary group (e.g., public school students, members of labor unions, senior citizens); no English department is known for its "noncreative" writing program; no English department is lauded for preparing teachers of literature and writing. No English department that I'm aware of makes room for those who want to bring literature to nonliterary groups, build powerful composition programs, and prepare *teachers* of literature and writing. In other words, literature might well have uses (to make humans more humane, to give them pleasure, to provide insights, to make people less violent and more loving), and I think that it does have such uses, but the political atavism of the English Department and the literary establishment discourages faculty from concern with "applications." And here I could, with a few flicks of my computer keys, assemble a lengthy chrestomathy of statements such as this archetypical one from Frye's *Anatomy of Criticism*:

> In literature, questions of fact or truth are subordinated to the primary literary aim of producing a structure of words for its own sake, and the sign values of symbols are subordinated to

their importance as a structure of interconnecting motifs. Wherever we have an autonomous verbal structure of this kind, we have literature. Wherever this autonomous structure is lacking, we have language, words used instrumentally to help human consciousness do or understand something else. (1971, 74)

As evidence of institutional rigidity and political atavism, consider the status of composition/rhetoric in virtually every English department in the United States. It is simply a fact that composition/rhetoric is now (and has been for some time) an important and lively part of the discipline that we call "English." That being the case, *the* English Department has the obligation to prepare students to understand the questions that derive from this field. The medical student, even though his or her goal is to specialize in, say, proctology, must understand the general principles of cardiology because that field is essential to medicine. The graduate student in English, whatever his or her area of specialization, must understand the general principles of composition/rhetoric because that field is essential to English.

It is unthinkable that we would certify a doctoral candidate who was absolutely unaware of issues in literary theory and history, and it is equally outrageous to certify a person who knows very little, if anything, about the history of composition/rhetoric and the issues that are currently debated in the field. Nonetheless, a rigid and politically atavistic establishment is impervious to arguments that would redefine "English" to include composition/rhetoric. (I was going to say "*actively resists* arguments that would redefine 'English,'" but that would be like saying that Hoover Dam actively resists Lake Mead.)

The Quest for Purity

"Buildings I have designed?" asks the testy professor of architecture. "I don't design buildings; I study the theory of buildings and their history."

"Patients?" says the puzzled med. school professor. "I'm concerned with advancing our knowledge of medicine, not with the application of this knowledge to people."

"Bridges and highways?" The professor of civil engineering scratches his left ear and then says, "I'm a theoretician. I'm not concerned with actual structures."

Poised and incisive, if perhaps just a bit smug, the English professor assures his colleagues that he *is* concerned with the "applications" of his discipline, bringing literature and literacy to the members of his society. "After all," he says, "don't I teach an under-graduate introduction to lit every semester? And don't I require two papers in every class that I teach? By the way, while I'm on the subject: students are becoming progressively more illiterate. The public schools just aren't doing their job. You should see the number of errors—misspellings, comma faults, agreement problems—on the papers that I receive."

Unlike architecture, medicine, and engineering (not to mention accounting, education, sociology, and law), English *is*, obviously, an applied discipline!

A Fable

The following story is, as two of its main characters said in *Theory of Literature*, "substantively beautiful and adjectivally true (i.e., doesn't conflict with truth)" (Wellek and Warren 1956, 34).

Once upon a mellow, golden October afternoon, René Wellek, Austin Warren, and I were sipping sherry and chatting about our profession. "Ah," sighed Austin, the gentle melancholy of the waning year (nearly beyond the season of mellow fruitfulness, yet still fecund and odoriferous, ripe apples hanging, yet unplucked) sounding in his voice, "ah, I just found out that the Physics Department is getting an eight percent increase in salaries this year. That's twice the amount we're getting in English. It's a goddamn shame!"

René raised his glass of sherry to the autumnal light radiating through the open window, took a pensive sip, set the glass back on the table, and said, "Ummh! Ate lunch today with a couple of philosophers. What an arrogant bunch! They told me that only tautological and empirically verifiable statements make sense. Those jerks would simply abolish esthetics and poetics."

Austin, warming to the occasion, drained his glass in two gulps, refilled it, and shoved the bottle across the table to René and me. "Yeh, and that psychology bunch—riding high with their stimulus-response crap. It makes me sick!"

Diffidently I summarized: "In other words, the philosophers and the social scientists have devalued literary knowledge. And the powers that be seem to think science is worth more than literature."

René: "Right on! They're a real bunch of barbarians."

Austin: "See, we get no respect."

René: "Lemme tell ya this. Literary scholarship has its own valid methods which are not always those of the natural sciences but are nonetheless intellectual methods"(1956, 16).

Austin: "Amen to that, pal. I've got a great idea. Let's write a book on the theory of literature. We'll show these philistines that literary scholarship is just as hard-assed as any other discipline."

René (as he uncorks the second bottle of Sandeman's): "Yeh, but they'll never read the book."

Austin: "Okay, so we'll prove to ourselves that we're just as good as that other bunch." And thus was founded the English-Department elite, the members of which (whom?) even at this moment (11:10 a.m., Monday, Sept. 28, 1992) are purchasing economy tickets to New York and are trying to find roommates to share expenses at the MLA headquarters hotel.

Notice the importance of the role that I played in this drama. Granted, my speaking part was limited to twenty-seven words, but how could the agon have played itself out *sans moi*, the compositionist? As Aristotle explained in his theory of comedy, without an underclass, there can be no elite.

Three Moments in a Career

I

My first encounter with English-department humanities was in 1948 during the first semester of my freshman year at the University of Nevada. I had read voraciously during high school: for example, all of Zane Gray; Forester's Hornblower series; *Of Human Bondage*; a great deal of Mark Twain; *Mutiny on the Bounty*; much of Wordsworth, Coleridge, Keats, Shelley, and Byron; virtually all of Robert Service; Fitzgerald's *Rubaiyat*; *The Three Musketeers*; quite a bit of Shakespeare; Dorothy Parker's *Enough Rope* . . . and I could go on and on. But my personal canon did not prepare me for the required texts in freshman composition: *Portrait of the Artist as a Young Man, Brave New World*, and T. S. Eliot's *Collected Poems, 1909–1935*. My instructor, fresh from defending her dissertation at Yale, very soon conveyed to me and, I suppose, to my classmates that our literary tastes sucked and that she had come to bring standards and culture to Reno and all of Nevada. Our first assignment was to write a ballad!

II

I was teaching composition while working on my doctorate in English at the University of Utah. By this time, I had been corrupted (by the influence of A. R. Kitzhaber at Kansas University, by *The Rhetoric of Fiction*, by my discovery of Kenneth Burke, by my growing interest in reading and writing in the agora), but no courses related even vaguely to the direction in which I had begun to hope my career would develop, and the faculty members simply disdained composition, freshman or otherwise. The director of freshman writing, wife of a senior professor of English, was a perfectly wonderful lady, doing everything she could to make our job easier and to improve the quality of instruction; all of us loved her. The composition staff met every Friday for brown-bag lunches, during which we discussed such matters as catching plagiarists, encouraging students to hand in more legible papers, overcoming the ever-present comma fault, and the virtues and limitations of casebooks as opposed to library research. The director always brought home-baked cake, cookies, or brownies.

III

The Los Angeles riots exploded, and Norma and I, safe in our Orange County refuge from The Inner City, watched TV in horror as the fires flared, the bricks flew, the glass shattered, the mobs kicked and pummeled, the looters looted, and the police chief alibied. Within six days, Mayor Bradley, President Bush, Vice President Quayle, Bill Clinton, Albert Gore, the Reverend Al Sharpton, the Los Angeles Police Department, the California National Guard, the California Highway Patrol, the FBI, and various other spiritual and civic leaders, organizations, governmental agencies, street gangs, and the American Red Cross had restored order and made it safe for me to drive the freeways to the central city, location of the University of Southern California.

In the English Department conference room and up and down the corridors of Taper Hall of Humanities, the talk was of the riot. I learned that a number of my colleagues had, admirably, shouldered brooms and shovels and marched off to join their fellow citizens in the cleanup. The consensus was that the University should establish closer ties with the community around it and should devote some of its resources to making Los Angeles a better place for all.

The week after the riots, at a meeting of English Department faculty, my colleagues waited patiently while I argued that we needed badly to develop a program for preparing teachers for the public schools and to hire someone in English education. After I had said my piece, the discussion became enthusiastically animated, as various members of the faculty advanced their notions about faculty that we would need for the future. The list that developed included a specialist in marginal writers, such as Djuna Barnes and James Branch Cabell; a Miltonist; a creative writer.

The Art and Craft of Rhetoric; or, Why I Disagree with Almost Everyone Nowadays

It seems to me that almost everyone nowadays misconstrues the art and craft of rhetoric, their theory and practice being driven by various ideologies and the longing for status within the institution that historical circumstances have made their professional home. However, in the following excursion, I want to be playful, stressing cooperation and identification rather than competition and division, yet to develop my argument, I must disagree with almost everyone. Imagine a group of us—you, Patricia Harkin, John Schilb, Jim Berlin, Patricia Bizzell, and Susan Jarratt—at a table in the lounge of a hotel where a CCCC convention is being held. It's about 9:30 p.m., and the day's meetings have ended. We order libations,[1] and I mumble a few words that sum up the thinking I've done as I've listened to the panels that my co-imbibers were on: "Jeez, Pat Harkin, you and John want to relocate composition, removing it from history and the traditions of rhetoric, its art. And, Jim, you, Pat Bizzell, and Susan want to substitute ideology for rhetoric." Well, these few words create a debate that lasts until after midnight. (Jim and I each finish three beers, and Susan Jarratt gets through three glasses of white wine.) By 12:45 we are all exhausted, but we agree to meet the next morning for breakfast so that we can carry on with the discussion.

Now your task, as reader, becomes difficult, for in the following I report only my side of the argument; you must provide the responses for Harkin, Schilb, Berlin, Bizzell, and Jarrat.

"You know," I say, "Hirsch first made the fatal error in *The Philosophy of Composition* (1977): composition is not a branch of rhetoric. Pat and John you bring us up to date with your Big Mistake. In your introduction to *Contending with Words*, you say that "composition itself is not 'an autonomous discipline' since it derives its methodology from diverse fields (such as behavioral psychology, linguistics, history, and even biology)." And with that, I make no further effort to quote from the drama based on real-life characters and an event that did not occur, but well might have, but I do refer you to Bakhtin, who will tell you that my "voice" is necessarily dialogic.

Harkin and Schilb present greater difficulties than Hirsch, who would now disown his claim that because the goal of composition should be to teach students to write with the greatest "relative readability," composition and rhetoric are separate disciplines (1977, 140). One could point out, for instance, that style is one of the traditional departments of rhetoric and that Hirsch has simply reduced rhetoric to style (or craft narrowly conceived) and by lopping off invention and arrangement (as well as memory and delivery, which don't have much to do with writing anyway) has done away with art. In any case, one assumes that Hirsch would now say composition has a cultural as well as a stylistic element (1987), though he has not, so far as I know, recommitted himself about the relationship between composition and rhetoric.

The "practical" consequences of removing composition from rhetoric will be dire. One hardly needs a history of literature to know that in the nineteenth century the canon was split, so that poems, stories, dramas ("imaginative" literature) gained transcendent value and such genres as autobiography, biography, history, essays, and letters (what I have called "other" literature) became devalued, even debased, within the establishment. And one hardly needs advanced mathematics to work out this equation: with the debasement of the "other" literature, came the debasement of composition. Elsewhere I have told the story of composition's debasement (Winterowd 1994); my point now is that willfully moving composition from rhetoric will further debase it. One can envision an efficient, utilitarian version of composition, which would have its advantages: the craft of strictly utilitarian writing (e.g., business letters, scientific reports) would gain value; teaching students to produce relatively readable prose (Hirsch 1987, 85–89) would be encouraged—and I am not being coy when I say that I greatly value the utilitarian and, like any good craftsperson, enjoy the work itself and take pride in the products. The loss to composition will be its primary claim to the humanist tradition. Even more important: the split between composition and "creative" writing diminishes both areas; we should have writing programs, not "creative" writing for the elect and composition for those plodding others.

When we begin to "define" composition as a discipline, then, we ask "What questions constitute the field (if it is a field)?" I would answer, and I presume not many "compositionists" would agree, that the master questions regard invention (*ethos, pathos, logos*), arrangement, style, and pedagogy. If that is the case, then composition is closely related to—if not a part of—rhetoric. Of course, some questions are unique to composition—for instance, those involving basic writing, writing across the curriculum, literacy in relation to society, writing as thinking, writing and ideology, the relationships of writing and reading, the technical details of coherence in an array in space as opposed to an array in time, the relationships of composition and "creative" writing, the ethics of literacy. . . . In divorcing composition from rhetoric and maintaining its position as a colonial field within the establishment, Harkin and Schilb have made a politically astute move. Dissociating themselves from the colonial underclass, they have begun to create for themselves positions as functionaries in the governmental bureaucracy.

Pat Bizzell and Jim Berlin abandon rhetoric for cultural criticism—and I know that both of them (in the imaginary dialogue in the hotel lounge) have reacted strongly to this statement. Pat has leaned forward and said sternly, "Now wait a minute, buddy!" Jim has stood up, walked five paces away, five paces back, and resumed his seat. "Now wait a minute, buddy!" he says.

Bizzell has stated the position that she shares with Berlin and others thus:

> I think it is important for academics to become cultural critics, or critical intellectuals as the practitioners are sometimes called, because I hope that the activity of cultural criticism will foster social justice by making people aware of politically motivated ideological concealments. Underlying this hope are two assumptions, that the present social order is unjust, and that becoming aware of how injustice is protected and promulgated ideologically will enable people better to resist and change it. (Bizzell 1989, 224)

Berlin offers a description of the composition course that results from the philosophy that he shares with Bizzell—and I must quote at length:

> The course is organized around an examination of the cultural codes—the social semiotics—that are working themselves out in shaping consciousness in our students and ourselves. We start with the personal experience of the students, but the emphasis is on the position of this experience within its formative context. Our main concern is the relation of current signifying practices to the structuring of subjectivities—of race, class, and gender formations, for example—in our students and ourselves. The effort is to make students aware of cultural codes, the competing discourses that are influencing their formations as the subjects of experience. Our larger purpose is to encourage students to resist and to negotiate these codes—these hegemonic discourses—in order to bring about more democratic and personally humane economic, social, and political arrangements. From our perspective, only in this way can they become genuinely competent writers and readers. (Berlin 1992, 26–27)

This course consists of six units: advertising, work, play, education, gender, and individuality (Berlin 1992, 27). And Berlin goes on to describe how the class deals with a 1981 essay from *The Wall Street Journal*, "The

Days of a Cowboy are Marked by Danger, Drudgery, and Low Pay"
(1992, 28). The class explores the context of the article and then establishes that the "cowboss" is in "binary opposition to the cowboys who
work for him as well as the owners who work away from the ranch in
cities" (1992, 28). In short, the students do a cultural critique of the text.

I am highly skeptical about this top-down approach of Bizzell
and Berlin, from ideology *supposedly* to the art and craft of rhetoric,
and as I will argue hereafter, composition should begin with rhetoric,
which will inevitably lead to ideological critique. We have the obligation to help students master the art and the craft that they must use in
their critiques. Furthermore, Berlin's course is apparently text-bound,
as if there were not a world out there to be "read" and critiqued.

Susan Jarratt (1991), like Gerald Graff (1992), would make
conflict—specifically, feminism—the center of the composition class.

> My hopes are pinned on composition courses whose instructors
> help their students to locate personal experience in historical
> and social contexts—courses that lead students to see how dif-
> ferences emerging from their texts and discussions have more
> to do with those contexts than they do with an essential and
> unarguable individuality. . . . When we recognize the need to
> confront the different truths our students bring to our classes—
> not only through self-discovery but in the heat of argument
> feminism—and rhetoric become allies in contention with the
> forces of oppression troubling us all. (115–116)

I would only remind Jarratt of her admirable study of the
sophists and would point out that Isocrates, for example, would take
exception to her vision of composition (as well as those of Harkin,
Schilb, Berlin, and Bizzell). Isocrates says,

> Since it is not in the nature of man to attain a science by the pos-
> session of which we can know positively what we should do or
> what we should say, in the next resort I hold that man to be wise
> who is able by his powers of conjecture to arrive generally at the
> best course, and I hold that man to be a philosopher who occu-
> pies himself with the studies from which he will most quickly
> gain that kind of insight. (1929, 335)

And that ability to arrive at the best course of action *through a mastery
of rhetoric* is precisely my goal as a teacher of composition.

A Voice of Reason Cries Out in the Wilderness

I appreciate Jim Berlin's openness in describing his composition
course (1992). So here is how I go about my trade (when I teach my

course in advanced composition). But first, two principles: one, since composition is a branch of rhetoric, I ground my courses firmly in the practice of rhetoric, not in an extrinsic ideology such as Marxism, feminism, or capitalism; two, I go beyond texts proper (books, articles, films, TV presentations) to the world out there, which I encourage my students to "read" critically, using the rhetorical methods that I teach. My course qualifies genuinely as cultural criticism, but, more important, it is a course in composition. Of course, my students soon learn that ideologically I'm a superannuated liberal, and I even tell them that I'm probably the only faculty member at USC who carries a labor union card. In the syllabus for the course is this statement, the ideas of which I reiterate (perhaps too insistently) throughout the semester:

Notes on the Craft of Writing

Like architecture, music, and sports (e.g., baseball), writing is an art, not a science, and one becomes a master at an art mainly through practice, though general principles or theories can be useful. For example, the little league player at batting practice gets tips from her coach: "Keep your right elbow higher." "Step toward the pitcher." "Keep your eye on the ball." The baseball player also watches other practitioners of the art, to see what techniques they use. In other words, the learner makes attempt after attempt, receiving *feedback* from the expert and from anyone else who observes the performance. Through this process of attempt-and-feedback, the performer (cellist, batter, writer) gradually improves the ability to perform. Like architects, cellists, and quarterbacks, writers never cease to improve their abilities.

For this reason, we will place heavy emphasis on revision, using first and second and even third drafts as the bases for crafting pieces of writing that we feel will achieve what we want them to. I will encourage you to bring your papers to my office both prior to submitting them and after you have received my judgment in the form of a grade and comments; to get the reactions of your colleagues in the class; to tamper with your papers, polishing, pruning; to enjoy the craft of writing.

From my point of view, narrative is the bedrock and basis of composition—not just narrative as self-expression (though, heaven knows, I cherish the expressive use of writing), but narrative as a rhetorical and conceptual tool. Furthermore, my upper-division students are, by and large, unable to write effective narrative. Thus, I start the class with several narratives such as Dillard's "The Interior Life" from *An American Childhood*; Conroy's "White Days and Red Nights" from *Stop Time*; Moorehead's "The Long Egyptian Night" from *The*

Blue Nile; Parkman's "The Platte and the Desert" from *The Oregon Trail*; Rodriguez's "The Achievement of Desire" from *Hunger of Memory*; and Rose's "I Developed the Ability to Read Closely" from *Lives on the Boundary*.

The master question about all the reading my students do is this: "Specifically, what did you learn about writing (narratives, explanations, arguments, business letters, or proposals) from these selections?" It has been my experience that students are more eager to discuss these "technical" matters than, say, the child's perception of the world (Dillard), family values (Conroy), colonialism (Moorehead and Parkman), education and class (Rodriguez and Rose), literacy (Rodriguez, Rose, and Conroy). Do these topics arise? Absolutely! And when they do arise, I let the discussion go where it will. But we do a good deal with specificity of detail, with coherence, with point of view. (It is so easy to demonstrate that concrete details—sights, sounds, smells, tactile sensations, or movements—are the heart and soul of narrative, and so difficult to get students to be concrete and specific!)

Evolving from these readings and the discussions is the first paper assignment:

> *Paper 1* (due Sept. 9): Keeping the essays by Rodriguez and Rose in mind (but not attempting to imitate them), write an account of a learning experience you've had during your time at USC. Your narrative may involve a class (e.g., science, social science, humanities, athletics), or it might well be something that has happened on campus—in the dorm or frat or sorority house, at the dining hall, in a student organization. . . .
>
> As you plan, and then as you write, keep a purpose in mind. Your narrative should be informative to the reader. For example, a student during fall semester wrote a fascinating account of *de facto* segregation at USC; using her own experiences, she explained how student organizations for minorities (blacks, Asians, etc.) exclude those who are not members of their ethnic and racial groups, and she compared the situation of blacks at USC with what happened at Rutgers, where she had been a student. Her personal narrative, then, was an analysis of a problem on this campus. *Unless you get specific permission from me, please choose a subject related to this university.*

For a variety of reasons, I ask the students to focus, whenever possible, on the university: we share knowledge of and interest in the institution; nontraditional texts are readily available (e.g., administrative policy statements, financial reports, admissions statistics, demographics of the student body); we can interview deans and faculty;

and we have ready access to the physical plant (cafeteria, athletic fields, library), an aspect of the subject that became, surprisingly, very important to one student, who argued convincingly that there are not enough open areas (e.g, for softball, Frisbee) and virtually no facilities for intramural sports. It comes as a great surprise to most of my students that they can "look things up" in places other than books and that they can critique not only novels and films, but also institutions and parts thereof.

The results of this assignment are usually heartening. Last semester, Miss Wilson used her experiences with Alpha Beta Nil as the basis for a critique of prissiness and elitism in sororities; Mr. Palm, a fraternity officer, wrote of the difficulty he and his brothers were having in achieving racial and social variety in their fraternity; and Mr. Weston questioned the morality of the university in regard to the homeless, who are hustled off campus when security forces find that they are present. In short, most of the students address significant issues regarding the institution that will, to a large extent, determine their futures.

When the students submit their papers, three of the students distribute copies of their papers to each member of the class. Thus, we are able to spend at least one whole class meeting—the one after the papers have been submitted—talking about the essays of three of our colleagues. These sessions are fascinating, both to me and to the members of the class. I ask each class member to have at least one specific constructive comment to make on each of the three papers. I also interject questions regarding *ethos, pathos, logos*, style, and form (of course, without using the jargon). "What sort of person is the writer of this paper—not Mr. Smith who's sitting in the back row of this classroom, but the Mr. Smith who emerges from the paper?" "Did the writer judge his audience correctly? From your point of view as readers, did he hit the mark or miss it?" "Does the writer convince you of his point? Do you at least grant that his view is reasonable?" "Do you find any stylistic problems? Could proofreading improve the paper? Do any sentences need rewriting?" "Might the paper be more effective if it were restructured?"

The second paper assignment evolves from readings such as Lopez, "The Country of the Mind" from *Arctic Dreams*; Matthiessen, "November 6" from *The Snow Leopard*; Eiseley, "The Angry Winter"; Thomas, "Late Night Thoughts on Listening to Mahler's Ninth Symphony"; Hawking, "The Nature of Theories" from *A Brief History of Time*; and Hurston, "How It Feels to Be Colored Me."

Paper 2: Write an e*xplanation* that relates to USC. You can explain an opinion, a process, an idea, or an object. I'm using Microsoft "Word for Windows," and the 848-page manual is an explanation of how to use that program. Remember that you must be an "expert" on the subject that you choose and also that your subject must be unfamiliar to your readers, for I cannot explain something to you that you already know. Here are some possible subject areas:

1. your reason for choosing USC;

2. your opinion about the quality of education you have received;

3. how to succeed socially or academically;

4. the method of studying or learning that you have developed;

5. your opinion about social life at USC;

6. how some aspect of USC could be improved;

7. relations with the community around USC;

8. the quality of life on campus;

9. your opinion about food service on campus; or

10. problems of commuting.

These are only suggestions and are not meant to restrict your choice, as long as your subject relates to USC. (By the way, the paper assignments in this syllabus are explanations.)

Just one example of a paper that this assignment—and a good deal of preparatory discussion—elicited. A couple of years ago, Ms. Braden, who, as a resident of a university dormitory was required to purchase a food service plan, did an extensive study of the economics of eating on campus versus taking meals in one of the many establishments just off campus in University Village. She compared food quantities, qualities, and prices, and she explained the University voucher system and the policy of not refunding the cost of meals that students miss. And I would stress the point that Ms. Braden did a great deal of research in the world "out there" as contrasted with cloistered research in the library, though my students also spent a good deal of time in the stacks, doing traditional research. (By the way, university food service came off very badly in Ms. Braden's paper, and we forwarded a copy of it to the food service manager.)

At about this point, I begin to stress "practical" matters, such as writing abstracts, one of the most useful forms that one can learn. The "practical" value of this skill in the business and professional world is obvious, and the usefulness to the individual learner and information-seeker is equally so. I also take periodic quick glances at *Guidelines for Document Designers*, a manual that explains and illustrates the use of visual features such as charts and graphs; the principles of readability; making maximally useful tables of contents; the use of subheads; and so on.[2]

The third paper results from a long discussion of the nature of problems, and in conducting this class discussion, I rely heavily on Young, Becker, and Pike, *Rhetoric: Discovery and Change* (1970). I find that my juniors and seniors have not been asked to think about the nature of problems and how to analyze them. Some of them find it difficult to differentiate a gripe from a problem that can be analyzed and thus at least partially understood. For example, one of my students did a paper on the way in which faculty members treat the custodial staff. She had a long and disheartening list of examples (considering that we academics are supposedly humane), but she said nothing about the dynamics of the problem. Another student undertook what at first appeared to be a real yawner, a topic that would not challenge any reader: parking on campus. However, the paper that resulted from her analysis and research turned out to be fascinating. She found that the number of permits in various categories issued by Parking Operations exceeded the number of actual spaces available on campus; she found out how much each space in a high-rise structure would cost; she located empty lots near the campus and learned how much it would cost the university to purchase them and use them for parking—in short, she did a convincing job of analyzing the parking mess at USC.

I have found that most students at my university, whether freshmen or seniors, are unable to argue convincingly, and if that is the case, all of their ideological and social consciousness will be largely in vain. Thus, for papers four and five, we modulate into argument, in many ways the most challenging of the assignments.

> *Paper 4:* It is impossible to create airtight categories for types of writing. For example, your second paper (an explanation) may well have fit the specifications for your third (the exploration of a problem), and it turns out that your first, second, or third paper may well fit the specification for number four, which is an *argument*. Most simply stated, the difference between an explanation and an argument is this: an explanation is intended to inform; an argument is intended to convince. You might clearly *explain* to me your opinion about racism on campus without *convincing* me that your opinion is valid. (In other words, I'd respond, "I see what you mean, but I don't agree.")

Or move argument one step further, and you have *persuasion*. Through argument you might convince me that your opinion about racism on campus is valid without persuading me that I should join you in taking action to remedy the situation. (It's not hard to *convince* people that cigarette smoking is a serious health hazard, but it's often very difficult to *persuade* them to stop smoking.)

For Paper 4, choose a topic about which to convince or persuade your readers.

In preparation for the assignment, students read and analyze several arguments. (Last semester, these included a tightly structured argument concerning vivisection; an article based wholly on examples, arguing that prizefighting should be more tightly regulated; and C. S. Lewis's "The Naturalist and the Supernaturalist"—among others.) And, with a good deal of coaching from me, they discuss the nature of arguments—in particular, two simple, but powerful, principles: arguments must have definition and uncertainty[3], and they must begin on agreement rather than disagreement (Perelman and Olbrechts-Tyteca 65).

The payoff of *imitatio* is gratifyingly evident in the results of this assignment. Students use the arguments that we have read and analyzed as structural models for their own arguments. One of the most interesting papers in this group last semester argued against a policy instituted by the new president of the university: Greek letter organizations were required to achieve a cumulative GPA of 3.0. The writer pointed out that the administration had not imposed this standard on other student organizations; in fact, said the writer, the administration would not dare to require the Black Student Union or the Young Americans for Freedom to achieve a cumulative GPA higher than that required for matriculation in the university, namely, 2.0. The writer was unsuccessful in his attempt to gain an interview with the president, but did include statements from the leaders of several organizations, the results of an interview with the director of athletics regarding the grades of team members, and the policy statement itself (a three-page document) in an appendix.

I have perhaps said enough to demonstrate how *I start with rhetoric* and how the students use that art to criticize the world around them, to help them understand that world, and to persuade others of their points of view, but to convey the texture of the class, I would need more pages than I can allow myself. Much of the class transpired in my office, with one or two or three students discussing their work and doing rewrites on the spot. (A computer and a printer are essential for the offices of composition teachers.) And much of the class took place on the telephone, students calling me to discuss their writing problems and, particularly, to use my influence to allow them access to sources of information (such as official, confidential statements regarding sexual harassment).

One more topic: grading. I explain that course grades result from a four-paper portfolio that students submit at the end of the semester. As I say in the syllabus, "You will choose four of your six papers to revise for the portfolio. The grade that you receive on the portfolio will be your final grade for the course." Interestingly, however, it is impossible not to assign a grade to each paper a student submits, even though these grades have no necessary relationship to the final grades for the course. Students are so grade-conscious that they become neurotic if they do not receive that kind of incisive evaluation on each piece of work. Summary comments and extended conferences simply don't suffice; students need A, B, C, D, or F.

Saving My Ego

This has been, essentially, a tragic story. For most of my career, my literary colleagues have kept me on the margin of the profession of English, in the ghetto of the English department and the MLA. Now my buddies, my allies—Berlin, Bizzell, Harkin, Jarratt, Phelps, and Schilb—are attempting to ghetto-ize me by shifting the professional substance from rhetoric to anthropology or cultural studies, or feminism, or whatever.

> Yes, I'm an old rhetorician,
> Nearly ready for the mortician,
> But before I go,
> I want you to know that

My marginalized position within my own department and within the establishment (e.g., MLA) has not destroyed my ego. Nor, after all these years, has my cantankerous, abrasive enthusiasm dimmed, for, as I have told my self through the decades and as I have announced publicly on more than one occasion, I may well be part of the scum of the profession, but, by gad, I'm the cream of the scum!

Notes

1. Berlin and I order beer. I don't notice what you and the others order. (Jim died after I had written this essay. However, because of his work, he will

always be a member of the group discussing composition rhetoric, and because of his warm humanity, he will always be a warm companion.)

2. This manual is in the public domain and is available from American Institutes for Research, 1055 Thomas Jefferson Street, NW, Washington, D.C. 20007.

3. That is, they must not be too broad, and they must not be resolvable by empirical evidence.

Works Cited

Abrams, M. H. 1953. *The Mirror and the Lamp*. New York: Oxford University Press.

Berlin, James A. 1992. "Poststructuralism, Cultural Studies, and the Composition Classroom: Postmodern Theory in Practice." *Rhetoric Review* 11 (fall): 16–33.

Bizzell, Patricia. 1989. " 'Cultural Criticism': A Social Approach to Studying Writing." *Rhetoric Review* 7: 224–30.

Brown, Stuart C., et al. 1994. "Doctoral Programs in Rhetoric and Composition." *Rhetoric Review* 12: 237–389.

Eagleton, Terry. 1983. *Literary Theory*. Minneapolis: University of Minnesota Press.

Emig, Janet. 1971. *The Composing Processes of Twelfth Graders*. Urbana, IL: NCTE.

Frye, Northrop. 1971. *Anatomy of Criticism*. Princeton, NJ: Princeton University Press.

Graff, Gerald. 1992. *Beyond the Culture Wars: How Teaching the Conflicts Can Revitalize American Education*. New York: Norton.

———. 1987. *Professing Literature*. Chicago: University of Chicago Press.

Halle, Morris, and Samuel Jay Keyser. 1971. *English Stress: Its Form, Its Growth, and Its Role in Verse*. New York: Harper.

Harkin, Patricia, and John Schilb, eds. 1991. *Contending with Words: Composition and Rhetoric in a Postmodern Age*. New York: MLA.

Hirsch, E. D. Jr. *Cultural Literacy: What Every American Needs to Know*. Boston: Houghton.

———. 1977. *The Philosophy of Composition*. Chicago: University of Chicago Press.

Isocrates. 1929. "Antidosis." Trans. George Norlin. *Isocrates*. Cambridge, MA: Harvard University Press. Vol. 2. 181–365.

Jarratt, Susan. 1991. *Rereading the Sophists: Classical Rhetoric Refigured*. Carbondale: Southern Illinois University Press.

Nietzsche, Friedrich. 1896. *Thus Spake Zarathustra*. Trans. R. J. Hollingdale. Reprint, London: Penguin, 1969.

Wellek, René, and Austin Warren. 1956. *Theory of Literature*. New rev. ed. New York: Harcourt.

Winterowd, W. Ross. "Literary Studies, Term Papers, and the World out There." Unpublished manuscript.

Winterowd, W. Ross, and Jack Blum. 1994. *A Teacher's Introduction to Composition in the Rhetorical Tradition*. Urbana, IL: NCTE.

Young, Richard E., Alton L. Becker, and Kenneth L. Pike. 1970. *Rhetoric: Discovery and Change*. New York: Harcourt.

21 Falling Into Narrative

Patricia Donahue
Lafayette College, Pennsylvania

In this essay, I will offer a narrative description of my pedagogical practice. I will describe who I am and what I do as a teacher of writing. This kind of activity—in which the self becomes a point of reference—is a familiar one for me. As a writing specialist teaching in a somewhat traditional English Department at a small liberal arts college, I am frequently called upon both to explain how composition functions as a teaching practice and to defend its disciplinary status, or at least its institutional legitimacy. To many of my colleagues, despite my good intentions and efforts to get the word out, the idea that composition constitutes a special field of study is a baffling one. For them, composition is neither fish nor fowl. At best, it is interdisciplinary, at worst, mystifying. To make its case (and my own) I have come to rely on the telling of stories. Stories allow me to demonstrate the efficacy of the professional discourse and to illustrate the enactment of theories into practice.

In telling stories, I am also giving into an urge widely felt by others in composition, if conferences and journals are reliable indicators—the urge to narrativize. Writing teachers everywhere are sharing stories of themselves as teachers (principles, procedures, and passions) and as people (problems, crises, and suffering). By claiming the authority of the "I," they are injecting what many believe is new knowledge into the field, and they are borrowing for their own purposes the seductive energy of storytelling.

But in the rush to write personal narratives, there are many who fail to be sufficiently critical of them. They argue that in "getting personal" they can liberate themselves from the constraints of more traditional academic genres. Their writing can be more authentic, cut closer to the bone. But the fact is that personal writing is as subject to regulation as any other discursive form; it, too, has its conventions, tropes, and stipulations. This is an issue I want to take up in more detail, and in a somewhat paradoxical fashion. I will share three stories of my own, but I will also—and simultaneously—examine the implications of an acritical deployment of narrative in composition. I think of this kind of analysis as "self-reflexive," because it not only generates new ideas but comments on the process of their production. If teachers want the stories they write to serve as learning opportunities, not only for others but for themselves, this kind of double-move is one they need to make.

The first story is a story of a conversation I had several years ago with a student in a freshman writing class. She came to see me in my office to discuss a personal writing assignment that the class had completed several weeks before. At the time of the conversation, I had reached a new stage in my thinking about the pedagogical application of personal writing. For several years, I hadn't assigned personal writing in any of my courses. I didn't believe that students could effectively transfer what they had learned about writing (and reading) from a personal context to a different one. Furthermore, the argument so prevalent in composition books—that college writing should begin with the personal essay because the "self" is what students know best—seemed simplistic. In my own experience, at least, the text of the self had always been the most difficult text to write: there is no creature more alien at times than the one we call "I." Yet, despite my reservations, I eventually yielded to my colleagues' arguments. The right kind of assignment, they insisted, could do everything I wanted it to do.

Whether or not the assignment I finally designed was the "right" one is debatable, but it did engage students in revisionary processes, encouraged them to think and to rethink, and to transfer skills. It consisted of three stages. In the first stage, students were to describe an experience they felt had a significant impact on them. (I placed no restrictions on the kind of experience they could select.) In the second stage, they were to add to their earlier piece new material, explaining why others might find the description of the experience significant to them. In the third stage, they were to produce two different versions of the second essay. In the first, they were to shift perspective from first to third person. In the second, they were to add to the third-person essay additional material relevant to the issue-at-hand, material taken from assigned texts which had been discussed in class. I should mention that in the next project, textual analysis, they were also required to shift perspective, but this time from third person to first person.

The student with whom I had the conversation had produced some of the best work on this project, the most thoughtful. So I was somewhat confused by her demeanor, her obvious discomfort. When asked why she had come to see me, she said that she needed to tell me something. She had "hated" the personal writing assignment. The problem wasn't its complexity or the amount of time it required, but the fact that she didn't think her life interesting enough to share with strangers: nothing exciting had ever happened to her, nothing dramatic. Having read enough to know that the best stories featured struggle and conflict, she felt that in order to hold her readers' attention (the importance of which I had stressed in class) and to produce a compelling tale, she had to "lie." And lying to me, she confessed, made her feel "crummy."

While the details of this conversation are a bit hazy (I've placed her actual words within quotation marks), I do remember that this experience was a significant one for me. It led me to review again—and in a more critical fashion than before—the contradictions that surround the discussion of personal writing in composition. On one hand, most teachers would concur that students occasionally lie (though I admit I was startled by my student's willingness to admit to it openly). They lie for several reasons: to fulfill expectations, to protect themselves from a loss of self-esteem, or to get by. Such lies may even be signs of deeper truths. From the perspective of poststructuralist theories like deconstruction (at least in its popularized and simplified version), it is even possible to say that lie is the necessary condition of language: all language is metaphorical, fragmentary, and conventional. On the other hand, when it comes time to assign personal writing or advocate its use or to extoll its virtues in composition textbooks, all these ideas are conveniently forgotten. The "I" is then defined as a special signifier presenting the "real" and "true" self, the person as he or she really is.

As a gloss on this story, I offer another. In an earlier draft of this essay, I constructed a chronological narrative of my development as a writing teacher, covering my early years as a graduate student in an English Department to my first full-time position as a writing specialist. I presented myself as a kind of hero (it was, after all, my story) who after receiving her Ph.D. in literature, made what had seemed, at the time, a courageous decision to specialize in composition, to reclaim pedagogy as a theoretical field of study, and to retool. It was a courageous decision because in my graduate program composition was considered an inferior field for inferior minds (this wasn't an unusual situation in English Departments in the early eighties). When I left this department to teach in the writing programs at UCLA, I entered a community of scholar/teachers who regarded writing instruction as the best and smartest work that one could do. Yet, despite this good experience and many positive ones that followed, I continued to regard struggle as the central theme of my professional life. Even when I had reached a stage of relative security, I felt I had to struggle to do work that others would recognize as important. Furthermore, my personal struggles seemed metonymically related to composition's struggle to achieve institutional legitimacy.

When I showed this earlier draft to a good friend, with whom I had worked closely in those early years, he told me that my self-representation was flawed. I had never been as naive, embattled, or isolated as my portrait would suggest. Early on, he insisted, I had found allies. He was one of them (he was chair of the French Department at the time). Other graduate students were also "struggling" to apply to their teaching of writing models of interpretation acquired in literature courses in order to bridge the gap between the fields. I was not alone, nor was my situation unique. While he stopped short of saying I had lied, his point was clear. As he saw it (and granted, his version may be as slanted as my own), I had been so eager to tell a good tale that I had fashioned my materials to emphasize struggle, conflict, and despair. Furthermore, he argued, if I had paused to examine my story as a complex and highly stratified text, if I had brought my training as a reader to bear upon my own story, I might have seen what to him was acutely clear. My story was not "original," but reproduced one of the most popular narrative frames found in literature, the *Bildungsroman*, in which a young person undertakes a journey from innocence to experience, vanquishes enemies, and reaches a stage of temporary rest. My story was subtended by a larger narrative pattern, which I could not control and did not even recognize. It was this pattern, rather than the "truth," that had been the driving force of my story. This meant that my story was not really "original" at all, at least not structurally. I had fallen into a particular narrative, and required the intervention of a corrective consciousness—this time presented in the form of another's story—to pull myself out. However, I did not then escape from narrative altogether; I merely employed a different pattern, in a more self-critical way. I told a different kind of story.

Perhaps a discussion of the term "narrative" is in order. While there are many competing theories of narrative, most of them agree on several points. For example, "narrative" and "story" tend to be interchangeable terms. (Some theories, however, define "story" as a sequence of events and "narrative" as the universal structures which frame them and establish significance.) It is also generally agreed that a story (or narrative) must consist of at least two events, real or fictional, conceptual or material. These events have to be organized in terms of a beginning, middle, and end. And taken together, these events must constitute a whole, a coherent subject. Many theories of narrative also claim that the patterns of narrative organization are limited in number; this means that many different stories will reproduce and utilize the same narrative pattern. Consequently, some patterns—such as the narrative of progress in which historical or scientific events are arranged in a line representing steady improvement—are repeated so often that they eventually strike us as "common-sensical," the natural order of things; their status as narrative—as something constructed—is forgotten. Another point of agreement is that narratives are not found only in imaginative literature, but are widely distributed across the discursive field, identifiable in any text organized temporally rather than topically—in news reports, gossip, myths, scientific articles, and even literary analyses. Finally, it is generally believed that narratives do not reflect reality but constitute it, transforming events into signifying parts of signifying wholes, imposing order upon life's messy details. Without narrative, it would be difficult for us to make our way and to communicate our experiences.

One final story remains, this time a pedagogical story in which I position myself not as hero or surprised interlocutor but as "self-reflexive" teacher engaging students and self in processes of discovery and critique. It is as subject as any other narrative to distortion, fragmentation, and exclusion. It also imitates—and brazenly borrows from—other instructional narratives. Those of Roland Barthes, David Bartholome, Wolfgang Iser, and Mariolina Salvatori come quickly to mind. I'm sure there are others.

In all the courses I teach (which include a first-year seminar, a first-year writing course, a course in Renaissance nondramatic literature, an introduction to literary study called "Literary Questions," and a seminar in literary criticism), my goal is to enact two pedagogical principles. The first is the belief that reading and writing are mutually interactive, interpretive processes. This means, at its simplest level, that writers must read what they write. But it also means that reading is a process of rewriting a text, a far more difficult idea to grasp, especially by those who perceive reading as a passive activity in which the reader receives the imprint of the text's intention, absorbs a message. From an interactive perspective, reading becomes a generative activity in which readers identify how a text establishes its intention and also how it undermines it. Readers do this by bringing into the "center" material that seems, in the text, to be marginal, by rearranging a text, by altering its course of events. This is not to say that readers control the text, or that they are more powerful than writers, but that, like writers, they have a role to play in the production of meaning and significance—they are not merely witnesses to another's performance. This is actually a principle a bit easier to teach than to define, for students these days are all too willing to "rewrite" a text to suit their own interests. The trick is to get them to see what may be there "in" the text itself, to encourage them to look at the words on the page.

A second principle is the idea that the articulation of difficulty constitutes genuine intellectual work. Difficulty is not formulated to be quickly resolved. It is embraced for what it teaches us, not only about specific texts but interpretive repertoires and protocols—what we bring to the critical act and how we have been taught to read. To establish difficulty we ask questions: why is this text difficult? Is it difficult because of assumptions we have about literature and language? I use the pronoun "we" to stress the idea that my relationship with my students is a collaborative one. I am not the "subject who knows" what the real difficulties are and how to resolve them. If difficulties are to be resolved, students must resolve them, usually by turning to another text for a new perspective (my debt to Mariolina Salvatori should be obvious here).

In a first year seminar entitled "Mindbenders: Ways of Knowing or a Course in Paradigms," I organize texts so that one can be used to comment and ultimately to "read" the other. This is how that story goes.

The first text consists of several chapters from Thomas Kuhn's highly influential book, *The Structure of Scientific Revolutions* (1962), which establishes a working definition of "paradigm." In this book, Kuhn argues that scientific change is not brought about through an accumulative process in which one discovery is added to another incrementally, but through paradigm shifts. But what is a "paradigm"? For Kuhn, the term refers to a mode, a set of theories which govern what kinds of questions can be asked in a particular scientific community and the procedures by which knowledge is generated. Any discovery that cannot be understood within the terms of a prevailing paradigm is dismissed as nonsense or labeled an anomaly— and then forgotten. Occasionally, however, an anomaly demands attention; it won't disappear. When this occurs—and such occurrences are rare—pressure is brought to bear upon the paradigm, so much pressure, in fact, that the paradigm is forced to change in order to accommodate the anomaly, to deal with it directly. This constitutes a "paradigm shift," and such shifts transform how scientific work is performed, evaluated, and discussed. They can also lead to "scientific revolutions." An excellent example is the Copernican Revolution, in which the motions of planets as observed through telescopes could not be reconciled with the existing model of a geocentric universe; the model had to change.

Now, as abstract and complex as Kuhn's text is, it helps my freshman students visualize belief systems in metaphorical terms, as a kind of container. To engage them in thinking firsthand about the process of constructing paradigms—and the limits inherent within any particular paradigm—I then construct a series of reading and writing acts. First, I ask them to formulate, in writing, their own personal paradigm or belief system and to consider its anomalies—what is inside and outside the conceptual box. We then read the *Gen-X Reader*, a collection of essays which examines the competing paradigms of the "nineties" generation. Once they explore this new paradigm, students return to their first essay and revise it, explaining how their personal paradigm conforms to and deviates from this generational model. Next, we read Primo Levi's *The Drowned and the Saved* (1988), a memoir of his years in Auschwitz, which, among many important ideas, offers a paradigm of subjectivity; identity in this book is determined in terms of one's position as an "insider" or an "outsider" within shifting realms (the concentration camp, Germany, the moral universe). Having read Levi, students produce a new piece of writing, determining what in their world constitutes "insider" status and how the "outsiders" they know are described and treated.

The last major text is Toni Morrison's *The Bluest Eye* (1984). We begin by formulating its difficulties (which we have done with every text, including the texts they have written). The difficulties most commonly identified include confusing plot details, a lack of knowledge about social milieu, and unfamiliar representations of race, class, and gender. We work through these difficulties by studying paradigms found in other texts and then applying them.

The first text that we turn to is Freud's *Civilization and Its Discontents* (1962). In explaining the nature and interaction of erotic and aggressive instincts, this book supplies a possible motive for the rape of the young girl, Pecola, by another character in the novel, Cholly Breedlove, her father. Because issues of gender are disregarded by Freud but prominent in Morrison's book, we read Berger's *Ways of Seeing* (1977). Berger argues that while men define themselves through performance, women see themselves as they are seen. Different dimensions of Morrison's text now become visible: Cholly's need to express himself through violence to prove his masculinity, and Pecola's attempt to redeem her invisibility through fantasy and psychotic retreat. Once the subject of cultural norms is introduced, we then consider Morrison's repetition of various elements of "Dick and Jane" stories. We read several examples to establish a paradigm of "family" that designates what is middle-class and white as normative. Then we examine Morrison's deconstruction of the family paradigm through the creation of various countertexts: the text of a father who rapes his daughter, a daughter who feels vilified, a mother who loves not her daughter but a little girl she is paid to love.

As they read, students also write: short pieces about difficulties and longer (five to seven pages) more formal "revisionary" essays, like the one I described earlier. In revisionary essays, students first produce a coherent reading of a text and then subject that reading to further analysis. They pose questions: Why have I emphasized these issues to the exclusion of others? What have I, as a reader, brought to this text in terms of literary, social, and cultural experience that will influence how I read it? What will my reader bring to my text? In their work, students may use "I," but not as a device to hide behind; their "I" is to signify the presence of a self-reflexive agent who takes nothing for granted.

What I've just offered could be called a narrative of instruction because it arranges pedagogical events in a particular order that is chronological and that emphasizes specific principles. While I am tempted to leave this story as it is, I will examine a few exclusions; for in order to tell a coherent story, I have had to leave out many details. For example, I had to leave out the difficulties I faced in writing a story about teaching that is faithful to the events (to the extent that such fidelity is possible), but also establishes their significance. Also, while the linear arrangement of the narrative suggests that a self-reflexive pedagogy unfolds in smooth and predictable ways, the reality is otherwise. Many "students" "resist" hearing that ideas have histories, that beliefs are paradigmatic, that no interpretation is complete (while I recognize that to refer to students in generic terms and to validate their behaviors as forms of resistance is problematic, these issues are beyond the scope of this essay; I plan to discuss them elsewhere). Furthermore, this narrative says very little about the classroom itself, ignoring the dialogics of teaching, the exchange of energy. It also excludes my struggle (as always, struggle is a theme) to teach students how to ask the kinds of questions that will lead them to generate ideas and to reflect on the generative process.

It would be a simple matter to conclude from this discussion that the production of narrative is more trouble than it's worth. That's obviously not the point I want to make. While it's not an easy enterprise to construct stories that tell the "facts," imbue them with significance, and also reflect on their production, it is a necessary one. For in telling such stories we make our work visible to others, we demonstrate the productive capacity of a professional language, and we assume the burdens of accountability. That last point is especially important, for if we are not accountable for the stories we tell, if we construct our stories so that they forestall rather than encourage critique, then they will fail to make the kind of contribution to the growth of knowledge in composition that we hope they will; they will not be able to be used by others. While I have stressed throughout this essay the benefits of sharing stories, I also want to say that it is the first reader of the story—who is, of course, the writer—who is in a position to learn the most from them: to identify his or her pedagogical (or personal) predilections and to make the necessary adjustments. If stories are to serve as occasions for self-instruction, however, they must be read critically, which means read as texts which borrow and reconfigure already existing conventions. For it is only when teachers become the best readers of the stories they write that they will be able to fall into narrative in relative safety, secure in the knowledge that they will not drown.

In writing this essay, I learned a great deal from conversations with Kathyrn Flannery, Richard Regosin, and Mariolina Salvatori. Special gratitude goes to Deborah Byrd, Monette Tiernan, and Lee Upton, my colleagues and friends, for commenting so wisely on earlier drafts. I owe a special thanks to Richard Larson, for his patience and excellent advice.

Works Cited

Berger, John. 1977. *Ways of Seeing.* New York: Penguin.

Freud, Sigmund. 1962. *Civilization and Its Discontents.* Trans. from the German by James Strachey. New York: Norton.

Kuhn, Thomas. 1962. *The Structure of Scientific Revolutions.* University of Chicago Press.

Levi, Primo. 1988. *The Drowned and the Saved.* Trans. from the Italian by Raymond Rosenthal. New York: Summit Books.

Morrison, Toni. 1984. *The Bluest Eye.* New York: Plume.

22 English in Education: An English Educationist at Work

Harold M. Foster
University of Akron

I walked across campus to visit the English Department yesterday. My students do this on a daily basis, but I had not been there for over a year. For I am an English educator in a college of education, far removed from the daily workings of the English Department.

My encounter with the English Department was eventful. I went there to use the resource room in search of the publisher's name of a poem I was using. Soon I encountered professor friends of mine who led me to a colleague who knew her poetry. While searching through her anthologies, she offered a few thoughts:

"One of your students asked me for an independent study on Chaucer, but she told me she didn't have time to read much."

I mumbled a few words of apology for my student and contended that I could not be held responsible for the actions of all our teacher candidates. After my comments, I was left with this:

"You people tell us we don't know how to teach teachers anyway." Surprised at this remark, I underarticulated something unintelligible, thanked her for her help and left. Then I remembered why I hadn't been there for a year. I have had my share of problems with the English Department.

I have my list:

- When the Ohio State Department offered money to the University to work with high schools to assess composition skills, the English Department jumped on the grant and left me out completely. I had friends all over the state tell me how my colleagues would gloat over the exclusion of the College of Education.

- A few years ago, members of the English Department proposed a Master of Arts in Teaching that would basically freeze my college out. One of my English Department colleagues threatened to take it to the highest level of administration if I refused to cooperate.

- At a seminar of English professors discussing English education, a colleague who is an English professor at another university opened the session complaining about colleges of education. "When are we ever going to do something about the root of the problem—education schools?" this professor lamented, citing an anti–college of education article from *The Wall Street Journal.*

- Often my brightest students are told by certain members of the English Department that they are too bright to become teachers.

Many arts and science professors do have these arbitrary attitudes about colleges of education, which they often express. But I am not completely isolated from my colleagues from other colleges.

- I meet regularly with English Department friends. We enjoy sharing stories about students we have in common, and I have learned to appreciate the problems of English departments that are divisive and painful, and have nothing to do with English education or me.

- I have, on occasion, aired my complaints to the English Department Chair, and he has been sympathetic and more than understanding about the strained relationships between our colleges.

- The former English Department Chair overlooked several of his department members and appointed me as the English Education liaison in the College English Association of Ohio (EAO), whose membership was comprised of English professors, except for me. Because they couldn't find me, I never did get any mail, but it was a good experience. EAO dedicated an entire weekend to English education and I told them they drove me crazy. The group broke into laughter and one of the members shouted, "we drive each other crazy as well." The English professors in this group were certainly not elitists, concerned only with educating the brightest. These were professionals trying to help many of their students overcome serious literacy problems.

- My extended English education community includes people from English Departments, people with joint appointments, and colleagues in colleges of education. No one cares where the professor is housed, and I find a healthy mix of viewpoints because of these differences.

- I have an informal network of friends who are English professors in my university. We seldom discuss English education business. We're just friends.

- I am director of the faculty development center at my university. I am responsible for aiding professors with teaching from all colleges and departments. My colleagues accept my expertise and I have not encountered an overt problem because I am in a college of education.

So my experiences with my colleagues from other colleges are by no means all negative. Some of us have managed to respect each other.

I, English Educationist

At this point, ten years ago, I may have made a plea for formalizing relations with the English Department, cross-teaching, collaborating. Now, I see it differently. I feel that things ought to stay the way they are. The English Department has a lot to do, the least of which is worry about me. And I can do my job as effectively as a full time College of Education professor as I could do it anywhere else. What are the options? Would I be better off as a full-time member of an English department? How are English educators treated in English departments? Are they given the same status and rewards as the Renaissance person or Eighteenth Century British Literature expert? Well, how about a dual appointment? How about splitting my time between English and Education? Would I have dual committee assignments? Would I have to go to two sets of meetings? Would I have to earn tenure in both places?

There are problems no matter where the English educator works. My problems are my isolation from the English Department and, to some extent, a lack of credibility because I am in a college of education. It would be very helpful if all my Arts and Science colleagues would treat my College with some understanding, which will never happen. But I have benefits as well. I am very independent in a college of education. I do not have to fight for my credibility or my status. And I provide some benefits to the College of Education. I present the humanist tradition in a college dominated by social scientists. I represent a different way of knowing from many of my colleagues. This adds to the general depth of the college.

No, I do not lament my position and I do not want more enfranchisement in the English Department. The English Education Program here was approved in the first round by NCTE for NCATE. To me that makes a statement not only for what I do, but also about the quality of experiences the English Department provides. In our separate ways, I feel we have combined forces to provide a topnotch English education program. The College of Education has given me the freedom to create a worthwhile English education program and the English Department has cooperated by offering top-line courses and experiences for English education students. What more could I ask?

I Do Not Teach English

The main reason I do not lament my position in a college of education is because I do not teach English. I would feel this way even if I was in an English department. For English education is different from English. I need students who are outstanding readers and writers: students who have read a wide range of literature and who have written widely and well and in many contexts. It is the role of the English Department to provide me with students with the above experiences. But my tasks are to help students develop a theoretical framework for how teenagers learn English—that is, reading, writing, speaking, listening, and viewing—and to help my students acquire the ability to transact the theory into appropriate secondary pedagogy.

It is my responsibility to figure out how to weave understandable theory, sensible pragmatics, and site-based experiences into a unified blend for the credit hours I am allowed to use for my English education courses. This is not English teaching. Also, this is not easy. I have been challenged for twenty years to create this blend of theory, simulated practice, and field experiences. I may come close, but I have never gotten it totally right and I suspect I never will.

My English Education Roots

My path to English education is probably typical. I was a college English major who got certified through a Masters program. I taught secondary English at all levels and then earned a Ph.D. in English Education. Then I became an English educator at a state university where I have been ever since. All of my experiences, including my elementary and secondary student days, have formed me as an English educator. Each of my experiences has added an element to my professional blend; however, two basic experiences created a professional English education baseline that has stayed with me throughout my career.

1. The first of these experiences was my days as a public school student. Unfortunately, my public school days were not characterized by

wonderful English classrooms. In my book, *Crossing Over* (1994), I describe in detail the impact of these days on me. All too often my English classes were segmented and boring. I read and wrote on my own time more than I did in class. I was talked at too much. My experiences included too much grammar, too many worksheets, too many drills, too many chapter quizzes, and too many literal questions.

I did have well-meaning teachers, but they were not well educated. They had not much to go on as far as how to teach English. I was in schools during the Sputnik days and this too often translated into mechanized English teaching. I will never forget my experiences as a public school student, which are locked into my long term memory and serve me as reminders of what kinds of English classrooms I want to help create and what kinds I want to avoid.

What these experiences taught me: Good English teaching centers around meaningful reading and writing experiences. Worthwhile English teaching is, whenever possible, holistic, whole, like in whole language.

2. The second major formative experiences for me were my secondary teaching days. I am sure every English educator depends upon teaching experience as a major source of inspiration and knowledge. These experiences are our greatest source of credibilty with those we prepare to teach and those teachers we work with and learn from. My teaching lessons are indelible.

What these experiences taught me: Teaching is a complex activity. I must remain humble in the search for answers. They are mercurial. I must always keep in mind the real problems classroom teachers face. Simplistic ideas will not help teachers with the numbers and natures of students they face. Many teachers perceive people like me, who do not meet kids in secondary classrooms everyday, as unrealistic. I must be ready to change based on what I see and do in secondary classrooms. Kids keep changing; so must my pedagogy.

These two experiences, my time in public schools as a student and as a teacher, are my baselines for English education. But these are not enough. I do have ideas about the development of literacy. And, although my ideas were formed before graduate school, it was the great learning theories I began reading as a graduate student that gave my ideas depth. I am grateful for all the reading I have done over the years. I feel the last twenty years have been outstanding years of research and theory for English education. Those of us in the profession have a common literature that is both deep and wide. Although reading cannot be everything, it gives me a sense of completeness as an English educator. When I model a teaching practice, I understand the roots of that practice.

What the learning theories of English education have taught me: What the roots are of the practices I model. Although my teaching practices change based on secondary classrooms, the ideas behind those practices stay stable or grow in the direction our research and theory grows. So classrooms change my ideas rapidly about teaching methodology, but they seldom change my ideas about learning theory. In other words, my view of language learning changes a lot slower than my view of how English is taught. For my learning theory to change or adapt, I must see other theory and research that is convincing. For my teaching methodology to change, all I need are some classroom failures.

So what I have just described are my roots as an English educator. The experiences I discuss above have led me to teach English education in the way I do. I find English education to be enormously complex with few concrete answers and constant problems and unresolved questions. But this is what makes my job so interesting and here are some of my attempts at solving the problems.

The Teaching of English Education

On Teaching Theory

I feel it is very important that my students attempt to develop thoughtful ideas about the teaching of English and I do this in two ways.

First, I model practice that springs from different theory bases, such as reader response or differing writing theory, and we discuss the theory behind the models.

This is very evident after I have finished our classroom performance of *A Midsummer Night's Dream.* Among the issues I discuss with my students after the production include: What has this taught us about learning to read? What do we now know about difficult texts? What have we learned about teacher expectations? Based on this experience, how do you define collaborative teaching? What are the advantages and disadvantages of collaborative education? Was it easier to read and understand Shakespeare by performance? If yes, why?

I base my teaching of writing course on six models—preparing the writing workshop; making assignments; freewriting; revising and editing for public writing; and evaluating writing. After each model, my students are asked to reflect on the ideas undergirding the pedagogy and to evaluate each model theoretically and practically.

My second approach to teaching theory is more direct. I spend time in one of my classes with a large unit on theory. I give direct lectures on theory; and my students have to read theory from the Cleary and Linn text *Linguistics for Teachers* (1993) and from the McCracken and Appleby book, *Gender Issues in the Teaching of English* (1992), and my students have to complete a series of essays based on theoretical questions such as:

- What are the theories of learning that support language arts instruction?

- What are the bases of the new approaches to language arts instruction—whole language, process writing, response-based literature teaching?

- What should teachers know about dialect and its influence on speaking, reading, and writing?

- What do we know about grammar and what are the best approaches to the teaching of grammar?

- What should teachers know about gender differences?

On Teaching Pragmatics

Almost all the pedagogy I teach my students is done through models. That is, I demonstrate almost every teaching idea or technique I want my students to learn. On the rare occasion I do not model a technique, it means I am in the process of developing a model for it. These are some examples of my classroom models:

- My entire teaching of writing course is based on the six models I mentioned above.

- I model discipline techniques where my college students simulate high schoolers.

- We hold a dozen reader response discussions based on young adult novels.

- I model a whole language unit on the teaching of *The Great Gatsby* as a model novel unit.

- My students and I deal with censorship issues through simulations including a unique real-life experience with *Huckleberry Finn.*

- Our poetry unit consists of reading and writing models both student-centered and teacher-centered.

- my students develop and simulate middle school English classes complete with interaction and structured group work.

- I am developing a reading workshop model.

It is obvious that I believe the only way I can teach pedagogy is by example. I may change my mind in the future. I try to remain humble in the face of the challenges presented by English education and I do not consider any classroom practice fixed forever.

I need to mention one other classroom practice of mine. I teach a school-based grammar unit using Warriner's *English Composition and Grammar* (1988). I don't like to do this, but I do it to protect my students from the nasty realities they all seem to face when they walk into schools. I use *English Composition and Grammar* not only for practical reasons, but because my students so easily see the inconsistencies and difficulties with this text. I, of course, in no way recommend this method of teaching grammar, but I feel negligent if I don't help my students face the grammar fascists they will encounter.

On Field Experiences

Over the years I have developed a network of friendly teachers in our area and we have been able to put together a complex field-based program we call the "Kenmore Project," named after Kenmore High School, where the project started. I can proudly add that the project won an NCTE Center of Excellence Award. My students are required to spend time in real classrooms in the semesters they take my courses. Most of my students spend time with Kenmore Project teachers who know how I teach and work very closely with me. As part of the project, my students may stay with their Kenmore teachers for student teaching if it is mutually agreeable. If this happens, we proffer these students the Kenmore Project Student Teaching award.

The Kenmore Project is worth articles of its own, so I can only write so much about it here. It is one of the professional accomplishments I am most proud of having achieved. The project gives my classes a depth I could achieve in no other way. The project allows me to hold some of my classes in real schools and allows high school teachers to visit the University to guest teach parts of my classes. Best of all, my students engage in dialogue with high school teachers about what my students have seen modeled in my classes at the University. The high school mentors provide my students with glimpses of reality that transcend anything I can manage to do in a university classroom. This project provides a depth to my English education program not achievable in any other way.

If I were asked what may be the most important task for a new English educator, I would respond, "Go out and get yourself English teacher friends in public schools. They will become your teachers as well as mentors for your students. And, also, ask them to allow you to teach their students on occasion. It will keep you humble."

Questions That Never Go Away

As I have stated before, I find English education to be a very complex field. I continue to have questions that require answers I search for:

- How do I transfer college classroom experiences into teaching skills for my students?

- What is the right mix of field experience with course work before student teaching?

- What is the place of theory in an English education program?

- What are the best ways of linking theory with practice?

- What do I have to offer teachers who are willing to work with my students?

- How do my theories of learning and teaching practices work with different school populations? Is there a difference between urban, rural, and suburban English teaching?

- How best can I help my students face diverse students?

- How do my teaching ideas work for nonnative English speakers and writers?

- How does technology impact the English classroom?

- What is the future direction of literacy and how will this impact English teaching?

- How can my students keep classrooms in control while allowing their students decision-making power over what they read and write?

- How important are film and television studies in English classrooms?

- How do I prepare my students to cope with peers and parents who may not understand their new ideas and methodologies?

- How do I convince some liberal arts graduates of the importance of considering the student in the classroom (see Clift 1987)?

- What changes do I need to make to improve the quality of my teaching and my program?

- How can I help my college grow in a good direction for teacher education?

- What is a good direction for teacher education? Is graduate teacher certification better than undergraduate? Is a field-based experiential program better than a college-based program, or is a combination the best model?

These and countless other questions remain with me as daily reminders of the difficulty of my job. In essence, these are the kinds of questions most English educators ask themselves all the time.

Joining Forces

Thus, I am no English teacher. I am an English educator who finds being close in proximity to the field experience office is every bit as important as being able to see the English Department Chair every day. Yet, on my best days on campus I feel a kinship with my colleague professors in all departments because we need each other. All university professors, particularly at state universities, need to wage in-common battles that we face nowadays. We can no longer afford to fight each other. There are powerful forces aligned against us, and the entire university for that matter. The issues we face include:

- The rethinking of the curriculum, particularly English, in the areas of reading theory, literature selection, and, of course, writing. I support this postmodern trend and I wish my colleagues success as they attempt to modernize and, to a large extent, democratize the curriculum. These painful changes of canon and methodology need support and I do my share in conversations with students and colleagues.

- The downward spiral of support, economic and psychological, from the public sector for higher education. No one I know has seen a crisis in higher education as large as the one we are now facing. Budget cuts have so drastically reduced funding that the existence of entire universities is threatened. Our state legislature is threatening to pass bills which redefine tenure, and would require every professor at a state institution to teach at least one additional course. The public mistrust of higher education has never been greater, brought on by sports scandals, improper research grant expenditures, a perceived deemphasis on teaching, and political correctness controversies.

- The numeracy and literacy problems that so many of our students bring to the university. Professors in all departments and colleges confront learning problems that need special attention.

So I feel there is plenty that English professors and education professors need to do. Both colleges are under siege in this terrible time for higher education. *ProfScam* and *Illiberal Education,* known to our legislators, were aimed at all of us. The battles aimed at both of us may prove deadly. We have our hands full.

Works Cited

Cleary, Linda Miller and Michael D. Linn. 1993. *Linguistics for Teachers.* New York: McGraw-Hill.

Clift, Renee. 1987. "English Teacher or English Major." *English Education* (December): 229–36.

D'Souza, Dinesh. 1991. *Illiberal Education: The Politics of Race and Sex on Campus.* New York: Free Press.

Foster, Harold M. 1994. *Crossing Over: Whole Language for Secondary English Teachers.* Fort Worth, TX: Harcourt Brace.

McCracken, Nancy and Bruce Appleby, eds. 1992. *Gender Issues in the Teaching of English.* Portsmouth, NH: Boynton/Cook.

Sykes, Charles J. 1988. *Profscam: Professors and the Demise of Higher Education.* Washington DC: Regnery Gateway.

Warriner, John E. 1988. *English Composition and Grammar.* 7 vol. Orlando: Harcourt Brace Jovanovich.

VII Making Connections

My experiences with teaching reasoning and critical thinking control my current teaching; I fear that they define me.

Richard L. Larson

23 Downshifting to Fourth

Toby Fulwiler
University of Vermont

1967

On a crisp September morning, I park my '61 Volkswagen in the faculty lot two blocks from Old Main, and walk, striding with all the confidence I can muster, new olive sportcoat, skinny green tie, creased khaki pants, wingtips, Masters degree, toward "American Literature: Colonial to 1865." Smiling, explaining ("You can call me Toby"), handing out, holding on, sitting, finally standing, and introducing thirty-five Stevens Point sophomores to Jonathan Edwards, Thomas Paine, and Benjamin Franklin. I will teach close reading of texts, assign one, draft papers, and collect out-of-class journals at the end of the semester. When the bell rings I ask, "Do you have any questions?"

My first mentor, Paul Freidman, who teaches creative writing, tells me the only comment he puts in the margins of student papers is "K" for "awkward," meaning the passage next to the K should be rewritten. My second mentor, Charlie Kempthorne, asks students to write something for ten minutes, then exchange with a classmate to "make it better," then reexchange again to "make it better," and then do it again. Paul and Charlie, along with Strunk and White, teach me that teaching writing is teaching rewriting.

1968

Melvin Laird, soon to be Secretary of Defense, is our congressman; Lee Dreyfus, soon to be governor, is our university president; they both support the war in Vietnam. Paul, Charlie, Bill Lutz, and I organize a teach-in called "Structure in Unstructure" (my title, I think) to protest the war. We hold these free university classes in the empty Ford dealership downtown, Lutz discovering "doublespeak," me analyzing *Time*style, and all of us writing, editing, and publishing *Counterpoint*, our underground newspaper, my first publication.

1969

Returning to Madison to finish my doctorate with Merton Sealts (a Melville man), I am hired by Bob Kimbrough (a Shakespeare man) to teach in the Integrated Liberal Studies Program (ILS), which keeps together one-hundred-some students for two years, twelve courses, and an interdisciplinary approach to knowledge. When Gretchen Schoff (a writing woman) visits my composition class one day, I spend the whole period teaching *The Tempest*, distinguishing proudly, as new critics were trained to distinguish, which minor character shouts which line revealing what, in the opening twelve lines of the play. After class, Gretchen notes that, when the play is actually produced, those twelve lines are delivered on stage, simultaneously, in about twelve seconds.

1970

A month before Wisconsin National Guard troops occupy Bascom Hill and Bascom Hall, ending everyone's semester with A's, the Teaching Assistant Association (TAA) to which I belong declares a strike, arguing that graduate students teach 62 percent of Wisconsin's classes and deserve a larger role in planning those classes. We also want a few more things, including access to the supply closet—yellow pads, paper clips, Scotch tape. I am shop steward for the ILS Department, Harry Brent for English, and Ira Shore is our parliamentarian. As picket captain, I lead a squad at the corner of Johnson and Park Streets trying to stop Teamster-driven trucks from delivering food to student dormitories in the wee hours of the morning. After twenty-eight days we sign a contract and return to teaching, losing educational planning, but winning the yellow pads, paper clips, and Scotch tape.

1971

A year after Megan is born, and two years before I finish "The Failure Story: A Study in American Autobiography" (revised for but never published by Greenwood Press), I help invent "Workshop Week," during which students offer relevant classes for faculty and faculty offer hobby classes for students. I enroll in "Music of the Doors," "Ten Speed Bicycle Repair," and offer "Introduction to Photography," setting up my Bessler enlarger in a dark room in the basement next to the boiler, the war in Vietnam fading as my concern for the craft of teaching continues to rise.

1976

Two years after Anna's birth—a real family of four now, one-year lectureships wearing thin—I drive the Squareback to the Palmer House, in Chicago, to interview with what I believe to be Michigan State.

Dean Powers, on his way back from an MLA Convention in California, interviews us four at a time—lucky for me, since his description of "three hundred inches of snow" and "the absence of stoplights within a hundred mile radius," do not jibe with my picture of East Lansing. What I am interviewing for, it turns out, is Michigan *Tech*, not *State*, on the southern shore of Lake Superior (so I heard it wrong on the phone). When Powers asks what I know about teaching composition, I tell him about Paul, Charlie, Gretchen, and *The Elements of Style*. When he asks me what else I know, I tell him about teaching photography. It's the photography (the boiler room class), that causes Tech to hire me as Director of Technical Communication. But in August, they hire Phil Rubens, a professional in technical writing, to direct that program. In September, new head, Art Young asks me to direct the composition program. And so I begin my life's work as a consolation prize.

1977

At the Rutgers NEH Summer Seminar, I first read James Britton, James Moffet, Janet Emig, Nancy Martin, Peter Elbow, Ken Macrorie, Don Murray, James Kinneavy, and Mina Schaughnessy in a workshop run by Lee Odell and Dixie Goswami—texts and teachers who add considerably to my stock of composition knowledge. Though Art sends me here to learn about directing composition, I come back with writing across the curriculum, holding the first Tech workshop for sixteen faculty on the screened porch of the Keweenaw Mountain Lodge, forty miles from campus, in October—a cold but heady time.

1978

When we ask the Engineering faculty to conduct a four-day workshop for the Humanities faculty, to explain what we should know to teach writing to their students, they teach me to use overhead projectors—which the British teach me to call "OHP's." An English teacher for ten years, afraid of high-tech inventions, I think "I can do that." At Vermont now, every writing classroom has an OHP chained in the corner—that, along with a designated motorcycle parking space next to Old Mill, my major victory.

1982

My survey American literature syllabus says, "No exams, formal papers, or quizzes will be given. Instead, each student will keep an interactive journal of ideas to be shared with instructor six times during the ten-week quarter, and to attend class faithfully. Students who write a good journal (good = lots of serious entries) will get good grades (good = A's and B's); students who do less (fewer or less serious entries) will get less (less = C's); students who do nothing ( ), will get nothing ( )." Grading is easy and nobody gets nothing and I learn that good teaching is anything you invent it to be.

1983

Together at Michigan Tech, Art Young and I have learned the secret of academic success: "Never finish one project before you start another—preferably two," a philosophy tough on family life, vacations, and personal hobbies. (During this period, I lose golf, fishing, and photography, putting in their stead reading, writing, and research. At the same time, I find quick relief from academic pressure in an old black BMW motorcycle that I ride in the short Upper Peninsula summers.) The publishing prevents perishing and racks up one hell of a vita, landing me, in 1983, a job in a literature department on the East Coast (associate professor with tenure), Vermont deciding to hire a writing czar, I'm later told, to get writing off the backs of the English faculty. For me, however, the move to Vermont is a move south, to give Laura, Megan, and Annie more room to grow than provided by the Houghton snow.

1989

At Vermont, my survey American literature syllabus says, "If you hand in ten good pages of your journal three times in the next fifteen weeks, 10 percent of your grade will be an A." Each meeting, the students form into six groups of five each; we start with journals. This everyday formation makes it difficult to attract and keep everybody's attention, even when I write profound and provocative things on the OHP, but easy for students to talk to each other, both asking and answering questions. Everyone writes three two-draft papers (critical, personal, and imaginative) and a take-home final exam (collaborative on a question of the group's own posing). The class works well, and I tell its story in the MLA book edited by Anne Herrington and Charlie Moran, me believing that teaching literature and teaching writing are two halves of the same whole. In spite of this belief, I am promoted to full professor by my department.

1990

At times I burn out, tire of being a traveling salesman for writing across the curriculum, organizing collaborative publication projects (*Community of Voices*, 1992; *Angles of Vision*, 1992), administering composition programs, and arguing with my department about hiring just one composition colleague. For a time, I quit all this and attend to my students, where I discover, much to my relief, that it's teaching makes me whole again.

In late August, I walk into the first-year writing classroom in Lafayette Hall, with twenty-five first-day students, waiting silently for their first college class to begin. I pass out lined paper, plug in the tape recorder, and begin playing Bob Marley, the students watching me closely. They are nursing, business, education, and engineering students taking a required writing class, expectations are low, and they do not want to be here. I continue to say nothing, but write on the OHP: "Welcome to English 1—a writing class. Get it? A *writing*—not a talking—class. Please spend the next seventy-five minutes getting to know each other and me by writing, not talking." Then I sit down, writing quickly, confidently, and passing notes, waiting for questions.

The first paper they write, based on personal experience, they write for seven weeks. After their first draft, every Tuesday they arrive in class with three to five pages of new copy from a different perspective: time limited to an hour or less (limiting), a whole draft in dialogue (adding), a draft switched to third person or present tense (switching), a new genre or form (transforming). At the end I lighten up, encouraging whatever version makes the most sense now, and then we begin a collaborative research essay, same process, and by term's end, I read the best student writing of my twenty-three-year teaching life. Teaching rewriting is teaching writing.

1991

In the spring, when I teach "Writing *The New Yorker*," a seminar for senior English majors, each student writes his and her way through the major *New Yorker* genres: a "Talk" piece, a "Profile," a "Reporter at Large," a "Review," a poem or story, a cartoon or cover (it was a lot simpler before Tina Brown took over the magazine). Instead of questions at the end of class, I mostly just hold on and get out of the way, English majors becoming manic writers when introduced to living subjects.

1992

On a crisp September afternoon, at 5:30, I walk out of the English Department faculty meeting before it is over. My colleagues have just refused, for the tenth consecutive year, to add one composition Ph.D. to our thirty-five member full-time faculty. I walk, striding with all the confidence I can muster, to the new white motorcycle parked in the lot next to Old Mill, buckle my helmet tight, crouch low, and ride the long way home, downshifting often to fourth, passing, with great satisfaction, everything in my way. At home, I pour a stiff vodka, and try again to remember why I came here and what I do. Later, I sit up in bed reading student essays—serious, sometimes funny, innocent, honest—and remember.

The last assignment I make in "Personal Voice" (an advanced composition class) requires these juniors and seniors to collect all of their own earlier writing, analyze it, and describe the evolution of their writing voice. Before they look at theirs, we all look at mine, a series of pages from my own professional writing going back ten years. The last piece I put on the OHP is an excerpt from my chapter, "Propositions of a Personal Nature," from Tom Waldrep's second volume of *Writers on Writing*. "Propositions" is written in what Winston Weathers calls "crots," short prose passages with white space for transitions—sort of "The Wasteland" in prose. Like Eliot, I too hate writing transitions, can't you tell?

1993

I write the syllabus for my graduate seminar, "Studies in Rhetoric and Composition," as a letter: "Dear Classmates _____" and sign it Toby. I invite (require) these MA candidates to write back weekly (two single-spaced pages): "Dear Toby," I respond to these Thursday letters in one collective letter, "Dear Classmates," and mail it back on Monday. They share concerns and questions about the class, the readings, the role of language in their personal lives, and learn that writing, once again, can be fun. The letters change the course and the lives of its inhabitants in every possible way for the better. At the end, each submits an edition of "collected letters," excerpts from fifteen weeks, complete with introduction, afterward, and a classmate-written preface—a graduate paper with all the trimmings.

1994

On the second sabbatical leave of my life, I go nowhere, except by motorcycle to nearby conferences. I attend to my writing; I keep in e-mail touch with colleagues who matter; I witness the publication of my four-year commercial project, *The Blair Handbook*; I avoid all matters departmental; and sometimes I miss my students. I also publish my first article about "riding" not "writing," in *BMW Motorcycle Owners of America News* (April, 1994). I've learned again, twenty-seven years after the *Counterpoint* teach-ins, that the writing and the teaching together make me whole. When I return in the fall, I plan to invite the students in "Personal Voice" to co-author with me "The Writer's Voice," an experimental advanced composition textbook (three credits and a byline).

Spring

I no longer have Upper Peninsula illusions that Vermont is south. Today it is April and cold and it actually snowed for a time. But I take the white BMW, anyway, for my weekly check of office mail. I ride carefully in the early morning traffic, downshifting no more than I have to, braking gently, steering with caution, watching the curves, with patience, for ice and gravel. My next teaching season, when I will trade my sabbatical leathers for Harris tweed, denim for corduroy, black boots for brown Oxfords, feels close, and that is OK. I am rested and ready and know the students are waiting.

Works Cited

Biddle, Arthur W., Toby Fulwiler, and Mary Jane Dickerson. 1992. *Angles of Vision: Reading, Writing, and the Study of Literature.* New York: McGraw-Hill.

Fulwiler, Toby. 1985. "Propositions of a Personal Nature." *Writers on Writing,* ed. Tom Waldrep. New York: Random House.

Fulwiler, Toby, and Arthur W. Biddle, eds. 1992. *A Community of Voices: Reading and Writing in the Disciplines.* New York: Macmillan.

Strunk, William. 1959. *The Elements of Style.* New York: Macmillan.

24 Connecting the Teaching of Reading, Writing, and Speech in Programs for Developmental Students

Judith Entes
Baruch College, The City University of New York

Wednesday is my favorite day. It was the day when, with the permission of my parents, I played hooky from school. My parents kept me from school; there was something more important, each and every year, that prevented me from attending classes—the theater. Even now, a ticket to a Broadway matinee performance costs substantially less than to other performances. Since I was one of four children, and my parents wanted to make going to the theater a family outing, attending evening performances was prohibitively costly, but attending in the afternoon was affordable.

And the circus, at Madison Square Garden (when it was on 50th Street, and also since it moved to its current location, on 33rd Street), every year offered Wednesday matinee performances for children at a discount. Often large groups of classes attended, many brought by buses. But I attended schools in Manhattan, and the schools never scheduled trips to the circus. So I was allowed to cut classes, and so were my cousins. And the group included my father's two brothers and their children.

Not only did my family value this activity, but so did others. All those kids whirling their lights in the darkness, illuminating this large arena—it shed some light on education, telling me that learning doesn't always take place in the classroom and dramatizing the need for collaboration and interaction. In the circus, in particular, the audience participated in the action. Individuals were chosen to ride on the animals or play with the clowns.

My parents also took me to folk concerts. Those didn't take place on Wednesday afternoons, but most often on weekends. And I was allowed to stay up late on a school night in February to attend the annual concert at Cooper Union celebrating the Presidents' birthdays; those concerts were later broadcast on radio station WNYC. The audience would join in and help the performer(s), often singing the chorus. And even now, these singers, Pete Seeger and Oscar Brown, are performing, and I join them, remembering and reminiscing about the connections—the connections between performer and audience.

There was a common thread among these live performances: the performers apppeared to love what they did. And I too wanted to find work that I loved. Teaching reading and writing in college, often to students who are the first ones in their family to attend college—this love affair has been going on for over twenty years.

Teaching is interactive, like the theater, and the processes of reading and writing depend on the audience, as in the theater. And to catch the attention of students, the teacher at times needs to perform, as in the theater. There are many links between teaching and theater, particularly the teaching of English. Throughout my academic studies, I specialized in "Reading" rather than the subject of "English." But the two are both concerned with the arts of language, with developing literacy. In my training, there was an emphasis on psychology, and in my doctoral studies, reader-response theory. The emphasis was upon involvement, particularly student participation. This focus appealed to me as I considered my teaching strategy. Rather than lecturing, I promoted student-teacher interaction. This practice supported the theory that there is not one correct response to literature; I recognize that there are many effective responses.

My philosophy of education, my insistence on creating a democratic, interactive community of learners, allowed me to develop a classroom where students could perform and also attend various cultural events within the college and outside.

As a child, I experienced with my family a great deal of attention to reading and speaking. Communication was considered extremely important, and my father felt so strongly that the television interfered with oral and written dialogue that he gave away the television set. He was particularly annoyed when, during visits to relatives on Sunday afternoon, his brother-in-law, instead of conversing with him, preferred to watch football. And it ruined the day for him when he visited his brother, and the evening snack tables were set in front of the TV, and instead of engaging in lively discussions we were hushed and sat in silence eating and watching Ed Sullivan. At our house, in the evening, we would all eat together and talk for hours. When most families would put on their TVs, we would read, play, and talk, and sometimes my father would write.

When I'm asked how I learned to read, I say that I learned from hearing my parents read to me each night—when I was a toddler, from children's books, and when I was older, from Sherlock Holmes and *Robinson Crusoe*. And during my adolescence I would read plays and act out different scenes or create puppet shows or musical revues. As a teenager I was employed by Mobilization for Youth, in which high school students worked together in creating theater, particularly inter-active performances. We performed on 2nd Avenue, in Off-Broadway houses that were the home of Yiddish theatre and burlesque. Those houses are closed, but there are still many Broadway, Off-Broadway, and Off-Off-Broadway theaters that I frequent regularly.

Often today, informally, I arrange for students to attend theater events, and, formally, in the spring 1988 semester, I organized a Cultural Enrichment Program under which students attended ballet, Flamenco dancing, museums, theaters, etc. Students read from *A Streetcar Named Desire* and saw the Broadway production of the play.

As a member of the Academic Skills Department (ASD, known until July 1991, as the Department of Compensatory Programs) at Baruch College of The City University of New York, I taught an intro-ductory reading course to freshmen. The department housed the SEEK Program (the acronym stands for Search for Education, Elevation, Knowledge). SEEK is a state-funded program that pro-vides "economically and educationally disadvantaged students with academic services."

I attended a lecture by Alan Dershowitz discussing his book *ChutzPah* (1991); he talked about Jewish values. He said that Jewish culture promoted education and helping others, often those less fortu-nate. Reflecting on my childhood, I realized that these values were instilled in me. My parents reminded their children of those values by practicing such behavior; they enrolled in courses throughout their life, and volunteered to help those in need. Professionally, my father represented individuals who were "underdogs" and were battling insurance companies.

I always felt very fortunate to be brought up in a loving family, and I was well aware that there were many less fortunate. I was able to help others, who mostly did not have family attending higher education and were mostly the first to take this journey.

For us, attending college never seemed to be a choice. It was mandatory—the natural next step after high school. My father would discuss his best years, attending City College and Columbia. Learning was fun. And now that I think back, I realize I was lucky to perform well on standardized tests. I was in elementary school at the time of Sputnik and I was one the few girls who scored high on the science test battery. My teachers praised me for my scientific ability though I did not study science in the curriculum, nor did I have much opportunity to demonstrate my "expertise." If memory serves, it was the third grade when I was in the ninety-ninth percentile and my grade level in reading was the equivalent of a senior in high school. It was then that I became suspicious of grade levels in reading; how, I wondered, could I be reading as if I was a senior in high school when I was an elementary school student? However, a high score allowed me to read what I wanted. There were some who were taken out of the class to read from the basals, and also to deal with the shame and suffering of being labeled "remedial."

The first course I taught at Baruch was Communication Skills (CCS), a required class for entering freshmen who did not pass the standardized Reading Proficiency Test. Students were block programmed; all of them attended the same English, CCS (the reading component), and Speech classes.

While teaching CCS, I interacted with English and Speech faculty members in planning the curriculum. Depending on the "team" members and their schedules, we met together, talked on the telephone, and gave each other feedback about teaching and students. We often tried to build our teaching around a common theme, and we tried to complement each other's activities. The benefits extended to both teachers and students. For us as teachers, we were not isolated. We could learn from each other, share, and even develop personal friendships. Even now, though we may not have seen each other for over a decade, when we do meet, there is a special bond, sort of like family. There was also a feeling of unity. We were committed to helping the students achieve success—students who were often labeled "at risk" and were not always embraced by the academic community.

The students, too, were able to develop friendships with classmates. They spent several hours each day with the same fellow students, since they attended at least three classes together. And they received instruction in courses with deliberate connections. We were knowledgeable about what was going on in each others' classrooms, and we coordinated the activities we planned. We tried to demonstrate to our students, who had been judged not prepared for college work in language, that reading, writing, and talking are interdependent activities that support and, indeed, crossfertilize each other.

CCS was terminated. Students were placed (by basic skills tests administered at entrance into college) in separate English, Reading, and Speech classes. It was unlikely that faculty teaching these classes communicated with each other regularly, or indeed had any contact at all, because the departments of English and Speech are separate units in the School of Liberal Arts and Sciences (LA & S) and ASD had been moved from LA & S to the School of Education and Educational Services (SEES).

For me, this separation is unhealthy: it weakens the instruction of the students most "at risk," most in need of coordinated instruction in language if they are to succeed in college and go on to productive lives. I have for over two decades tried to teach collaboratively with colleagues to give the greatest benefits to students most in need. I am convinced that working closely with colleagues and students on the teaching of reading, writing, speech, and the subject matters of academic study is essential to our efforts teaching these students.

But I am also concerned about how these students are placed into their courses. And now documents recently published by the National Council of Teachers of English and the International Reading Association state that multiple measures are needed for fair assessment. Yet, at the college level, placement is often determined by one single test, a test that is not necessarily measuring what college students need to know and be able to do.

What is even more frightening is that beginning in the fall of 1993, the score on the Writing Assessment Test (WAT) will carry even more weight than ever since students will be placed in a range of remedial English *and* Reading classes based on that score. In addition, I am confused about how students are labeled as ESL (English as a Second Language) based on their WAT scores; students so labeled are required to take at least eight contact hours of instruction with no credit.

I question why these tests are being administered. What is their purpose? Why are the decisions made to use them? And who makes these decisions? Students are placed in my class because of a low score on the Descriptive Test of Language Skills (DTLS), but my curriculum is not based on having students read stilted paragraphs and having them select only one correct response to each question about the paragraph. This kind of examination is in conflict with "reader-response" theory, which holds that more than one answer may be considered appropriate. Within my classroom I ask students to develop working portfolios, collecting and reflecting upon their reading and writing, and using authentic materials—real readings and writings required of them in the academy and at home and at work. There are many assignments; students read works by many different authors and must write many different kinds of papers. Portfolios have long been used in assessment by the arts community. We can learn much in education from the arts.

The arts also recognize the need to collaborate. Artists depend upon others. My favorite kind of show is the musical, and when I am home, I try to bring back in memory a show I have just seen by singing the songs, or trying to. When I was a child, I learned the music of Rodgers and Hammerstein, Lerner and Lowe, Comden and Green, Kander and Ebb, Bock and Harnick, Schoenberg and Boubil, and Bernstein and Sondheim. These teams created classics still sung today. And when interviewed, members of these teams often said that they couldn't have produced their work without the help of the other team member. Yet some of these teams dissolved, and members found other partners.

Most successful creative ventures are not carried on in isolation. But the classroom is often isolated, the activities there carried on in isolation by teacher and students. The teacher is isolated; classroom instruction is not integrated with the work of other classes, and language activities are disconnected from each other. The natural connections among academic fields should be articulated. And the interrelatedness and interdependence of reading, writing, and speech should be highlighted.

There is in American higher education a movement toward interdisciplinary studies. Some English departments house, for example, cultural studies, women's studies, and business writing. And if these courses are not offered within the English Department, faculty coordinate and cosponsor or coteach courses in these areas. But I am not aware of English departments integrating their course offerings with Reading classes. Reading departments generally offer courses for no credit and their faculty are often marginalized.

At my college, in 1993, reading and writing are taught in isolation. The educational partnership between these central activities of literacy is dissolved, and there are no other partners.

That dissolution runs against my experience, especially my experience of theater. Those of us who have the opportunity to see Shakespeare performed know how much more powerful the experience becomes than when we just read the texts—how much is achieved when collaborating actors deliver aloud Shakespeare's words, speaking the language of kings and queens, against the background of an artfully designed set as illuminated by skillful lighting. I still remember performances of *The Taming of the Shrew* staged in Stratford, Connecticut, a theater-in-the-round, the outdoor performances of the Delacorte Theatre in Central Park, Mike Nichols's production of *Hamlet* on Broadway. Memories of those performances are still sharp for me today.

If in my free time I attend the theater, is this then an activity my students would enjoy? In polling my students, I found that most of them had never attended a theatrical event. And so, for many, my arranging to have the class attend a theatrical event is their first such experience—and one that they remember long after they leave the college.

To my amazement, theater producers are extremely supportive in arranging for groups of students to attend performances at a discounted rate. Sometimes it is for Wednesday matinees, and also for alternative days and times. The first class trip was to Circle Repertory, then located on Sheridan Square, under the artistic management of Marshall Mason. The production was the "Life of Richard Cory." Before the performance, the students read the poem "Richard Cory," by Edward Arlington Robinson, and I taped the Simon and Garfunkel song "Richard Cory." Besides introducing students to the song, I also introduced other songs by the same team, and told students about the group's history, their split, and their individual accomplishments. Though the students listen to music regularly, they were not familiar with the music of Simon and/or Garfunkel. Simon won a Grammy Award for his album *Graceland*. He donated some of his profits to help end apartheid, and though many of my students are African American they were not familiar with his interest in South African music or his campaign.

His interest allowed us to discuss the issues of enslavement and empowerment of peoples. And like most subjects, they are springboards for lots of topics on which students can read, write, and talk.

The power of literature is the universality of what it vividly represents. Many of the themes represented in literary texts speak to us all. Men and women can identify with the characters and situations represented in great works of literature as enacted by skillful performers, and can come to a deeper understanding of human experiences.

Ideally, it would be a better world if nations could be at peace with each other, working together toward a common goal. So, too, in the academy. But in the academy, what is best for students and for teachers is not always practiced. Though CCS no longer exists, I try informally to keep in contact with faculty from other departments so I can coordinate my teaching with theirs as they ask students attending their classes to engage in the performance of reading and writing and listening and speaking.

Stephen Sondheim wrote the music and lyrics for the songs in *Company*. If he had had a collaborator, that person might have influenced his song, "The Ladies at the Matinee" so that it would have become the "Children and/or Students Attending Wednesday Matinees." I hope to continue to arrange to have students attend performances of theatre and see the language arts interact.

But regardless of whether I can coordinate my teaching with that of other faculty and can encourage students' attendance at the theater, I am committed in my classroom to creating an environment where the connection is maintained between reading, writing, and speech, just as in drama and in the musical theater many specialized talents interact to create the experience we share during a performance.

Works Cited

Dershowitz, Alan. 1991. *Chutzpah*. Boston: Little, Brown.

25 Reuniting Grammar and Composition

James L. Collins
State University of New York at Buffalo

This essay tells the story of how I made my peace with the issue of grammar and composition. I tell how growing up a stutterer in a society that laughs at Porky Pig prejudiced me against correcting or otherwise commenting on outward characteristics of language. That prejudice is consonant with what the dominant ideology in English education tells us about grammar and composition, and it certainly influenced my work as an English teacher where for about a decade I consistently refrained from commenting on grammar and usage in my students' writing. My real purpose in this piece, however, is to argue that the profession's oppositional stance to teaching the conventions of written language is inappropriate. I use my personal triumph over stuttering to show how language use is the source of power needed to capitalize on the symbolic value society assigns to language, especially written language. In company with Lisa Delpit (1987, 1990) and other critics, I argue that instructional methods, such as whole language and process writing, do a disservice to nonmainstream students by not teaching the editing skills necessary to control those matters of form and usage which are crucial to symbolizing status and power. Finally, I offer suggestions for a new integration of language conventions and composition in the teaching of English and English education.

Almost twenty years ago, an article called "Stuttering Pencils" appeared in the *English Journal* (Stoen 1976). The article described stuttering as learned behavior and argued that writers can learn to stutter just as speakers do. In this view of the etiology of stuttering, children go through a period of normal nonfluency during early stages of language acquisition, and sometimes overanxious parents become alarmed by a child's hesitations and repetitions and tell the child to slow down, start over, pronounce words carefully, and so on. With time, such advice teaches the child to think of himself or herself as a stutterer. Experiences in school can reinforce that self-perception, as when other children find the stutterer's struggle to read aloud amusing. From Wendell Johnson's *People in Quandaries* the article borrows the term *diagnosogenic*, which Johnson coined to describe his finding that the diagnosis of stuttering is one of its causes. The article implies that diagnosing writing problems may help to create them. Just as a child can learn to have difficulty saying certain words fluently if he or she is consistently told to slow down and repeat the words, children can learn to have difficulty with writing if teachers emphasize correctness too much.

My own experience supported the "Stuttering Pencils" argument. "James has a tendency to stutter," my mother wrote in a note responding to my second-grade teacher's request for information about why I was so quiet, and what followed then and intermittently through junior high school was "speech therapy." A tall, gray-haired man, for example, would appear outside of my second-grade classroom, and his appearance at the door was the signal for me to put away my things and leave with him. My recollection of our sessions is that he would have me talk and try to figure out what was wrong with me. I remember him stopping me on one occasion, making me freeze while stumbling over a word, and saying something about my tongue being stuck at the roof of my mouth. And without him telling me to, I tried for a considerable time after that to hold a piece of gum under my tongue so that I might talk without my tongue touching the roof of my mouth. Later I discovered that Socrates, also a stutterer, tried the same trick, only with pebbles instead of gum. The gum did not help my speech, and in retrospect, I now believe that failure probably reinforced my stuttering by making the condition seem more permanent. Diagnosis became a contributing cause.

My early experience with stuttering and schooling left me strongly opposed to forcing kids to read aloud, to pulling kids out of classrooms, to ability grouping (which for me had too often meant *dis*ability grouping), and especially to correcting speakers. I carried these beliefs into my work as an English teacher. Above all, I was opposed to teaching grammar and usage because I wanted my students to listen and read for the message behind the words, for what people are saying instead of how they are saying it. I tried to persuade my students that the outward appearance of language has very little to do with the discovery or communication of meaning. My "anti-grammar and usage" position was, of course, consistent with what most current teachers of writing believe. The success of the writing-process movement has been to free composition from grammar study in textbooks

and workbooks, and this success was achieved by stripping the traditional preoccupation with rules of grammar and usage away from
composition instruction. The writing-process movement has had a
positive influence on the teaching of writing, if for no other reason
than because it liberated the profession from its overwhelming preoccupation with rules of format and correctness.

For me, though, the writing-process movement has gone too far.
Not all concern for the quality of written products and for adherence
to writing conventions deserves to be thrown out with old-fashioned,
overly prescriptive rules. Writing is a process, to be sure, and it is a
process of discovering meaning just as Graves (1983) and Atwell
(1987) and Elbow (1973) and the other process people tell us, but it is
also a process of exercising power. Writing is rule-governed, and using
writing as an instrument of power and not only as a tool of discovery
necessarily involves attending to the fixed and inviolable aspects of
written language, including matters of format and convention. Again,
I have come by this realization autobiographically. The influence this
time is not so much the fact that I once had "a tendency to stutter," but
rather the more important fact that I overcame that tendency.

Stuttering is a prison. Imagine not being able to pronounce your
name in front of a group of people, then add the feeling of extreme discomfort when some members of the audience begin to laugh, as if they
think you can't remember your name. Gradually the stutterer learns to
avoid speaking to anyone but family members and close friends.
Beyond a circle of intimates, socially inspired and enforced silence
becomes a way of life. This is especially true of classrooms where language is too frequently a measure of performance; the stutterer comes
to believe that teachers have kids talk primarily to try to figure out
what's wrong with them. And speech therapy provides little help; in
fact, like ability grouping or tracking or pull-out programs in general,
speech therapy, in my experience, is one of education's ways of trying
to make individual differences disappear from the regular classroom,
as if being "normal" is what school is really about.

I stopped stuttering because I wanted to. The change was
extremely gradual and involved making myself speak in acceptable
ways in a widening circle of friends and an expanding variety of contexts. It also involved, I am absolutely certain, the realizations that no
one's speech is perfectly fluent and well-formed and that the outward
appearance of speech—my own or anyone else's—is to a large extent
determined by the degree of comfort the speaker feels, the sense of
belonging or not in the particular speech situation, the personally felt

balance of power and the solidarity among participants in the speech community. In other words, my triumph over stuttering was not accomplished by overcoming a deep-seated shyness or some other anomaly. The cure, like the problem itself, was social, not psychological.

Therein resides the meaning of my experience for the teaching of writing. Language differences are social, not psychological, in origin. Patterns of language use are signs of group membership, indicators of degrees of familiarity and belonging, signs of status and power within and across cultural groups. Language has symbolic value beyond representing thought and word; it also tells who we are and what relation of power or solidarity is at work in a given communication situation. To borrow an economic metaphor from Bourdieu (1980), language standards have cultural capital because they are symbolic of knowledge and status; the conventions of standard language carry culturally significant attributes, such as prestige and authority, and like all language conventions, standard ones create a consensus within a community as to the significance of the social world. Whether we English teachers like it or not, language symbolizes power and status, and it does so in a manner that is deeply ingrained in cultural values. Correctness in language may be arbitrary in abstract theory, but in the real world, correctness is culturally determined and serves as one of the major ways discourse communities symbolize power relations and legitimate status. Given the fact of a dominant, standard language system, the choices for language users are only three: to not participate in the dominant language system, to participate in a manner that violates conventions, or to participate in conformity with conventions. For me, the first choice has meant silence, the second deviation, and the third power.

Obviously, I have lived and rejected the first two choices and selected the third one. My real point, however, is that democratic language education should make sure that every student gets to choose which of these three basic language options to pursue. Process writing and whole language may not be preserving that choice. Critics of such approaches to writing instruction, such as Delpit (1987; 1990), Gee (1990), and Kutz and Roskelly (1991), repeatedly focus on the difficulties implicit instruction—teaching which does not make expectations for language forms and conventions explicit—can pose for students whose discourse strategies diverge from mainstream literate discourse. By neglecting written products and conventions too much, the writing-process movement may be inadvertently reserving the primary benefits of literacy instruction for writers who are already familiar with literate language conventions. If so, the movement favors writers who are already experienced in the literate language of the dominant culture.

Whether or not to teach the conventions of written expression is not the issue. Of course we should teach students how to make their writing conform to the standards of educated prose. The real question is how to teach the conventions in a way that preserves dignity and comfort for learners, in a way that neither deprives nor embarrasses students, that does not reinforce incipient negative beliefs by implying that difference is caused by disorder in need of diagnosis and treatment. A crucial first step toward teaching language conventions in this manner is the realization that it is not the rules themselves that make grammar-based writing instruction ineffective so much as the direct teaching of the rules apart from genuinely literate activities. Mina Shaughnessy supports this latter view:

> It may well be that traditional grammar-teaching has failed to improve writing not because rules and concepts do not connect with the act of writing but because grammar lessons have traditionally ended up with exercises in workbooks, which by highlighting the feature being studied rob the student of any practice of seeing that feature in more natural places. (1977, 155)

Rules have been traditionally taught as a body of knowledge, a set of "narrow prescriptions" (Rose 1984, 96). I take the position, as do many writers and teachers, that it is better to teach conformity to conventions as an integral part of writing, not as a separate set of rules. In this analysis, we are not teaching correctness, we are not in the least concerned with spoken language, we are not focusing on writing problems isolated from acts of writing, and we are not separating editing from writing and revising. We are instead teaching students that editing is an integral part of writing and that editing has really only one rule: *Change your writing only to improve it for your audience*. As one editor writes, "whatever changes you make should be for accuracy, clarity, felicity, or just plain intelligibility" (Blair McElroy, quoted in Plotnik, 1982, 39).

The best argument I can offer for making editing an integral part of writing, for putting grammar and composition together again, is that literacy is the source of language standards in the first place. We have no academy-governed, arbitrary source of usage standards in this country. The closest we come to an official body of language overseers takes the form of usage panels, as when dictionaries assemble a panel of experts to rule on levels of usage for particular words. But how do these experts make their decisions? The authority they appeal to is literate language itself, since that is where we acquire our working sense of language standards. To quote Plotnik's *Elements of Editing*:

> A mastery of good syntax—how words are strung together well—can come in only two ways: by spending the first twenty-five years of one's life in a drawing room with E. B. White, Vladimir Nabokov, Elizabeth Bowen, Gabriel García Márquez, Saul Bellow, Eudora Welty, John Fowles, Langston Hughes, Joyce Carol Oates, James Baldwin, and John Updike—or by reading their works and those of other writers whose choices of words and word arrangement establish our standards of literate communication. (1982, 37)

If language conventions are best learned through writing practice, and if literature is the best authority on the conventions of written language, then it makes sense to have students write in a variety of styles from literary models. I want to be clear in recommending literary models that I am *not* advocating the reductive analysis and imitation of professional models used in so many English 101 textbooks. Rather, the idea I am advancing is that the "ingrained ear for language" that English teachers and other highly literate people acquire intuitively as a by-product of reading widely can be learned consciously by practicing writing in the ways and patterns of professional writers. What follows, for example, is an exercise in writing to study conventions of sentence construction that I have used with graduate students in English education. The example is an excerpt from a longer piece in which an English teacher, Niecy Felser, wrote in imitation of a professional writer, Annie Dillard, in *Pilgrim at Tinker Creek*. Here is Dillard's original text in which she describes her observation of a frog in a tiny pond:

> He didn't jump; I crept closer. At last I knelt on the island's winterkilled grass, lost, dumbstruck, staring at the frog in the creek just four feet away. He was a very small frog with wide, dull eyes. And just as I looked at him, he slowly crumpled and began to sag. The spirit vanished from his eyes as if snuffed. His skin emptied and drooped; his very skull seemed to collapse and settle like a kicked tent. He was shrinking before my eyes like a deflating football . . . . I gaped bewildered, appalled. An oval shadow hung in the water behind the drained frog; then the shadow glided away.
>
> I had read about the giant water bug, but never seen one. . . . The frog I saw was being sucked by a giant water bug. I had been kneeling on the island grass; when the unrecognizable flap of frog skin settled on the creek bottom, swaying, I stood up and brushed the knees of my pants. I couldn't catch my breath. (1974, 5)

And here is Niecy's imitation of Dillard's text in which she describes her observation of a shopper in a giant suburban mall:

> At the edge of the curb, I notice a short, elderly woman in a pink pantsuit. She is barely visible, hidden by a mound of bags and packages which surround her. I creep closer and am just able to make out the label affixed to her breast pocket. "HELLO, my name is: Mildred," it reads. She is a pale old lady with red drooping eyes. And just as I look at her, she slowly crumples and begins to sag. She is shrinking before my eyes like a deflating balloon at T.G.I. Friday's. I stand, open mouthed, as she slumps over onto a J.C. Penney shopping bag. I had read about people who "shopped 'til they dropped," but never seen it. Unable to catch my breath, I stagger toward the heavy glass doors hungry for the solace which lays beyond.

I think it is obvious how this exercise involves conscious imitation of part of a professional writer's work in constructing and perfecting sentences. Dillard herself sees value in paying close attention to the construction of sentences: "The reason to perfect a piece of prose as it progresses—to secure each sentence before building on it—is that original writing fashions a form" (Dillard 1989, 15). Dillard believes writing is perfected at the level of the sentence, an idea that flies in the face of the process approach where generally teachers and students are advised not to worry about sentence-level matters until the text level of writing production is under control. In spite of the imperatives of process, however, the fact remains that postponing attention to sentence form until a separate editing stage of the writing process, after the construction of text, is very close to the traditional notion that sentences should be worked on in isolation from the production of text, in practice exercises in handbooks or workbooks. Dillard instead views the sentence as the main building block of meaning, as a unit of thought and memory and understanding. Her advice to "perfect a piece of prose at it progresses" treats sentences as formative elements of the writing process. The writing-process approach, on the other hand, is more likely to view sentences as worthy of attention at the editing stage, a view that separates conventions of syntax, mechanics and punctuation from the construction of meaning.

Putting literature in the service of improving writing skills is a natural for English classes, since English teachers are responsible for both literature and composition, and the deliberate imitation of literary models approach teaches sentence craft and sentence conventions. Still, the imitation of literary models is not the only way of practicing the conventions of written language. I have found that *Time* and *Newsweek*, for example, also do an excellent job of modeling the conventions of educated writing for secondary and college students. In fact, any writing practice that puts process and conventions together gives writers access to the language of power in American society.

Works Cited

Atwell, Nancie. 1987. *In the Middle: Writing, Reading and Learning with Adolescents*. Portsmouth, NH: Boynton/Cook.

Bourdieu, Pierre. 1990. *The Logic of Practice*. Trans. Richard Nice. Stanford University Press.

Delpit, Lisa D. 1987. "Skills and Other Dilemmas of a Progressive Black Educator." *Equity and Choice* 3.2 (winter): 9–14.

———. 1988. "The Silenced Dialogue: Power and Pedagogy in Educating Other People's Children." *Harvard Educational Review* 58: 280–98.

Dillard, Annie. 1974. *Pilgrim at Tinker Creek*. New York: Harper's Magazine Press.

———. 1989. *The Writing Life*. New York: Harper and Row.

Elbow, Peter. 1973. *Writing without Teachers*. New York: Oxford University Press.

Gee, James Paul. 1990. *Social Linguistics and Literacies: Ideology in Discourses*. New York: Falmer.

Graves, Donald H. 1983. *Writing: Teachers and Children at Work*. Exeter, NH: Heinemann.

Kutz, Eleanor and Hephzibah Roskelly. 1991. *An Unquiet Pedagogy: Transforming Practice in the English Classroom*. Portsmouth, NH: Boynton/Cook Heinemann.

Plotnik, Arthur. 1982. *The Elements of Editing: A Modern Guide for Editors and Journalists*. New York: Macmillan.

Rose, Mike. 1984. *Writer's Block: The Cognitive Dimension*. Carbondale, IL: Southern Illinois University Press.

Shaughnessy, Mina P. 1977. *Errors and Expectations: A Guide for the Teacher of Basic Writing*. New York: Oxford University Press.

Stoen, Don. 1976. "Stuttering Pencils." *English Journal* 65: 40–41.

26 Confessions of a Teacher Who Has Not Learned about Teaching

Richard L. Larson
Lehman College, City University of New York

The essay that follows reflects on how I came to adopt a particular approach to the teaching of reasoning and writing, and how that approach became the flimsy foundation of a teaching career. The essay tells of where, and to some extent why, I began to employ that approach, of how very slowly I came to understand what I was trying to teach. And it tells of what I did not learn—and still have not learned—about how to relate what I teach to the needs of students, or about the value to students of what I have tried to teach. And it tells of totally unsuccessful efforts at another kind of teaching—leading a staff of teachers to the emphases I was trying to establish. Finally, it tells of puzzlements I confront even today in my teaching. Writing the essay has forced me to reappraise the work of some forty years of teaching, and to confront questions/problems I have not been wise enough to address or to answer.

Without knowing it, I was ripe and ready for an approach to the teaching of writing that departed substantially from the kind of teaching I had experienced in high school and in my first years in college, where the subject matters of writing in English courses were mainly two: personal experiences and literary texts. But my private reading in high school had consisted mainly of detective stories, legal casebooks, and Blackstone's *Commentaries* on the laws of England; I was convinced that I would study law and enter the legal profession. But in my second year at Harvard College I developed doubts, mainly about the integrity of those in that profession. (In the 1940s in Massachusetts, such doubts were easy to develop.) But I liked to read, and as a result decided to major in English as an undergraduate, then to attend graduate school in English and enter college teaching.

My first professional job was as a part-time section man and tutor in the Harvard English Department. In the 1950s, section men (there were almost no women) and tutors were self-taught. We were given a syllabus and list of students and told to go teach. So I improvised, trying to teach students what I thought I had learned as an undergraduate and as a graduate student of English literature. I devised rather detailed assignments in the written explication (often through line-by-line commentary) of literary texts, focusing the assignments and my responses to students' papers on the structures of language and the development of themes and characters in the texts we were studying. (In that era, when the study of literature was heavily indebted to what was called the "New Criticism," such assignments fit exactly the conventional expectations for the course I was teaching.) I had some notion of what I wanted to teach students about reading literary texts: I wanted them to learn to focus attentively on the resonance and significance of individual words and idioms in context, and on patterns of words and images in the text. I wanted them to recognize the "interinanimations of words" (the semanticist I. A. Richards's term; his *Practical Criticism* (1935) was an influential volume). But I had little sense of how to *teach* students to write about literary texts; I merely asked them to focus sharply on the language of the texts, to be as clear as possible about how they read the texts, and to support their analyses with specific references to and elucidation of the texts—lessons I'd had to learn in my own course work. For me, "assigning" papers and leading class discussions was "teaching." I had not heard of "prewriting" or of asking students to collaborate (except in class discussions). I never thought about asking students for revisions of papers; students simply moved to the next assignment.

When I had completed my allowed number of years as a teaching fellow at Harvard, a position opened at the Harvard Graduate School of Business Administration for a person who would teach sections of a course called "Written Analysis of Cases" in the first year of the two-year M.B.A. program. I was encouraged to interview for it because the Chair of English at Harvard thought it would be good for me to retain easy access to Harvard's libraries. I was duly hired as an instructor. Two or three people jokingly compared me to a man from an English Department who had been hired many years earlier to be a reader of papers at the Business School and had stayed on to become a distinguished professor of marketing, as if I might have some delusions about following a similar path.

My work at the Business School, which extended for seven years, was, as I reflect on it, the turning point of my professional life. Teaching at the Business School was unlike any teaching I had done before, or indeed had ever experienced in school, college, or graduate school. Instruction at the Business School was carried on through the study of "cases," written presentations of data, prepared by case writers, about a business organization—the data disclosing and giving extended information about a "problem" on which an executive had to make a decision, or several decisions, and take some action. The curriculum of the first-year program was at that time divided into seven courses (students took all seven), including principally Marketing, Control (i.e., Accounting), Finance, and Production (of manufactured goods), Administrative Practices (essentially human relations in a business context), and the course I taught. All courses were built mostly around cases, occasionally supplemented by explanatory "technical notes" sketching the substantive information, or the technical procedures, a student needed to know in order to address the cases.

The faculty did not lecture, though teachers occasionally explained concepts that arose during the discussions. Classes held ninety students, all of them men until after my time at the School, and met in rooms built like amphitheaters with five or six rising rows of seats, arranged in such a way that all students at all times could easily turn and face any other students or the instructor. Classes, usually eighty minutes long, were almost entirely devoted to recitation (the student giving in detail his analysis of the assigned case) or discussion. The focus was consistently on the questions, "What should Mr. X (the executive whose problem was in focus, almost always male) do in this situation? Why?"

To answer these questions, students had to recognize and identify the "problem" implied in the case data: they had to perform complex cognitive acts, including predicting the consequences of possible decisions and of taking no action. Sometimes the problem was verbalized in the case document, but more often the student had to make inferences about the problem from data the case presented; that is, they had to perceive that there was a choice to be made in that situation, and/or had to perceive that "something is going wrong here" and had to verbalize what that "something" was and perceive why that condition had arisen. Often students had to undertake extended and quite subtle analysis of the data just to locate the problems: there were often several problems, interrelated. (To show how deeply I was immersing in the emphases of the School, I recall that my first publication was an article on the definition of administrative problems, in the *Harvard Business Review* (1992), based upon my experience with the cases we taught.) Then, students had to make further detailed analyses, quantitative (e.g., costs and returns on investments) and non-quantitative (e.g., of the "culture" of a particular company, the history of the efforts to sell a product, the relationships and motivations of persons involved) to recognize possible decisions and choose which ones to recommend that the focal executive should take.

In class, faculty members regularly called on students without warning for their analyses of the case assigned for that day, and then called on other students to respond to their classmates' analyses. If, for instance, a case presented a situation where an executive had to decide which of several expensive pieces of equipment his company should buy, a student might open the discussion by saying what sort of return the company might expect on the investment it would have to make in each piece of equipment. Another student might respond by challenging the first student's assumptions: What are you assuming, student two might ask, about the efficiency of each available machine in turning out what it was to produce? What are you assuming about how often each machine would be "down," unusable? If the case included data that might suggest some resistance among production workers to using the machine, student two might ask what steps student one would propose to counter this resistance, and how much those steps might cost, and so on. These dialectical processes, the challenging of assumptions, the pointing out of implications of a line of reasoning (much as philosophers argue), the demand for details about how a given action might be carried out and difficulties overcome, could continue for much of a class period. They constituted what, for me, was a new and stimulating process of teaching.

The course I taught reinforced through regular written assignments many of the lessons students had to learn in order to succeed in the six substantive courses. My course met in sixteen full-class meetings over the year (in contrast to the other courses, which met fifty or sixty times) and made fourteen writing assignments (some of them discussed in class, many not discussed), most of them to a word limit of 1,300 words each.

For a reason that probably relates to my temperamental affinity for studying issues and how decisions are made, I found myself attracted to that nondirective teaching method—"nondirective" in the sense that the instructor implicitly expected the student to select and follow his own way of looking at a case without overt guidance from the instructor or a set of written guidelines. (Many faculty took pride in their ability at "nondirective" teaching, sometimes leading the student very subtly, as he talked, by asking questions, but never telling the student how to proceed or pronouncing judgments on his comments.) I was attracted to that teaching more than to the subtleties of explication of texts and structural analyses of literary works. Cases had no "answers," and students were never shown a "preferred" resolution. A good analysis was one reflecting incisive understanding of issues raised in the case, mastery of the often extended and complex data presented in the case, and cogent predictive reasoning in support of the student's decision. (Since the cases required the making of decisions with uncertain outcomes, students had, in effect, to predict as well as possible, with their reasons, the outcomes of possible actions and of inaction, and also to say what they would do if their predictions proved wrong.) Students were never told specifically *how* to approach a case. They had to draw on their perceptivity as readers, their ability to make inferences from what they were told in the printed case, their growing familiarity (from class discussions, instructor's comments, and technical notes) with the subject matter of the courses. Analyzing a case was and is an act of inferential reading: it required students to understand the "literal" sense and the implicit possible significance of the words, phrases, and numbers they read, to construct an estimate of what might happen in future time, under different conditions.

The task of defining a problem in the real world fascinated me. (Cases were not fictional; though names and sometimes data were disguised, cases were "real" descriptions of business or governmental situations, written by faculty and research assistants on the basis of on-site observations and interviews.) That effort engaged my interest more than the task of explicating literary texts; the task of recognizing problems and defending recommendations about what to do, based on data, I came to consider a major analytic and rhetorical challenge.

But I did not initially understand the disciplinary bases of the mental activities we were teaching. Only after I had taught at the Business School for several years did I slowly begin to realize what I was teaching: mainly deliberative rhetoric (which I had never studied formally) and what we now call "critical thinking," now usually taught in the discipline of philosophy but practiced in many disciplines. (I had encountered the tenets of critical thinking in a philosophy course on "Logical Technique of Thought and Argument.") I was also teaching "problem-solving," which traces its roots to mathematics and statistics.

And, had I but known the discipline, I could have drawn more wisely on psychology, since our cases placed people, with diverse motivations, personalities, world views, and goals, into action, and knowing something about these features of people would have assisted the analyses.

My course, in effect, reinforced what the other courses were teaching through intensive class discussions, by asking the students to write their analyses of assigned cases for readers to review. Students' papers were graded, on the same scale used for quizzes and examinations in substantive courses, by a staff of specially trained readers. (These days we frequently discuss the wisdom of grading students' writing, particularly in light of Peter Elbow's distinction between "ranking" and "describing" [1993]. But at the Business School, where the student's purpose in writing was to demonstrate fitness to be an aspiring executive, the purpose of grading was indeed to make summative judgments and to rank students.)

Grading was based on the student's perceptivity in identifying the problem(s) presented in the case document, the student's ability to recognize the meanings of data, the reasonableness of the student's proposed solution to the problem, the cogency of the student's argument in favor of his decision, and the clarity of the writing. To achieve a satisfactory grade, the student had to make a strong case for his or her solution, showing that it indeed answered, fully, the problem(s) confronting the focal executive, that it was preferable to other possible solutions, and that it did not entail unacceptable adverse consequences. Students had to infer the value of these heuristic probes from the instructor's responses, their classmates' reactions, and readers' comments on their papers. Also, the student had to present his decision cogently in clear, compact writing with appropriately detailed quantitative exhibits when needed. Though I was not at the time perceptive enough to think about the papers in these terms, students had to demonstrate high abilities in the inventional and organizational strategies of rhetoric. Students received written comments on their papers that would, we hoped, guide them to improved performance on the next assignment. Students were never asked to revise the analyses they had submitted, but the readers conducted interviews with them if the students so requested.

The program and the techniques and emphases of the teaching worked: they did make a difference; from comparing the features of students' thinking and writing in May with what they had displayed in September, we could see that the first-year program, taken as a whole, had indeed helped to improve the depth and complexity and sophistication of students' analyses, the forcefulness of their organization of ideas, the vigor and clarity of their expression. Though we conducted no formal assessment of the instruction we had given (probably we would not have known what "assessment" meant in that context), as the year progressed, the course faculty, mostly advanced students in the School's doctoral program, could see the impact of their work.

The changes were due, as I now recognize much more than I recognized at the time, to the sharp and intense focus of the instruction; the efforts of all faculty were geared to helping students develop their ability at decision-making and forceful communication. Furthermore, the faculty collaborated deliberately in that effort. Two examples: first, for each case assigned in our course, an appropriate member of the subject matter faculty met with our staff, discussed the case with us, helped us to see the specific issues raised and any specific analytical techniques required of students, and discussed with us sample student papers. And, a second example, the faculty working with each ninety-man section met regularly over lunch to discuss, often in penetrating detail, the progress—in class discussions, and in written work—of every student in the section. True, mine was the only course in which the student regularly had to set forth in writing, done out of class, his reasoning on issues in a case. But other courses gave quizzes and examinations, which were case analyses written under pressure of time. Students, too, and occasionally their wives, recognized and commented on the changes that had come over them during the year.

But the students who entered the first-year class at the Business School, however successful they had been as undergraduates (many had been very successful) had had a great deal to learn, about reading, interpreting detail, reasoning, arguing, and writing. They were quite willing to jump to conclusions not warranted by the data they saw, to make unrecognized assumptions, to ignore significant data, to ignore possible counterarguments, and to ignore possible consequences of their arguments. Recognizing and reflecting at length on this need, I decided that I would like to work in an undergraduate writing program. Helping to prepare students as writers for the professional world outside college after graduation, and for later professional study, I thought, might be an important role for a college teacher of English. I decided to look for a position teaching undergraduate writing courses when I was to leave the Business School. The University of Hawaii invited me to become director of its composition program and

I accepted, naively thinking that I could influence undergraduate writers and undergraduate teaching of writing.

But though I had, in effect, been teaching administration for seven years—through discussion of cases that often required analysis of administrative problems (one faculty member defined "administration" as the "art of getting things done through working with people") and asking students to write about situations in which changes in practices and procedures were called for, I, in effect, ignored whatever I had taught about administration. I ignored the human context in which action had to be taken. I ignored the fact that the students in Hawaii were undergraduates (many of them the first people in their families to attend college), not graduate students. I ignored the fact that few, if any, of the students had firm, or even tentative, career plans, and that probably few could see the importance for them of the kinds of reasoning and writing I had spent the last seven years teaching. And I ignored the cultural as well as the ethnic differences between students in the Boston area and students in the mid-Pacific, many of them of Asian or Hawaiian descent, with different values and attitudes from the well-to-do, mostly white students in Massachusetts.

And I ignored the teachers. Hawaii had only a small graduate program in English at the time; writing courses were taught by full-time and part-time instructors, many of whom had lived in the state for years, had taught at the University for years, and were well satisfied with the work that they did. What's more, many of them were conscientious and capable teachers. To try to effect change in the main writing course at Hawaii, even assuming (an assumption by no means wise, but one I never questioned) that what I had come to think students should learn was indeed appropriate for students in Hawaii, would have required much greater wisdom, much greater knowledge about students, much greater knowledge about how language and discourse work, and, especially, much greater skill and sophistication in working with experienced, intelligent colleagues, than I as a new Ph. D. in literature from an Ivy League university could have any hope of possessing. Nor was I able to acquire that wisdom in my ten years in Hawaii, particularly since I did not think directly when I was there about the points I have just discussed. I had taught data analysis and writing in a context where all colleagues shared essentially the same goals in their teaching: they knew what they wanted their students to become. But in Hawaii, each individual member of the composition staff had his or her own well-founded perceptions about students' needs and about how discourse should be taught to those students;

most were not about to accept the radically new priorities of an intruder from the Ivy League. And I had no evidence of the success of my teaching procedures and emphases, even on the fertile ground of Harvard's Business School.

As a result, my efforts to redirect the program toward close reading, analysis of data, evaluative and critical thinking, and deliberative rhetoric had very limited success, despite my memos to staff and draft commentary on possible assignments—which at least one instructor told me I should not even be distributing. (She called them "coercive.") Even though I shortly became a participant in the recruitment and selection of instructors, whom the University at that time began to bring mostly from the mainland for three-year terms, I had little success making my vision of a writing program prevail. If I had my agenda for what the courses should teach, many of the other teachers had their own agendas.

Many of those agendas were political, and deeply felt. This was the 1960s, the United States was at war in Vietnam (noisy tanker planes flew nightly over Honolulu on the way southwest), and the women's movement was increasingly winning converts among staff members. Many of the instructors we recruited focused their curricula and teaching emphases on these issues. I tried to focus the writing course on the study of language, on analysis of data, on the systematic exploration of difficult questions, and on rhetorical communication (I wrote out teaching notes on these matters for the staff), not on large political topics. I could, if I had had the wit to think of doing so, have used the political issues to show the staff how students might carry on critical thinking, analysis of data, and deliberation. But I lacked that perspicacity. In proceeding as I did, I inspired near rebellion among the staff.

I did succeed in redesigning the first-year program to offer separate courses in different kinds of writing, among them one in writing about issues requiring analysis and deliberation—a course which did attract the interest of some staff members. But I had no success in redirecting the thrust of the overall writing program. I never learned to apply in the context of Hawaii what I had been helping to teach in the Business School—about critical thinking, about people's needs and motives, about the processes of securing cooperation among diverse colleagues and of achieving change in the writing curriculum among staff members of widely different backgrounds, preferences, and convictions.

The time came when I wished to return to the mainland. Lehman College of CUNY offered me the opportunity, and, after twelve years as a senior administrator (ten of them as a dean of a division of Education) I joined the Department of English at Lehman. Since that time, almost all of my teaching has been based on models for problem-solving: what the Business School emphasized and what I tried to teach there. Even my classes in "Introduction to Literary Research" asked students to locate "researchable" literary "problems," define them carefully, plan approaches to solving them, and search out the primary data (not just the opinions of critics and commentators written years after the primary texts had been completed) that would lead to solutions to those problems.

And in my courses in first-year composition, Advanced Exposition, and Report Writing, I continue teaching how to define problems, analyze data, adjudicate issues, and conduct argument in support of judgments, evaluations, and action. My experiences with teaching reasoning and critical thinking control my current teaching; I fear that they define me. My assignments in Advanced Exposition require of students the definition of problems (mostly social problems, such as the meaning and value of "affirmative action," the place of resistance to authority in our society), the collection of suitable data, and the choice of ways to come to terms with these problems. In my classes in Report Writing, I also assign students to locate problems in business and other professional settings, find data concerning these problems, and present findings to superiors (or to clients or lenders of money), whom the student must carefully identify and characterize. I'm not sure I've seriously considered alternative teaching strategies and emphases for the teaching of writing; I might not have known what such alternatives were.

I find that the students show a need (as did those early in their first year at the Business School) to learn what constitute "data" and "evidence," and to identify what they would say, and how, to the audiences to whom they write. Furthermore, writing is, obviously, a social process, not an activity engaged in by individuals oblivious to the people and conditions around them. Anticipating the needs and wishes of an audience, what I think is called "decentering" (i.e., getting outside oneself to consider how another person might see a situation, what that other person or persons might expect to learn from a given report, or might regard as a cogent argument about an issue in dispute), continues to seem, as I reflect on students' work, the most difficult single challenge these students face as writers entering upon professional careers.

And yet, however much of my teaching career has been devoted to urging students to pursue data in order to solve problems and to formulate problems precisely enough to permit useful analysis, I do not know whether my approaches to the teaching of rhetoric, and writing, are wisely chosen and effective for my undergraduate, heavily minority, students in an urban public college. And I can't argue to another person that they are. I do not know whether my teaching has made a difference for my students, however much I am convinced intuitively of the value of what I have been teaching. Nor have I yet collected information, or even considered how I would seek information, to tell me. I do not know whether my students carry useful processes and techniques into subsequent courses and out into the world of work. I have come to conclude that I have a major problem of learning the value of what I have been doing; I should not simply assume its value. I need to address that problem. But first I need to find out *how* to address it.

Still, teaching analysis of data, decision-making, rhetorical communication (writing addressed to individuals and groups, designed to evoke a particular response), sensitivity to the resonance of language and to the ways in which language creates a social context and an environment for discussion, and alertness to the needs, wishes, assumptions, and values of one's readers—these efforts at this moment, whether or not they are worthwhile or successful, define my professional self. Some of these emphases are not "English" as most of the contributors to this volume (to judge from their essays) would probably define it. But I do think that they are essential abilities for a citizen in this country and a member of almost any profession, and I think it may have been worthwhile to devote a major share of my work as a teacher and scholar to helping students develop the abilities I have enumerated.

Works Cited

Elbow, Peter. 1993. "Ranking, Evaulating, and Liking: Sorting out Three Forms of Judgment." *College English* 55: 187–206.

Larson, Richard. 1992. "How to Define Administrative Problems." *Harvard Business Review.*

Richards, I. A. 1935. *Practical Criticism: A Study of Literary Judgement.* New York: Harcourt Brace.

VIII Finishing Touches

Today I find myself trying to deflect my authority and transfer as much of it as I can to my students.

Charles Moran

27 Teaching and Learning English: Two Views

Charles Moran
with
Pinkal Amin, Liz Ying Feng Chin, Terri Cocchi, Kelly Donahue, Vernard Fennell, Sean Lally, Andrea Lemay, Alex Parker, Claudia Prodan, Alison Sisitsky, Joseph Smelstor, Nathan Smith, Kristina Soares, Melissa Walters, Li Wu

University of Massachusetts at Amherst

I began teaching English in September 1958. From what I can remember and reconstruct, I was a then-conventional stand-up teacher, working in a room with desks bolted to the floor, set in rows, giving regular quizzes and occupying the teacher-place in the room, behind the dark wood desk, under the clock. My overriding agenda, I distinctly remember, was maintaining my rather fragile authority over students no more than five years younger than I was. Where I really helped students then, I believe, was in one-to-one conferences on their writing.

Today I find myself trying to deflect my authority and transfer as much of it as I can to my students. Further, I rely less and less on the individual conference, focusing instead on community-building and collaborative projects, of which this writing is an example.

When I try to account for this change, I see a number of forces at play. First, our profession's pedagogy is itself moving in this direction, and I'm going with the flow. We've broadened our perspective, looking outside English and there seeing that in the sciences and in workplaces, writing is often, and profitably, collaborative. Second, I'm fifty-seven now, thirty-six years older than I was in 1958, an aging professor with children ten years older than the students I teach. I have so much authority that it gets in the way. To get anything done, I have to deflect some of this authority and convince students that I am on the same continuum of humanity as they are. Third, my students and I are working in very different physical space: no rows of student desks but a room filled with computer terminals arranged in pods, where we communicate both "F2F" and online. Fourth, I am in daily contact with young teachers who are trying new kinds of teaching and, in my presence, reflecting upon this teaching. In such a setting I am both encouraged to experiment and to reflect. And fifth, I have as colleagues Anne Herrington and Marcia Curtis, whose naturalistic studies of classroom cultures have helped me see that my "story" of what happens in my classroom needs to be seen in the light of the stories told by students, and Peter Elbow, who has supported me in my belief in the power and value of student voices.

To gather the materials that my students and I present here, I kept my own teacher-journal, focusing on what seemed to be good moments in the semester. I asked the students to reflect, too, on what seemed to them to be good moments. I believed that in this way we could assemble our individual definitions of the "good teaching" and "good learning" that was happening in this English class. The writing of the essay was entirely collaborative. I acted as editor and assembler; the students contributed text and suggested changes and edited the final manuscript. What we found surprised us all. My "good moments" had almost nothing in common with the students' "good moments"—and yet their "good moments" were everything I had hoped for. Uncharitably construed, we were two trains passing in the night. Charitably construed, I am a teacher in transition, enacting one pedagogy while remembering another.

The course we were all involved in was "English 113, College Writing." The course has as its goal the development of young writers. To that end, student writing is the principal text in the course; the "reader" is a monthly student publication that includes writing from each person in the class. My own goals in this English class were consonant with the course's goals. I wanted each person in the class to consider himself or herself, even if only for this semester and within the boundaries of this course, a writer. I wanted, further, to have us feel that we were a community—granted, a bogus community, one assembled by the University Writing Requirement and a computer program that registered students into this section according to their schedules and the alphabet—a bogus community, but still as real as most. We could, if we worked at it, become as legitimate a group as a dormitory unit, or an intramural team, or an English Department. In this community I hoped that writers would come to see that it is normal and productive to rely on others for feedback, response, for help of all kinds.

These goals were present, but not fully understood by me, at the beginning of the semester. They emerge from my journal entries—of which these are a sample.

September 23, 7:40 A.M.

Didn't think of this until after the class, next morning, in the shower—when I do my best thinking, it seems. Received phone call from Claudia Sunday; she told me her father had died and that she'd miss class for two weeks. We agreed that she could write—perhaps about this experience—and when she came back this writing would "count" as writing for the course. I announced Claudia's absence, and the reason for it, to the class—saying that she was still with us, part of the community, and that I sensed she needed us and that's why she'd called. Wanted them to know that she was still with us, though she'd not be there for two weeks. Nathan: suggests that we send a card. Alison: wonders whether Claudia had done a draft for her editing group.

What's interesting is that I remembered feeling strange when I made the announcement to the class. I felt not accustomed to this role, vaguely embarrassed to be presenting a conversation with a student to other students. Yet I thought I believed that the class should be a community. In the past I'd have kept Claudia's absence, and the reason for it, to myself, and dealt with it as "teacher." Here I was turning to the class as a community, and reporting the absence, and the reason for the absence, of one of our members. I deal with the situation, and they deal, too. Or, more accurately, *we* deal.

It is interesting too that in my journal entry written right after the class, I did not think what I'd done worth recording. It wasn't part of "English." Not until the next morning, in the shower, was I permitted a glimpse beyond my own categories.

September 22

Just had a good class today. 2 hours 45 minutes of class plus lab. The best part: working with Vernard, Kelly, and Jason on speaking their language aloud. Had fun. They all had sentence boundary problems. They'd had lots of correction, too, it seemed. And they were not excited about grammar lessons—which I believed wouldn't have worked anyhow. Each of them read one another's prose aloud and repunctuated. Then I sent them off to read and repunctuate their own writing. Then back to the group to check it out. Most had found 50 percent of the errors. Pretty good day's work. What I told them: this won't work right away. It's not a magic glove. But it's a technique that they can use to improve their own sentence-boundary-punctuation.

What they seemed to like most was my telling them that they were writing rhythmically and grammatically sophisticated English (all true) and the problem was not their knowledge of the language, which they were using expertly, but the marks they were putting between words—punctuation—a minor but highly-valued skill in our tiny piece of the world.

September 25

Reflecting on yesterday's class: I was really pleased by a moment: I'd just distributed published books from last year's classes, telling this class that as of next week they'd begin moving toward their first publication. Sean Lally comes up to me as I type at my station: 'Can we have some time to clean up our drafts before they get published?' The common sense of it all—writing for publication, 'real' writing. Someone but me will see this stuff. Suddenly it comes clear: Now it's time to proofread! On the same day I go to a conference on portfolio evaluation, and a teacher raises the 'teaching grammar' and 'proofreading their work' question. Bruce Penniman—once a student of mine, now a seasoned teacher and presenter at this conference, says it clearly: proofreading matters when it matters. In his journalism course, because the course publishes the school newspaper, final copy has, finally, to be perfect. Students know this; they make it so."

So these are the moments that I thought were the best—"good English"—for me. But what would the students think? Seven weeks into the semester I asked them to reflect on the work we'd done together. I asked them in these words: "Thinking back through the semester so far, what were the 'good moments,' for you? Moments when you felt good about what was happening to you as a writer? In making your choice, consider at least these possibilities: moments when you were writing; moments when you were reading others' work; moments when you were discussing or listening; moments when you were reviewing your own work, or the work of others."

Not one of the students focused on the moments I had focused on: my announcement (sharing?) of Claudia's message; the beginnings of the in-class publication; the sentence-boundary-punctuation drill. What they did focus on was perhaps related to these "moments" that I had picked out, but only if one read these "moments" as contributing to an atmosphere that permitted writers to work and grow, individually and together.

In their responses, students most often focused on "writing" moments, sometimes moments when they felt freed from constraints. Here is Vernard:

> I can remember one time when I was writing this semester, I was writing about just some of the things that I was thinking about, and worried about at the time. I think that this was one of the more delightful moments of this semester, not just for this class but for all of my classes. I really felt as though I was free— that I could and did say exactly what I was feeling. I had that luxury all the time, but this was the first time I had really done it. It was like a breath of fresh air, like I had released something that had been in hiding. As I stated in my writer's autobiography, I would write all of the time when I was younger—until I started to have to write for grades, until I started to take my first English course. When I did this writing I felt as though I was again a child with nothing to care about except my writing.

Often the students spoke of writing as discovery or breakthrough. Here is Kris:

> I do believe that one of my best moments has been while I was working on essay four. I believe that my writing has changed and taken a turn for the better. For the first few essays I felt like they were a little dry, boring and without meaning. Of course I didn't realize that until I wrote one that was not like that. I was happy with my first essays—I just feel like I have moved onto another level now. I feel like essay four opened a part of me and that my writing can only get better from here. Whether or not that is really true remains to be seen. Writing this essay brought out a different side of me. I was writing about something close to me and not just another mechanical essay. This time I did not look at the essay as a paper with a deadline. It was different, and new, and wonderful. This essay also helped me in other ways. By writing it I opened lines of communication with myself and others that I thought had been lost. I have now begun to talk about my feelings more, and I now have a different perception on things.

Pinkal Amin's "moments" included both the discovery of a subject and the effect on her of her readers' responses:

> I began with the simple and brief thought of a village. I had dreamed recently about a village. It was very blurred, but some-how I felt like writing about that dream. . . . My ideas became more clear and strong when I got the three responses to my writing. I started to write the real essay on the computer as a free writing about a village. One of the main reasons I wanted to write about this issue was that I was really stressed out and

drained after midyear exams. I was so angry that I thought of a
place where I could get complete peace.

Many students connected the value of their writing to the fact that it
was not assigned, but self-sponsored. Here's Nathan:

> I honestly believe that the times that I was able to sit down
> and simply write about anything on my mind were unmatched.
> As a writer, I learned so much about concentrating on the things
> that I am interested in that I feel I have begun to realize the
> importance of starting out from scratch in every work that I do .
> . . . Another good moment for me was when I was reading one of
> my rough drafts. I was ready to burn the thing and suddenly all
> of these ideas came streaming from my head. I didn't know how
> it happened, but I know that I was really shocked by the whole
> thing and I think that I will remember it for a while. Soon I real-
> ized that the reason that all these ideas came into my head was
> because I was writing about what I wanted to. Therefore it was
> easy for any thought about the topic to come into my mind.

And Terri, too, finds that self-sponsored writing has value to the writer:

> One good moment in class is when I finish a paper and I
> actually like it. It's not just another paper passed in, but it's
> something that means a lot to me. Writing about things that
> bother me I find is a good way to get them out into the open and
> sorted out. Sometimes it helps me figure out how I feel or helps
> me make a decision. This is good, because without the oppor-
> tunity to write freely on our own chosen topics, I probably
> wouldn't have bothered to write about some of things that I
> wrote about.

Most students said that the best "moments" included times when they
read and responded to each other's writing. Here's Alex, who speaks
of how he enjoys reading others' work:

> Reflecting back on the semester I can think of a few good
> points which I would like to discuss. One that comes to mind in
> particular is writing comments to the people in my editing
> group. This is always fun because the essays are so interesting to
> read. First Andrea always writes about things in great color with
> excellent vocabulary. Sometimes I do not even know what she is
> trying to say. This is what makes reading her papers so interest-
> ing. Next Alison writes about some kind of personal thing.
> These essays are interesting to read, because I know that they are
> true. It is almost like she is sharing her personal issues with the
> editing group. Then Joe's papers. These are always a joy to read.
> I find them most amusing and I get a touch of his personality in
> every essay. . . . When I am reading essays like this I have no

problem writing a comment. They make writing comments easy because I know that they will take it into consideration.

Liz, too, learns from reading others' writing. She says that in this class she comes to "know" her colleagues through their writing.

> I really enjoy reading others' work. I can learn more new ideas and different ways to approach a writing. I like the writing subjects in this class because we can write anything on our mind. We can express our own ideas and opinions freely. For this reason, we will know one another from our writings. You can tell what kind of person one is by reading the writing.

Kelly finds working with others' writing valuable too; she speaks of it in terms of "helping" others:

> Good moments include helping people with their work. Writing responses to other people's work makes me feel good. I feel that I am helping them make their work more interesting to the reader and helping them make their work better for them. I also like discussing my work with my group; they always give me good advice and help me in tough spots.

And Andrea highlights the experience of *being* read:

> I constantly write my thoughts but never have had a chance to let others read them. This class gives me a chance to gather opinions and views from others. Also, the criticism allows a more diverse view to form toward whatever I am writing. I never had any confidence in my writing, but being in this class has developed a sense of worthiness in me—that actually what I think is of importance or originality and worthwhile to read. Every time someone reads a piece that I have written, that moment contributes to my sense of self-worth. . . .

Claudia has experienced both the power of writing to "clear up" her thinking, and the value of her readers' approval of her work:

> One of the good experiences that I've had in this class was writing about what I was feeling during the two weeks that I was home for my father's funeral. I was writing without thoughts about grammar or having to have other classmates analyze my writing. I was trying to express myself in words, and I wasn't sure if I was bringing my thoughts over on paper as I wanted to. Charlie looked them over and because he approved of my writing I somehow, because of his acknowledgement, had a feeling that what I had written had meaning. I might also never have written about this difficult time in my life if it hadn't been for the writing class and that helped me clear up certain ideas.

I also felt that it was worthwhile to write, when one day some of my friends got hold of one of the essays I had to hand in and laughingly told me that my writing was expressed exactly the way I thought. They told me that if they had read it without knowing that I had written it, it would have reminded them of me. This made me realize that I might be acquiring skills that, although they might not make me a great writer, do let me express what I think in my own personal way.

Many of the students wove together two strands: their sense of themselves as individual writers, and their sense of themselves as members of a community. Joe had this to say:

I like the way this class is run—not too much lecture, but enough so you know what is going on. You give us the chance to write our papers and correct our mistakes ourselves through your comments and our peers' comments. Also all the relationships in this class seem to be great, both between student and student and teacher and student.

They often noted the value of self-sponsored writing, and then followed with a comment that noted the value of writing in a community. "Good moments" were sometimes moments when they, as writers, found voice and subject. "Good moments" too were when they made connections with other writers. Missy writes this:

I was very happy when I found out I could write about anything I wanted to. I have never had a course that allowed me so much leeway. I really like the freedom. Other "good moments" were when we were given the to opportunity to be able to read our peers' essays. I realized that I had a lot in common with my classmates. It also helped me out to know that a lot of people who were writing were going through the same things I was. It made me realize that we were all in the same boat, and we all wanted to keep this boat afloat! The goodness of this is that I now knew that my classmates and I were all on the same wavelength, and we were all here to help each other.

Li, too, notes the value of community to him:

This English course is basically concentrated on one thing: that is, writing essays. It is all one piece of work that helps you develop your writing skill and build up a very strong writing. It might help on typing as well. With students working in a group, that helps students to know one another better. The relationship between student and teacher seems very close when we have conferences, which gives a chance for a student and the teacher get to know each other. Also we can get comments from others and these help me to change my essay to a better one.

And Sean speaks of the writer as both individual and social:

> There were a few moments in this class or outside of this class when I was very happy or pleased with myself and my work. When I was finishing my final draft on number three I thought that I had written a good paper and I felt good about handing it in. Another good feeling that came from it was that of finding what exactly the problem was that I was writing about, and because of that I spent the time I needed to think about it. By thinking the problem through, I knew where I wanted to go with it and what needed to be done. Other good moments that come a little more often are when you're reading other people's papers for them and you get to see what is affecting them and how they are relating to the same situations that you're in. These are moments that make you realize that you're not alone, in the sense that other people are also feeling the same way and having the same problems.

Alison writes about a social moment on "Interchange," an online, synchronous discussion:

> My favorite moment was when the class was entering the topics of our next essays into the computer for everyone to read and respond to. At this point in the semester, everyone is very familiar with the writing techniques and capabilities of their peers. As the topics came up on the screen, I felt a closeness to various people in the sense that I knew what their intent was going to be and I knew how to respond to them. It showed me that we really do not know anything about anyone in the class, yet we know so many personal things about everyone from reading their work. This moment was very good for me because I realized the amount of trust between each other and no one was afraid to be judged. Most of us have not discussed the problems we deal with in our essays, yet I have gained an understanding of each individual and what is important to them right now. This is a bond that is not easily created.

And she writes about herself as a writer too:

> Another favorite moment was reading my completed essay about my mother and her problems. I, for so long, have had to deal with pent up emotions, and could never really explain them in words. After hearing the professor open up and tell about his own personal difficulties, I felt the ability to open up and express myself. My "peer editing group" responses also encouraged me by them telling me they were interested and had dealt with similar situations. A feeling of relief filled me when I finished that topic, making it a very enjoyable moment.

So what does our story tell us about English? About teaching and learning? To the teacher, "good English" has to do with teaching—being in a role, "doing" things. Charlie thought that a "lesson" or a "thing he did" was important—and maybe it was. But the student writers speak of the power they find in writing—not always, but often enough. To the students in this class, "good English" has to do with two different, but somehow related, activities: learning through writing about their own experience, in language they feel is theirs; and learning through social exchange—both through reading the work of others, and having their work read by others. For the students, writing is discovery, and writing is social action. That, for us this semester, has been English. And it is a great deal, indeed.

28 The Way I Was/ The Way I Am/ And What I Learned in Between

Lynn Langer Meeks
Utah State University

I graduated from college in 1968. I had gone to college for three reasons: (1) to marry a doctor; (2) to get away from the farm; (3) to marry a doctor. I majored in English because I liked to read. I decided to become a teacher because even thinking about giving someone a shot made me nauseous, and I couldn't type. I figured on having a ten-year career: just long enough to get "the doctor" through medical school. Then I'd spend the rest of my life pursuing genteel hobbies, charitable works, and driving my precocious children to various lessons and scouting activities.

So much for dreams of the '50s; they quickly turned into the reality of the '60s and '70s. "The doctor" disappeared, and I found myself teaching school, not with a career in mind, but because I needed a job. I had to pay off my National Defense Loan, and if I taught for five years, the government would forgive half of it.

I have often longed for an opportunity to publicly apologize to all my former students who were subjected to my primitive attempts to teach English. I want to apologize for those one hundred-question, multiple-choice tests that I gave you, the sentences I made you diagram, the boring and useless lectures I gave, and the essay tests in which I made you parrot back all those boring and useless lectures. I want to apologize for ignoring those of you who were less-than-perfect students or who were discipline problems. I know that my child-abuse method of teaching English convinced many of you that you were not only terrible writers, but that you were also stupid *and* suffering for irreversible character flaws. My only excuse is that I was doing the best I could with what I knew at the time. The truth is I just didn't know that much about how students learned to read and write.

I began teaching high school when subject matter was all important. I taught English grammar and literature (pronounce that *lit–er–ah–cha*). The focus was on content and correctness, and I taught my way through textbook after textbook, beginning with the Anglo-Saxon period in September, making it to the Victorian period by May, following the axiom that the only good writer is a dead writer. I knew my students weren't learning very much, but I didn't know what else to do. I was just trying to survive for five years while I paid off my National Defense Loan.

By 1977, I'd gotten a master's degree in English literature; at the time I thought learning more content would make me a better teacher. So I indulged myself in seminars on famous dead writers and wrote endless pseudoscholarly papers on arcane topics, delighting in every class. I remember my seminar on Henry James most fondly. My professor had devoted himself to the study of Henry James's life and work. He told us about Henry James while he chain-smoked Turkish cigarettes tightly between his tobacco-stained thumb and index finger, the smoke curling about his hooded eyes. I inhaled the secondary smoke along with his theories. It was glorious to be young and intellectual.

However, I still didn't know any more about teaching English than what I'd read in journals and learned at various local conferences. These "process" ideas sounded interesting, but I was skeptical and full of the "yeah, but's": *Yeah, but* if I don't grade every paper, what will make students write them? *Yeah, but* if I don't give reading tests, how will I know my students have read the assignment? *Yeah, but* if I put my students in groups, won't the brightest students do all the work? *Yeah, but* if I don't lecture, how will my students learn what is true and beautiful?

Also there was a subtext: I was inordinately proud of being a teacher of English *lit–er–ah–cha*, an intellectual who enlightened with my insightful analyses of plot, character, and literary criticism. I liked the power; I liked thinking of myself as an intellectual. Had I been able to smoke while teaching high school, I would have chain-smoked Turkish cigarettes, grasped tightly between tobacco-stained fingers, the smoke curling slowly about my hooded eyes.

The turning point in my English teaching career came in the summer of 1978 when I participated in the Greater Phoenix Area Writing Project. To explain the effect of this four week course—even sixteen years later—I can think only of religious metaphors. Born again, saved, enlightened, healed, renewed, and recommitted, I went back to my classroom after those four weeks with a messianic zeal that made me unpopular with many members of my English Department.

The scales had fallen from my eyes. I knew the truth, and I was determined to set my colleagues free.

Fortunately for my colleagues, my fervor soon wore off and I left them alone, but my ideas about teaching and learning had been fundamentally changed. For the first time in my life I had been asked to consider how students learned instead of what students learned. The whole idea of process writing made sense after I had to write and examine my own writing process. I learned how peer response groups worked by being in a peer response group. Because I was both a student and a teacher during those four weeks, because my classmates and I were co-investigators, because no one tried to teach me anything—just set up situations in which I could learn—I learned more about teaching English in four weeks than in all the years of undergraduate, graduate school, and teaching combined, and since then, I have never stopped learning about teaching English.

The Greater Phoenix Area Writing Project changed the direction of my professional life. As a result, I got serious about graduate school and earned a Ph.D. in 1985. After three years of teaching English at a university, I became a state language arts consultant. Now I spend my time working with teachers and school districts to improve the teaching of English language arts. I serve on committees, help to develop courses of study in English language arts, and conduct inservice workshops on various topics relating to the teaching of English language arts.

As I work with teachers in my state and provide guidance and support for their growth and development, I continue to reflect on my own growth and development as a teacher and teacher educator. What follows is an analysis of my experiences as a classroom teacher, graduate student, and consultant in which I discuss what I consider essential conditions for learning—conditions that I think must be present if we are to continue growing and developing—and I also show how I teach now.

Easily Accessible Information

I lived seven miles away from a university with an exceptional English Education Department. I taught high school English during the day and took classes at night. I could attend the university whenever it was convenient—after school or later in the evening. The classes I wanted to take were usually available, a major research library was accessible and open late, and I could take one class every semester and two during the summer if I felt like pushing myself. The cost of credits was reasonable, and often the school district I worked for picked up the bill. It took me seven years to get to get an M.A. and another to get a Ph.D., about the same amount of time Jacob put in for Rachel. It was hard work to teach school and attend graduate school, but each had a tempering effect on the other. The theories that I had learned by night had to stand up to the cold reality of 150 twelfth-graders by day. On the other hand, when I got the "yeah but's" and needed help understanding how to implement a particular theory, help was there from colleagues, the library, and mentors.

Mentoring

Of course, without ready access to instruction it is extremely difficult to learn, but even with ready access, I could never have continued my education without a mentor. My first mentor eventually became my major professor in graduate school, but when I initially met him I was supervising one of his student teachers. At the time, I was happily teaching high school English and heavily involved in coaching the girls' gymnastics team. In truth, I was more interested in winning the state championship than I was in taking more classes. I had become worse than a stereotypical coach and had turned my classroom into the film festival capital of the high school. I had the lights off in my classroom so much that I finally had to get a reading light for my desk so that I could work on my meet lineups while my students watched the movie *du jour*.

Recognizing my obsession with winning the girls' gymnastics championship, my mentor had a serious talk with me: "Lynn, if you want to continue coaching gymnastics and teaching high school English for the rest of your career, that's a fine choice. But if you want to do something else, then quit coaching and come back to school. You have to make up your mind, because you can't coach, teach, and work on a Ph.D."

A Ph.D.? Me? He thinks I could do a Ph.D.? I'm not smart enough. I'm too old. It will take too long. I'm not smart enough. But he thinks I could do a Ph.D. I don't think I'm smart enough. But he thinks I'm smart enough. Maybe I am.

So in 1978 (after my team won the state championship) I went back to school again. My mentor gave me guidance and support for seven years. He provided opportunities for me to attend and present at national conferences. He encouraged me to publish. He helped me with scholarships for summer study. He introduced me to his colleagues in the profession whom I had formerly known only as end notes in my papers. He, to paraphrase Frank Smith, helped me join the English Education Club. Whenever I was plagued by self doubts, personal problems, or overwhelmed with the enormity of what I had committed myself to, and I sat in his office, snuffling noisily into a sodden Kleenex, he soothed my fears with his unshakable confidence. He believed in me, and he expected me to succeed. How could I let him down?

Community Of Learners

There were many others who supported me as I continued to learn and develop as a teacher and teacher educator. There were my classmates in the graduate program and the colleagues I met during the Greater Phoenix Area Writing Project. We met before and after class to study together. We met on Saturdays; we attended conferences together. We became involved in our state NCTE affiliate and worked together to plan a regional English conference. We "hired" each other as consultants for out district writing projects. We hung out; we even had slumber parties. Once a year we'd check into a local resort for the weekend, lie around the pool during the day, then put on our jammies, eat junk food, and tell secrets all night. When things weren't going well—either professionally or personally—we had each other. These colleague-friends were especially important to those of us who couldn't go to graduate school full time: we saw each other struggle to balance teaching, graduate school, family, and professional responsibilities. We were role models for each other and when one succeeded, it gave us all a boost of confidence.

Teaching Others

Gradually I began to rethink myself. For all my life—except when I was teaching high school students—I had thought of myself as *only a student*. But as I began to take a more active role in the profession, to serve as a consultant, and to be a specialist in language arts for school districts, I began to think of myself as a knowledge-maker rather than a knowledge-taker. Often, in my role as a K–12 state language arts consultant to school districts, I was asked questions on a language arts–related subject that I didn't know very much about. Reading is a good example. As a secondary teacher, I'd never taken any courses that specifically had to do with teaching reading to elementary students. As a secondary English teacher, I expected kids to be able to read, and if they couldn't, it wasn't my responsibility. (A regrettable stance, I now realize, but it typified my attitude in those years.)

However, as a state language arts consultant, I couldn't take that attitude. I had to become knowledgeable, and I didn't have time to take classes. So I read, and talked with many elementary reading experts. My need to know compelled me to learn an amazing amount of information with supercharged intensity. The same thing happened with spelling. I quickly absorbed current research on teaching spelling after I received a telephone call from a superintendent, and could neither answer one of his questions nor suggest appropriate reading material.

Involvement in the Profession

For the first seven years of my high school teaching career, I didn't attend one professional conference or belong to a professional organization. I thought conferences were run by university professors who could have nothing to say to me because they didn't teach 150 students a day, and presenting at a conference myself seemed ludicrous. The idea of me telling other English teachers what I knew made no sense. I thought all English teachers knew what I knew—and knew it better than I did. Besides, I had too many papers to grade and too many gymnasts to coach.

My first involvement in the profession was at the local affiliate level. A friend asked me to co-edit the affiliate newsletter. I started attending the local affiliate's business meetings, and I was asked to be the liaison to NCTE. I had no idea what that meant or what my responsibilities were, but I did know it meant attending the NCTE convention in Boston, so I accepted the appointment. When I attended my first NCTE business meeting, I just sat and watched, hoping I looked like I knew what was going on. I truly understood none of the issues being discussed and had no idea which way to vote. After the first year as an NCTE liaison, I became better informed and more interested in participating directly in NCTE. Later, I became editor of an affiliate newsletter, liaison to SLATE, and then I was appointed to a number of NCTE committees.

I consider my professional involvement of utmost importance to my continued growth and development as a teacher and teacher educator. I was appointed to committees chaired by highly competent, knowledgeable people who served as role models for me. As a committee member, I was asked to develop surveys, write abstracts, chair workshops, and publish newsletters. On the committees I met dedicated professionals who, like me, had plenty to do but were still willing to spend time on behalf of the organization. My involvement in

NCTE also broadened my view of the importance of a professional organization. I began to realize that the problems in my classroom were only one of a multitude of issues that NCTE was addressing.

Discontent

I don't remember ever being satisfied with my teaching, even when all I knew was the child-abuse method of teaching composition and the guru model of teaching *lit-er-a-cha*. Even within my limited repertoire of teaching techniques, I spent a serious amount of time trying to figure out how I could be a better teacher. The first two years that I taught, I commuted forty-five minutes each way. I was fortunate to share the ride with another novice teacher. We talked teaching methods nonstop going and coming and that helped me reflect on my own teaching practices and modify my techniques, such as they were.

Later, after my summer at the Greater Phoenix Area Writing Project and through graduate work, I continued to modify my teaching practices, constantly looking for new and better ways to do things. By then I had established certain criteria for the new methods I experimented with: (1) less work for me and (2) more work for the students. A good example is peer response groups. The students did the writing, the students did the revising, the students took the responsibility, and I didn't have to spend so much time grading papers. I was so enamored of peer response groups, I used them as the topic for my dissertation.

However, I have never stopped fiddling with the peer response group concept. For every composition class I teach, I have figured out a new combination or permutation of peer response. Mutation may be a better description. I'm experimenting with peer response all through the composing process rather than just at the end for proofreading or editing. And I'm still not satisfied. I can hardly wait until next semester so I can try out a variation of peer response groups that I invented last week.

The Way I Am

So what does my classroom look like today? In my composition classroom, students sit at tables, often at computers. They sit in groups of three and four, facing each other, not me. My "lesson plans" are written out on the board, so that the students know exactly what's going to happen in class. I begin by explaining my "lesson plans" and what each activity will include. What follows is a typical agenda for the beginning college composition class I met once a week for three hours on Monday evenings. This lesson plan is for a class midway in the semester. My lesson plans and directions to students are in italics; my explanations are in regular print.

Write about issues or concerns that came up this week as you were writing. Do you have any specific questions you would like to ask me? Is your homework done? Do you have copies of your draft for everyone in your group? If you are not prepared, what can you do next week to ensure that you are?

I usually begin class by asking students to write about issues or concerns that developed during the week as they were writing. Since I only met my class once a week, I looked for ways to have "conversations" with them. I asked them to answer the above questions in writing. Then I use these questions as the basis for opening class discussion. I also collected their answers and responded to their concerns in writing.

General comments on students' drafts turned in the previous week: Listen to each essay as the author reads his or her draft; jot down questions and comments to share. I'll comment too.

Since I use a workshop method to teach composition, my students write weekly, but much of what they write turns out to be drafts that they may or may not choose to expand and revise for a polished paper. Out of a sixteen-week semester, students usually turn in two or three papers for a formal evaluation from me. Most of their weekly work is experimental in that I encourage them to try out and try on ideas and writing styles to see "how they work." Therefore, my comments on most of their weekly papers tend to be quite general.

I have found that if I am too specific or too critical with my comments, then students may discard a perfectly good draft because "they think I don't like it." I have discovered that if I read all their papers and then choose three or four of the best drafts to read the class and comment on, students are much more willing to take risks and explore ideas. I have also learned that students look forward to hearing their peers' papers, and their peers' and my general comments. True, some students complain that I don't give them enough written comments, but I refuse to (a) write their papers for them or (b) regress into my old dysfunctional habits of child-abuse English teaching.

Peer Response Groups: Learning to give and take suggestions about writing.

As I have worked with and in peer response groups over the years, I have changed my emphasis on how I use them in my classroom. Early on, I used peer response groups to ensure correctness: I wanted students to read each other's papers and "fix" them so there were fewer grammatical or spelling errors for me to correct. If students could help each other improve content, so much the better, but I called the groups "peer editing groups," and that's how I thought of them.

Now I use peer response groups as a writing forum—a place where students can exchange ideas about writing: their own and their peers'. Therefore, I am more interested in students' conversations about writing than their actual editing skills. I want students to read each others' writing to generate ideas and to see how another person addressed the same theme. Also, I want students to practice giving and receiving responses. I have found in my own job as a language arts consultant for a department of education, that often I am called upon by my colleagues to respond to their writing. Because my colleagues and I write many documents that have political impact, we have begun to realize how much we need—in fact, must have—each other's candid responses, whether we are writing documents individually or together.

Read drafts of your essays to members of your peer response groups: Take notes on their comments.

As they work in peer response groups, I ask my students to follow a model of response demonstrated in a video produced by Word Shop Productions: "Student Writing Groups: Demonstrating the Process" (which I purchased from NCTE). Each student reads his or her paper to the group, and then each group member responds in turn—and without interruptions from any other group member—while the author of the paper takes notes. This method provides an opportunity for every student to speak, and the author walks away with several pages of notes to use when revising.

I monitor each peer group closely and listen to the degree of sophistication and focus of the students' comments. I have found that I can learn a great deal about a student's conceptual understanding of composing by the comments that they make on other student's papers. My informal research tells me that, depending on the developmental level of the student, there is often a month gap between their being able to articulate a suggestion about composition and their being able to begin to "practice what they preach." In fact, I think that the oral part of the peer response, which forces students to listen and comment on each other's writing, may be more important than the comments they receive.

Get ready for next week's class: Discuss reading assignments; in your small groups, brainstorm for your next essay. Share your ideas with your group. "Steal" any that sound good.

Because I believe so strongly that in writing, as well as in architecture, form follows function, I set broad general themes for students to consider. Then they write experimental drafts about these themes for several weeks before choosing one draft to extend, expand, and polish. To help with generating ideas and to serve as professional models, I assign three or four essays per week for my students to read. The book that I use, *75 Essays: An Anthology* (McGraw-Hill 1993), groups essays around broad general themes such as "Growing Up, Growing Old," "Cultural Rules of Behavior," or "Science and Technology."

I ask my students to write within these broad general themes, using the essays in the book as models of excellent writing as well as idea generators. Then, depending on the purpose and audience, the form will naturally take shape. I find it too artificial to teach "forms." I have never, in the six years I have been at the department of education, been asked to write a process essay, an argument, or a description. I have, however, on countless occasions been given an audience and a purpose, and I've had to figure out which form or combination of forms will best help me accomplish the purpose.

Portfolio review: Look over your portfolio and select a draft that you would like to expand and polish.

I use "the Meeks model" of portfolio assessment, in that the portfolio functions both as an archive for the students' writing and—at the end of the course—a record of their growth and development. Every third or fourth week, the students review their portfolio and select a draft of an essay that they would like to spend more time on. They then develop this essay into a more polished work for me to make extended comments on. Early in the semester, there is not much in the portfolio to choose from; students are still trying to understand the concept of exploring ideas and then discarding them for a while or maybe forever.

At the end of the semester, students look through their portfolio and choose one essay to make final revisions on to turn into me for a grade. The essay that they choose to revise is, in their judgment, the best work that they have done all semester, the essay that represents everything that they have learned about composition to date. I "grade" this essay and it counts as sixty percent of their grade in the class.

Scoring standard: Use your scoring standard as you revise your essay to help you focus on your areas of strength and weakness.

I use a scoring standard that has been developed at the state level to evaluate students' writing. I give students a copy of the scoring standard at the beginning of the semester. Students use the scoring standard in their peer response groups as the basis of their response, and later as they revise. I also, of course, use it as the basis for comments on their drafts, and to score their final paper. I also ask students to use the scoring standard to analyze their own work.

I am sold on using a scoring standard. For one, I can trace student progress very easily because a scoring standard clearly describes levels of proficiency. I can also show students where they "fit" on a scoring standard, and using a scoring standard, together (in conferences) we set specific goals for improving their writing. Using the same scoring standard over the course of the semester means there are no "surprises" when it comes to the final grade. Students are so adept as using a scoring standard, they can easily predict their grade. Usually, my final assessment is little more than a verification of their self-assessment.

Self-assessment: Giving responsibility for learning to the student.

Every week, I ask students to fill out a self-assessment of their writing and attach it to their essay. I ask them to respond to the following:

Write down three things you are most proud of in your paper. Assuming you will rewrite this paper, what three things should you do to improve it? Using the scoring standard, give yourself a score and justify it.

I find that I read the self-assessment with almost more interest than the paper. I become most concerned when a student doesn't recognize what he or she could do to improve the essay. After all, my goal for instruction is to help students understand what it means to be a good writer and what good writing is. I know that coming to this understanding takes time. A student needs ample opportunity to figure it out for himself or herself through reading, writing, and reflecting.

Baby Steps

In the 1990 movie *What About Bob?*, Bill Murray plays an obsessive-compulsive acrophobe who seeks help from psychiatrist Richard Dreyfuss. The Dreyfuss character has written a book called *Baby Steps*. The book's thesis is that anyone can overcome debilitating compulsive behavior through taking one step at a time, no matter how miniscule or unsteady the steps. Murray uses "baby steps" as his mantra, chanting it to himself as he tries and eventually succeeds in curing himself. Although he does drive the Dreyfuss character crazy in the process, the analogy, I think, is sound.

As I look back on my teaching career, I have engaged in what many might call obsessive-compulsive teaching behaviors, behaviors I engaged in because they made me feel smart, in control, or safe. To change those behaviors, I had to engage in the baby step philosophy. I took faltering, wobbly steps, not willing to let go of one practice until I was pretty sure I had control and understanding of another. And I never tried to change too much at one time. I was too scared. Also, I was too skeptical.

For example, the first time someone explained to me the concept of "whole language," I laughed. I knew "it wouldn't work." But over the years I began to try whole language concepts, implementing them slowly and then building on my success. At the same time I investigated theories on how children learn language. It's taken nearly twenty years for my practice to reflect current research on students' language learning, and I am still not satisfied with my level of understanding or application.

Another analogy that I think helps explain my growth and development as a teacher and teacher educator is the process I go through when I write. When I write, I use typical writing process strategies, trying to focus on my audience and purpose. Then I get feedback, and I revise some more. The whole process of my learning and development as a teacher and teacher educator has been one of brainstorming, drafting, and revision. For example, take this article I'm currently rewriting for the umpteenth time; I'll never actually be done with it. The main difference between this article and learning is that I have a deadline. With learning, I can revise forever.

As I look back on my growth and development as a teacher and teacher educator over the last twenty-five years, I marvel at where I was and how much I've changed in my theory and practice. And I plan to continue changing. In twenty-five years I hope to be writing a similar article, apologizing to my students and decrying my ignorance about teaching English language arts in 1994. In the meantime, I've learned some valuable lessons through examining my own growth and development as a teacher and teacher educator.

What Do I Think I Know Now?

I've learned some things about teaching English language arts since 1968. One thing I've learned is that students learn by doing and that most teacher-talk is wasted. I try to structure each class period so that I only talk 10 percent of the time. The rest of the time I try to make sure that my students either write individually or with partners, talk to each other, or in other ways take an active part in a lesson. I try to spend most of my class time walking around, peering over shoulders and eavesdropping.

I've also learned that I'm more effective as a "coach" than a guru. When I first began teaching, I thought I should be the center of attention and everyone should listen to me. Now I see myself looking on from the sidelines. When necessary, I call "timeout," offer some advice, *metaphorically* pat my students on the rear, and send them back into the game.

I've also realized that students need to learn to work in groups and think of themselves as part of a community of writers. That means being able to solicit advice about writing as well as give it; it also means learning how to write with someone else. And it also means that I have to create a classroom environment based on cooperation rather than competition.

Furthermore, I have found that students need to see a variety of models for writing. They need to read examples of good writing—both from their peers and from professionals. In addition, they need to see me as a writer; I must share my struggles, frustrations, revising strategies, and finished products with them.

Another thing I've begun to understand is that students need to talk to each other; they develop and extend their ideas as they speak, and they learn from other students. When a student can tell another about a specific strength or weakness in an essay, the student either can or will soon be able to apply that knowledge to his or her own writing.

I have also discovered that students learn best in a "risk-free" environment. Students need many opportunities to experiment without penalty. That means that I must develop a course of study and a method of assessment in which students' attempts are valued as much as their final draft. If I want students to experiment with language, forms, ideas, styles, and audiences, I must find ways to reward them for their experimentation. I've found that if I "grade" everything, then students feel they are being penalized for their risk-taking, and their writing tends to become sterile and formulaic, i.e., safe and dull.

Finally, I've begun to realize that students must take responsibility for their own learning, and it is my job to set up situations in which they can. That means letting students decide what they will write about and how. It also means asking them to do frequent self-assessments in which they have to evaluate themselves as learners and evaluate their work for its level of proficiency. (I am not saying that all students buy into this approach. I still have many students who just want me to tell them what they "need to do to get an A." But most of them come around when they understand that I want them to learn how to learn.)

As a state English language arts consultant since 1988, I've learned that I need to provide easily accessible information on teaching English language arts. For a rural state such as mine, that means inservice workshops for teachers in their schools, on school time. Many teachers would like to continue their education, but the demands of their job and commitment to their families make it difficult, if not impossible.

I've also learned that I need to assume the role of mentor more often. I need to support teachers and create situations in which they have opportunities to attend conferences, give workshops, publish, and become resources for their own schools and school districts.

Another thing I have learned to do is encourage teachers in my state to become more professionally involved. Especially in a rural state, the yearly affiliate conference, the affiliate newsletter, and the *English Journal* may be the only chances some teachers have to stay current in the profession or involve themselves in a community of learners.

Will I ever be contented? Perhaps that's the nature of the English teacher: we are by nature discontented. We're usually looking for new, more effective, easier, different ways to do things.

When I think about the teacher that I was in 1968 and compare her to the teacher I am today, I find no similarities either in theory or in practice. Yet, I am the same person and any changes that I have made have been made hesitantly, one step at a time, one wobbly foot in front of the other, using a great deal of support. Slowly, over time I have been able to capitalize on my discontent and use it to create a sympathetic and caring environment that encourages risk, change, and responsibility not only for my students, but also—perhaps most importantly—for me. You see, both as teachers and as students, in order to change, we must begin taking those baby steps without fear of driving ourselves—or each other—crazy.

Works Cited

75 Essays: An Anthology. 1993. 4th ed. New York: McGraw-Hill.

Student Writing Groups: Demonstrating the Process. Videotape. Workshop Productions.

What About Bob? 1990. Directed by Frank Oz. With Bill Murray and Richard Dreyfuss.

29 Collaborative Computer Encounters: Teaching Ourselves, Teaching Our Students

Gail E. Hawisher
University of Illinois at Urbana-Champaign

Cynthia L. Selfe
Michigan Technological University

Here are the three letters for those pieces you asked me to respond to. I'll send them if you have e-mail addresses or you can forward them if you want. Make any changes you think needed—don't be shy.

Cindy, the delighted
(e-mail message, October 28, 1996, 10:37 A.M.)

Thanks! I wonder (and this may not work) whether some sort of visuals in Geoff's text would help address the problem of writing a text that, after all, fails to move in Duchamp's sense—that, when all is said and done, reproduces traditional academic writing (not sooo traditional really ;-). It makes one want to be able to insert holograms. . . .

Gail
(e-mail message, October 29, 1996, 10:29 A.M.)

As English educators and teachers who grew up in the '50s and '60s and entered the profession in the '70s, neither of us started teaching with computers; we learned as we went. And what we learned convinced us that computers were becoming increasingly important in educational settings—not simply because they are tools for writing (they are not *simply* tools; they are, indeed, complex technological artifacts that embody and shape the ideological assumptions of an entire culture), but rather because these machines can serve as powerful catalytic forces in the lives of teachers and students. Although the machines themselves mean little to us, the work they support and the range of discourse they give us access to mean a great deal.

It is through our own work with computers, for example, that we continue to rediscover an essential truth about our profession—that teaching is an inherently social and political activity, and that the human exchanges resting at the heart of teaching take place not only among educators and students, but among teachers and other teachers. Teachers do their best work when they can write together and think together about what they do. And if our current system of education often serves to isolate teachers from one another—limiting collaborative teaching projects (as too expensive and not efficient), restricting teachers' travel to conferences (by eliminating travel monies or refusing to support substitutes), and keeping teachers in their own rooms or their own offices (through increased class loads and increasing fear of liability)—computers can help teachers re-establish connections with colleagues, share the important stories of teaching, and reflect in critical ways on the work and profession that they share. The changes, supported by technology, however, are not without complication, and they have their own price for teachers.

The electronic mail messages that begin this paper were extracted from correspondence about our most recent collaborative writing project—a collection of essays for the University of Illinois Press on literacy issues for the twenty-first century. We're surprised to note that 1996 marks a decade of professional collaboration between two teachers that began in 1986 and that still continues ten years later. Despite the remarkable changes in computer technology that remind us daily of the passage of time, it doesn't feel like ten years. But a whole series of joint projects tells us that this is the case—our collaboration has a history; it is sustained through daily electronic exchanges; it shows little sign of stopping and, indeed, seems to expand as computers touch more aspects of our professional lives. During this period, our work together has spawned two book series; a book co-authored with friends on the history of our field; three co-edited collections of essays; six co-authored articles; joint conference presentations extending from Boston, Massachusetts, to Auckland, New Zealand; and a number of projects—like the about-to-be-published technology reader for Prentice-Hall—that exist in various stages of development and that we hope, with time, will reach fruition. All of these projects have been supported by computers in some way. Through our collaboration, we have made friends in Estonia, Australia, England, and Japan—to these other teachers, we can talk on a daily basis given access to computer technology. As collaborators, we have worked together on *Computers and Composition: An International Journal for Teachers of Writing* and have also completed a four-year term as editors for the *CCCC Bibliography of Composition and Rhetoric*. Our professional collaboration also touches our teaching and our students despite our two universities being more than five hundred miles apart.

We consider this collaborative activity important as much because of what it tells about teaching and the profession of English education as because of the outcomes of the various projects. In this chapter, we chart our professional collaboration to trace the ways in which it has been shaped and changed by the rapid developments in computer technologies. For us, computers and their use in the teaching of writing have provided both the content and the method for joint projects. We study computers and writing, and we also use computers to write together, to talk together, to think together. The use of computers has, in effect, enabled our collaboration with each new technological development contributing to the collaborative processes we bring to the task. We suggest, furthermore, that our collaboration has changed as our theoretical perspectives on teaching and writing have changed and that the nature of our theories of teaching are inextricably bound to the new technologies and the challenges that they present. So what we include here is really part of a larger history[1] that we alluded to earlier—it is a history of a collaboration that affects our scholarship and our teaching, a history that relies on chance encounters, mistaken notions, and the optimistic belief that computers can serve as powerful and positive catalytic forces in our professional lives.

Yet, if each of our collaborations have begun with an optimistic perspective, we have usually come to find our belief slightly misplaced—that computers can be used profitably, yes, but the outcomes—the research, the edited collections, the coauthored articles, the teaching—have never evolved in ways that we expected or predicted. More often than not, we found that our collaborative computer enterprises have taken on lives of their own, lives that, furthermore, tended to grow out of misconceptions that we brought to the task. In the sections that follow, we tell stories about our collaborations and frame them by first identifying the misconceptions we initially formed about technology itself—the subject of our scholarly work—and then discarded or modified. We then go on to discuss what our collaborative experiences of the past years might suggest for the preparation of teachers of English.

Misconceptions, Teaching, and Technology

Misconception #1

Computer-assisted instruction (CAI) would transform English classrooms by making us better teachers and our students better writers. And if CAI didn't do it, word processing software or electronic conferencing software certainly would.

When we met in 1984 at the Computers and Writing Conference hosted by Lillian Bridwell-Bowles and Donald Ross in Minneapolis, we were doing independent software development and research on computers. Cindy was at work on a software program, Wordsworth II, which eventually gave her the material for her first NCTE book, *Computer-Assisted Instruction in Composition* (Selfe 1986), and Gail was at work on writing the proposal for her dissertation study, "The Effects of Word Processing on the Revision Processes of College Students," later published in part in *Research in the Teaching of English* (Hawisher 1987). Each of us believed fervently that we were on the brink of new discoveries in English teaching and that they would transform our paper-based writing classes into exciting new electronic learning spaces where students' writing improved dramatically. Wordsworth II led students patiently through the writing process by presenting them with modules aimed at different kinds of college writing. The module on writing narratives, for example, asked students before writing their drafts to "identify aim and purpose," "identify audience," and "consider organization."

While Cindy was busy testing the benefits of Wordsworth II, Gail continued to work on her research, modeling a study of computers and revision, in part, on Bridwell's landmark study (1980) of revision. Students in her first-year writing class produced and revised drafts with and without the help of word processing software, and she classified and counted the kinds of changes they made. She then submitted the essays to a group of trained raters who judged the quality of the writing. While she still remembers classifying over four thousand revisions on eighty different essays, the results of the study indicated that students neither revised more nor wrote better essays on computers with word processing capabilities than they did with pen and typewriter. Although students in the Wordsworth II and word processing study reported anecdotally that they enjoyed writing with computers, neither investigation indicated the patterns of improvement we had thought we would find. And our experiences with computer-supported teaching were being corroborated independently by writing teachers all over the country. Generally, these teachers worked alone—as sole computer advocate in a school, district, or college—and could share stories of their teaching only when they came together at conferences or professional gatherings to talk about the uses of the new technology. Although the hopes for computer-supported instruction were high and the enthusiasm great, the results proved less than conclusive. Computers did not necessarily improve the quality of students' writing: they helped teachers encourage more drafts and allowed students to increase their fluency. In many cases, the technology encouraged an improved attitude toward the task of writing; technology alone, however, did not improve the nature of students' writing—teachers and the ways they used the technology emerged as an increasingly important focus.

Indeed, sometimes computers encouraged a sort of temporary amnesia among teachers during the early '80s, supporting a return to the kind of skills-based instructional programs that were popular in the '60s. Despite the promise of radical change associated with the new technology, many English composition teachers employed computers within highly traditional contexts for conservative educational purposes: among them, grading and evaluating papers, providing drill and practice grammar tutorials, identifying stylistic problems, checking spelling, and providing practice with sentence structures.

The conservative trend in instructional strategies during this period was exacerbated by the work being done in teacher-education programs. At this point, most schools lacked teacher-education programs that devoted time to examining technology from critical perspectives. Few teachers, moreover, had access to any post-service education that helped them think critically about the use of computers within instructional settings. Without such education—and faced with administrators who demanded a speedy and cost-effective integration of computers into English programs—English composition teachers often resorted to the readily available computer-assisted software packages prepared by commercial vendors. The packages were frequently authored by software developers who had very little experience in the teaching of English. Moreover, as Paul LeBlanc (Hawisher et al. 1996) has pointed out in his scholarship on software development, programs designed for English classrooms—such as style and spelling checkers—often served a highly conservative function themselves in that they reinforced the back-to-basics movement that supported (and continues to support) traditional authority structures within educational settings. Thus, teachers in those early years came to adopt computers, but nevertheless resisted meaningful change by using computers to reinforce older and unproductive ways of thinking about learning. The computers were, in effect, no more than electronic versions of the printed grammar handbooks that came before them. Computers were seen, in essence, as a means of reducing student-generated error in composition and literacy classrooms.

From these early experiences with computers, we developed a deep distrust of easy answers and clear directions. We learned, separately—as did many teachers who were experimenting with technology in those early days—that computers were not panaceas for students' writing and English instructors' teaching. We learned that unless the profession brought to its research and its teaching a critical perspective that informed every aspect of its work as English teachers and computer professionals, little real change would occur. When we met again at the 1986 Computers and Writing Conference in Pittsburgh, we decided to collaborate on a co-edited collection we entitled *Critical Perspectives on Computers and Composition Instruction* (Hawisher, Selfe 1989). By rethinking and re-examining our own enthusiasm for computers from a critical perspective and by asking others to examine their teaching and research by thinking against the grain of their own enthusiasm, we hoped to make a major contribution to the young field of computers and composition studies.

And, in many ways, the essays in that collection adopted the critical stance we thought appropriate at the time and agree with still. Andrea Herrmann (1989) argued that many public high schools fail to provide adequate staff development opportunities for teachers and thus prevent the integration of good CAI and word processing into existing curricula; John Thiesmeyer (1989) questioned the kinds of CAI software that prevailed in English classes, arguing that such software focused on what the computer can do rather than on what students can do; and Ron Fortune (1989) suggested that teachers tap the potential for computers to enhance visual learning rather than concentrating only on students' verbal abilities. Along with these chapters was another excellent piece by Michael Spitzer (1989) describing a new technology that promised to create an online meeting place for teachers and students: the computer conference. Spitzer told us that because paralinguistic cues, such as facial expressions, one's appearance, and one's standing in the particular community or class, are not apparent in online conferences, students can concentrate more on *what* is being said rather than on *who* is doing the saying. Although the two of us had experimented in 1985 with electronic conferencing on the

"Fifth C," an early electronic bulletin board for writing instructors sponsored by New York Institute of Technology, we had never used it with students for our teaching. For the next several years, we were to experiment with the electronic conference as a means of improving our teaching and our students' learning. And, predictably perhaps, we brought the same unbridled enthusiasm to our work with online conferences that we had earlier brought to CAI and word processing.

Misconception #2

The use of computers, especially online computer conferences, would decenter the teacher's authority in writing classes, provide students with their own spaces for learning, and ultimately democratize English classes.

Both of us began using computer conferences—exchanges of written commentary among groups of students—in the late '80s, setting aside electronic spaces for students in our classes to converse over the networks. We believed that this writing on computer networks would allow students to assume a greater degree of authority in their discourse and that the networks could also prompt students to become independent learners, relying less on their teachers for approval and more on their classmates. Reporting on her research with computer conferences, Cindy noted—along with Marilyn Cooper in "Computer Conferences and Learning: Authority, Resistance, and Internally Persuasive Discourse"—that online conferences demonstrate "expressive, informal language and show evidence of a frank engagement with content" (848), and that "such conferences are capable of making student-teacher and student-student exchanges more egalitarian, reducing the dominance of the teacher and the role of accommodation behavior in discussion" (851–52). Somewhat later, in a review of research on electronic conferences, Gail wrote that "the majority of studies [on online conferencing] in education environments see learning as the result of active engagement and interaction among the participants where no one person or instructor dominates" (Hawisher 1992, 95). Each of us had come to understand the potential for online environments to serve as alternative learning spaces that could inspire a sense of experimentation and exploration among students, encouraging them to develop an online authority that was often missing from traditional English classes. This same optimistic perspective also marks our coauthored "Tradition and Change in Computer-Supported Writing Environments" (1993), in which we suggest that electronic conferences, along with new developments in hypermedia, might well give us the opportunity to change our dominant modes of teacher-centered behavior in the English class. Both of us—while understanding the need to think in increasingly critical ways about the uses of computers in writing-intensive classrooms and the kinds of instructional environments we were trying to shape with our applications of technology—may have been too ready to accept the value of computer-supported conferences.

This particular fact became patently clear to us when we collaborated on a joint research study of online conferences, using two undergraduate English classes that we were teaching at the same time on descriptive grammar and editing as the focus of our study (Hawisher 1992). When we read over the entries in the two online conferences—conducted at two separate university sites in connection with two separate classes—we noted that we, as teachers, were referred to more often than any student in our classes. Furthermore, we saw that students engaged in the same teacher-pleasing behavior that characterized our traditional English classes. A student in Gail's class wrote, for example, "I like the way everyone gets involved in the [oral] discussions—I'm looking forward to learning both with you and from you." (This was addressed to the whole of the class.) Another student wrote, "There have been few other classes that I have taken that encourage participation as much as this one." Cindy's class also viewed the classroom context positively, but somewhat differently. One student commented, "The way to overcome the oppressive system is to challenge the authority of the system. There is one person in our situation who retains power—Cindy. Take it up with her—she's not unreasonable; she'll listen." Another wrote, "Back to resistance. I think that part of the problem is figuring out *what* to resist. Like with grammar. We need to figure out what is important and what of the important things could be improved or changed for the better."

What interested us about these comments is how prominently we figured in the students' online discussion, a conversation we thought we had made theirs. We also noted how quickly they recognized and adapted to our teaching approaches. Over the past several years, each of us has tried to change our teaching. Gail has tried to create a classroom atmosphere in which both she and the students become learners-in-progress, all tackling new problems and ideas, building on and contributing to the ideas of others, and making new knowledge. Cindy has also tried to change her teaching. She has become increasingly concerned with the inequities that surround teachers, and believes fervently in her responsibility to democratize the classroom with technology and to address issues relating to race, class, and gender. Both sets of students demonstrated, in these conferences, that they had been very much influenced by each teacher's theory of teaching, which we have independently cultivated and developed over the years.

Of all the insights we gained from our joint study, then, the most startling to us was that even when English teachers set aside these electronic spaces for their students, believing that they will become places where students assume authority, the teacher, at least in our cases, retains her presence every bit as much as in the traditional classroom. The students hailed each of us more than any of their classmates, despite neither of us participating in the conference. In our article in *College Composition and Communication*, "The Rhetoric of Technology and the Electronic Writing Class" (Hawisher, Selfe 1991), we wrote about the need for a critical awareness of the networks for all of us working in computers and composition, a need that was underscored dramatically by our own teaching and research of the undergraduate classes.

Misconception #3

The new technologies would streamline our work as writers, collaborators, editors, and teachers, making us more efficient and productive.

Here we feel the need to comment on a *partial* truth—that the new technologies, especially e-mail and desktop publishing, have indeed streamlined our collaborative work. In editing *Computers and Composition*, the two of us send e-mail back and forth between Michigan Tech and the University of Illinois with an ease unavailable to us in the '80s. Many reviewers for the journal, futhermore, send us their responses to manuscripts online, and we forward them blind to those of the authors who are also online. The journal itself has grown from a stapled newsletter of ten pages—produced on an electronic typewriter—to a perfectly-bound journal of over a hundred pages—one designed and edited primarily online with the support of a full-featured word processing program, chart- and graph-generation programs, document-design and page-layout programs, optical-character and line-art scanners, modems, and electronic mail. For the work we undertook on the *CCCC Bibliography on Composition and Rhetoric*, we were able to transport completely formatted End Note files back and forth, and read them as though we had just created them on our own office or home computers. We hope that the *Bibliography* will soon be available to subscribers online, for we believe that the electronic medium will allow English teachers to search for sources in ways that print simply does not permit.

Despite—or perhaps, because of—the ways in which computers have supported our work, we also find ourselves increasingly overloaded with technological detail: keeping track of hardware and software improvements, managing projects involving technology, and making changes associated with technology. Because we are now dependent on computers for collaborative projects, we are forced to find funding for rapidly changing equipment and software—and in times of budget cuts, such efforts cannot continue to be well received. Given our dependence on technology, we also have to remain fairly current with the increasingly rapid pace of change in the field of electronic publication, if only to keep up with the graduate-student assistants who frequently seek our advice and guidance in improving the appearance of publications and the processes of publishing. Because we can be more "productive" and "efficient," we can also do more, and our work continues to grow at what seems, sometimes, an exponential rate.

Because students work on computer-supported collaborative projects with us, we have begun to converse with them over e-mail as well, and we are not sure when conversation stops being idle talk and becomes teaching. The boundaries between the two universities seem less fixed than they once were as our students, too, begin talking to one another, discussing their programs of study, their classes, their writing, and their teachers. The new technologies permit us, indeed encourage us, to work with students at both institutions and have our students collaborate with one another. For the classes we are now teaching, we have felt obliged to learn—and then to introduce students to—the Internet (a worldwide system of linked computers), its World Wide Web (the Internet's hypertext interface), and a range of tools that will help them use this vast network: gophers (programs that provide access to information and files at thousands of sites), file-transfer protocols (that allow individuals to send and receive all forms of digitized information), MOOs and MUDs (virtual spaces existing on the Internet that individuals use to interact in real-time), listservs (that send e-mail to groups of people and maintain online group conversations), and newsgroups (that provide access to more than five thousand topical discussions involving participants from all over the world). Although none of these changes represents a step in the wrong direction, we often wonder whether the new technologies indeed streamline what we do or whether they overwhelm us, and other teachers, with the possibilities they present. This complex set of challenges, we know, is not ours alone—in fact, they interest us most because they are increasingly shared by other teachers and collaborative teams, many of whom have access to less technological support than we do.

Computer Encounters and the Preparation of English Teachers

As we write this, we recognize that our computer encounters, our electronic collaborations, have implications not only for teachers currently in the classroom, but also for students who are preparing themselves to shape educational environments as teachers. Some of these implications are unsettling. If English teachers once believed that their formal learning concluded with certification, they must now come to terms with a technological learning horizon that recedes constantly. Teacher preparation programs are just beginning to recognize that they must prepare teachers to be lifelong learners in technological environments. The stories we tell here, and the misconceptions around which we frame our stories, illustrate repeatedly that we have been engaged in an ongoing process of discovery. Our stories also demonstrate that teachers should be prepared to learn not only from their firsthand experiences with technology, but also from observing their students' experiences with technology. Our students' experiences with online conferences provided a check on our own teaching and told us that we were not providing the kinds of new intellectual online environments that we thought; we were instead merely mirroring—in new learning spaces—the kinds of student-teacher relationships that have long characterized English teaching. Teacher-research methods should go hand-in-hand with preparing new English teachers to be lifelong learners.

Teacher preparation programs, moreover, need to think about providing models for prospective English teachers by introducing them early to the new technologies and to electronic collaboration. We're thinking here of James Levin's work with the "tele-apprenticeship," a model of student-teacher interaction in which students collaborate with faculty on professional research (Levin, Waugh, and Chung 1992). Levin and his colleagues pair undergraduates with faculty to observe and practice how professors use e-mail in their work. The students first immerse themselves in e-mail, reading before becoming full writing participants, and then finally go on to respond to colleagues and contribute to joint projects. Although the two of us never formalized the tele-apprenticeship model in our own work with students, it essentially represents our many collaborations with students as we work together on *Computers and Composition.*

Finally, despite our many misconceptions, we believe that our work with computers has underscored the pleasures of collaboration for both us and the students with whom we work. As we write our collaborative essay, taking turns, sending various drafts back and forth across the network, we no longer are isolated scholars working alone to produce a finished manuscript.. We are, instead, co-conspirators, borrowing freely from online files that the other has written, producing a text that no longer reveals which one of us did the actual writing. And our collaboration does not stop with our writing—it is now a part of our in-person as well as our online teaching. Cindy visits the University of Illinois to talk to students and faculty in WITS (Women, Information Technology, and Scholarship), a group of feminist scholars; Gail goes to Michigan Tech to help with Tech's annual two-week workshop for English teachers. In between the visits, each converses via e-mail with colleagues and students at the other's university.

To close our collaborative essay, we include a passage from Michael Schrage's *Shared Minds: The New Technologies of Collaboration:*

> Over time, collaborative technologies will reframe personal experiences and perspectives as dramatically as the clock changed society's perception of time and television reshaped the experience of entertainment. Collaborative technologies will dramatically enlarge our vocabularies of interaction and, most importantly, will evolve into something we all take for granted. Many of our most important relationships will be viewed through the prism of these evolving tools. (1990, 186)

Our use of computers—our reliance on collaborative technologies—encourages us to rethink constantly the ways that we edit, write, do research, and teach. Despite the misconceptions that inevitably mark our beginnings and our continued seeking, computers enable us to collaborate together in ways that were once not possible. Our teaching, we believe, is the better for it.

Note

1. With good friends Charlie Moran and Paul LeBlanc, we compiled a history of the first fifteen years of computers and composition studies

(Hawisher, LeBlanc, Moran, and Selfe 1996). In the book, we tried to trace the threads of this history through the complexly related contexts of composition studies as a set of related academic programs, and through the development of computer technology as a series of cultural and commercial phenomena.

Works Cited

Bridwell, Lillian. 1980. "Revising Strategies in Twelfth Grade Students' Transactional Writing." *Research in the Teaching of English* 14 (October): 197–222.

Fortune, Ron. 1989. "Visual and Verbal Thinking: Drawing and Word-Processing Software in Writing Instruction." *Critical Perspectives on Computers and Composition Instruction*, ed. Gail E. Hawisher and Cynthia L. Selfe. New York: Teachers College Press, 145–61.

Hawisher, Gail E. 1987. "The Effects of Word Processing on the Revision Strategies of College Freshmen." *Research in the Teaching of English* 21 (May): 145–59.

——. 1992. "Electronic Meetings of the Minds: Research, Electronic Conferences, and Composition Studies." *Re-Imagining Computers and Composition*, ed. Gail E. Hawisher and Paul LeBlanc. Portsmouth, NH: Boynton/Cook, 81–101.

Hawisher, Gail E., Paul LeBlanc, Charles Moran, and Cynthia L. Selfe. 1996. *Computers and the Teaching of Writing in American Higher Education, 1979–1994: A History*. Norwood, NJ: Ablex.

Hawisher, Gail E., and Cynthia L. Selfe, eds. 1989. *Critical Perspectives on Computers and Composition Instruction*. New York: Teachers College Press.

——. 1997. *Literacy, Technology, and Society: Confronting the Issues*. Upper Saddle, NJ: Prentice Hall.

——. (in preparation). *Reflections on Literacy and Technology in the 21st Century*. Urbana, IL: University of Illinois Press.

Hawisher, Gail E., and Cynthia L. Selfe. 1991. "The Rhetoric of Technology and the Electronic Writing Class." *College Composition and Communication* 42 (February): 55–65.

——. 1992. "Voices in College Classrooms: The Dynamics of Electronic Discussion." *The Quarterly* 14 (summer): 24–28, 32.

——. 1993. "Tradition and Change in Computer-Supported Writing Environments: A Call for Action." *Theoretical and Critical Perspectives on Teacher Change*, ed. Phyllis Kahaney, Joseph Janangelo, and Linda A. M. Perry. Norwood, NJ: Ablex, 155–86.

——. 1997. "Wedding the Technologies of Writing Portfolios and Computers: The Challenges of Electronic Classrooms." *Situating*

Portfolios: Four Perspectives, ed. Kathleen Blake Yancey and Irwin Weiser. Logan, UT: Utah State University Press.

——. 1997. "The Edited Collection: A Scholarly Contribution and More." *Publishing in Rhetoric and Composition,* ed. Gary A. Olson and Todd Taylor. Albany, NY: SUNY Press, 103–18.

Herrmann, Andrea W. 1989. "Computers in Public Schools: Are We Being Realistic?" *Critical Perspectives on Computers and Composition Instruction,* ed. Gail E. Hawisher and Cynthia L. Selfe. New York: Teachers College Press: 109–25.

Levin, James, Michael Waugh, and Haesun Kim Chung. 1992. "Activity Cycles in Educational Electronic Networks." *Interactive Learning Environments* 2 (March): 3–13.

Schrage, Michael. 1990. *Shared Minds: The New Technologies of Collaboration.* New York: Random House.

Selfe, Cynthia L. 1986. *Computer-Assisted Instruction in Composition: Create Your Own.* Urbana, IL: NCTE.

Spitzer, Michael. 1989. "Computer Conferencing: An Emerging Technology." *Critical Perspectives on Computers and Composition Instruction,* ed. Gail E. Hawisher and Cynthia L. Selfe. New York: Teachers College Press: 187–200.

Thiesmeyer, John. 1989. "Should We Do What We Can?" *Critical Perspectives on Computers and Composition Instruction,* ed. Gail E. Hawisher and Cynthia L. Selfe. New York: Teachers College Press: 75–93.

IX Attitudes

English and English education professors have to examine and revise our own teaching so that it represents an effort to model a coherent, principled pedagogy.

Collett Dilworth and Nancy Mellin McCracken

30 Ideological Crosscurrents in English Studies and English Education: A Report of a National Survey of Professors' Beliefs and Practices

Collett Dilworth
East Carolina University

Nancy Mellin McCracken
Kent State University

At nine o'clock on Monday morning I hear that Shakespeare was the greatest writer of all time; at ten o'clock I laugh along with my professor about the obvious limitations of a canon of dead white men; at noon I revise my essay in accord with Professor Smith's directions; at two o'clock I listen to my methods professor tell us not to appropriate our future students' texts. On Tuesdays, I visit the schools where they tell me to pay no attention to what they say at the U, since anyone not in the schools every day has no idea what's going on in the real world.

—English education student

Each academic discipline harbors variant beliefs about its means and ends. These differences are usually subtle, esoteric and intramural, but occasionally major new intellectual currents develop and begin to reshape a field. Such times tend to invigorate the professoriate, for we grant that our most robust means for achieving progress is a forum within which competing ideas are put to the test.

Reprinted with permission from *English Education* 29:1 (February 1997): 7–17.

Yet our students, the future citizens of the disciplines, find such times troublesome as they search for their own coherent vision of English studies and English education.

Throughout the country, state legislatures and executive branches have charged that education authorities should specify standards in literacy and acculturation and should devise means for achieving the standards. When educational leaders at state and local levels respond to these mandates, they develop curricula, and that is when their variant ideologies vie most conspicuously. Meanwhile, college English departments and schools of education prepare students to teach in the schools and to assume curricular leadership. And here, too, value systems compete to specify what English should do for people and how. In these crosscurrents, students of English education must struggle to gain a repertoire of values and tactics that will serve them in the schools where other crosscurrents await.

Somehow those who study to be English teachers must construct a theory of English while garnering wisdom from all that the discipline currently offers. Studies of college students' epistemological development, e.g. Perry (1970) and Belenky et al. (1986), suggest the complexity of "finding a place for reason and intuition, and the expertise of others" (Belenky et al., 133). Our students may ask professors of English studies and English education how they should behave when they get in the classroom or in central offices, but what they really need from us, what we do that educates them more profoundly than any good advice, is our response to this implicit request: "Show me who to be." And here, manifest values, ideology in action, is everything. We exert compelling influences in the way we teach Composition, Renaissance Literature, Literary Theory, Introduction to Linguistics, History of Rhetoric, Methods of Teaching English in the Secondary School, and Student Teaching Supervision.

And lasting consequences may result when we professors reveal our hostility toward alternative ideologies. Few English educators on university faculties have not felt the sting of contempt from colleagues whose specialties are in the traditional literary epochs. Few have not felt encouraged by other colleagues from those same fields. And few do not despair at least a little as they observe their student teachers befuddled within the melange of competing and contradictory values surrounding them.

Recognizing the challenging discord in English studies and English education, NCTE's Conference on English Education formed a Commission on English Studies and English Education charged to investigate significant differences within the English community and to find ways to encourage communication among disparate groups. This information might help construct a way to choreograph discord into harmony. Such a charge, however, begs the question of how to identify groups and their beliefs:

- Are there sets of professional values in the English professoriate?
- Do these value patterns define like-minded groups of believers, and if they do, how can we characterize the varying ideologies?
- Do those engaged in English education hold different patterns of beliefs about the profession from those who characterize themselves as primarily literature specialists, linguists, or rhetoricians?
- Most important, is there common ground on which to build a reconception of English studies and English education?

To begin to answer these questions, the Commission sponsored a survey of English professors' beliefs and practices (Dilworth and McCracken, 1992).

The Survey

To gain a representative sample of professors of English in the United States and a benchmark group of English educators, we identified forty-eight professors who were members of CEE committees or the CEE Executive Committee. These represented major research institutions, full-service universities, and four-year colleges from all regions of the country. We sent packets of questionnaires, directions and return envelopes to these colleagues, whose job was to gather and return data from the English departments on their campuses. They also responded to the questionnaire. Forty-four of the forty-eight CEE colleagues completed questionnaires. The total number of usable questionnaires returned was 457.

In constructing the questionnaire, we attempted to elicit responses to relevant constructs in the teaching of English by presenting strongly opposed pairs of position statements for each of four aspects of English studies: composition, language, literature, and pedagogy. Twelve such statements were printed on a single page, and participants were asked to respond using a six-point scale of agreement from strongly agree to strongly disagree. The two statements about composition focused on "the most important" methods of instruction (note that topically paired statements were not adjacent on the questionnaire):

1. For the teacher of composition, the most important activities are to provide exemplary texts as models, to prescribe rhetorical virtues, to proscribe rhetorical vices, and to give detailed critiques of students' completed essays.

7. For the teacher of composition, the most important activities are to foster apt prewriting strategies, thoughtful drafting, and clear-sighted revision by guiding and encouraging students' performance of these processes.

The pair of items on assessment were designed to reveal attitudes toward criterion-referenced and norm-referenced evaluation:

6. The most valid evaluation of achievement in the English curriculum will tend to separate students into high, average, and low achieving groups. Many students, therefore, should make the average, "C," some should make "D" and "B," and few should make "F" and "A."

10. The most valid evaluation of achievement in the English curriculum will reflect how well students have met distinct criteria. An assessment might legitimately show most students making "A" (excellent). An assessment might just as validly show most students making "B" (good) or "C" (fair) or "D" (poor).

The position statements aimed at the study of literature focused on two aspects; first, the primary purpose for literary study and the literary canon:

5. The foundation of the literature curriculum should be those great works whose merit has been established by the cumulative judgments of the civilization's most sensitive readers.

11. The English curriculum should focus less on notions of literature's intrinsic merit and more on literature's social and political implications.

The second pair of related statements about literature focused on the notion of the ultimate truth, or meaning, in texts:

3. The presence of an ultimate meaning at the heart of a text, a meaning relevant to basic truths, is an illusion generated by readers vainly believing in objective reality.

12. As agents of the humanities, English teachers should develop in their students the skills and sensitivities required to conduct a lifelong search for fundamental truth.

The position statements about linguistic study focused on two commonly expressed beliefs about the purpose for such study:

2. If the curriculum in language does nothing else, it should develop students' knowledge of standard English and their understanding of "the best word in the best place."

8. The main reason for including the study of language in the English curriculum is to teach students the legitimacy and power of their own language in their own lives.

A sixth pair of statements focused on the perceived value of pedagogical theory and training:

4. Apprenticing a college graduate to a good teacher is the only essential pedagogical preparation for teaching.

9. Formally studying the theory and practice of teaching is crucial in teacher education.

In order to study identified patterns of belief in relation to college professors' primary fields of teaching and research as well as their professional background and involvement in teacher education activities, a second page of the questionnaire asked the following questions:

13. In what academic unit do you serve? (English department, education school or department, both, other)

14. What do you consider your primary specialty? (literature, composition, linguistics, English education, other)

15. Have you ever been certified to teach English?

16. Have you had experience teaching grades 6–12? (none, 1–2 years, 3–5 years, over 5 years)

17. Have you been involved with English/language arts teachers or curriculum in elementary, middle, or high schools in your area in the last three years? (workshops, contest judging, consulting, research)

18. Have you been involved in the last three years in any significant ways with the English department faculty (if you are in a school of education) or with the education faculty (if you are in an English department)? (informally several times a year, formally at least once a year)

19. Do you believe that coursework in English should be different for English teaching majors than for nonteaching majors? Please explain.

20. Do you believe that graduation requirements for coursework in other liberal arts and sciences should be different for English teaching majors? Please comment.

21. In the literature/composition/linguistics classes you teach, are you usually aware of which of your students are planning to teach?

22. What difference, if any, have you observed between your students who are teaching majors and those who are non-teaching majors?

23. How, if at all, do you adapt your literature/composition/linguistics courses for teaching majors?

Data Analysis

We applied three statistical procedures for the responses to the strong position statements, items 1 through 12: a) a factor analysis discovered sets of items which intercorrelate to suggest that an underlying value or "factor" accounts for the professors' reactions to those items, b) a cluster analysis sorted the questionnaires so as to identify groups of professors whose patterns of responses to the factors tend to be alike, and c) a comparison of descriptive information from items 13–23 and responses to items 1–12 enabled us to determine professional experiences and practices of the members of each cluster.

The factor analysis suggests four concerns governing the responses:

1. How should we teach the construction of significance?

2. How should we construe academic achievement?

3. How much can we gain from formal pedagogy?

4. Where should we locate the student in relation to the curriculum?

The Ideological Patterns: Seeking Common Ground

The cluster analysis suggests that, rather than a global bipolar split—such as liberals vs. conservatives, new critics vs. deconstructionists, or literary scholars vs. teacher educators—there are five clusters of like-minded people each including specialists in literature, linguistics, composition and rhetoric, and English education. The patterns of response show that any given professor is likely to have adopted a solution to the concerns identified by the factor analysis in such a way that he or she will find relatively comfortable membership in one of five groups of comparable size, each group significantly different from the rest. The members of each group will tend to manifest the crucial values inferred below. In manifesting these values, the professors implicitly respond to the request of their English education students, "Show me who to be."

Group 1. Professors in this group believe that texts have frames of reference within themselves, and that at the core of any given text is a meaning whose particular worth is discernible by apt readers. They believe that the task of the writer is to construct frames according to certain principles required by an ultimate meaning, and that the task of the reader is to reconstruct these frames so as to access ultimate meanings. Professors in this group believe that in the study of literature, social and political phenomena are relevant only to the extent that they are contained within texts. They believe that we can teach the principles and techniques of textual construction/reconstruction, but students' abilities to learn them are normally distributed (i.e., they expect a bell curve).

Professors in Group 1 feel we need not rely on formal pedagogy to make these principles and tactics as apprehensible as possible, and students with sufficient aptitude can apprehend them to the depth permitted by their aptitude. Just as they believe that curriculum inheres in texts and principles, so these professors find little merit in focusing the curriculum on students' discourse processes and personal lives.

Group 1 has the smallest percentage of English educators, the largest percentage of literature professors, and the least prior experience and current involvement in K–12 schools of the group. They are least likely to advocate an English curriculum different for teaching majors than for nonteaching majors. They are least likely to adapt their course requirements for teaching majors enrolled, most likely to consider teaching majors inferior to other English majors, and least likely to consider them superior.

Group 2. At the opposite end of the spectrum, college students encounter professors in Group 2 who believe that a text is a sociopolitical construct whose significance emerges as each reader transacts with the text. These professors believe that the task of writers is to compose and revise according to their evolving purposes in relation to an anticipated reader, and the task of readers is to construct significance within their ideology while construing the ideology of the writer. Because these professors believe that the significance in a curriculum is that which is constructed within students, they believe that curricula should be designed based on students' own experiences and discourse processes. Since these processes are seen as being shaped by the student's social context, sociopolitical implications are viewed as integral to the curriculum.

Professors in Group 2 believe that just as we should focus the curriculum on the individual's socially constructed consciousness, so should we focus academic achievement on how well individuals' work meets socially constructed criteria. These professors believe that norms freeze students into a status quo, but applying criteria can help ensure each student's optimum growth. Finally this group believes that formal pedagogy is essential because it provides the means of designing curriculum and instruction tailored to the psychological and social mandates of education.

Group 2 includes 80 percent of the English educators among the respondents and twice as many composition professors as Group 1. Members have twice the prior experience in teaching grades 6–12 and twice the current involvement in K–12 schools that any other group has. They are most likely to envision an English curriculum different for teaching majors than for nonteaching majors, e.g., including required courses in adolescent and minority literature. They are more likely to know which of their students are teaching majors and to adapt their English courses to their needs. They are more likely than other groups to consider teaching majors superior to other English majors and least likely to consider them inferior.

Group 1 and Group 2 are the most widely separated groups. It would not be difficult to label these two groups with any of the bipolar terms current in debates about English studies and English education: Old paradigm/new paradigm (Hairston 1982), language as artifact/language as social construct (Gere et al. 1992), structural curriculum/poststructural curriculum (Cherryholmes 1988). From another perspective, these two groups have been characterized as those who hold high standards vs. those with no standards; those who seek order vs. those who choose chaos. Internally, these groups are often characterized as us vs. them, good guys vs. bad guys. Although the English educators who populate Group 2 and literature professors who populate Group 1 disagree on most matters of importance in English studies and English education, the survey uncovered an important area of common ground.

Despite their strong differences, both groups agreed with almost 80 percent of all the professors surveyed that, "As agents of the humanities, English teachers should develop in their students the skills and sensitivities required to conduct a lifelong search for fundamental truth." This statement seems to have served as a rallying point for all but one of the groups, Group 3.

Group 3. These professors are in close agreement with Group 2 in all its convictions but one: a mixed group of literature, composition, linguistics, and English education professors, they believe that we should certainly not try to develop in our students "the skills and sensitivities required to conduct a lifelong search for fundamental truth" (Questionnaire item 12). Some of the professors in this group underlined the word "fundamental" suggesting the rejection of essentialism as their reason for disagreeing with the statement. Professors in Group 3 might argue that since all meaning is socially constructed and mutable, we have no business sending our students on a wild goose chase for fundamentals. Rather, the profession should adopt a phenomenological stance toward reality.

Group 4. Professors in this group ally themselves with Group 1 on the matter of how significance should be constructed in reading literature and in composing, so we infer they generally teach students to comprehend meanings inherent in texts. Unlike Group 1, however, members of this group tend to believe it is a mistake to ignore students' own experience and discourse processes, so it makes sense to these professors to base curricula on students' current aptitude and knowledge. Group 4 professors report modest agreement that formal pedagogy is worthwhile, and they tend to believe that students should be evaluated according to individual progress. Applying criteria to performance makes more sense to these professors than expecting the bell curve of norm-referenced assessment. We might characterize these individuals as traditional in their approach to the discipline and student-centered in their approach to the classroom.

Group 5. Professors in Group 5 agree with Groups 2 and 3 in their convictions that significance should be constructed in reading literature and in composing, and they agree that it is right to focus on students' own experience and discourse processes. Group 5 professors, however, see more value in apprenticeship than in formal pedagogy, and because they do not differentiate between criterion- and norm-referenced evaluation, they may have reflected little on the function of evaluation. Group 5 seems to comprise professors who are content to explore the discipline with their students while reflecting relatively little on teaching.

Implications for English Education

The survey belies the notion that professors live in dualistic camps. Knowing this would be a help to prospective teachers who must work their way through the intellectual crosscurrents that characterize English studies and English education. Belenky et al. (1986) and Perry

(1970) trace the complex developmental task of college students as they move from "authoritarian dualism" to committed "constructed knowledge." Many students arrive in college believing in simple right and wrong answers. They quickly discover major differences in outlook among their English and English education professors, differences not only about what is significant in the discipline but also about the fundamental procedures for construing significance. These divergences are not often publicly debated or even acknowledged in the curriculum. Within each class of their English studies, our students must learn to appreciate ambiguity, to trust their own instincts as they read and write, and also to conform to the conventions and procedures for rational inquiry and public communication. The profession expects that finally, if all goes well, the students will construct for themselves a coherent philosophy and pedagogy of English.

In our experience, all does not always go well. The students in our English methods classes—like the student quoted at the beginning of this article—find the task of making a coherent vision out of their English studies daunting, if not impossible. Our students deserve some help in constructing a coherent pedagogy. This central developmental task should not be, and need not be, left to chance. Having surveyed professors of English education and English studies, finding a wide array of differences as well as common ground, we are in a better position to describe the changes necessary in most English education programs to make the learning environment more conducive to prospective teachers' intellectual development.

1. As Gerald Graff (1990) has argued, differences in theory should be highlighted for students. The students already perceive strong differences in practice, but they do not get to hear the open discussion of the theoretical bases for these differences in practice. English and English education professors can help our students build bridges among the theories and pedagogies they experience in college. If any group of English majors needs a clear overview of critical theories, it is English education majors who, because of their pedagogical work, must tie theory to practice. To a general reader of literature, different critical theories may be purely academic. To a teacher of literature, whose responsibility it is to help students create the richest possible readings of the most significant literature, the theoretical matters are central. For example, a reception theory approach to *The Adventures of Huckleberry Finn* is more than a marginal critical approach for the teacher of young African American readers. Reader response theory is extremely practical for those who teach Kate

Chopin to young women who initially blame Chopin's heroines for the conditions of their lives.

2. English professors must share the responsibility with English education professors for teacher education. Teaching is central to the discipline of English, yet the survey shows that 44 percent of English professors do not know which of their students are prospective teachers, and many do not want to know. Almost 24 percent believe that those who seek certification to teach English are inferior students in college English classes (9 percent find teaching majors superior, however). While there is not a strong conviction among most respondents that "formally studying the theory and practice of teaching is crucial in teacher education," relatively few surveyed agree that "apprenticing a college graduate to a good teacher is the only essential pedagogical preparation for teaching." Unless professors of English incorporate discussion of teaching and learning in all their courses, the entire burden of methodology and philosophy falls to the one or two methods courses students take in their major area. Yet, most professors (59 percent) report that they make no adaptations for their students who are preparing to teach. Still, almost 30 percent of the professors surveyed say they do model different teaching techniques, 18 percent ask students to focus on teaching in some assignments, and 15 percent recommend additional readings related to teaching in their English courses.

3. English professors must find time to meet together with English education professors regularly in order to acknowledge and explore perceived differences and to discover our common ground. Most of the professors surveyed report no formal liaison with colleagues involved in English education outside their own department. About one fourth of the professors surveyed report informal encounters between professors of English studies and English education during the school year, and nearly 20 percent serve together on masters and doctoral committees, but only 11 percent meet formally at least once a year to discuss curriculum. Clearly professors in English departments tend to have little connection with professors in education departments even though they share the same students who must somehow construct a coherent, principled pedagogy.

4. English and English education professors need to examine and revise our own teaching so that it represents an effort to model a coherent, principled pedagogy. The survey shows a significant pattern of unexamined beliefs in the profession. For example, one important

distinction in pedagogy is that between "norm-referenced" and "criterion-referenced" testing. Whether or not a professor has learned to use those words, he or she might be expected to have thought carefully about assessment in English. Professors conscious of their assumptions should be able to differentiate at least these two convictions: (1) Intelligence is rare in the classroom and thus the task of assessment consists of dividing the sheep from the goats, in which case 'C' will be the mean and the mode, and the bell curve will validly describe the distribution of grades; and (2) intelligence is rife in the classroom and thus assessment is a matter of recording instances when it is manifest, in which case (depending on assessment criteria, students, curriculum, and instruction) the average grade might legitimately be any letter grade, and the bell curve would be an artificial imposition. In constructing the survey we expected those who agreed with item 6 would disagree with item 10, and Group 2 did respond clearly in the expected manner. But other groups did not so clearly differentiate their responses to these two items, suggesting that many college English professors may need opportunities to construct a coherent philosophy of assessment.

5. English and English education professors need to help our students build bridges from the theories and pedagogies they experience in our colleges to the children and young adults with whom they will work in schools. The survey shows that most of the respondents had not been involved in area schools in the last three years other than in the role of presenters or judges. Just 15 percent of all the professors surveyed (but 58 percent of English education professors) had been engaged in collaborative projects with teachers in schools where they might have a chance to learn enough to assist their college students to build the necessary bridges from theory to practice English studies and English education.

The national survey of English studies and English education professors reported here is strong evidence for the need for local and national colloquia on the relationship of English studies and English education. The first such colloquium, entitled "English Studies and English Education: Language, Literacy, and Public Policy," was sponsored by CEE at the Fall NCTE Convention in Chicago.

Note

1. The authors thank the members of the CEE Commission on English Studies and English Education for help with distributing the questionnaire

and Nancy Prosenjak of Metropolitan College of Denver, Colorado, for assisting with the qualitative analysis of the data.

Works Cited

Belenky, Mary F., B. M. Clinchy, N. R. Goldberger, and J. M. Tarule. 1986. *Women's Ways of Knowing.* New York: Basic Books.

Cherryholmes, C. H. 1988. *Power and Criticism: Poststructural Investigations in Education.* New York: Teachers College Press.

Dilworth, C. B., and N. M. McCracken. 1992. The CEE Commission survey of beliefs and practices of professors of English studies and English education. Technical Report available from C. Dilworth, East Carolina State University.

Gere, A. R., et al. 1992. *Language and Reflection: An Integrated Approach to Teaching English.* New York: Macmillan.

Graff, Gerald. 1990. "Teach the Conflicts." *The South Atlantic Quarterly* 89: 51–67.

Hairston, M. 1982. "The Winds of Change." CCC. National Council of Teachers of English. Guidelines for the Preparation of Teachers of English Language Arts. Urbana, IL: NCTE.

National Council of Teachers of English. 1987. *Guidelines for the Preparation and Certification of Teachers of English.* Urbana, IL: NCTE.

Perry, W. G. 1970. *Forms of Intellectual and Ethical Development in the College Years.* New York: Holt, Rinehart and Winston.

Conclusions: Interpreting the Stories

31 Interpreting the Reflective Stories: The Forces of Influence in Our Essayists' Lives

Richard L. Larson
Lehman College, City University of New York

How to organize the wealth of insight and reflection in the essays and stories in our volume? Because of their richness, no single plan can adequately suggest how our essays might be read most productively. Indeed, as David Bleich suggests in talking about literature in his account of how he developed his approach to reading and interpretation, each reader is encouraged to follow his or her perceptions of dominant themes and emphases in these essays, without feeling the impulse to have a single way of reading win out over other ways of reading; readings are not in competition with one another for superiority.

In what follows, then, I discuss one way of seeing these essays—one way of grouping them which, I hope, responds fairly and productively to their emphases. In any group a reader will meet writers whose reflections might as easily be placed in a different group; my placement of them reflects the emphases I perceive to be established in their writing.

I begin with a group that features the importance of family relationships, friends (who might also be teachers, but who seem to have been friends first), and community in their authors' development—the impact of the social environments in which the writers formed their sense of who they were and what they wanted to be. David Bleich and Judith Entes speak of the social environments of their upbringing in talking about the growth of their self-perceptions.

Writers in my second group highlight the importance of influential teachers and colleagues in their growth. The teachers may be memorable individuals, such as those discussed by Shafer, Stewart, and Monseau (for whom Elliot Eisner's ideas set a course for her work with student teachers), or important colleagues, such as those described by Cynthia Selfe, Gail Hawisher, Lynn Meeks, and, notably, Art Young, who responded in a community of colleagueship and fostered the continuing of such a community.

Alongside colleagues, I array students and our authors' perceptions of students as formative influences on their growth. Hence my third group includes the work of Brenda Greene and Charles Moran. The teaching of both is shaped, though in different ways, by their perception of students' needs and the responses of students to instruction. For Charles Moran, indeed, the students are his coauthors, and the essay is made up substantially of comments they offer as writers studying and practicing writing. Both authors illustrate—not that other authors do not—what our profession refers to as "student-centered" teaching.

From the influences of persons I move, in my discussion of clusters of essays, to the influences of the subjects we study in English and English Education. Among those subjects, an obviously central one is literature. Mike Angelotti's title suggests that promotion of and response to literature is a focus of his reflections. Mary Savage takes stories as her focus, and Jane Tompkins draws on her experiences with literature, notably T. S. Eliot, in discussing the distresses she felt and her ways of relieving, resolving, those distresses. For these people, of course, literature is not just an object of study; it is a morally and educationally formative force in their lives.

We are, of course, shaped by other subjects within the broad scope of English; some of those elements are the emphases of Patricia Donahue, Rhonda Grego and Nancy Thompson, Sandra Stotsky, and myself. For Patricia Donahue, a theory of narrative helps her in evoking and understanding personal stories from her students, some of whom question the truth of their stories. Grego and Thompson find their teaching shaped by feminist theories of the self and by psychologists' guidance in retrospection. For Sandra Stotsky, advanced study in reading and in language, which she pursued later in her career from an international perspective, directed her thought and impelled her teaching. My own largely unsuccessful efforts to develop a focused style of teaching come from influences I felt in a professional school—influences rooted, though at the time I did not perceive it, in cognitive theory and in rhetoric. Insights into our various subjects led us to who we have tried to become.

Many of us, including some I have elected to place in other groups, remind our readers that our paths toward who we are encountered conflicts and oppositions—tensions within ourselves and with those around us. Peter Elbow speaks of the oppositions he felt between himself and some of his teachers, and draws those perceptions into an exploration of "resistance," "giving in," and clashing with those whose view of teaching depends heavily on ranking students. James Collins recounts his effort to overcome stuttering, and to overcome the arguments of those for whom "grammar" is not a suitable subject for the classroom. Harold Foster and Ross Winterowd, who seeks to identify himself as "the cream of the scum," tell of painful, even destructive, interactions with colleagues. My co-editor, Tom McCracken, tells of resisting clichés and bromides about teaching students, in the process of defining his stance toward teaching. And Joe Milner, in a discussion with echoes of Harold Foster, defines the continuing tension, the conflict, if you will, between teaching the elements of our subject and teaching about teaching.

I reserve for a final grouping—not that each piece could not be thought of equally well in a different group—those pieces in which the writers tell of having learned much through reflection on the processes of their teaching, their successes and sometimes the want of success. The striking essays here, for me, are those of Gordon Pradl, reflecting on his interactions with prospective college teachers of writing, and particularly on his perception of what he was trying to accomplish or was not accomplishing, and Susan Hynds, whose conclusion, drawn from her wealth of experiences at different levels, sums up what, for her, it means to be a teacher.

I have added here a sort of coda (which indeed could appear in the group on opposition and resistance, but does not because it is not a personal reflection, but a report of a survey whose authors are detached, not discussing themselves): an account of points of conflict between the views of teachers of English and those of English educators. If the essays in our volume reveal, and many do, differing views of professional responsibility, that survey may crystallize at least some of those differences.

Our authors have taken widely different paths toward their professional selves, and my effort at clustering the essays may indeed be futile. Generalizing about the essays may also be dangerous. But I will conclude by offering one generalization: Our authors are talking about self-reflection—how they made, as they advanced in their careers, their own choices, and decisions, about how to proceed. For the most part, they did not follow directions or textbooks or curriculum outlines; they are substantially self-taught, as indeed any teacher of any subject must be. I invite our readers to reflect on the influences that energized them, and on the choices they made in becoming the professionals they are today.

32 Interpreting Stories: Rebels in the Professoriate

H. Thomas McCracken
Youngstown State University

One theme that runs through or hovers about these thirty essays particularly interests me, although it is not new in the profession. It is a continued tension between those who are interested in studying teaching and learning in "English" and those who believe that "English" represents some body of information or art which takes precedence over the teachers' and students' stance toward it. More tension exists between English studies and English education than one might be led to believe from publications on college teaching. And that tension does not derive only from differences between departments, as we learn from the survey by Dilworth and N. McCracken and from other essays in the volume. The tension also derives from the fact that both groups (or all groups) care about the subject of English and care about their students. I want, in this brief essay of interpretation, to explore that theme and to give a brief rationale for the categories into which the essays have been placed in this volume.

Rebellion against and periodic marginalization by the very academy to which these writers aspired characterize a large number of writers in this volume. Hynds spends her seventh grade "out in the hall"; McCracken drops out of high school; Elbow drops out of college; Tompkins reacts against her previous behavior in following the dictates of the academy; Savage finds the academy irrelevant; and Foster and Winterowd react against departmental intolerance of their work. They apparently speak for many more in the profession from whom we hear only silence. For example, two well-known professors who originally had intentions of writing for this volume about the tensions and frustrations they experienced in English departments (they were in English education and composition), decided not to alienate their colleagues and withdrew their offerings. There are others in this volume who speak directly of such tensions and marginalizations, including Donahue, Bleich, Meeks, Milner, and Pradl.

All learned from their studies, in major part it seems, by their resistance to authority and, it seems to me, what they learned was leadership. I do not, of course, mean any kind of administrative leadership, but rather an intellectual leadership, one that might be characterized as showing how to define teaching as a "profession of ideas and action." Learning in the context of institutions is the only game in town for most of them, so it was not a question of rejecting the general environment of the academy. They simply wanted the academy to live up to its ideals. Their fight was and is over **how** learning is to take place and, as a by-product, **what** learning is to take place. At this point in their careers, they have established elbow room for themselves and others in the academy and have made their ideas felt throughout the profession.

The NCTE/NCATE Guidelines require college English and English education teachers to model the pedagogy expected of the prospective teachers in their classes, so there is some pressure on departments to pay attention to teaching in that way. Still, universities having research as a primary goal feel differently about the study of teaching from, say, a university whose English teaching majors constitute 75 percent of the department. Nevertheless, the NCTE/NCATE Guidelines expect English and English education departments to establish a joint program for prospective English teachers. My experience in reviewing hundreds of such programs from 1988–96 shows that such cooperation is less than it might be. English departments are themselves a "loose confederacy" of American studies, linguistics, peace studies, cultural studies, English education, literature, composition, writing centers, and, occasionally, developmental studies. And secondary education departments also comprise a loose confederacy of fields, such as reading, curriculum and methods, and, about half the time, English education. Connections have to occur formally between English departments and English education departments. Success in making connections occur requires hard work and steady maintenance. The contents in the volume point to both the "interdisciplinary" nature of the subjects we call English and the competing disciplines in which most of us work. However, the strong spirit of persistent joy in working with students that surfaces in many of the stories seems to be the antidote for any long-term argument for failure. Where teachers and students learn from each other, optimism and hard work overcome competition and lack of sufficient rewards.

Because preparing the educators of future elementary, secondary, and college teachers is where English studies and English education intersect—both groups teach the same students—greatest tensions are situated there. The two groups intersect least, though, in preparing college teachers, another way it seems that fate tries to keep distance between them. Some colleagues prefer to ignore those tensions and center on what makes them survive and prosper as people and professionals. Others deal directly with "interdisciplinary" relationships. All of the essays, however, are grounded in individual experience and reflection woven into professional perspectives, and that is what makes this volume different: it tells us in great measure who college English and English education teachers are and what they value. If there is common ground in the professions of teaching English and English education, it is here in this volume.

I assume that good readers create their own texts from rich readings. When they "read" our text, they will be creating it, based upon their own psychologies and biographies. Open categories seem to stimulate rich readings. The more specific and literal headings become (e.g., toward an Army manual), the more boring/less imaginative is the reading. All an editor can do for readers is to offer a reading, make a sample model for them, and simultaneously invite them to create their own readings. The way to do that, I believe, is to keep the categories open. I therefore prefer **loose connections** over controlling categories.

I. Ways We Have Been Affected (Tompkins, Young, Stewart, and McCracken)

Tompkins has been so profoundly affected by a one-headed scientific logic [the male academy, which she doesn't name as such] that she eschews the whole system. But the real question for the reader is not whether she has been affected, but why it took twenty-seven years to break free. I found her piece especially moving. **Young's** career, as he explains, was profoundly "affected" by the invitation to become a Freshman Composition instructor. His essay is a reflective story about what that decision meant in his life, showing readers what key decisions and turning points mean for an academic life. This is one of the most useful essays on the department that I have read. **Stewart** could fit into "Going Along" or this category. His great professional turning point, what he was most affected by, was his entrance into Kansas University. Everything for Stewart emanated, as he says, from his working with Ken Rothwell at Kansas (and, a little, Albert Kitzhaber) and from marrying his wife. Those are the things that most affected him. **McCracken** was affected most by teachers in his life who seemed to care about him as a person, rather than a disembodied mind. As an undergraduate, he was influenced by reading Earl Kelley (the structure of his essay is built around Kelley's principles). He describes the resistance paradoxically necessary to become educated by the academy. By implication through Kelley's principles, he alludes to his own philosophy of teaching currently.

II. Going Along (Bleich, Bayer, Hudson-Ross, and Smagorinsky)

Bleich's essay is strikingly about gender, using his own example as a way of showing what the academy has been about, how and why he came to it and learned to prosper in it. The key for him was patronage and he has now come to see this as injurious to women. All males and females who teach in the university will recognize and understand that phenomenon by the quotation alone. Bleich "goes along" with the male system in the academy, the phrase also invoking Speaker of the House Sam Rayburn's old line: "To get along, you have to go along." Bleich gets along just fine and shows us how it was done, but is now reassessing that experience. **Bayer's** essay fits loosely with Bleich's by both her opening reference to feminism and her working through the system *without* patronage, *without* help. She develops, she says, from "maybe this [teaching] is a career" phase to "teaching as a profession" phase. She builds her essay from these concepts. She "goes along" with the degree system, but she survives through her discoveries in *teaching*, something no one in the "male system" shows her. **Hudson-Ross** looks back, having gone along. She encounters Gloria Steinem's *Revolution From Within*, then "goes alone" (opposing "going along"). Like Bayer, she gets no inspiration or support (patronage for Bleich) from the system. She gets her knowledge from teaching itself, in spite of the system. And that is what "going along" did for her: not much. **Smagorinsky** invokes his reading and research learned from the University of Chicago, launched by his English education background, a good example of "going along." Smagorinsky's friends are his mentors in the male system. The very title of his essay suggests the similarities with Bleich.

III. Finding Rewards (Elbow, Pradl, Shafer, and Monseau)

Elbow started out searching for academic rewards in the two schools in his title. He failed; he later sees they failed him. He finds rewards in his writing and his students. **Pradl** chastises the system, particularly the "delivering of information" bias—the transmission of the discipline (thus, he is speaking of "departmental" categories) and says, in effect, "no rewards here." **Shafer** found his rewards through the system (often the historical modes are variations of "Going Along") and from some of the memorable figures in our profession. **Monseau** says you can find rewards in helping students see and practice other ways of teaching by becoming connoisseurs, following Eliot Eisner's metaphor.

IV. How We See Ourselves (Hynds, Stotsky, and Milner)

   Stotsky is surprised to find the academic world which she enters uninformed in certain ways. She sets out on a path of exploration, Mary Kingsley-like, protecting traditional values (product over process; logic over feeling). She relies on her own "assessment of what seemed to work well or not work." It is her stance that jumps out past the descriptions of her work. She sees herself very differently from **Hynds** and **Milner** who see themselves, finally, as part of a teaching community (English education), as evidenced by their strong stances toward that community.

V. Telling Different Kinds of Stories (Savage, Grego, Thompson, Greene, and Angelotti)

   Savage sees the academic community much as Elbow did (and many others), but she has a different kind of courage and tells a different kind of story because she leaves the academy and doesn't come back. **Grego** and **Thompson** tell a different kind of story because they collaborate on research that reveals ways they work together and teaches them more about writing and students. **Greene's** story is different because of its conservatism in the larger academic community, but its radicalism for her students. **Angelotti** tells probably one of the four or five very different stories in the volume because he engages us in his teaching in the community, in class, and centers on a genre at the same time.

VI. Professional Relationships (Foster, Donahue, and Winterowd)

   Foster's outspokenness, like **Winterowd's**, represents a very large number of college teachers who will suffer neither insult nor injustice meekly. Their positions also represent many who are afraid to speak up for all the usual reasons (concern about promotion, tenure and reluctance to confront authority). In Foster's case, it is English education that bothers English department folk because they see themselves as serving the liberal arts, not a particular vocation, and especially not one that purports to apply teaching theory. **Donahue** fits this category because she is working in the same milieu. She says, "in my graduate program composition was considered an inferior field for inferior minds (this wasn't an unusual situation in English departments in the early '80s)."

VII. Making Connections (Fulwiler, Entes, Collins, and Larson)

This category was taken from **Entes'** title, a metaphor she uses effectively as applied to her subject. **Larson** fits the category particularly well because of the central connection he makes between teaching the case method at the Harvard Business School and his subsequent use of it in teaching and academic outlook in the rest of his career. **Collins** makes connections between an early personal problem and his subsequent learning and teaching. **Fulwiler's** connections are made as he weaves through his jobs, learning as he goes ("Grading is easy and nobody gets nothing and I learn that good teaching is anything you invent it to be").

VIII. Finishing Touches (Moran, Meeks, Hawisher, and Selfe)

It seemed to me appropriate that we finish with (a) students speaking (**Moran**); (b) a particularly lively overview of what has been central to the volume: how the writer got to where she teaches today (**Meeks**); and (c) a conclusion that looks toward a new way of seeing teaching through collaboration, the very place the profession thought it would fall apart using the new hardware and softwares (**Hawisher** and **Selfe**).

IX. Attitudes (Dilworth and McCracken)

As a way of approaching the survey (Section IX) the reader might read or reread **Moran**, **Pradl**, and **Hynds** to see the ideal in classroom practice for those academically inclined toward English education.

Editors

H. Thomas McCracken is in his fortieth year of teaching, the last twenty-eight of them at Youngstown State University. He has been Chair of NCTE's Conference on English Education (1986–88); he is currently NCTE's Representative to NCATE and has served two terms (six years) on NCATE's Specialty Areas Studies Board. He is currently serving a term on NCATE's Executive Board. For further information, see his essay in this volume.

Richard L. Larson is Professor of English at Lehman College of the City University of New York, where for several years he served as Dean of the Division of Professional Studies. He is a former Chair of the Conference on College Composition and Communication, and a past editor of the journal *College Composition and Communication*. He has served as Chair of the NCTE's Standing Committee on Teacher Preparation and Certification, and has just completed a term on the editorial board of *Research in the Teaching of English*. Before coming to New York, Larson taught at the University of Hawaii in Honolulu. He is the author of a monograph, *The Evaluation of Teaching: College English* (MLA-ERIC), and has edited an anthology entitled *Children and Writing in the Elementary School: Theories and Techniques* (Oxford).

Judith Entes is Associate Professor in the English Department at Baruch College, City University of New York. When she wrote her chapter for this volume she was a member of the Academic Skills Department at Baruch; that department was eliminated in July, 1995. Reading and writing are no longer taught in two different departments at Baruch.

Entes began work for this volume as a contributor. She then helped to develop the book and became more actively involved, to help ensure that the book would become a reality. Her most recent publication (1996) is "Students Becoming Their Own Advocates," in *Advocacy in the Classroom*, edited by P. M. Spacks (St. Martin's Press).

Contributors

Michael L. Angelotti is an English Education faculty member in the College of Education of the University of Oklahoma, Norman. He also serves as a resident poet for the Oklahoma Arts Council and is Director of the Oklahoma Writing Project. He is past-president of ALAN, and has served on the CEE Executive Committee and the NCTE Standing Committee on Teacher Preparation and Certification. He currently chairs the CEE Commission on Methods Teaching and conducts the annual NCTE Convention Fountain of the Muse poetry readings each fall. He has published in NCTE journals such as *The ALAN Review, English Education, English Journal,* and *Research in the Teaching of English,* and in the professional literature of other organizations. His poetry has appeared in books, journals, and literary magazines.

Ann Shea Bayer is on the Graduate Faculty in the Department of Teacher Education and Curriculum Studies, College of Education, University of Hawaii at Manoa. Her publications include *Collaborative-Apprenticeship Learning: Language and Thinking Across the Curriculum, K–12,* as well as various articles published in journals such as *Research in the Teaching of English, Language Arts,* and *Mind, Culture, and Activity: An International Journal.* Bayer is a former member of the CEE Executive Committee, and has been active with the National Writing Project, most especially with the Bay Area and Hawaii Writing Project sites.

David Bleich teaches in the English Department, Women's Studies, and Jewish Studies programs at the University of Rochester. His forthcoming book from Heinemann-Boynton/Cook is: *Know and Tell: Disclosure, Genre, and Membership in the Teaching of Writing and Language Use.*

Rita S. Brause is Professor of Language and Literacy Education at Fordham University's Graduate School of Education and a teacher at New York City Community School District #3's Center School. Responding to the challenge offered by NCTE's designation as a "Promising Researcher," she has authored numerous articles and book chapters about teaching and learning in *Language Arts, English Journal, English Education, Research in the Teaching of English* and *Anthropology and Education Quarterly.* She has most recently published *Enduring Schools: Problems and Possibilities,* a reflection on teaching and learning and school reform in elementary and secondary schools, published by Taylor and Francis. In addition, she has written *Search and ReSearch: What the Inquiring Teacher Needs to Know* (with J. S. Mayher) and *An Investigation into Bilingual Students' Classroom Communicative Competence* (with J. S. Mayher and J. Bruno). An active member of NCTE, Brause has served in numerous capacities including CEE Program Chair for the Spring Conference in Washington, DC and Chair of the Committee on English Education and English Studies.

James L. Collins has been a professor for almost twenty years at the State University of New York at Buffalo, and before that he was an English teacher for ten years in Springfield, Massachusetts. His main research interest is in studying how teachers can help low-achieving students learn to control their own writing through writing strategies. Jim is the author of numerous books, articles, and chapters and has presented workshops and a videoconference for the National Council of Teachers of English. His latest book is *Strategies for Struggling Writers.*

Collett Dilworth directs the composition program for the English Department at East Carolina University, where he has taught English and English education for twenty years. He has also taught and served as curriculum coordinator for the Fayetteville, N.C. schools. He has authored numerous articles for NCTE publications and has coauthored two textbooks for commercial publishers. Currently he serves as executive secretary of the North Carolina English Teachers Association and edits that organization's newsletter.

Patricia Donahue is Associate Professor of English at Lafayette College, where she teaches first-year writing, advanced writing, Renaissance literature, and critical theory. She also directs the writing across the curriculum program, a program she created twelve years ago. She is co-editor of *Reclaiming Pedagogy* (SIU 1989); has published essays and reviews in *College English, CCC, Reader,* and *Shakespeare Bulletin;* and is currently working on a book-length project on the disciplinization of composition studies.

Peter Elbow is Director of the Writing Program and Professor of English at the University of Massachusetts at Amherst. He has taught at M.I.T., Franconia College, Evergreen State College, and SUNY Stony Brook—where he also directed the writing program.

Elbow has written *Oppositions in Chaucer, Writing without Teachers, Writing with Power, Embracing Contraries, What is English?,* and (with Pat Belanoff) a textbook, *A Community of Writers.* He has published numerous essays on writing and teaching and evaluation. In 1986 he won the Braddock award for "The Shifting Relationships Between Speech and Writing." In 1994 he won the James A. Berlin award for "The War Between Reading and Writing—and How to End It." He served on the Executive Committee of the Modern Language Association and the Executive Committee of the Conference on College Composition and Communication.

Harold M. Foster is Professor of English Education at the University of Akron. His latest book is *Crossing Over: Whole Language for Secondary English Teachers,* published by Harcourt Brace. He serves on numerous NCTE and CEE commissions and committees. He is currently a member of the NCTE Commission on Media and the Standing Committee on the Preparation of English Teachers. Foster has received an NCTE Center of Excellence Award for his school-university collaboration, the

Kenmore Project. He has written two other books and several essays and articles, many of which have appeared in the *English Journal* and *English Education.*

Toby Fulwiler has directed the writing program at the University of Vermont since 1983. Before that he taught at Michigan Tech and the University of Wisconsin where, in 1973, he also received his Ph.D. in American Literature. At Vermont he teaches introductory and advanced writing classes. His most recent book is *When Writing Teachers Teach Literature,* co-edited with Art Young (1996). In addition he has written *The Working Writer* (1995) and *Teaching with Writing* (1986); edited *The Journal Book* (1987); and co-edited *Programs that Work* (1990), *Community of Voices* (1992), and *Reading, Writing, and the Study of Literature* (1989). He conducts writing workshops for teachers in all grade levels and across the disciplines, riding to workshop sites, weather permitting, on his BMW motorcycle.

Brenda M. Greene is Professor of English and Chair of the Department of Languages, Literature, Communications and Philosophy at Medgar Evers College, CUNY. The major focus of her research and writing has been in the areas of basic writing, multicultural literature, and writing across the curriculum. Her most recent publications have appeared in *When Writing Teachers Teach Literature, English Education,* and *Voices in English Classrooms.* She is co-editor with Lil Brannon of *Rethinking American Literature.* An active member of NCTE, Greene has participated in workshops and forums and has served on the Editorial Board and the College Section Committee.

Rhonda C. Grego is currently Associate Professor of English at Benedict College, South Carolina, where she teaches undergraduate courses in composition, rhetoric, and critical theory. She is also co-PI (along with Dr. Christopher Chalokwu, Dean and Professor of Geology) and Director of the Bridges Writing Program, a three-year (1997–2000), FIPSE-funded project exploring the implications of alternative learning environments and participatory inquiry approaches for African American writing development and research on college teaching and learning about writing. Her publications include "Writing Academic Autobiographies: Finding a Common Language Across the Curriculum" (in *Pedagogy in the Age of Politics,* edited by Patricia Sullivan and Donna J. Qualley), and "Repositioning Remediation: Renegotiating Composition's Work in the Academy," with Nancy Thompson (*CCC* 47.1/February 1996).

Gail E. Hawisher is Professor of English and Director of the Center for Writing Studies at the University of Illinois, Urbana-Champaign. With Paul LeBlanc, Charles Moran, and Cynthia Selfe, she is author of *Computers and the Teaching of Writing in Higher Education, 1979–1994: A History.* She is also co-editor of several books focusing on a range of theoretical, pedagogical, and research questions related to literacy and technology. With Cynthia Selfe, she edits *Computers and Composition:*

An International Journal for Teachers of Writing. Her articles have appeared in the *English Journal, College English, College Composition and Communication,* and *Written Communication,* among others. She is currently a member of the MLA Committee on Computers and Emerging Technologies and is Assistant Chair of the College Section of the National Council of Teachers of English.

Sally Hudson-Ross teaches secondary English Education at The University of Georgia. After exchanging jobs with a high school teacher during the 1993–94 school year, she and school and university colleagues devised a new, year-long teacher education program based on teacher research and collaborative inquiry. She and her colleagues have written about those experiences in articles published in *English Journal* and *English Education* and in a forthcoming book, *Growing Together: Student Teaching and Mentoring in a Collaborative Inquiry Community,* jointly published by Teachers College Press and NCTE. Sally has served on NCTE and CEE committees and was local arrangements chair for the 1990 convention in Atlanta.

Susan Hynds is Professor and Director of English Education at Syracuse University. Before beginning her university career, she was a teacher of English, speech, and drama on the middle school and high school level in Nashville, Tennessee for nine years. Her work with teachers focuses on the areas of language across the curriculum, writing, and literary reading. She has written articles and book chapters on language teaching and has authored four books: *Perspectives on Talk and Learning* (with Don Rubin); *Developing Discourse Practices in Adolescence and Adulthood* (with Richard Beach, ABLEX); *Making Connections: Language and Learning in the Classroom*; and *On the Brink: Negotiating Literature and Life with Adolescents*.

Nancy Mellin McCracken is Associate Professor of English Education at Kent State University. She is currently Vice-Chair of the Conference on English Education. She has published *Gender Studies in the Teaching of English* and numerous articles in *English Education.* She is Director of the Northeast Ohio Writing Project.

Lynn Langer Meeks is Director of Writing for the English Department at Utah State University in Logan, Utah, where she teaches courses in composition, Children's and Young Adult Literature, and English Education. She was the English Language Arts Coordinator for the State of Idaho Department of Education from 1988–94 and prior to that taught at Scottsdale and Saguaro High Schools in Scottsdale, Arizona. Her article, "When World Views Collide, the Curriculum Explodes" won the *English Leadership Quarterly's* Best Article Award for the 1996 academic year. She is coauthoring *Frameworks 9–12 Core Course* with Brian Cambourne, Jan Turbill, and Andrea Butler and is a national trainer for Frameworks Language and Literacy Program. She has been the Chair of the Committee to Review Videotape and Film for Inservice Materials and a member of the Commission on Media. She lives with her husband Norman L. Jones, their dog Blue, and their three cats: Scotsy, MacCavity, and Ashlee.

Joseph Milner serves as Chairman of the Department of Education at Wake Forest University and is the director of the eight-site North Carolina Writing Project. He served from 1992 until 1994 as Chair of the Conference on English Education and as a member of the Executive Committee of the National Council of Teachers of English. He has been a member of The National Faculty since 1984 and was Editor of *North Carolina English* from 1992 until 1994. He serves on the Editorial Board of *Children's Literature in Education* and other publications. He, with his wife, authored an English methods text, *Bridging English,* and he has written books and essays on English education, children's literature, aesthetics, linguistics, and American literature.

Virginia R. Monseau is Professor of English at Youngstown State University, where she regularly teaches graduate and undergraduate courses in young adult literature, children's literature, and composition. She has also taught the English Methods course and has supervised student teachers in the field. The incoming editor of *English Journal,* she is a past president of NCTE's Assembly on Literature for Adolescents and a member of the Commission on English Education and English Studies. She has published numerous articles, book chapters, and book reviews on young adult literature, children's literature, and English education and has co-edited two collections of essays. Her most recent books are *Presenting Ouida Sebestyen* for the Twayne Young Adult Authors Series and *Responding to Young Adult Literature,* published by Boynton Cook.

Charles Moran is Professor of English at the University of Massachusetts-Amherst. The coauthors—Pinkal Amin, Liz Ying Feng Chin, Terri Cocchi, Kelly Donahue, Vernard Fennell, Sean Lally, Andrea Lemay, Alex Parker, Claudia Prodan, Alison Sisitsky, Joseph Smelstor, Nathan Smith, Kristina Soares, Melissa Walters, and Li Wu—were students in a first-year writing course, "College Writing," taught by Moran in the fall of 1992. Teacher and students cowrote this chapter as part of the work of the course. Moran continues at his University; the coauthors have gone on to useful and productive lives in such fields as medicine, education, social services, and business.

Gordon M. Pradl teaches English education at New York University. From 1986 to 1992 he served as Director of Staff Development for the university's Expository Writing Program. Co-editor of *English Education* from 1985 to 1992, he coauthored *Learning to Write/Writing to Learn* (1983) and edited the essays of James Britton, *Prospect and Retrospect* (1982). His most recent book, *Literature for Democracy* (1996) addresses his ongoing concern about authority relations in the English classroom.

Mary C. Savage is Associate Professor at Hofstra University, New York. She is the founder of the Parent Storytelling Workshop of Henry Street Settlement in New York City.

Cynthia L. Selfe is Professor of Composition and Communication and Chair of the Humanities Department at Michigan Technological University. Selfe is Associate Chair of the Conference on College Composition and Communication. In addition, she has chaired the College Section of the NCTE, served as a founding member and Chair of that organization's Assembly on Computers in English, and served as Chair of the organization's Instructional Technology Committee. She has also been recognized as an EDUCOM Medal award winner for innovative computer use in higher education. Selfe has authored, coauthored and co-edited various books and collections of essays regarding computers and education. Selfe and Hawisher are the founders and current editors of Computers and Composition Press, which sponsors the publication of books on computers of interest to English composition teachers.

Robert E. Shafer was Professor of English Education at Arizona State University for twenty-five years. He had been retired for six years upon his death at the age of seventy-two in 1997. He was Vice-President of NCTE (1967–68), and he received NCTE's Distinguished Service Award in 1995 at the San Diego Convention.

Peter Smagorinsky is Associate Professor of English Education at the University of Oklahoma. His interests include how literacy is defined and assessed in high schools, and how the social contexts of schools influence teachers' decisions. His work is currently funded through the National Research Center on English Learning and Achievement (CELA). He is currently co-editor of *Research in the Teaching of English.*

Donald C. Stewart was Professor of English at Kansas State University for twenty-four years until his death at the age of sixty-one in 1992. He was Chair of the Conference on College Composition and Communication in 1983, a member of NCTE's Editorial Board (1975–78), edited *Kansas English* (1971–80), and was President of the Kansas Association of Teachers of English (1984–85).

Sandra Stotsky is Research Associate at the Harvard Graduate School of Education and the Boston University School of Education. From 1991 to 1996, she served as editor of *Research in the Teaching of English,* the research journal sponsored by the NCTE. She has taught or subbed at every grade level from kindergarten through high school, as well as at the undergraduate and graduate levels. In the past five years, she has served as a consultant on teacher training to Polish, Lithuanian, and Romanian educators in Eastern Europe on the content and pedagogy for programs in civic education in their public schools. She has served as co-chair of a committee appointed by the Massachusetts Commissioner of Education to prepare a final version of the English language arts curriculum framework for the Commonwealth of Massachusetts. This document sets forth academic standards for the English language arts for K–12.

Nancy S. Thompson is Associate Professor at the University of South Carolina, where she has worked with Rhonda Grego on the Writing Studio project. She has published on the topics of basic writing, literacy, media, imaging, and research methodology, in addition to articles with Grego on the Writing Studio: "Repositioning Remediation: Renegotiating Composition's Work in the Academy" in *CCC* and "The Writing Studio Program: Reconfiguring Basic Writing/Freshman Composition" in *WPA*. At present she is working on a book-length project on Sylvia Ashton-Warner's contributions to literacy education.

Jane Tompkins is a writer, teacher, and workshop leader who teaches at Duke University. She is published in the fields of literary theory, American literature and is the author, most recently, of a memoir on teaching and learning, *A Life in School, What the Teacher Learned* (1996).

W. Ross Winterowd is the founder and was the long-time director of the doctoral program in rhetoric, linguistics, and literature at the University of Southern California. That program is now, lamentably, defunct, but more than fifty graduates throughout academia carry on the work begun at USC. Winterowd's most recent work is *The English Department: A Personal and Institutional History*.

Art Young is Campbell Chair in Technical Communication, Professor of English, and Professor of Engineering at Clemson University. He has co-edited several books on writing across the curriculum, including *Language Connections: Writing and Reading Across the Curriculum; Writing Across the Disciplines: Research into Practice; Programs that Work: Models and Methods for Writing Across the Curriculum;* and *Programs and Practices: Writing Across the Secondary Curriculum.* He is also the co-editor of *When Writing Teachers Teach Literature: Bringing Writing to Reading* and *Critical Theory and the Teaching of Literature.* He has served as a consultant to colleges and universities in the United States and Europe.

This book was set in Palatino and Helvetica by City Desktop Productions.
The typeface used on the cover was Officina Serif.
The book was printed on 50-lb. Williamsburg offset paper
by Versa Press, Inc., East Peoria, Illinois.